RETROSPECTIVITY AND THE RULE OF LAW

Retrospectivity and the Rule of Law

CHARLES SAMPFORD

Foundation Professor of Law and Research Professor of Ethics, Griffith University
Director, Institute for Ethics, Governance and Law
(a joint initiative of the United Nations University and Griffith University)

with the assistance of
Jennie Louise, Sophie Blencowe and Tom Round

OXFORD
UNIVERSITY PRESS

UNIVERSITY PRESS

Great Clarendon Street, Oxford OX2 6DP

Oxford University Press is a department of the University of Oxford.
It furthers the University's objective of excellence in research, scholarship,
and education by publishing worldwide in

Oxford New York

Auckland Cape Town Dar es Salaam Hong Kong Karachi
Kuala Lumpur Madrid Melbourne Mexico City Nairobi
New Delhi Shanghai Taipei Toronto

With offices in

Argentina Austria Brazil Chile Czech Republic France Greece
Guatemala Hungary Italy Japan Poland Portugal Singapore
South Korea Switzerland Thailand Turkey Ukraine Vietnam

Oxford is a registered trade mark of Oxford University Press
in the UK and in certain other countries

Published in the United States
by Oxford University Press Inc., New York

British Library Cataloguing in Publication Data

Data available

Library of Congress Cataloging in Publication Data
Sampford, C. J. G. (Charles J. G.)
Retrospectivity and the rule of law / Charles Sampford ; with the
assistance of Jennie Louise, Sophie Blencowe, and Tom Round.
p. cm.
Includes bibliographical references and index.
ISBN-13: 978–0–19–825298–6 (hardback : alk. paper)
1. Retroactive laws. 2. Rule of law. 3. Judicial process. I. Louise,
Jennie. II. Blencowe, Sophie. III. Round, Tom. IV. Title.
K566.S26 2006
340′.11—dc22
                                          2006001573

Typeset by Newgen Imaging Systems (P) Ltd., Chennai, India
Printed in Great Britain
on acid-free paper by
Biddles Ltd., King's Lynn

ISBN 0–19–825298–6   978–0–19–825298–6

1 3 5 7 9 10 8 6 4 2

Preface

This book has been a long time in gestation. It arose out of interests generated in 1984 and I proposed it to Oxford University Press in 1989 after the publication of my first monograph. I expected it to be the next book project—to follow no later than my next sabbatical. The publishers have waited with more patience than an author has any right to expect and I would like to emphasize my gratitude to the editors who have been patient in the face of the many projects I have felt obliged to start and complete in the interim. While the list of activities were always acknowledged to be worthy—from starting a law school and the establishment of research centres at Melbourne, Griffith and now the United Nations University, to an array of large research projects that were central to the success of those centres—I marvel at the patience of the world's greatest academic publisher accepting yet another deferment in a series of serial delays.

There is a great irony in the length of the delays. As an undergraduate and postgraduate student, I occupied the traditionally rarefied areas of legal, ethical and political philosophy. I completed my law degree following strong advice from a philosophy mentor rather than my law lecturers—reflecting, in part, the quality of education offered by law schools in the 1970s; a matter which I considered to be a lost cause until the late 1980s.[1] My doctorate sought to deal with the issue of whether legal theory was more or less helpful in seeking to understand law in terms of systems—a question which I sought resoundingly to resolve in the negative.[2] While, like most doctorates, it occupied a central element in the sorting of my ideas and the development of my thoughts which I still apply on a daily basis, it was a work of high theory seemingly removed from much of the work that has followed.

The irony is that it was the issue of retrospective law making that led to that fundamental shift—from a largely theoretical interest in jurisprudence to an application of law, ethics and other disciplines in the humanities and social science to current issues of practical concern. It was that shift that led to the range of other projects interrupting the natural process by which one monograph follows another.

This led to projects on legal education, applied ethics, corruption and integrity systems, public law, *coups d'etat*, restoring the rule of law in the Asia Pacific, the ethics of intervention, and sovereignty and intervention. It also led to an invitation to start a law school (at Griffith), the establishment of a research centre in

---

[1] See Legal Education: New Foundations, Cavendish, London, 1998 (with Jack Goldring and Ralph Simmonds).

[2] I learnt many things from my supervisor, Professor Colin Tapper, but one thing he did do was to cure me from seeking to split my infinitives.

Melbourne (the Centre for Philosophy and Public Issues), and a sequence of increasingly larger research centres at Griffith (the National Institute for Law, Ethics and Public Affairs; the Australian Research Council Key Centre for Ethics, Law, Justice and Governance and the United Nations University Institute for Ethics, Governance and Law). These undertakings led to much writing and grant getting but allowed precious little time for the project that stimulated my 'applied turn'.

My first writing on the Rule of Law was a review essay of Professor Geoffrey de Q. Walker's tome on *The Rule of Law* in 1989 (Melbourne University Law Review and then Public Law). My first paper was presented at the Australian Law and Society Conference in December 1990, which led to a research project and report for the Victoria Law Foundation in 1991 and the publication of two articles with Andrew Palmer, then a Research Fellow at the Centre for Philosophy and Public Issues. It also led to an extensive seventeen-page book plan with the sequence of arguments by which I would establish the case. However, a month after I delivered that paper, I was invited to come to Queensland to become Foundation Dean of Law and I sought the first of many extensions from my patient, if increasingly less expectant, publishers.

I would like to thank those who helped with the research for the book and did the first drafts of some of the text—Andrew Palmer, Dr Tom Round, Dr Jennie Louise, Hugh Breakey, and Sophie Blencowe. While I had written an early paper and prepared an extensive seventeen-page book plan as early as 1989 setting out the sequence of arguments, many contributed to the fleshing out of those arguments and the search for legal cases and jurisprudential writings that supported and, more importantly, contradicted the positions taken and the conclusions drawn.

While acknowledging contributions, I take full responsibility for the final arguments. Nevertheless, the value that I place on their contributions mean that the text refers to 'we'—not out of quasi-regal, professorial arrogance, but out of collegial respect and appreciation.

No acknowledgement by a modern academic would be complete without the genuine recognition of the sufferance of families for the increasingly quixotic eccentricity of those who persist in thinking that the academy is a place where people should, as in this book, pursue their ideas wherever they take them. In the first monograph that I wrote, I acknowledged the forbearance of my young son who had accepted a lesser dose of paternal participation in his life because of the book I was writing; and I apologized in that Preface that it did not have as many pictures as the books he was used to. In the intervening years, I have completed many books and articles without any noticeable increase in pictorial content. Fortunately, he and his sister are no longer in need of picture books, studying philosophy themselves. To them and their long-suffering mother, I dedicate this book.

Contents

Table of cases

Table of legislation

Introduction

Nothing is more certain to cause apoplectic explosions of fear and loathing among some lawyers than the mere mention of the dreaded word 'retrospectivity'.[1] Few topics can be better guaranteed to produce conflict without resolution, heat without light. The term 'retrospectivity' is often used in the loosest possible way to refer to just about any change that affects the interests of those involved. While debate may seem to resemble philosophical disputation, terms like 'human rights', 'justice', 'democracy', and 'the rule of law' are often used for effect rather than argument. But despite the lack of rigour with which the public debate is conducted, the issues do reflect and exemplify genuine philosophical and theoretical problems about the way we handle legal change in what we hope to be, or make, 'well ordered societies under law'.[2]

It is natural that the examples of retrospective rule making that catch the headlines and generate wide debate are of the rarer and more exotic variety. Some of them are truly outrageous but this should not lead us to assume that all retrospective rules, under some very tenuous definitions, are bad. However, one should not be misled into thinking that retrospective rule making is rare, confined to extreme and exotic cases. As we shall see, retrospective statutes are relatively common and, in some cases, deservedly uncontroversial. Nor should the frequency with which conservative lawyers attack legal changes they dislike on the grounds of retrospectivity and its supposed inconsistency with the rule of law lead one to think that retrospective legislation is the preserve of impatient, left-wing reformist governments dissatisfied with past iniquities. As we shall see in this book, retrospective law making is not at all uncommon and is not confined to any one part of the political spectrum. Indeed, the debate in Australia about retrospective legislation was stimulated by retrospective tax legislation passed by conservative treasurers in 1977 and 1982 to counter two particularly artificial tax schemes.

Two decades later, the second of those treasurers, John Howard, is Prime Minister of Australia and supporting some, but not all, retrospective legislation

---

[1] For example, Geoffrey de Q Walker calls retrospective tax legislation one of 'a series of legislative attacks on constitutional rights and civil liberties, any one of which would have been considered unthinkable in more normal times'. See, 'Ending Constitutional Drift: A Democratic Agenda for Change,' in Suri Ratnapala, Geoffrey de Q Walker and Wolfgang Kasper (eds), *Restoring the True Republic* (Centre for Independent Studies, St Leonards, 1993), 11. Daniel Troy claims that the 'overwhelming majority of laws that are retroactive in form are unjustifiable', *Retroactive Legislation* (American Enterprise Institute, Washington DC, 1998), 3.

[2] A term used by Mark Sagoff, *The Economy of the Earth: Philosophy, Law and the Environment* (Cambridge University Press, Cambridge, Mass., 1988), 192.

dealing with issues involving 'border protection' and terrorism. Although Prime Minister Howard has passed no retrospective criminal legislation of his own, he has expressed an ambivalent public attitude to retrospective criminal provisions introduced by the Presidents of Indonesia and the United States, which verges on tacit personal approval of these measures.

The Tampa tantrum

On 26 August 2001, the *MV Tampa*, a Norwegian container ship acting on an Australian request, rescued 433 persons who claimed to be Afghan or Iraqi refugees and/or asylum seekers. On 28 August 2001, SAS troops boarded the *MV Tampa*. Two days earlier, the Captain had taken the *Tampa* into Australia waters following a statement.[3] The SAS troops having taken control of the ship, the *Tampa* was ordered out of Australian territorial waters. The rescuees were forcibly removed from the *Tampa* and then taken by Australian naval vessels to Nauru with a minority going to New Zealand (which granted asylum to all those it processed).

That evening, the government introduced the Border Protection Bill 2001 to retrospectively validate all actions taken in relation to the matter. It passed the House of Representatives within one hour but was rejected by the Senate. Litigation followed immediately. Two of the four Federal Court judges who considered the matter held that the rescuees were detained by the respondents on board the *MV Tampa* without legal authority and were entitled to a remedy in the form of an order of release on the mainland of Australia—Justice North at first instance and the Chief Justice of the Federal Court, Justice Michael Black, on appeal. The other two appellate judges upheld the Government's appeal and the High Court did not give special leave on the basis of government claims that the rescuees were, by that time, no longer in the hands of Australian government officials.[4]

---

[3] See North J's statement of the facts in *Victorian Council for Civil Liberties Incorporated v. Minister for Immigration and Multicultural Affairs* and *Vadarlis v. Minister for Immigration and Multicultural Affairs* (2001) 182 ALR 617. See, for example, *Australia and Refugees, 1901–2002: An Annotated Chronology Based on Official Sources*, Dr Barry York—Social Policy Group, 16 June 2003; and V. Rajanayagam, 'The Tampa Decision: Refugee Rights versus the Executive's Power to Detain and Expel Unlawful Non-citizens' (2002) 22 *University of Queensland Law Journal* 1.

[4] The High Court made it very clear, when it dismissed the application for special leave, that it was doing so on the limited ground that the relief sought under section 75(v) of the Constitution was not available to the applicants because of a change of circumstances and that the relief was no longer relevant to their position. It expressly left open the issue of the executive and prerogative power that was examined in the Full Court and which was subject to debate in the Full Court. It also left open the question of the validity of part 2 of the *Border Protection (Validation and Enforcement Powers) Act 2001*. Submission and subsequent questioning of Mr Angus James, Lecturer in Law at the University of Canberra, *Commonwealth of Australia Official Committee Hansard Senate Legal and Constitutional References Committee Reference*: Migration Legislation Amendment (Further Border Protection Measures) Bill 2002, p. 26.

Despite (or possibly because of) this close result, the government introduced, and gained passage of, revised legislation which was supported by the Opposition. Its retrospectivity was plain and to the point: 'All action to which this Part applies is taken for all purposes to have been lawful when it occurred'.[5] That action included: Any action taken during the validation period by the Commonwealth, or by a Commonwealth officer, or any other person, acting on behalf of the Commonwealth, in relation to:

(a) the *MV Tampa*; or

(b) the *Aceng*; or

(c) any other vessel carrying persons in respect of whom there were reasonable grounds for believing that their intention was to enter Australia unlawfully.[6]

This retrospective legislation validated taking control of a ship from its captain and to take 433 people claiming a right to asylum under international refugee law and the government's own *Migration Act 1958* (Cth) out of Australian territorial waters against their will and eventually to a Pacific atoll. On one view of the law, this could be characterized as retrospectively validating what would otherwise be crimes of violence by government officials, committed for the purpose of denying the rights of refugees under international and Australian law let alone against the captain of a ship. While no one was physically injured, the seriousness of the issue is underlined by what would have happened if the Captain and/or the asylum seekers had taken a similar view to that of North J and Black CJ. If they had considered that the threatened use of force was unlawful and acted in what they believed to be self-defence, bloodshed could have easily resulted—with interesting questions of criminal liability arising for the soldiers and the government.

The Bali bombers

On 12 October 2002, Islamic extremists detonated a fertilizer bomb in a truck outside the Kuta Beach nightclub in Bali, Indonesia. The explosion killed 202 people and maimed more than 300 others. Astute work by the Indonesian police led to the suspects being quickly arrested and charged. The first to be tried was Amrozi bin Nurhasyim, a 41-year-old mechanic; a five-judge court found him guilty in August 2003 and sentenced him to death.

Apart from the propriety of the death penalty, few would disagree that the conviction was just. Deliberate murder of hundreds of unarmed civilians is a crime in every legal system known, and Amrozi's complicity was not in doubt: he

---

[5] *Border Protection (Validation and Enforcement Powers) Act 2001* (Cth), s 6. [6] Ibid, s 5.

purchased the truck and the chemicals for the bomb. However, Amrozi's lawyers filed an appeal against the decision on the grounds that it was unlawful. The reason for this claim was that Amrozi was charged with the crime of terrorism, under regulations made on 18 October 2002—days *after* he committed the crime.[7] Of course, he could have been charged with a number of pre-existing crimes against Indonesian law (murder, arson, grievous bodily harm), but he was not. And it was only the newly declared crime of terrorism that carried the death penalty.

In July 2004, Indonesia's Constitutional Court ruled the anti-terrorism laws unconstitutional due to their retrospectivity. In post-Suharto reforms to the Constitution of Indonesia, an Article was added declaring that 'the right not to be prosecuted under retrospective laws [is a] basic human right that may not be diminished under any circumstances'.[8] This ruling overturned the conviction of one of the Bali bombers, Maskur Abdul Kadir, and led to the dismissal of charges against Idris, who had confessed to taking part in the bombings. It also paved the way for 33 other convicted bombers, Amrozi among them, to appeal their convictions. The bizarre assertion of some Indonesian officials that the convictions were safe, because the prohibition against retrospectivity also forbade the 'retrospective' application of the Constitutional Court's rulings,[9] did not carry much weight.

The Indonesian government had argued that because terrorism can be considered a 'crime against humanity', the anti-terrorism laws may fall under the category whereby international law allows an exception to the prohibition against retrospectivity; or alternatively, that they may be justified as protecting 'the rights of others' under Article 28J of Indonesia's Constitution. However, the categorical wording of the anti-retrospectivity clause made these interpretations difficult to maintain, and the Constitutional Court held that the bombings were not gross violations of human rights.[10] Thus, combined with the Indonesian criminal law's long-standing prohibition against double jeopardy, and tactical bungling by the prosecution, the Indonesian Constitution's safeguard against retrospective law could mean that unrepentant mass murderers walk free.

---

[7] *Perpu 2/2002 on the Eradication of Criminal Acts of Terrorism in Relation to the Bomb Explosion Incident in Bali, 12 October 2002*. A *Perpu* is a 'Government Regulation in Lieu of Law' and can be issued by the President 'in the event of a compelling emergency,' provided it is ratified by Parliament in its next session (Constitution of Indonesia, Article 22). See Ross Clarke, 'Retrospectivity and the Constitutional Validity of the Bali Bombing and East Timor Trials' (2003) 5 (2) *Australian Journal of Asian Law* 2–32; Angus Martyn, 'The Amrozi Bali Bombing Case: Is Indonesia's Anti-Terrorism Law Unconstitutional?', *Research Note No 14*, Australian Parliamentary Library, Canberra, 7 October 2003, at URL http://www.aph.gov.au/library/pubs/rn/2003-04/04rn14.pdf; AAP, 'Difficult and messy appeal will send Amrozi to firing squad: expert', *Sydney Morning Herald*, 8 August 2003.

[8] Article 28I(1), inserted 18 August 2000.

[9] Greg Sheridan, 'Constitutional Terror', *The Australian*, 28 August 2004.

[10] Sheridan, 'Constitutional Terror'.

Guantanamo Bay and the Australian 'Taliban'

Similar issues—terrorism, Islamic extremists, and retrospective criminal law—also caused debate in Australia a few months later. In February 2004, the US Government repatriated five British citizens and one Dane who had been held in detention at the US base at Guantanamo Bay, Cuba, after having been allegedly captured fighting with the Taliban/Al-Qaeda forces in Afghanistan. Many Australians had been lobbying for two Australian citizens—David Hicks and Mamadouh Habib—to be similarly returned to their home country. However, the Bush Administration claimed that the Dane and Britons had been returned to their home countries only because they could be tried and punished there under domestic law.[11] This was not said to be true of Australia: The problem is that Australian laws were never framed to deal with something as bizarre as the David Hicks case. Training with al-Qaeda, or fighting for a group like the Taliban, does not appear to be an offence under current Australian law. The closest applicable law is the 1978 *Crimes (Foreign Incursion and Recruitment) Act* that made it a crime to fight as a mercenary overseas. This states that a person must be involved in a 'hostile activity against the government' of a host country. But Hicks was fighting with the Taliban, the then government of Afghanistan, not against it. Another option might be to charge Hicks with treason because he was fighting against a coalition that included Australia. However, this is complicated by the fact that Australia was not formally 'at war' with Afghanistan—a requirement under the treason laws.[12]

After Hicks and Habib were taken prisoner (in 2001), Australia enacted laws defining terrorism more specifically. However, this legislation was not made retrospective, despite statements by the then Opposition leader, Mark Latham, that Labor would support any moves by the Government to backdate the 2002 Act on the grounds that the prisoners would be better off avoiding a potential death penalty, facing normal court procedures and serving any penalty in Australia. One Labor frontbencher suggested that such backdating might be unconstitutional and both the Prime Minister and the Minister for Foreign Affairs ruled out retrospective criminal legislation.[13]

The irony was that under United States jurisdiction Hicks and Habib would have faced trial for breaches of rules set out by an Executive Military Order that

---

[11] In fact, none were charged and all Britons were released within 24 hours. In January 2005, days after an affidavit alleging that he was tortured was lodged in a US Court, the US government announced it was releasing Habib.

[12] Cameron Stewart, 'Nowhere man: While alleged terrorist David Hicks sits in a cage in Cuba, his case sits in the too-hard basket of international diplomacy', *Weekend Australian Magazine*, 6–7 April 2002, pp. 15–17.

[13] Sophie Morris, Dennis Shanahan and Andrew McGarry, 'Latham backs off new law for Hicks', *Weekend Australian*, 21–22 February 2004.

was passed retrospectively; that is, after the alleged offences were committed.[14] This was not apparently objectionable to the Australian Government.[15]

Meanwhile . . .

While the above examples indicate the 'headline' examples of retrospectivity, retrospective law making is a legislative practice that elected Australian representatives engage in frequently and deliberately. At the same time, courts are refining and revising law all the time.

This book

This book offers an answer to a puzzle: why are retrospective laws so trenchantly reviled, but so frequently used? How can a practice, which is so frequently said to undermine the rule of law, be compatible with the generally and relatively well-ordered societies under law in which it occurs?

It will commence by an analysis of the various meanings given to 'retrospectivity' and the rule of law, noting the differences and their potential significance, and avoiding definitions that prove too much or too little but allow the debate for and against retrospectivity to be mounted. In particular, it will be shown that retrospectivity is not an absolute but a relative term. Chapter 3 seeks to analyse the many arguments against retrospectivity and finds that they can be effectively reduced to one that can be put in terms of justice, fairness, equity or the rule of law. This very strong argument is that the law operates most effectively and fairly if the direct legal effects of an individual's action are determined using texts

---

[14] The Executive Order 'Detention, Treatment and Trial of Certain Non-Citizens in the War Against Terrorism, 13 November 2001, does not formally establish new offences, seeking to establish military commissions to try 'violations of the laws of war and other applicable laws' (section 1(e)). However, the charges laid against Hicks seem to indicate that the charges include some that would not have been entertained by a US court (let alone an Afghan court) at the time they were alleged to have been committed. Richard Ackland, 'Why throw Hicks to the wolves', Sydney Morning Herald, 21 January 2005, attacks the vagueness of the charges. 'It's worth remembering that the charges against Hicks are of the most vaporous quality imaginable: conspiracy, attempted murder by an unprivileged belligerent and aiding the enemy. The claimed conspiracy relates to Hicks joining 'an enterprise of persons who shared a common criminal purpose', that is, terrorism. The attempted murder charge says that he 'attempted to murder diverse persons by directing small arms fire, explosives and other means intended to kill' coalition forces in Afghanistan. There is precious little detail in the charge of aiding the enemy, only that he 'intentionally aided the enemy, to wit al-Qaeda and the Taliban, such conduct taking place in the context of and associated with armed conflict'. However, the point at issue for us here is whether the breadth of such charges indicate a significant extension of existing US law—especially the imposition of attempted murder charges on those fighting for countries with which the United States is at war. It may be that the real problem is that the procedures and composition of the court and the lack of review makes it possible to run with such broad, vague and unprecedented charges. See Chapter 4 (4.6 Retrospective Criminal Legislation).

[15] See more detailed discussion in Chapter 4 (4.6 Retrospective Criminal Legislation).

discoverable in advance. By this process, the law guides action and those who respond to its guidance can generally rely on rational and legitimate expectations that this will happen.

Chapters 4 and 5 show that retrospective rule making is common in legislatures and almost universal at the senior judicial level. Chapter 6 then examines some of the general justifications for retrospective rule making—especially legislative—and Chapter 7 considers what this means for the rule of law. Does it have to be abandoned, modified, or demoted? Or does it need to be reconsidered and reconceived?

This book, therefore, presents a far more complete picture of the uses and abuses of retrospectivity than have been attempted before. Seen in the context of its actual use, retrospectivity appears to be a legitimate but limited tool for dealing with some of the problems which confront legislatures and governments—especially, but not exclusively, in non-criminal matters. Furthermore, while there are undoubtedly examples of unfair, even evil, retrospective legislation, such examples are rare and are probably far less prevalent than examples of unfair prospective legislation.

In this book, we will consider some of the problems involved in calling legal rules or other legal statements 'retrospective' and the variety of arguments made against some of the arguments that are, or could be, made for and against retrospective legislation under its various definitions. We compare these with the arguments for and against retrospectivity in judicial decision-making and the various conceptions of the appropriate constraints under which it does or should operate.

Our argument is that most of the arguments against retrospective legislation are unfounded, of little importance, or reducible to the one strong reliance argument that is very strong but not universally compelling. The argument is that, when a citizen contemplates an action, he or she is entitled to rely on the expectation that the legal consequences of that action will be determined by the legal rules that were discoverable at the time the action was taken. However, this argument is neither overwhelming nor unequivocal. Reliance weighs against retrospectivity in many cases, but it (or the principles underlying it) actually justifies retrospective legislation in others. This has important consequences for traditional concepts of the Rule of Law and even suggests a complete reconceptualization of the ideal.

1

Defining retrospectivity

1.1 Introduction

The widespread feelings of hostility towards retrospective law noted in the Introduction might leave some under the misapprehension that there is a general understanding and agreement on what retrospectivity is. In fact, there is no agreed definition of retrospectivity; most definitions appear to have either serious flaws or, at least, significant limitations. Indeed, there are genuine difficulties finding such a definition.

It is not, of course, uncommon for the villainy of the cavalierly condemned to be imprecisely defined. It is easier to condemn on charges that do not have to be specified and contradicted. Ironically, such condemnation is against one of the key tenets of the 'rule of law' which retrospectivity is accused of offending. It is, of course, an irony, that those accused of retrospectivity are not always accorded the rule of law protections that the charge be defined and known in advance.[1]

This chapter provides a brief overview of the history of retrospectivity then turns to the attempt to define it. After evaluating the strengths and weaknesses of a number of definitions, it concludes that retrospectivity does not appear to be an all-or-nothing characteristic of laws, but rather is a matter of degree. This has significant implications for the 'absolutist' opponents of retrospectivity who seek to reject all retrospective law making.

1.2 A historical overview of retrospectivity

Concern about retrospective law making has a long history. The idea that there is something wrong with punishing people for conduct which they engaged in before its proscription is an ancient one, although it is often conflated with other aspects of legal unfairness. The democratic Athenian polity established by Solon and Cleisthenes was based on the ideal of *isonomia*, or 'equality of laws to all manner of persons and a certainty of being governed in accordance with known

---

[1] While a concept does not have a human right in itself, the rule makers against whom the accusation is made do—as do any whose rights the rule maker is trying to preserve.

rules'.² Greek jurists expressed disapproval of excessive changes to the laws (which are objected to on the same grounds as retrospective law). Demosthenes claimed that the Locrians were 'so strongly of the opinion that it is right . . . to preserve the institutions of their forefathers . . . that if a man wishes to propose a new law, he legislates with a halter round his neck'.³

Indeed, to the Greeks, changes to the law were essentially undesirable because they were seen as undermining the laws' moral authority. Placing their faith in the educative value of laws and *mores* rather than their deterrent power (as Machiavelli, Hobbes and Bentham did), the Greeks were suspicious of changes that diluted the antiquity of laws and hence cast doubt upon the wisdom of their ancestors. Frequent or retrospective changes were therefore undesirable for this reason, and not primarily for the reason usually assumed today (namely, that retrospective laws do not give notice to those affected by them).⁴ As we shall see, arguments for stability and against retrospectivity are often related. Many of those who strongly condemn retrospective laws broadly conceived really want the law to stay the same—whether because they prefer the old law or the source from which it came.⁵ While recognizing this tendency, this book will argue that there is a perfectly defensible general and individual interest in the stability of law that should be respected and taken into account by all lawmakers. This is related to but separate from the general and individual interest in the prospectivity of law which must likewise be respected and considered carefully. Each increases the capacity of law to guide citizens by making it possible to know in advance the laws that will be applied to their actions. Retrospectivity reduces this by changing the rules after the citizen has acted; frequent prospective legal changes reduce this by making it harder for the citizen to keep up with the rules that will be applied.⁶

The Roman republic and Empire clearly distinguished retrospective from other new law making. In the Roman Republic and Empire, jurists propounded the twinned maxims *nulla poena sine crimen* (no penalty without a crime) and *nulla crimen sine lega* (no crime without a law). Retrospective laws were contrary to the spirit of these ideals. Such laws were unknowable at the time of the alleged offence. This was a source of criticism that went beyond retrospective laws.

---

² Geoffrey de Q Walker, *The Rule of Law: Foundation of Constitutional Democracy* (Melbourne University Press, 1988) 93.

³ Demosthenes, 'Against Timocrates', Section 139, repr. in JH Vince (trans) *Against Meidias, Androtion, Aristocrates, Timocrates, Aristogeiton*, Loeb Classical Library No 299 (Harvard University Press, Mass., 1951) vol. 3, 463.

⁴ Walker, p. 242. Although this reason may also have played some part in the measures they imposed to curtail new legislation.

⁵ That more authoritative source may be, in addition to ancestors: God, Reason, the founding fathers (especially popular with literalist constitutionalists), and legislature (for those who oppose judicial law making). However, those who take 'education' and 'notice' seriously note the difficulty of communicating and explaining law to those to whom it applies.

⁶ As we will see, these are only generalizations. Some retrospective changes will restore the law to that which the citizens thought it was when they acted and some changes to law can make it easier to understand.

According to Blackstone, the Emperor Caligula was criticized for allegedly writing laws 'in a very small character, and hung them above high pillars the more effectually to ensnare the people'.[7] Interestingly enough, Caligula's ploy indicates that even he recognized the undesirability of retrospective criminal laws!

The Romans were not, however, averse to new laws and were the first Europeans to codify law—providing an exemplar for later European states. Such codes were intended to give clear notice to the public of the laws that applied to them. In general, however, the trend over time was toward greater codification of laws (and hence, more emphasis on giving notice). Such codification did not mean that laws were necessarily reasonable or just[8] (let alone comprehensible). But the very fact that ancient lawmakers (Hammurabi, Moses, Solon, Justinian) took pains to codify laws indicates that written advance warning was thought desirable. It probably was not regarded as *necessary*, however, being seen more as either a gracious supererogatory act on the part of the sovereign (reflected in the commonly used reference to such codifiers as law-*givers*). However, it would be surprising if at least some did not see it as a wise move to make law more effective by making it more predictable and thereby making it easier for the lawgivers' subjects to modify their behaviour in the way desired by the lawmaker.

In the Christian tradition, the concept of Natural Law produced a tension between the desirability of notice and the idea that such notice is not necessary for just punishment. In his Epistle to the Romans, Saint Paul wrote that 'where there is no law, neither is there any transgression.'[9] Despite this, Gentiles who had not heard of the Ten Commandments were still thought to be accountable for violating the Natural Law that is 'written in their hearts, their conscience also bearing witness'.[10] Thomas Aquinas held not only that 'promulgation is necessary for the law to obtain its force', but also that 'the Natural Law is promulgated by the very fact that God instilled it into men's minds so as to be known by them naturally'.[11] By such arguments they could recognize the importance of notice but claim that notice had been given.

Protestants have traditionally been more ambivalent about Natural Law[12] and other traditions are hostile. Islam traces its very foundation—the giving of the Qur'an to the Prophet Muhammad—to Allah's insistence that 'we never punish

---

[7] Sir William Blackstone, *Commentaries on the Laws of England*, 1765, repr. (University of Chicago Press, Chicago, 1979) vol. 1, 46. This, again, emphasizes the importance of notice—that the problem with retrospectivity is essentially one of notice—that it is hard to discover the text of a law that has not yet been made. However, it should also be noted that it was not impossible to read the text and it is not impossible to predict the kinds of changes that lawmakers may choose.

[8] Babington, p. 7.   [9] Romans 4.15.   [10] Romans 2.15.

[11] Aquinas, *Summa Theologica*, chapters I–II, Question 90.

[12] Peter J Leithart, 'Natural Law: A Reformed Critique', 3 (2) *Premise*, 29 February 1996 at 4. See also C Stephen Evans, 'Apologetics in a New Key: Reviving Protestant Anxieties over Natural Theology', in Mark McLeod and William Lane Craig (eds), *The Logic of Rational Theism: Exploratory Essays* (E Mellen Press, Lewiston, NY, 1990); and John Calvin, *Institutes of the Christian Religion*, Geneva, 1539, Book 2, Chapter 8, Section 1, trans. Henry Beveridge (Eerdmans, Michigan, 1989) 317. This may be partly explained by the different relationship between man and God. While

[humankind] before I have sent a messenger' (ie a prophet bringing written scriptures).[13] Jewish scholars have largely traditionally rejected the idea of a Natural Law discoverable by reason alone; although some (for example, Joseph Albo, 1380–1444) concede that acts such as theft and murder are *intrinsece malum*, others source even these prohibitions to divine revelation.[14]

The Roman maxims cited above can be seen to imply a ban on retrospective criminal laws and we saw above that even Allah reportedly bound himself to a principle of non-retrospectivity. However, firm rules against retrospective criminal laws are relatively recent in the West. In the English Courts, the presumption against retrospectivity was a canon of interpretation only rather than a ground of invalidity.[15] A stretched interpretation of Lord Chief Justice Coke's celebrated and controversial dictum in *Dr Bonham's Case* that the common law would 'adjudge . . . to be utterly void' any Act of Parliament that was 'impossible to be performed'[16] could perhaps be read as encompassing retrospectivity.[17] Lord Chief Justice Coke was certainly expounding some key rule of law principles—going beyond the principle that no person should be judge in their own cause (the issue in *Dr Bonham's Case*) to impossibilities and absurdities. However, it is not clear whether retrospectivity as a subject matter was in fact within his ample field of fire—or whether common law judges can ever be too precious about the retrospective law-making of others given the inevitably retrospective effect of judicial decision-making (see Chapter 5). The English *Bill of Rights 1689* included no prohibition of retrospective laws (this was probably because it was not a particular abuse that was, or could be,[18] committed by the Stuart kings, and also because Parliament was concerned with asserting rather than limiting its own

Catholics continued to believe that there was one earthly institution that could authoritatively (and, much later, 'infallibly') interpret God's will and God's law, Protestants believed in an individual relationship with God mediated, at best, by a local congregation or presbytery. Thus, any Protestant version of divinely inspired natural law would mean that there could be many claimed authoritative statements of Natural Law. While this was fine with a Protestant view of 'conscience' and ethics, it was bound to create difficulties for law.

[13] Qur'an, Su'rat 17 ('*al-Israa*'), v15.

[14] J David Bleich, 'Judaism and Natural Law', in Martin P Golding, (ed), *Jewish Law and Legal Theory* (New York University Press, 1993) 94.

[15] For detailed discussion of the interpretation of retrospective law see DC Pearce and RS Geddes (2001) '*Statutory Interpretation in Australia*, Butterworth pp. 250–270; or (1988) 99, 180–195.

[16] (1610) 77 ER 638, 8 Coke's Reports 107a, 2 Brownlow's Reports 225 at 113b.

[17] On the basis that Parliamentary sovereignty is 'always limited by Parliament's ability to express its legislative intentions with sufficient precision and clarity'. Douglas E Edin 'Rule Britannia', 2002, available at <http://www.utpjournals.com/product/utij/523/523_edlin.html>, referring to comments by Lord Hoffmann in *R v Secretary of State for the Home Department, ex parte Simms* [2000] 2 AC 115 at 131. Also see discussion of different interpretations of Coke's comments in Geoffrey de Q Walker, *The Rule of Law: Foundation of Constitutional Democracy* (Melbourne University Press, Melbourne, 1988), 117–119; and Mark D Walters, 'Common Law, Reason, and Sovereign Will', 2003, available at <http://www.utpjournals.com/product/utlj/531/531_walters.html>.

[18] As the *The Case of Prohibitions* (1607) 12 Co Rep 63 stripped them of the ability to make law through judicial decisions and *The Case of Proclamations* (1611) 12 Co Rep 74 stripped them of independent legislative power.

legislative supremacy).[19] Thus, although the common-law presumption against retrospectivity was well established, it was regarded as only a guide to ascertaining the legislature's intent, not as a ground for setting aside that intent if expressed unambiguously.

For Blackstone, the common law presumption against retrospectivity and the sovereignty of Parliament were both well established. Clearly expressed retrospective laws were valid. But for Blackstone they were clearly wrong. After citing Caligula's ploy mentioned above he wrote:

There is ftill a more unreafonable method than this, which is called making of laws ex poft facto; when after an action is committed, the legiflator then for the firft time declares it to have been a crime, and inflicts a punifhment upon the perfon who has committed it; here it is impoffible that the party could forefee that an action, innocent when it was done, fhould be afterwards converted to guilt by a fubfequent law; he had therefore no caufe to abftain from it; and all punifhment for not abftaining muft of confequence be cruel and unjuft. All laws fhould be therefore made to commence in futuro, and be notified before their commencement; which is implied in the term 'prefcribed'.[20]

American lawyers fighting for independence were much influenced by Blackstone. They took on board his revulsion for retrospective criminal laws but were in revolt against the sovereignty of Parliament. Unlike the 'glorious' revolutionaries of 1688, they saw Parliament as well as King doing wrong and sought to constrain the federal legislature that they created and the colonial legislatures that they reformed.

The prohibition of retrospective laws began early, with Delaware passing a Declaration of Rights and Fundamental Rules in 1776, article 3 of which provided 'That retrospective Laws, punishing Offenses committed before the Existence of such Laws, are oppressive and unjust and ought not to be made'.

Jefferson was against all retrospective laws[21] but the prohibitions in other states and in the Federal Constitution were, like Delaware's, confined to retrospective criminal statues. Although Madison raised an extension of the ban beyond criminal laws during the Constitutional debates, it was not pressed when Dickinson consulted Blackstone and announced that Blackstone's definition only covered criminal cases.[22] This was apparently sufficient to determine the matter.[23]

---

[19] It should be remembered that the 1689 Bill of Rights is still a pre-enlightenment document—emphasizing the collective rights and privileges of an institution along with its members and beneficiaries, the Parliament, against the sovereign rather than the individual rights of citizens against a legislature.

[20] Greg Bailey *From Revolution to Reconstruction: A Biography of William Blackstone (1723–1780)*, available at <http://odur.let.rug.nl/~usa/B/blackstone/blackstone.htm>.

[21] 3 US 386 (1798) PER Chase at 391 and per Paterson J AT 396.

[22] Blackstone's Commentaries, Introduction, Section the First, On the Study of Law, 1765, p 46, available at <http://www.yale.edu/lawweb/avalon/blackstone/introa.htm>.

[23] For example see Joseph Story (1833) *Commentaries on the Constitution of the United States* 3: §§ 1338–39 'The general interpretation has been, and is, that the phrase applies to acts of a criminal nature only'. This commentary and others available at <http://press-pubs.uchicago.edu/founders/>.

Subsequently, in *Calder v. Bull*[24] Justices Chase and Paterson made reference to Blackstone's definition as applying to 'crimes and nothing else' in determining that the *ex post facto* clause was indeed limited to criminal laws.[25]

While the Constitution confined itself to banning retrospective criminal laws, it went further in also banning Bills of Attainder. Although the link between the two seem strong to some commentators who are strongly influenced by that document,[26] it was not apparently clear to Jefferson who apparently drafted a Bill of Attainder for the Virginia legislature that would have executed an English loyalist.[27] The courts refused to enforce the Bill and insisted on trying the 'attainted' under normal processes.

At the time, Bills of Attainder were still occasionally used by the British Parliament (as well as the related, if milder, procedure of 'impeachment' which the Americans retained while the British let it fall into desuetude for politicians, finding the 'no confidence' motion sufficient for removing unwanted politicians and leaving serious charges to the courts). Both measures might be defended from charges of retrospectivity on the grounds that they generally claimed breaches of law by those who were punished by attainder or dismissed by impeachment.[28] Jefferson's Bill alleged high treason, murder and arson—crimes that had long stood, though their application to those fighting a war, especially one in defence of the previously accepted sovereign, was as doubtful then as it was in the Hick's case cited in the introduction. The Bill of Attainder can be seen as a survival from the mediaeval origins of the 'High Court of Parliament' when law making and adjudication were not clearly distinguished and the parliament's role was to declare law rather than to make it. As such, the principal problem with Bills of Attainder is a breach of the concept of the separation of powers that emerged in the seventeenth and eighteenth centuries rather than retrospectivity as such. However, the breadth and novelty of some of the grounds that could be cited meant that Bills of Attainder were often, effectively, retrospective and can be argued to be contrary to the rule of law as generally interpreted.

The French revolutionaries followed the New World ban on retrospective criminal laws. The French *Declaration of the Rights of Man and of the Citizen* of August 1789 declared (in Article 8) that 'no one shall suffer punishment except . . . by virtue of a law passed and promulgated before the commission of the

---

[24] 3 US 386 (1798) per Chase at 391 and per Paterson J at 396.

[25] Greg Bailey *From Revolution to Reconstruction: A Biography of William Blackstone (1723–1780)*, available at <http://odur.let.rug.nl/~usa/B/blackstone/blackstone.htm>.

[26] For example, Geoffrey de Q Walker, *The Rule of Law*, pp. 316–322.

[27] For example, see Joseph Story (1833) *Commentaries on the Constitution of the United States* 3: §§ 1338–39 'The general interpretation has been, and is, that the phrase applies to acts of a criminal nature only'. This commentary and others available at <http://press-pubs.uchicago.edu/founders/>.

[28] Thomas Jefferson, 'Bill to Attaint Josiah Phillips 28 May 1778', in Julian P Boyd et al (eds), *The papers of Thomas Jefferson* (Princeton University Press, Princeton, 1950), Papers 2, pp. 189–91; available from The Founders' Constitution, University of Chicago Press, Volume 3 Article, Section 9, Clause 3 Document 4 at <http://press-pubs.uchicago.edu/founders/documents/a1_9_3s4.html>.

offence'. Although intended as a permanent standard by which to judge the legitimacy of later statutes, the *Declaration* was not judicially enforceable against the legislature (like the 'glorious revolutionaries' the framers of the Declaration saw the problem as the King and the solution as the legislature, with the latter expected to follow its own grand declarations of principle). It is not entirely clear whether the framers of the American Constitution expected their prohibition on passing any 'Bill of Attainder' or '*ex post facto* law' to be judicially enforceable. The ability of courts to exercise judicial review to invalidate statutes was something that was only later (and retrospectively?) determined by Chief Justice Marshall in *Marbury v. Madison* in 1803.[29] By that time, France's constitutional experiment had been converted into a military and imperial dictatorship.

In the twentieth century, human rights charters drafted by international bodies and common-law jurisdictions have sought to limit retrospective laws. The 1948 *Universal Declaration of Human Rights* (UCHR) guarantees, in Article 11, that 'no one shall be held guilty of any penal offence on account of any act or omission which did not constitute a penal offence, under national or international law, at the time when it was committed. Nor shall a heavier penalty be imposed than the one that was applicable at the time the penal offence was committed'. This was subsequently amplified in the 1966 *International Covenant on Civil and Political Rights* (ICCPR). European Union nations are bound by Article 7 of the *European Convention on Human Rights and Fundamental Freedoms* 1950 (ECHR) which prohibits retrospective laws except in relation to acts deemed criminal at the time of commission according to 'general principles of law recognised by civilised nations.'

These instruments, being matters of international law, do not have direct domestic effect in all systems. But their terms have been followed in most if not all post-1945 Bills of Rights. For example, a suspicion of retrospective law is reflected in the *Canadian Charter of Rights and Freedoms* 1982, the *New Zealand Bill of Rights Act* 1990, and the UK *Human Rights Act* 1998,[30] with constitutional effect. Article 11 of the Canadian Constitution also requires that for a person charged with an offence to be found guilty, the act must have constituted an offence under either Canadian law, international law or have been 'criminal according to the general principles of law recognized by the community of nations' at the time it was committed. In France, the prohibition of retrospective criminal laws (except where they benefit the accused) in the Declaration of the Rights of Man and Citizen now enjoys constitutional status by virtue of being incorporated into the preamble of the current Constitution.[31] Article 28(I) of the Indonesian

---

[29] (1803) 5 US 137.

[30] It should be noted, however, that while in all three countries these prohibitions are legally enforceable, in the last resort they can still be suspended (Canada) or even repealed (NZ, UK) by a normal legislative majority.

[31] Letter to Isaac McPherson, 13 August, 1813, available at <http://www.answers.com/topic/ex-post-facto-law>.

Constitution prohibits prosecution under retroactive application of law as this is considered a human right that may not be derogated from in any circumstances. Under Article 54 of the Constitution of the Russian Federation laws instituting or increasing liability have no retroactive force. An individual will not be held liable for the commission of an offence if it was not recognized as one at the time the act was committed and retroactive effect of a law applies only where liability has been lifted or the penalty reduced. Article 20 of the Indian Constitution provides protection from conviction for violation of a law that was not an offence at the time of the commission of the act and from a penalty greater than that under the law in force at the time. The Japanese Constitution, under Article 39, protects persons from being held criminally liable for an act which was lawful at the time it was committed. Article 35 in the Bill of Rights of the Constitution of the Republic of South Africa provides protection for an accused person from conviction where an act or omission was not an offence at the time it was committed under either national or international law. The Constitution of Argentina under section 18 mandates that punishment without trial based on a law enacted before an act was committed is not permitted.

The widespread use of rules or presumptions against retrospective law, particularly in modern times, may give the impression that there exists a clear, universally accepted and philosophically sound definition of retrospectivity. This is, however, very far from being the case. There is a great deal of disagreement on how retrospectivity ought to be defined. Indeed, there is even disagreement over how the search for a definition ought to proceed: whether it is better first to identify what is bad about retrospectivity and then proceed from there to a definition, or whether it is better to settle on what retrospectivity is before trying to decide what is wrong with it?[32]

As this book argues that retrospectivity is not universally bad and even occasionally a positive good (performing an indispensable role in a well-ordered society under the Rule of Law), we obviously take the latter view. It is generally better to settle the definitional question before tackling the normative one. Indeed, it is hard to meaningfully say that 'X is bad' or 'X is not bad' if X is already defined by its evil character. Sometimes the vehemence of the attack on retrospectivity seems to indicate that, for some, retrospectivity amounts to whatever they dislike about laws which are taken to be retrospective.

Even in the absence of pejorative distortion, defining retrospectivity is not an easy task. While most would prefer a definition which would give both necessary and sufficient conditions for a law to be retrospective, this may be an unattainable standard in practice. Under such circumstances, a good way to proceed is by a process of reflective equilibrium; that is, moving back and forth between a proposed definition and our pre-theoretical judgements concerning particular

---

[32] Eule, 'Temporal Limits on the Legislative Mandate: Entrenchment and Retroactivity' (1987) *Am. B. Found. Res J.* 380 at 436n.

laws. If our definition includes retrospective laws which we are not prepared to regard as such, or (conversely) excludes laws which we are convinced *are* retrospective, then the definition is, to that extent, unsatisfactory. If, on the other hand, a definition does a very good job of tracking our most confident judgements, then we may be led to revise those more marginal intuitions which are incompatible with the definition.

In the remainder of the chapter, we therefore consider several proposed definitions of retrospectivity. In Chapter 1.3 and 1.4, we examine initially plausible but fatally flawed definitions of retrospectivity: one very broad, and another very narrow. Unfortunately, we cannot, as Goldilocks found in the little bear's porridge, find a definition that is 'just right'. However, in Chapter 1.5 we arrive at a relatively satisfactory definition of a retrospective law: namely, one alters the future legal consequences of past actions or events (or, to put it another way, that at least one of the laws that are used to determine the consequences of an action was not potentially discoverable at the time the action was taken). One result of this definition is that it shows that retrospectivity is not an all-or-nothing matter, but rather a question of degree; we explore this implication in Chapter 1.6 and 1.7.

Before we proceed, however, a brief note is in order. In the literature on retrospectivity, it is common to see a number of terms—especially the words 'retroactive' and '*ex post facto*'—in addition to 'retrospective'. Sometimes these terms are used to denote different aspects of retrospectivity; at other times, they appear to be used as interchangeable labels for the same phenomenon. Additional neologisms are also sometimes introduced to mark out various aspects of retrospectivity. This profusion of distinctions and terms poses a difficulty for a discussion of retrospectivity. To adopt any particular existing usage risks distorting others' arguments, either through misinterpretation or by forcing their arguments into definitional lines they were not originally intended to fit. On the other hand, to introduce new stipulative definitions of our own would only introduce more clutter into the conceptual landscape. We have, therefore, chosen to use the word 'retrospective' generally to cover all such permutations. However, in discussing writers who regularly attempt to make the distinction, it is easier to use the 'retroactive' to refer to retrospective laws whose retrospective effect is formally and explicitly stated by indicating that an enactment is to take effect before its promulgation. Laws so expressed will often, but not necessarily, have more and greater retrospective effects than other retrospective laws.

1.3 The broad definition

At one extreme of definitions of retrospectivity is the broad one suggested (though perhaps no longer advocated) by Professor Dennis Pearce; according to this definition, a law is retrospective if it 'impairs an existing right or obligation'.[33] A similar definition suggests that legislation is retrospective if it alters the market value of a pre-existing asset. Thus, many tax reforms in the USA during the 1980s were labelled as retrospective because they removed tax shelters without saving or preserving benefits accruing to existing investments in these shelters (that is, 'grandfathering').

The latter definition is obviously inadequate (since it would not encompass laws which do not concern or affect assets), but is not, in any case, intended as a comprehensive definition of retrospectivity. The former definition, by contrast, is quite comprehensive, covering all types of legislation. It locates the defining feature of retrospectivity in the fact that it is rights and obligations which have arisen in the past that are affected by new law.

This definition seems to be *too* comprehensive. Indeed, it might be argued that this definition would define *all* legislation as retrospective. After all, the *raison d'etre* of legislation is to create new legal rights and obligations, or vary existing ones; indeed, unless a right or obligation is altered, one wonders if any legal change has been made at all. It might be argued that laws are only retrospective on this definition if they *impair* existing rights or obligations, which means that they will not be retrospective if they enhance or add to existing rights and obligations.[34] But this, in fact, makes the definition *more* problematic, for it implies that laws which enhance or add to existing rights and obligations *cannot* be retrospective, even if they explicitly state that such rights are deemed to have had legal force—and ought to have been respected—from the beginning of time. Some laws which are *clearly* retrospective by any common-sense judgement would not be retrospective by this definition.[35] Of course, this objection is easily overcome by modifying the definition: legislation would be defined as retrospective if it *altered* existing rights or obligations. But then it *is* true that this definition of retrospectivity encompasses all legislation. This renders the definition counter-intuitive and useless: it is not part of our common-sense concept of retrospectivity

---

[33] DC Pearce, *Statutory Interpretation in Australia* (2nd edn, Butterworth, Sydney, 1981) 49. This definition, however, was omitted from the 3rd edition, which may indicate that Pearce no longer accepts it.

[34] This deals a fatal blow to the attempted distinction between laws that enhance and impair rights. The first problem with such a distinction is that it is very rare for the rights of one person to be enhanced without the impairment of the rights of others. This does not mean that law making regarding rights is a zero-sum game, so that enhancing or adding to one right will always have to come at the expense of impairing another right. However, there are very few purely Pareto efficient laws, unless one considers that an impairment of the rights of the state can be ignored, even when such an impairment directly affects the rights of others (as taxpayers, welfare recipients and beneficiaries of government action). And it is not particularly relevant here: if all legislation necessarily involves impairing rights, then the definition will include all legislation; if it does not, then the definition is even more problematic and will have to be modified in any case.

[35] The alteration of rights and obligations typically devolves around allocation and alteration of property rights. However, it also applies to criminal law. The classically prospective criminal law imposes penalties on future action and warns of their future imposition. These alter (by increasing) the obligations of those who are warned and alter (by increasing) the rights of those who benefit from the deterrence effect of the threatened penalties.

that all legislation is retrospective. This means that the definition is not capable of doing the work we would want such a definition to do: namely, that of distinguishing a class of laws which has a particular feature not shared by law in general.

The only motivation for adopting this problematic and inadequate definition may, in fact, be a rhetorical one: it would enable the application of the label 'retrospective'—along with the associated stigma—to almost any piece of law making that displeases the speaker. In other words, given the prejudice against retrospectivity, the ability to brand a particular piece of legislation as retrospective is useful to those who oppose that piece of legislation. However, under this broad definition, the label 'retrospective' will not pick out a feature which distinguishes that piece of legislation from any other, so to call that legislation 'retrospective' is to object to it only on grounds which would equally be an objection to all other pieces of legislation. It is only under a narrower definition that it would be possible for retrospectivity to be particularly objectionable. Thus, those who would adopt a broad definition in order to call a law retrospective, but also attempt to retain the negative associations of retrospectivity (which would require a narrow definition), would be guilty of equivocation: that is, using the same word with different meanings in order to make the desired conclusion appear to follow.

1.4 The narrow definition

We have seen that the broad definition of retrospectivity is inadequate because it labels far too much legislation as retrospective. An attempt to give a satisfactory (and narrower) definition might, therefore, proceed by focusing on what legislation we ought to *exclude* from the category of retrospectivity. Thus Fuller,[36] for example, claims that legislation imposing tax on past financial gains (which were non-taxable at the time they accrued) is not retrospective, because such laws always operate prospectively: that is, they tell the taxpayer how much tax to pay in the future, even when the amount is calculated on the basis of past transactions.[37]

---

[36] In fact, critics of retrospectivity often turn out to dislike legislation in general, preferring to rely on courts to declare common-law rights case by case. See FA Hayek, *Law, Legislation and Liberty Vol 1: Rules and Order* (Routledge and Kegan Paul, London, 1973) 97 ff; Walker, pp. 115, 182, 313, 362, 391–2.

[37] It is ironic that, in 1982, when the Senate was debating proposed legislation against 'bottom-of-the-harbour' tax avoidance schemes, Senator Noel Chrichton-Browne (Liberal, WA) distinguished himself as one of the few Australian parliamentarians to cite a jurisprudential philosopher by quoting Lon L Fuller's view that making retrospective rules was one of the ways *not* to make law. [Australia, *Hansard*, Senate, 1982, vol. 96, p. 2599; citing Lon L Fuller, *The Morality of Law* (Yale UP, New Haven, 1964; 1969 rev. edn), 39.] However, he missed two points about Fuller's argument. One was the argument above that none of his arguments against retrospectivity applied to tax legislation. The other was that Fuller was arguing, not that all retrospective legislation was inevitably bad, but rather that if all law were retrospective then there would be no law. Only in an ideal world (where all laws are clear, well-publicized, never-changing and fully known in advance) could laws also be, and be expected to be, completely prospective.

ALP parliamentarians made an apparently similar argument in legislative debates over 'retrospective' taxation bills. It was argued that, because tax liability does not arise until the end of the financial year, no retrospectivity is involved if the Government changes the tax rules for the *entire* period at any time before it ends.[38]

The proposed benchmark of what *excludes* a law from the class of retrospective laws could, therefore, be said to be that it tells people what to do in the future. And from this we can derive a principle concerning which laws *are* retrospective: if a law that tells people what to do in the future is *not* retrospective, then a retrospective law must be one that tells people *what to have done in the past*.

This definition might be thought to be problematic on grounds which are precisely the converse of the objection to the broad definition: that is, according to this definition *no* laws will qualify as retrospective. It might be objected that even the most uncontentious and obvious examples of retrospectivity—that is, retrospective criminal laws—will not qualify as retrospective according to this definition, since they merely tell the courts what to do in the future (or tell people what penalties or legal consequences will apply to them in the future). To take an extreme example, Parliament might re-introduce the death penalty for certain crimes. Since no one is liable to this penalty before he or she is convicted, it could be argued—on the narrow definition—that it would not be retrospective to execute those who committed these crimes during the period before the legislation was enacted.

In fact, this is not entirely accurate: it would still be *possible*, in principle, to make retrospective legislation. Retrospective tax legislation would tell people, not how much tax they will have to pay in future as a result of the new law, but rather how much tax they *have to have paid in the past* as a result of the new law.[39] Similarly, it might be thought that a law which decreed that past conduct (legal at the time) is now decreed to have been criminal would still be retrospective on this definition.

This, however, shows that while it is, in principle, possible to make retrospective legislation under this definition, no *actual* legislation would ever qualify as retrospective, for it would be pointless and absurd to make such legislation. And this means that the definition is inadequate generally, since it fails to count as retrospective many pieces of legislation which are clearly and unequivocally retrospective according to our pre-theoretical judgements.

The motivation for adopting a narrow definition such as this is likely, as with the broad definition, to be a strategic one. In Fuller's case,[40] it seems to have been due to a total lack of sympathy for tax avoidance which led him to an ill thought out distinction. But the cost of this was to weaken the definition so that there was no law that could be retrospective.

---

[38] Fuller, 1964, p. 59.

[39] For example, Shadow Treasurer Ralph Willis, *Hansard*, Australian Commonwealth, House of Representatives, 1978, vol. 109, p. 1902; Senator Peter Walsh, *Hansard*, Australian Commonwealth, Senate, 1978, vol. 77, p. 2417.   [40] Cf. Fuller, p. 59.

What the discussions of both the broad and narrow definitions of retrospectivity have shown is that neither definition is adequate: the broad definition includes as retrospective pieces of legislation which are clearly not retrospective according to our pre-theoretical judgements; the narrow definition excludes pieces of legislation which *are* clearly retrospective according to our pre-theoretical judgements. Such definitions are not capturing our settled common-sense judgements concerning retrospectivity. The need for equivocation in using these definitions against particular pieces of legislation also shows that they do not even do the strategic work required of them by absolutist opponents of retrospectivity.

1.5 Capturing what we mean by 'retrospectivity'

We have seen that both the broad and narrow definitions of retrospectivity fail to identify or capture what it is that makes a law retrospective. Both the broad definition and the narrow definition fail to do justice to our pre-theoretical intuitions that some laws are retrospective and some are not and that it makes sense to debate the desirability of retrospectivity.

Driedger, who ends up identifying a number of ways in which a law can be retrospective, makes a more plausible proposal concerning the defining feature of retrospective laws. According to Driedger, there are two broad categories of retrospective law: firstly, *retroactive* law, which 'operates as of a time prior to its enactment', and secondly, *retrospective* law, which 'operates for the future only. It is prospective, but imposes new results in respect of a past event'.[41] This second kind of retrospectivity is further broken down into three subclasses:

(a) statutes that attach benevolent consequences to a prior event;

(b) statutes that attach prejudicial consequences to a prior event;

(c) statutes that impose a penalty on a person who is described by reference to a prior event, but the penalty is not a consequence of the event.[42]

As Driedger goes on to show in discussion of particular cases, this composite definition does very well in capturing our pre-theoretical judgements concerning retrospectivity. However, it must be pointed out that the distinction between *retroactivity* and *retrospectivity*, while describing a real difference in the verbal form in which retrospective law is expressed, lacks normative and practical significance. In other words, the distinction fails to mark out any difference in the actual *effects* of retrospective law, since these effects are the same for both.[43] Other writers have

---

[41] Elmer A. Driedger, 'Statutes: Retroactive Retrospective Reflections' (1978) 56 *Canadian Bar Review* 268.   [42] Driedger, at 271.
[43] Even though some legislation does state that it takes effect before the date of its promulgation, the legal consequences are not altered until that promulgation. Consider a court which is considering a case in February 2005 that concerned events which occurred in July 2003. If a retrospective Act of

noticed this essential similarity: Fisch claims that the distinction is 'analytically incoherent',[44] and Graetz writes that 'because all changes in law, whether nominally retroactive or nominally prospective, will have an economic impact on the value of existing assets or on existing expectations, the distinctions commonly drawn between retroactive and prospective effective dates are illusory.[45]

Thus, although this distinction is made by many of those analysing retrospectivity,[46] it is not as important as ordinarily assumed. The separation of (broadly) retrospective laws in to 'retroactive' and 'retrospective' is not due to the operation of different 'retrospectivity-making features', since the practical effects are the same. As Driedger himself notes, all such laws have one thing in common: namely, they attach 'new consequences to an event that occurred prior to its enactment'.[47] This, then, can be used as a general definition for *all* kinds of retrospective laws, with one caveat: because it is useful to draw attention to the fact that retrospective law may remove expected consequences as well as imposing unexpected ones, a slightly different phrasing may be preferable. We can, therefore, define retrospective laws as laws which *alter the future legal consequences of past actions and events*.

Moreover, the reason for the consequences being altered is the same in all cases. It is because the legal texts that will be applied to determine the legal consequences of an action at a hearing in the future are not the same as the texts that were discoverable at the time the action was commenced. Between the action and the hearing, a new text has been created and it is used in substitution for, or in addition to, the texts which the individual affected could have discovered at that time. The legal consequences of actions may be altered by a text which is facially prospective (but which has retrospective effect) as well as those which are retroactive.

This definition certainly captures the pre-theoretical conception of the workings of retrospective laws: the common picture of retrospectivity being that of a person performing a discrete and completely lawful action on one day, and on the next having a sanction attached to their action despite the fact that it is already in the past. It also captures those laws which are commonly regarded as paradigmatic examples of retrospective legislation. In the Australian case, these are:

- The *Taxation (Unpaid Company Tax) Assessment Act 1982* (Cth). In this case, a combination of transactions occurring in, say, 1978 had the legal effect,

Parliament covering such events occurring after January 2003 has passed through all stages and received Royal Assent but is awaiting Proclamation in the Government Gazette, the court cannot apply the new law.

   44 Jill E Fisch, 'Retroactivity and Legal Change: An Equilibrium Approach' (1996–1997) 110 *Harvard Law Review* 1056 at 1069.

   45 Michael J. Graetz, 'Retroactivity Revisited' (1984–1985) 98 *Harvard Law Review* 1820, 1822. See also Louis Kaplow, 'An Economic Analysis of Legal Transitions' (1985–1986) 99 *Harvard Law Review* 509 at 510, 518–19.

   46 See, for example, W David Slawson, 'Constitutional and Legislative Considerations in Retroactive Lawmaking' (1960) 48 *Cal. Law Review* 216 Section 1 216–220; Stephen R. Munzer, 'A Theory of Retroactive Legislation' (1982–1983) 61 *Texas Law Review* 425–6.   47 Driedger, at 276.

when they occurred, of avoiding liability to be taxed. But after the relevant legislation was passed in 1982, the legal effect was that a new liability to pay tax had arisen.

- The *War Crimes Amendment Act 1989* (Cth). In this case, prior to the enactment of the legislation, actions performed in Eastern Europe in 1944 (for example) had no legal consequences under Australian law at the time they occurred, even when followed by emigration to Australia. But the enactment of the legislation added the legal consequence of liability for conviction and sentencing in an Australian court.

On our definition, such laws are retrospective because they attach new consequences to actions or events that have already occurred. At the time, such actions (that is, entering into the relevant transactions, committing war crimes, or emigrating to Australia having committed war crimes) did not have the legal consequences of incurring tax (in the former case) or incurring liability for prosecution in Australian courts (in the latter case). The legal consequences were created after the acts were performed or the relevant event occurred.

Many laws have partially retrospective effects. The issue is not whether those effects are retrospective but the nature and extent of those effects and the reasonableness of their imposition.

1.6 Applying the definition

We have seen that our proposed definition of retrospectivity seems to do a good job of capturing the 'paradigmatic' cases referred to above. These, however, are straightforward examples involving discrete events occurring at specifiable times. In addition, each amendment specified direct legal consequences: a liability to pay tax in one case, a criminal penalty in the other. But neither the law, nor the lives that law is intended to regulate, are always so simple. First, human life is not always episodic: some transactions extend over time, and to achieve our most treasured goals we must typically plan and carry out a series of related actions, the consequences of which may take years to unfold. This is true of most economic goals: building a business, acquiring a customer base and building our assets. The economic goals that can be gained in a day or a week (the clever trade, the quick deal, the rearranging of assets and the tax avoider's sleight of hand) are, rightly, valued less. If this is true of our most respected economic goals, it is doubly true of our non-economic goals: building our relationships with those we love and care about, raising a family, seeing our children through to a safe and prosperous future, building an institution (for example, a law school or a research centre), pursuing a career, gaining the respect of our neighbours, 'making a difference' and leaving the world a better place. Similarly, the law rarely attaches legal consequences to a unique, isolated event. Usually, a combination of events is necessary to trigger a legal liability.[48]

Because of this, the question of whether a law is retrospective is often difficult to answer. In the case of extended plans or courses of action, a law may be enacted after the first action or event has occurred, but before the last has been completed; or it may be unclear whether the final event which triggers the liability occurs before or after the law is enacted. Such laws may be retrospective from one point of view, but prospective from another. Indeed, even in the relatively straightforward case of the *War Crimes* amendment, both the wartime conduct and the postwar voyage to Australia are necessary to trigger legal liability. This means that if a person committed war crimes in 1944, but emigrated to Australia *after* the enactment of the legislation, this legislation is, in a crucial sense, prospective in relation to that person. Indeed, it might even be said that a war criminal resident in Australia could have left the country while the retrospective law was going through the parliamentary process.

The problem is especially common in the areas of taxation and economic regulation (many of which fall under a category known as 'transition problems', discussed below in Chapter 5). Many investments (and virtually all that are profitable) are long-term. Someone who decides to buy a bond or build a factory does this in order to achieve future profits. Such profits will be the intended result of the original investment decision (alone, or in combination with subsequent decisions) and often investors are *de facto* committed once they make the original decision. Obviously, a change in the way these profits are taxed (made after the initial decision has been made) can significantly alter the consequences of the decision. An initial decision might be made because of, and with a reasonable expectation of, certain consequences following from a course of action initiated by this decision, but such consequences may never eventuate because of an intervening change in the law. Indeed, unplanned and undesirable consequences may instead be the result. And the person may have no opportunity to avoid such consequences, because the first event in the series—the initial decision to invest— is now long past.

Consider, for example, an Australian manufacturer who builds a widget factory at a time when the tariff on imported widgets is 45 percent. If that tariff is later reduced to 10 percent, or if a change in monetary policy causes the value of the local currency to rise sharply, the manufacturer may become unable to compete with imports. The manufacturer's chance of making any profit from the factory is thus eliminated.[49] In an alternative scenario, where the manufacture of widgets

---

[48] Pierre Schlag, 'Normativity and the Politics of Form' (1991) 139 *University of Pennsylvania Law Review* 801 at 931.

[49] Something like this happened in the first three disastrous years after Britain's 1979 election. High interest rates drove up the pound, despite inflation (reaching 22 percent at one point). This caused manufacturing output to nosedive—it did not return to pre-inflation levels until 1987—and unemployment to treble.

results in environmental pollution, the widget factory may be built at a time when emission-control standards are lenient. If these standards are later tightened, the widget factory may no longer be able to operate profitably.

Such examples show not only the difficulty of individuating past actions and events (and the consequences thereof) in a way which allows us to tell when the legal effects of these are altered by a change in the law. It is not just that *retroactive* laws do not exhaust the category of retrospectivity, and that facially prospective laws can have retrospective effect. Retrospectivity is also usually contingent on the particular history and circumstances of a given policy. A statute that declared that 'from the first of January next year, no person shall drive an automotive vehicle using leaded petrol' is prospective on its face, and would also be prospective were it enacted in the Australia of 1890 (or 2100). However, if enacted by an Australian legislature in 1950 or 1990, this seemingly prospective law, in fact, has a retrospective operation, because it affects the future consequences of a past action or event (namely, that of having bought a car which uses leaded petrol).

A similar example concerns the re-introduction of tertiary fees in Australia in 1989. The Higher Education Contribution Scheme (HECS) officially applied prospectively: students were charged only for subjects that they enrolled in after the relevant legislation took effect. However, in practice, the impact of the new scheme was heavily retrospective. A student about to complete the final year of a degree, and faced with the choice of whether to pay to complete the course, faced the loss of an investment of several years' study if they chose to drop out. Arguably, even a first-year student might be 'locked in' by their choice of senior school subjects nearly three years previously.

A supporter of HECS could argue that the retrospective effect is not, in fact, as significant as suggested above, since the re-introduction of some form of student fees had been on the political agenda since 1986 when the Commonwealth Government introduced a $250 'administration fee'. But this merely raises the question of how specific advance notice must be when given in non-legal form. When what is known is not the precise form of the statute, but only the general policy intentions of the Government, can a person be deemed to have made their plans with reasonable notice of future legislation?

There are also various kinds of retrospective effect. One such effect occurs where a facially prospective statute has retrospective operation by attaching consequences to some voluntary conduct for which a 'head start' is useful: that is, it advantages those who have already undertaken a certain form of conduct relevant to the statute. For example, when the Australian Parliament in 1983–4 amended the *Commonwealth Electoral Act 1918* to provide for registration of political parties, it included a reservation that for the first three months after the amendments took effect, only parties with at least one representative in the Commonwealth parliament could register. Parties satisfying the alternative criteria—one State or Territory parliamentarian, or 500 voters as members—had to wait until this grace period expired. Since party names were reservable on a first-come, first-served basis, this promoted the legitimate public goal of preventing, say, a small fringe group from registering the name 'ALP', 'Liberal Party', and so on at the expense of much larger and better-established bodies publicly recognized under those titles. Nonetheless, it did have a retrospective operation.[50]

The above scheme effectively created a new legal right on the basis of actions that had already been completed. In so doing, it imposed limitations on the actions of others. This can happen more generally when property regimes are created or altered. The imposition of an intellectual property regime would be one example. Important legal consequences are created because of past inventions or creative works. A similar effect is created when property regimes are changed by domestic policy or international agreement. This can happen, for example, where the length of copyright is extended (as in the Australia–US Free Trade Agreement)[51] or when zoning changes increase the density of housing permitted on a particular area or site.

Other examples occur when activities are licensed for the first time. It is common, when doing this, to license those who are already lawfully carrying out the activities in question. This provides a benefit to those who were already carrying out those activities, but is also potentially a detriment to those who were planning to do so. However, to the extent that a license is limited in duration or scope, this may be seen as reducing the scope of the activity currently engaged in.

Discussion of retrospectivity tends to concentrate on laws which have the effect of reducing the value of past acquisitions or transactions because they are the ones that generate the greatest complaints. A law may, on its face, leave legal title to some action or property untouched, while at the same time reducing the personal or economic value of that title. Statutes imposing *de futuro* restrictions on land use or disposal (to protect, for example, the environment, or the rights of traditional indigenous owners) have been criticized for having such retrospective impact. Constitutional prohibitions against uncompensated takings (USA Fifth Amendment) or acquisition on unfair terms (Australia, Section 51) guard against this form of implied retrospectivity when combined with an element of 'attainder'—for example, if number 10 Smith Street is singled out for eminent domain while numbers 8 and 12 are left untouched, due to the exigencies of freeway construction. However, constitutional regulation of 'takings' or 'acquisitions' does not cover cases where a facially neutral government decision has the effect of lessening a title's value.

Although this problem is often discussed in economic terms, using property rights as an illustration, it is equally applicable to personal rights and liberties. It might be argued that the economic aspect of the problem is more acute because items of property (including intangible but objectively valuable things such as

---

[50] It also verged on being a 'closed class' law, saved only by the fact that it was possible—if highly unlikely—that enough MPs might change their party allegiance before the three months ended to upset the pattern estimable at the time the amendments were passed.

[51] See <http://www.ilaw.com.au/public/ftaarticle.html> 2 March 2005.

a university education) are harder to change or revise than other life plans; indeed, their very fixity and scarcity contributes to their value. A statute declaring that from 1 July next it shall be lawful for persons other than legal practitioners to undertake conveyancing of land has the effect of devaluing, to some degree, the investment that admitted barristers and solicitors have put into obtaining their law degrees, articles of clerkship, admission and practising certificates. Similarly, a decision to increase New York's quota of taxi medallions may likewise have the effect of devaluing the investment taxi drivers have made in their business.

It is not clear that this emphasis on property rights is justified. While there may be some for whom the acquisition of property is at the centre of their life plans, for most, such acquisition is a means to other ends. To be sure, it is a necessary means to many ends. However, there are many ends which the possession of property might assist but which could be threatened more directly by prospective laws. Laws against 'inter-marriage', for example, can take purely prospective form (as did the early Nazi laws and most of the South African ones), but far more effectively shatter the plans of those affected (couples planning to marry) than, say, the imposition of environmental constraints on a factory which has managed to externalize the costs of the pollution it creates for much of its life.

In many cases, retrospective effects are not the goal (or at least, the primary goal) that the legislators desired to achieve. They are, at most, side effects, and may be genuinely regretted as such. But to deny that such laws do have retrospective operation would be to appeal to something like the 'doctrine of double effect', and this seems unreasonable, since such laws do impose a new burden as a consequence of past actions or events. Although as Oliver Wendell Holmes (Jnr) once noted: even a dog can tell the difference between being tripped accidentally and being kicked deliberately; it is still not happy about either.[52] Thus, our definition has the advantage of allowing that a law may be retrospective even when this is not explicit in its wording. Indeed, it shows how retrospective effect can arise from the interaction of two different kinds of *prospectivity*: the prospective law and the prospective consequences of one's actions. Both the action and the law have consequences in the future only, but a prospective law can operate retrospectively by changing the prospective consequences of an earlier action.

Status

Some laws do not attach legal consequences to actions and events, but to statuses. On one interpretation, such laws are not retrospective, as can be seen from the court's ruling in the case of *Re a Solicitor's Clerk*.[53] This case concerned provisions under the *Solicitors' Act 1941 (UK)* for the making of orders prohibiting a person from being employed by any solicitor if they had been convicted of larceny. The solicitor's clerk argued that the application of such an order to himself was

[52] Oliver Wendell Holmes (Jnr), *The Common Law* (Little, Brown and Company, Boston, 1881).
[53] [1957] 1 WLR 1219.

retrospective, since he had committed the offences prior to the statue; prohibiting his being employed by a solicitor constituted a retrospective increase in the penalty for his crime. The court held that the application of the statute did not have retrospective effect, since the new consequences did not attach to the clerk's past acts; rather, they attached to his status as a person convicted of larceny.[54]

A different interpretation, however, might be thought to be implied by the ruling in another case, *Bakker v. Stewart*.[55] This case concerned a statute which removed the court's power to release on bond persons convicted of drink-driving offences. As in the case of the solicitor's clerk, it was argued that the new statute should not be applied to those who had committed their offences prior to its enactment. In this case the court agreed, holding that the application of the new law in such cases would amount to a retrospective increase in the penalty for their offence.

Pearce and Geddes try to reconcile the two judgements by focusing on the 'interconnection between the offence and the penalty'.[56] Similarly, Driedger holds that a distinction can be made, relevant to these cases, between laws which attach new legal consequences to past acts or events, and laws which attach new legal consequences to characteristics that arose in the past.[57] According to Driedger, only the former kinds of laws count as retrospective. In the case of the solicitor's clerk, the law was not concerned with the act of larceny, but rather with the characteristic of being a person convicted of larceny. In *Bakker v. Stewart*, however, the law was concerned with the penalty for the *act* of drink driving. It was not attached to the characteristic of 'being a person convicted of drink driving offences'. (It was not proposed, for example, to impose any new consequences on people who had been convicted of drink driving—and released on bond—under the old statute.)

It seems, however, that the distinction between attaching new consequences to actions or events, and attaching new consequences to characteristics, might not always be so clear. Even in the above example of the solicitor's clerk, it might be thought that the statute, while intended only to apply to a characteristic, did effectively attach a new consequence to the act of committing larceny—namely, that of being prohibited from being employed by a solicitor. And it might be pointed out that in many cases, it would be possible to re-describe acts or events in terms of characteristics: a statute which applied to the performance of certain acts might be re-described to apply to people who had the characteristic of having performed such acts. This is especially true if we are talking of penalties, which are imposed on conviction, and might therefore be described as attaching either to the offence the person committed, or to the person's status as a person convicted of committing the offence. Therefore both such acts fall under our

---

[54] Driedger, at 270–1.   [55] [1980] VR 17.

[56] Dennis C Pearce and RS Geddes, *Statutory Interpretation in Australia* (3rd edn, Butterworths, Sydney, 1988) 182.   [57] Driedger, at 271.

definition of retrospectivity. This does not mean that they are necessarily acceptable or not—and if the latter whether the objection to them is based on their retrospectivity.[58]

Matters of degree

Whether a law is retrospective is not a simple matter of timing. Rather, retrospectivity will be a matter of degree, and will depend on how the actions and events occurring before the enactment of the new law relate to those occurring afterwards. We could even devise a rough 'metric of retrospectivity' by asking how long in advance the average individual would need to be informed before the consequences (that is, costs and benefits) of a law would no longer be considered *new* (unexpected or unforeseen) consequences of the actions to which the law applies. For example, if the typical Australian citizen owns a car for ten years before selling it, then a law declaring that all cars must run on non-leaded petrol, effective immediately, would have a 'retrospectivity score' of ten years. Alternatively, we could calculate this 'retrospectivity score' in terms of the loss in value of a person's leaded-petrol car once the statute is enacted. Similarly, we could equate the 'retrospectivity score' of a law changing the penalty for murder from life imprisonment to execution with the average time between commission of the offence and conviction/sentencing (on the first way of calculating),[59] or the difference between the average sentence under the old law and the average sentence under the new law (on the second way).

One problem with this, however, is that the costs (or benefits) are often speculative, particularly in the case of laws altering the value of past acquisitions or transactions. Determining the effect of a law on an individual often depends upon a counter-factual guess about the use the owner *would* otherwise have made of their property. Take, for example, a law forbidding the clearing of currently undeveloped land. If the owner of such a piece of land had intended to leave the land undeveloped as a wildlife sanctuary, then the law does not as a matter of fact attach any new consequences to their actions in acquiring the land. However, if the owner had planned to create a new subdivision and construct a bridge to connect it to other land owned on the mainland, and would not have bought it otherwise, then the law, in forbidding the building of the bridge, forecloses the

---

[58] Some rules which are clearly attached to statuses will be objectionable regardless of whether or not they are retrospective.

[59] Some people might object that the 'retrospectivity score' of such a law ought to be zero, since no one's *legitimate* plans are disrupted. However, this is to beg the question concerning the justifiability of retrospective laws; assuming that illegitimate plans cannot have 'retrospectivity scores' seems to assume that the application of such a law to murderers is not retrospective because it is not objectionable. What such an objection seems to be *really* saying is that the 'retrospectivity score' of illegitimate plans should not be given any *weight* in determining the justifiability of the law. But if we are trying to determine, not whether the law is justifiable, but rather *how retrospective it is*, then such questions are beside the point.

intended usage of that land.[60] Where it was previously a consequence of acquiring or owning the land that one would have the ability to build a bridge on it, this is no longer a consequence; instead, a new consequence has followed (namely, that one's investment has decreased in value).

While a person's intentions or future plans are an objective fact—'the state of a man's mind is as much a fact as the state of his digestion'[61]—they are not the sort of facts that can be determined with great reliability, especially when it may be in a person's interest to claim that they did or did not have a particular intention. This means that the 'retrospectivity score' of particular laws may not be determinable in practice. However, we may be able to get around such problems by measuring the retrospectivity of a statute according to how much notice the person would have required to reduce their costs (or benefits) to zero assuming they *did* intend to realize the consequences now being altered.

The common feature of retrospective and retroactive laws is that the legal consequences of actions taken in the past are determined in the future by legal texts that have been created in the interim and hence were not discoverable at the time the action was taken. The grievance felt against retrospective legislation comes from those who expected to gain certain benefits from past acts on the basis of the law as it then stood and would have acted differently had they known that the legal texts would be changed. In some cases, expected benefits have been built into the price of assets and others have paid that price.

Such individuals have a clear interest in the texts that are applied to an action being the same texts as those that were discoverable at the time the action was taken. However, that interest is effectively in the stability of law rather than its retrospectivity. This is a legitimate interest that should always be recognized and respected. However, stability is not the only virtue of law—and there can be many good reasons to change the law—including the interests of others. The question is when an interest that should be recognized and respected should also be protected. There are many such arguments that privilege certain interests on the basis of rights, democracy and the Rule of Law. Chapter 3 will consider the major arguments that have been put forward against some or all retrospective rule making. However, the issue is not whether the law is retrospective but which interests should be respected and what degree and form of protection for those interests should be provided.

1.7 Threshold points—legislation

Our definition of retrospectivity may be objected to on the grounds that it entails degrees of retrospectivity; that is, it fails to classify laws straightforwardly and in

---

[60] As, for example, in the Hindmarsh Island Bridge case, Hugh Morgan, Western Mining Corporation head, in 1991, criticized a decision to protect an Aboriginal sacred site because it meant that 'ultimately, any religious nut, no matter how weird, can effectively expropriate property rights anywhere'.   [61] *Edgington v. Fitzmaurice* (1885) 29 ChD 459, per Bowen LJ.

a black-and-white fashion as merely 'retrospective' or 'not retrospective'. In fact, we think it is an advantage of our account that it acknowledges the shades of grey present in disputes over whether or not particular laws are retrospective. This approach neither begs any questions by ruling in or out instances of disputed laws (that is, where there is disagreement over whether or not a law is retrospective), nor attempts to wield too wide a brush by assuming that, if a law is in any way retrospective, it is not different in any relevant respects from the most absurd instances of retrospective laws.

Not everyone, however, will be comfortable with the idea of retrospectivity as a continuum concept. Such a continuum is not appealing to those who want to say that all retrospective laws are bad. However, for those who find actual cases of retrospective laws varying from wicked, to regrettable, to excusable, to necessary, it may have real appeal. As Fisch notes: seeing retrospectivity as a matter of degree 'converts the evaluation of retroactive lawmaking from a binary issue into a quant-itative analysis. Rather than asking whether retroactivity is appropriate, we should ask what degree of retrospective impact is appropriate'.[62] Thus, the norm-ative question concerns not the justifiability of retrospectivity, but rather the amount of retrospectivity that is justifiable. And because of this, it might be argued that there is some threshold point beyond which a law really is, for all intents and purposes, prospective. This threshold will be the point in time at which, given a law concerning the act of Φ-ing, the application of the law to a person's Φ-ing *at that time* ceases to be retrospective.

Surprisingly, little attention has been given to this 'threshold' question; yet, it is helpful in considering the degree to which, if any, the laws are retrospective. Depending on the time selected as the threshold, some laws that are commonly criticized as retrospective might, in fact, be (officially) entirely prospective. For example, if the date of passage through all legislative houses is given as the thresh-old, then a statute taking effect on that day (that is, its application to a person's Φ-ing on that day) is not retrospective, even if it has not been signed into law by the head of state. At the other extreme, if the threshold is set as the earliest time at which the citizen can avoid any disadvantages under the statute by altering their conduct at minimal cost, then some statutes that appear prospective in form might not cease to be retrospective until months, even years later (for example, laws phasing out leaded-petrol cars or analogue mobile phones); some might *never* cease to be retrospective (for example, changes to pensions or HECS laws that stagger benefits available according to date of birth).

In trying to identify a 'prospectivity threshold', we would be trying to identify a point at which a person, in deciding to Φ, can be taken to have enough knowledge of the content of the law to be aware of the consequences it attaches to their Φ-ing. Applications of the law to Φ-ing after that point in time can be taken to be prospective, since the law is not imposing any new (unplanned or unexpected)

---

[62] Fisch, at 1072–3.

consequences on past actions or events. The point determined by the legislature as the time an enactment takes effect can be taken as an attempt to stipulate such a 'prospectivity threshold'. In fact, however, there are a number of claimed times at which a person is taken to have enough knowledge of the content of a law to rebut any claim of 'retrospective effect'. And, as we will show, none are totally satisfactory: that is, none completely avoid any retrospectivity, and some have other difficulties.

Consider, then, the following alternatives for a 'prospectivity threshold' (concerning, for the sake of illustration, our law affecting Φ-ing), in order from furthest back in time to furthest forward in time:

1. *When the law is knowable by ordinary use of conscience or right reason*

i. This is the earliest time claimed as the point at which the application of a law affecting Φ-ing becomes prospective. The threshold is set at the point at which it is obvious to 'common right or reason', or can be deduced from it, that Φ-ing is prohibited, and punishable. Clearly this does not apply to all laws: it would be difficult to deduce a system of traffic regulations, or a scale of tax rates, from the 'laws of Nature and of Nature's God'.[63] However, for those laws that do fall into this category, the 'prospectivity threshold' can be extended quite far back indeed. If the 'pre-statutory law' is equated with the *Tao* or *Logos* of Natural Law, it can be said to originate at the beginning of time itself. More modest claims for its origins can set it at a more recent time that is still before the defendant was charged, or even born: for example, the 'first great principles of the social compact',[64] the 'ordinary expectations of fellow members of society',[65] or 'the common law of the Commonwealth'.[66]

2. *When the law is embodied in some instrument exterior (and usually superior) to the legal system*

i. This threshold requires that there be warning by some written instrument, but one that need not be a statute (or even the Constitution) of that particular jurisdiction. For instance, in the days before slavery was abolished in the USA, it could be argued that the practice was, in fact, unconstitutional (except where the Constitution's language, construed very strictly, allowed it) because it contradicted the promises of the Declaration of

---

[63] US Declaration of Independence. However, while particular rules such as a 60 km/h speed limit or the rules for giving way on roundabouts might be too speculative to be enforceable in the absence of positive enactment, a *general* duty to drive reasonably could probably be deduced by 'exercise of right reason' from the 'natural' prohibition against endangering the lives or safety of fellow humans.   [64] *Calder v. Bull* (1798) 3 US 386 (Dall.).

[65] *Shaw v. DPP* [1962] AC 220: *R v. Elizabeth Manley* (1933) 1 KB 529.

[66] *R v. Kidman* (1915) CLR 425.

Independence.[67] Likewise, the judges in *R v. Dudley and Stephens* made use of the Bible; they held that shipwrecked sailors should have known that necessity was no justification for murder and cannibalism because (*inter alia*) of 'that Great Example we profess to follow'. A modern, secular equivalent is the *International Covenant on Civil and Political Rights* (1966) and similar international declarations. In particular, the ICCPR, and some national Constitutions (for example, that of Germany), endorse 'retrospective' criminal statutes against acts that constitute a violation of international law.[68]

3. When the intended introduction of the law is announced

i. This threshold locates the required notice within the particular legal system; indeed, in a stage of the legislative process itself: in other words, one is taken to have sufficient notice of the new law's effect on Φ-ing at the point when the intention to introduce a statute concerning Φ-ing is announced to the legislature. This method, commonly referred to as 'legislation by press release', has been criticized on many grounds, and I will discuss it at greater length in Chapter 4. Whether sufficient warning is given, however, may depend on how likely it is that the legislation will actually be passed, and there are substantial differences among democracies in the extent to which all Houses of the legislature are likely to grant the executive its desired legislative package.

4. When the law is introduced to the legislature (as a formal bill)

i. This threshold is a refinement of the previous one. If a press release, memorandum or Second Reading speech is not sufficient notice (being studded with bloated political rhetoric), then perhaps a properly drafted legal document will suffice. Thus, backdating an Act to have effect from the first time the corresponding Bill was introduced into the legislature can be defended on the grounds that at least the citizen has been informed in precise statutory language. In addition, it could be argued that the citizen can now assume that the final version will not differ so substantially from the initial Bill as to make this notice nugatory; if the legislature is so opposed to the Bill's main thrust that it would want to amend it in any significant way, it might as well reject the Bill outright. And although minor amendments do make the final operation of the original Bill harder to predict accurately, they are unlikely to be any worse in this regard than the possibility of

[67] JM Balkin (ed), *What Brown v. Board of Education should have said: the nation's top legal experts rewrite America's landmark civil rights decision* (New York University, 2001) 130.

[68] However, a statute would still be required, even a retrospective one. A restored democratic government could not simply stage its own Nuremberg-style trials by executive fiat, without some kind of statutory authorization for the trial, conviction and punishment.

unexpected judicial interpretations. Clearly, however, there is still scope here for retrospective effect, even if it is relatively trivial.

5. *When the law is passed by the legislature*

i. Another possible threshold is the time the Bill is approved by the legislature—that is, by the requisite number of legislative houses.[69] But the problem with this point as the threshold is that whether the date of passage (rather than assent) can be considered the time at which sufficient notice is given would have to depend on whether the Head of State is authorized, or likely, to wield their veto power so as to stop the Bill or force amendments to it. In Westminster jurisdictions, the version of the Bill that leaves the legislature is almost certain to make it onto the statute book in identical form, but this is not the case in the USA. This would mean that, say, a law that took effect on the day either the House or the Senate (whichever was later) approved it would be retrospective in the USA but not in Australia. It is not impossible for differences in substantive constitutional doctrines to vary so greatly with differences in structure, but generally it would seem better to assume consistency where possible.

6. *When the law is signed into law by the Head of State*[70]

i. Virtually all liberal democratic constitutions set this at the point at which a Bill becomes law (although the Head of State's refusal to give assent is usually either politically unthinkable, as in Westminster jurisdictions, or subject to legislative override, as in America and France).[71] It is also the point at which a potential veto by either legislative chamber (or by Head of State) becomes *functus officio*. Even if an Act's effect is deemed backdated to an earlier time, it has no legal effect at all unless and until it reaches the point of being signed into law. This proposed threshold, therefore, has a certain intuitive appeal.

ii. The problem, however, is that the legislature cannot dictate the time at which the Head of State signs the Bill (not down to the day, at any rate). The effective date of an Act is usually specified within the Act itself,

---

[69] In Westminster jurisdictions, the Crown or its vice-regal representative is legally defined as an element of the legislature. However, in the USA the President is not an element of Congress, which consists only of the House of Representatives and Senate. This exclusion is ironic as the US President has far greater practical influence on legislation than the British Monarch and his/her viceroys. For consistency, 'legislature' is used herein to mean only the House or Houses, excluding the Head of State, whose role is primarily executive and whose legislative powers are incidental to this.

[70] For brevity, 'Head of State' in this context means a President or Monarch, and includes Governors-General, Governors, Lieutenant Governors, and Administrators who represent the Head of State (and carry out functions analogous to those performed by the President or Monarch) within a particular jurisdiction. 'Assent' is used here for both republics and monarchies.

[71] Switzerland and the Australian Capital Territory are rare exceptions where, because there is no separate Head of State, the head of government certifies that a Bill has been enacted.

although if none is mentioned the Act will usually (by default) take effect on the day of assent, which can then be appended to the published act as a marginal note. But if the giving of notice is a concern, it seems arbitrary to leave potentially crucial transactions hanging on whether the President has time for a signing ceremony in the White House garden or whether the Governor-General's schedule at Yarralumla is full this week. Even a delay of a few days might be disruptive.

7. *When the law is promulgated in the official gazette or register*

   i. This is set under the Commonwealth *Acts Interpretation Act 1901* as the effective date for regulations and other subordinate legislative instruments.[72] The *Government Gazette* is published approximately every three days. Another option might be to specify the date at which copies of the Act are available from the Government Printer—or, today, on the Internet. This seems to be the most reasonable or lenient threshold: it is, if anything is, the point at which people ought to be aware of new consequences of a law. However, this threshold would have the absurd side-effect of making legal liabilities potentially depend on the vagaries of the printery, of the government's website designer, or of the postal service.

   ii. It is also possible to fix a date for commencement that is derived from, but later than, the day of assent (that is, 30 days after it is signed into law). It may be unwise for the Bill itself to specify its own commencement date in case unforeseen circumstances (for example, preparation for a massive compliance campaign as with the GST) make it impracticable, and an extension would require further legislation.

8. *At some point after the law is signed or promulgated*

   i. Some jurisdictions postpone the commencement of a statute for some substantial minimum time after it is enacted, signed and promulgated. For example, California and Switzerland both impose a 90-day delay, in order to allow for voter-initiated referendum changes. Sri Lanka has an analogous provision, in which a grace period is reserved during which any citizen may challenge a new Act's constitutionality in the Supreme Court.[73] Note, however, that in both cases where an intervening delay is required after promulgation, the reason is not so much to give the individual citizen notice of the obligations imposed by a valid statute, but rather to test (via referendum or judicial review) whether the statute will be valid at all.

None of these suggestions present themselves as an obvious demarcation point between retrospectivity and prospectivity: all would still allow for some retrospective

---

[72] *Acts Interpretation Act 1901* (Cth), Section 5 (Commencement of Acts); *Statutory Rules Publication Act 1903*, Section 5. See also Queensland Criminal Code, Section 22 (3).

[73] *Constitution of Sri Lanka* (1972), Sections 48 and 54.

effect, and some would present other problems if adopted as the marker of prospectivity. In general, however, there is obviously lesser degree of retrospectivity the further forward one moves in time. Any presumption against retrospectivity can therefore be supposed to increase in force the further back in time the effects of a piece of legislation.

1.8 Threshold points—judicial law making

The preceding section dealt with potential threshold points in legislation and the various landmarks along the legislative process from the first rumblings of discontent until the promulgation of the Royal Assent. When judges overrule earlier precedents, there is a high degree of retrospectivity. However, even here there are matters of degree. When a precedent is overruled, it is rare that it is a complete surprise. Whether or not courts deliberately signal likely changes, there are almost always warning signs. Unlike the legislative process, there is no single time line. However a number of signals that case law is uncertain, at risk of change and likely to be modified can be identified. Such signals could include:

1. Some academics or senior barristers are politely critical of a line of precedents.
2. Litigants seek to distinguish the line of authority.
3. Some judges consider the possibility of restricting some of the precedents (while others continue as before).
4. The precedents are distinguished regularly and some judges are 'confining it to its facts'.
5. Senior judges doubt the line of authority in *obiter*.
6. The line of authority is increasingly distinguished.
7. Lawyers before the highest court which supported the line of authority give leave to argue that it be overruled.
8. In argument, some of the judges seem to indicate that the line of authority will be overruled.
9. The authorities are overruled.

Intertwined with this legislative or judicial progression towards legal change are the series of events by which citizens carry out the plans that will eventually be affected by the change of legislative and or judicial texts—and the degree to which citizens are, or could reasonably be assumed to be, aware of the coming change. The degree to which citizens are committed to a course of action whose future legal consequences are affected by the new legislative or judicial texts will thus vary along with the growing probability of the change in text.

1.9 Conclusion

We have seen that retrospectivity eludes simple definition. Nor is it always an easy matter to determine if—and in what way—a law is retrospective. Retrospectivity is not always apparent from the wording of a law, and the actual retrospective effects of a facially prospective law may be difficult to measure. It is even difficult to stipulate a point at which a person's awareness of the substance of a new law can be deemed sufficient for the consequences imposed by the law to have been known and accepted. In practice, however, we can usually identify those cases where the consequences of past actions and events are sufficiently altered so as to create concern.

We have used a fairly broad definition of retrospective laws as laws which *alter the future legal consequences of past actions and events* because the legal texts that will be applied to determine the legal consequences of an action at a hearing in the future are not the same as the texts that were discoverable at the time the action was commenced. Between the action and the hearing, a new text has been created and it is used in substitution for, or in addition to, the texts which the individual affected could have discovered at that time. This allows us to focus on the kinds and extent of such altered consequences and, in later chapters, on the reasonableness of expectations that the legal consequences will not change, the notice given of a change and the reasonableness of such changes.

2

The Rule of Law

2.1 Introduction

In the first chapter, we examined the concept of retrospectivity and advanced what we consider to be the most useful definition. In this chapter, we will undertake a similar task with respect to the 'Rule of Law', a concept which figures so prominently in arguments against retrospectivity considered in the next chapter.

Defining the Rule of Law is, unfortunately, not any easier than defining retrospectivity itself. The 'Rule of Law' is one of those 'hurrah words' that conservatives,[1] centrist liberals, and radicals are all eager to claim, while importing different (if frequently overlapping) elements into their use of the term. Moreover, there is some disagreement about the *normative force* of the Rule of Law—how much it prohibits, and how much weight should be given to it in the face of potentially valuable conflicting goals.

In this chapter, we will examine several proposed definitions of the Rule of Law and show that, despite disagreement over precisely what is included under the term, there is a fairly wide consensus on certain necessary elements. We will then discuss those things which, it is commonly agreed, are forbidden by the Rule of Law—that is, those things which are usually supposed to be incompatible with it. Finally, we will discuss the major criticisms of the Rule of Law, and evaluate their validity. At the end, we will outline what we take to be normative significance of the claim that retrospectivity fails to conform to the Rule of Law.

2.2 The meaning of the Rule of Law

At its simplest, the 'Rule of Law' (and its European equivalents of the *Rechstaat* and *Etat du Droit*) can be taken, as Raz points out, to mean 'literally what it says: the rule of the law'.[2] However, this does not tell us very much. One of the simplest

---

[1] The word is used in its traditional (conservative?) meaning of the term—those who wish to conserve existing institutions and practices and, while prepared to change for good reason, are sceptical of arguments for change because of oversold reforms which failed to achieve their stated aims and generated damaging unintended consequences. They are not to be confused with 'neo-conservatives'—a strangely oxymoronic linguistic oddity (that is, why would a true conservative be 'neo'?).

[2] Joseph Raz, 'The Rule of Law and its Virtue' (April 1977) 93 *Law Quarterly Review* 196.

and most enduring versions of the idea of the rule of law centres on an evocative but impossible ideal: 'the rule [or government] of law[s], not the rule of men' (or of women, or indeed of any fallible mortals).[3] According to Blackstone, law is 'not a transient sudden order from a superior to or concerning a particular person; but something permanent, uniform, and universal.'[4]

Taken literally, this is nonsense. Laws are not and cannot be self-creating or self-enforcing edicts. Unlike the laws of gravity or thermodynamics, they need human beings to create, interpret and enforce them. A more feasible meaning for this ideal is that all humans (especially officials of the state) are subject to law rather than arbitrary exercises of state power. Sovereign authorities rule through human beings, but the rule of law ensures that the process is, as far as possible, channelled through the means of rule making and attempts at faithful rule implementation. In other words, it ensures that individual citizens have a fair warning about the rules to be applied to the actions they choose to take (and the opportunity of a fair hearing to determine what legal consequences of those rules are). They are not simply punished without any (or with insufficient) regard to the laws at the time they acted.

For many, the law and the rule of law are inextricably linked. Joseph Raz argued strongly that this version of the rule of law was crucial to the nature of law itself.[5] He saw law as a two-stage decision-making process, where rules are first made by the legislature and then interpreted by the executive and judiciary. Ideally, the officials applying the law at both stages view themselves as part of an enterprise in which the state has attempted to make rules that guide citizens; therefore, officials conscientiously seek to draw their own reasons for decision from these rules. There are, of course, imperfections in the way rules are made and interpreted, but those who are involved in both stages of the process still endeavour to be true to their ideal function. This does not mean that judges can pretend that the answer is always clearly, unequivocally and uncontroversially found 'in' the rules that have been made at the first stage, nor that there is no creative role. What Raz means is simply this: it is not the judge's role to think, afresh, what the right answer should be, but to find the right answer already determined—or at least bounded— by the rules set down in advance. Judges use these rules as the basis for their decision-making.

This idea is linked to Raz's 'sources' thesis—that all legal rules have sources, and it is at the source of each that the first stage of decision-making occurs. This offers

---

[3] The term appears to have first been used by the English republican writer James Harrington, in his tracts *The Prerogative of Popular Government* (1657) and *The Commonwealth of Oceana* (1656), and in slightly different terms: 'an empire of laws and not of men'. The revised version is widely used: cf, for example, J Toohey [Justice], 'A Government of Laws, and Not of Men'?, Paper presented to the 'Constitutional Change in the 1990s' Conference, Darwin (6 October 1993), reprinted in: Justice John Toohey, 'A Government of Laws, and Not of Men'? (1993) 4 *Public Law Review* 158. The term originated with James Harrington (1611–1677), a leading Parliamentarian in the English Civil War, as 'an empire of laws, not of men'. See Richard A Posner, *Problems of Jurisprudence* (Harvard University Press, Massachusetts, 1990) 23.   [4] W Blackstone Volume 1, p. 44.
[5] J Raz, *The Authority of Law: Essays on Law and Morality* (Clarendon Press, Oxford, 1979).

a more realistic revision of the 'rule of laws, not men' formulation: the law comes from a source outside the officials who are applying it. It need not be Divine, or natural, or otherwise superhuman in origin; it is enough that those who enforce the rules are not the same people that make them.

Another recent re-formulation of this enduring ideal is Ronald Cass's idea of 'fidelity' to rules. According to Cass, decision-makers should be faithful both to laws as a whole, and also to the principles and standards contained in them. Indeed, the principles make the rules coherent and allow a judge to act faithfully with law as a whole as opposed to a series of disconnected edicts.[6] Cass' view is very similar to Ronald M Dworkin's famous view of 'Law as Integrity', which calls on officials, especially judges, to make every statute and common-law rule the 'best it can be'.[7]

2.3 Coke

An early assertion of the rule of law in English case law came at the start of the seventeenth century—a century that was generally better for absolutism than the rule of law and hopeless for democracy. The religious wars and the opportunistic interventions to protect co-religionists from the very real oppression by princes of different religious persuasion led to the mid-century pragmatic compromise found in the Treaty of Westphalia (1648) that such interventions generally created more misery than the tyrannies they were designed to alleviate. However, while almost all European states became more autocratic, with France leading many towards absolutism, England moved dramatically in the other direction despite having a far more centralized state and starting with a much more powerful monarch than France in 1600. This is not the place to speculate on whether this was due to inherent features of the common law and other British institutions, to Stuart incompetence or merely the fact that Elizabeth died without issue and the English elite would not accept from a Scottish king what they had taken from strong Tudors and might well have taken from a strong Tudor like Henry VIII or Elizabeth I.[8] Certainly, Coke records himself as saying something to James that he would hardly have contemplated saying to Henry or Elizabeth:

Then the King said, that he thought that the law was founded upon reason, and that he and other had reason as well as the judges: to which it was answered by me, that true it was, that God had endowed His Majesty with excellent science, and great endowments of nature; but His Majesty was not learned in the laws of his realm of England, and causes which concern the life, or inheritance, or goods, or fortunes of his subjects, are not to be decided by natural reason but by the artificial reason and judgement of law, which law is an act which requires long study and experience, before a man can attain to the cognizance of it; that the law was the golden met-wand and measure to try the causes of his subjects; and

---

[6] See n. 33. [7] RM Dworkin, *Law's Empire* (Duckworth, London, 1986) 379.
[8] If so, the common law world can thank her for saving us from two scourges—the Spanish Armada and her own house.

which protected His Majesty in safety and peace; with which the King was greatly offended, and said, that then he should be under the law, which was treason to affirm, as he said; to which we said, that Bracton saith, *quod Rex non debet esse sub homine, sed sub Deo et lege* [the King ought not to be under any man, but under God and the law].[9]

As we saw in Chapter One, Coke made other contributions to the enunciation of the rule of law with *Doctor Bonham's Case* emphasizing another key element of the rule of law, that no person may be judge in their own cause.

2.4 The Dicean tradition

While Coke's reported exchange may be popular with legal historians, English influenced discussions of the Rule of Law always used to commence with the views of influential nineteenth century lawyer Albert Venn Dicey. As one British critic has observed, 'Dicey's work has, in some respects, become the only written constitution that we have',[10] which is perhaps ironic given Dicey's defence of the lack of a written constitution in the UK. Dicey considered Victorian England to be exemplary in its observance of the Rule of Law, and used it to illustrate his outline of the concept. According to Dicey, the Rule of Law has three main aspects, which can be summarized as follows: (1) only ordinary laws enforced by ordinary courts; (2) all persons equally subject to the laws; and (3) rights guaranteed in practice rather than on paper.

Dicey explains these three aspects thus:

[The Rule of Law] means, in the first place, the absolute supremacy or predominance of regular law as opposed to the influence of arbitrary power, and excludes the existence of arbitrariness, of prerogative, or even of wide discretionary authority on the part of the government. Englishmen are ruled by the law, and by the law alone; a man may with us be punished for a breach of law, but he can be punished for nothing else.

It means, again, equality before the law, or the equal subjection of all classes to the ordinary law of the land administered by the ordinary law courts; the 'rule of law' in this sense excludes the idea of any exemption of officials or others from the duty of obedience to the law which governs other citizens or from the jurisdiction of the ordinary tribunals; there can be with us nothing really corresponding to the 'administrative law' (*droit administratif*) or the 'administrative tribunals' (*tribunaux administratifs*) of France.

---

[9] The Case of Prohibitions (1607) 12 Co Rep 63. Readers of the case who define repartee as 'the reply you think of in the car driving home afterwards' will marvel at the feisty response and wonder whether Coke really said it quite so brilliantly or later rephrased—the exchange hardly matters. One account of the interaction indicates that Coke ended on his knees but was still only saved from the Tower of London on that occasion (he spent time there later), by the intercession of another Privy Councellor—see JP Somerville *Politics and Ideology in England (1603–1640)*. Case history is a history of winners and this case note could only have entered and stayed in the reports if the judges had not become winners. What matters was that he, and the other common lawyers seeking to restrain the King, were successful.

[10] Ferdinand Mount, *The British Constitution Now: Recovery or Decline?* (Heinemann, London 1992) 47.

The notion which lies at the bottom of the 'administrative law' known to foreign countries is, that affairs or disputes in which the government or its servants are concerned are beyond the sphere of the civil courts and must be dealt with by special and more or less official bodies. This idea is utterly unknown to the law of England, and indeed is fundamentally inconsistent with our traditions and customs.

The 'rule of law', lastly, may be used as a formula for expressing the fact that with us the law of the constitution, the rules which in foreign countries naturally form part of a constitutional code, are not the source but the consequence of the rights of individuals, as defined and enforced by the courts; that, in short, the principles of private law have with us been by the action of the courts and Parliament so extended as to determine the position of the Crown and of its servants; thus the constitution is the result of the ordinary law of the land.[11]

This explication of the Rule of Law has drawn much criticism. Firstly, Dicey's opposition to wide discretionary powers has been criticized as failing to appreciate that such powers are often crucial to government, particularly if they are to be effective in promoting such goals as public health and safety. Secondly, it is claimed that Dicey's standard of equality before the law ignores the extra rights and powers that public officials (for example, members of parliament, policemen or tax inspectors) may enjoy, even though they are equal before the law in the sense of being liable for their crimes. And thirdly, Dicey is accused of ignoring the role which written guarantees of rights (such as the US Bill of Rights) can play in upholding the Rule of Law.[12]

Some of these criticisms are misguided. Dicey's opposition to wide administrative discretion was due to his feeling that such powers failed to provide citizens with sufficient guidance as to what was required of them. He also pointed to the arbitrary use of power inherent in some exercises of discretionary powers: for example, the authorization of non-judicial detention or punishment in France. In any case, as Walker notes, some disagree that the granting of discretionary powers is the only, or best way, to solve the kinds of problems usually cited as justification for them.[13]

Regarding the second criticism, it is true that equality before the law is not absolute; obviously, public officials will possess special powers which the ordinary citizen does not. However, the underlying idea Dicey brings out is that these legal differences should be *minimized*. The additional powers are attached not to the person, but rather to the office or position, and they are interpreted narrowly (as being justifiably exercised only for public benefit). As Brian Simpson puts it:

The inequalities of power only apply to part of the official's life, the official part. The British Ambassador in Paris is my superior when it comes to issuing me with a replacement

---

[11] A V Dicey, *Introduction to the Study of the Law of the Constitution* (10th edn, Macmillan, London 1924) chapter 9, pp. 202–3.
[12] Geoffrey de Q Walker, *The Rule of Law: Foundation of Constitutional Democracy* (Melbourne University Press, 1988) 130–2.   [13] Walker, p. 135.

passport, but if he tries punching me on the nose when we meet on holiday in Cornwall he will find that for that purpose we remain equals.[14]

Similarly, Cabinet Ministers and other MPs are subject to the civil law and may end up (as many have) going to jail. Dicey also points out that special tribunals (such as those set up by Napoleon to try government officials) may serve as a mechanism for allowing those subject to them to get away with breaking the law. This criticism is reflected in the widespread public suspicion of the specialist tribunals set up by professional associations (such as in medicine and law) to determine disciplinary charges against their members. These are often accused (with or without justification) of letting their members off with, figuratively, a slap on the wrist. Dicey was particularly worried about special tribunals for government officials.

Finally, it is not precisely true that Dicey thought written guarantees of rights useless in upholding the Rule of Law; indeed, he praised the US Bill of Rights. However, he was concerned that such rights be prior to (and be recognized in the courts as prior to) their codification. For him, it was important that rights be recognized as originating, not from a written document such as the Constitution, but rather from the actual workings of the legal system. In Britain, the courts had for hundreds of years consistently enforced principles such as the presumption of innocence and the right to *habeas corpus*. This was a much more effective guarantee against state interference with rights than a written document. It would be very difficult, for example, for a dictator to persuade the judiciary to set aside their convictions that such rights existed independently of the constitution; whereas, if judges only enforced rights on the basis of their being stated in the Constitution, then these rights would be much more easily distorted or set aside, either through narrow interpretation or by amending the Constitution in an illiberal direction. It is, therefore, only of secondary importance to Dicey that rights are guaranteed by a written instrument. In fact, this view—described by Professor James Crawford as 'a method of protecting rights by seeming to ignore them'[15]—is still widely shared today.

There is, however, a further problem in Dicey's formulation. Geoffrey de Q Walker, who defends Dicey against the first three criticisms, nonetheless holds his conception of the Rule of Law to be inadequate in a crucial respect: namely, his acceptance of the absolute sovereignty of Parliament and his failure to adequately address the resulting inherent conflict with the Rule of Law.[16] In other words, the absolute power of parliament to make new law or alter existing law threatens the Rule of Law itself. Walker considers the explanation that Dicey thought that absolute parliamentary sovereignty 'was no threat to the rule of law because the powers conferred by a statute were confined by the interpretation put upon the

---

[14] AWB Simpson, *Invitation to Law* (Blackwell, Oxford, 1988) 18.
[15] James Crawford, 'Australian Law After Two Centuries' (1988) 11 *Sydney Law Review* 447.
[16] Walker, p. 137.

statute by the judges'.[17] However, in the end he seems unconvinced by this reply; Walker remains concerned that

while conveying fairly well the outlines of the underlying spirit [of the Rule of Law], Dicey's exposition left the 'incarnate' rule of law as a largely procedural formula, a matter of form and habit, a fragile construction that parliament could sweep away at any moment with impetuous or vindictive legislation.[18]

Like so many nineteenth century Englishmen, he was overly proud of the achievements of the English legal tradition and insufficiently alive to its weaknesses.

2.5 Fleshing out the epigram—twentieth century 'thin theories'

The twentieth century offered some more promising attempts to flesh out the epigrammatic ideal of the rule of law not men. Three great twentieth century theorists—Friedrich Hayek, Lon Fuller and Joseph Raz—seem to converge upon the same basic core.

Friedrich Hayek gives the following characterization of the Rule of Law:

Stripped of all technicalities [the Rule of Law] means that government in all its actions is bound by rules fixed and announced beforehand—rules which make it possible to foresee with fair certainty how the authority will use its coercive powers in given circumstances, and to plan one's individual affairs on the basis of this knowledge.[19]

For Hayek, the Rule of Law safeguards freedom by allowing agents to act with the knowledge that the law binds the authority as much as the individual. Agents can act confidently in the knowledge that governmental interference is only permitted when a person is in breach of a general law, impartially applied. Thus the Rule of Law implies that laws must be general, predictable, and must apply to everyone equally. However, it is considered that Hayek takes the requirement of generality and universality too far. Elsewhere he states:

The conception of freedom under the law . . . rests on the contention that when we obey laws, in the sense of general abstract rules laid down irrespective of their application to us, we are not subject to another man's will and are therefore free. . . . As a true law should not name any particulars, so it should especially not single out any specific persons or group of persons.[20]

As Raz points out, such a strict requirement on generality and abstractness leads to arguably absurd results, since it would mean there could be no laws concerning, for example, women, racial minorities or disabled persons. Hayek is aware of this problem, and attempts to overcome it by stipulating that special rules refer to 'properties that only some people possess . . . Only a woman, for example, can

---

[17] Walker, p. 138.   [18] Walker, p. 130.
[19] FA Hayek, *The Road to Serfdom* (University of Chicago Press, Chicago, 1944) [1975] 72.
[20] FA Hayek, *The Constitution of Liberty* (Routledge, London, 1960) 153–4.

be raped or got with child'.[21] According to Hayek, such laws 'will not be arbitrary...if they are equally recognized as justified by those inside and those outside the group'.[22] However, as Raz notes, this concession threatens to import into the concept of the Rule of Law the requirement of 'a form of government by consent', which puts us on 'the slippery slope leading to the identification of the rule of law with the rule of the good law'.[23]

Lon Fuller[24] explains his version of the rule of law through the parable of a king ('Rex') whose eight attempts to make laws for his subjects end in such abject failure that they do not even amount to law, because he:

1. tries to make special rules for everyone to suit their particular needs. But this only arouses confusion and anger at differential treatment;
2. fails to publicize them so nobody knows what laws to follow;
3. makes all his laws retroactive;
4. enacts vague or obscure rules;
5. enacts rules that contradict each other;
6. enacts rules that could not be followed;
7. fails to apply rules consistently;
8. changes his laws so often that his subjects cannot rely on them to plan their actions.

From this parable, Fuller derives eight 'virtues of law'. Ideally, all or most laws should be general, publicized, prospective, clear, non-contradictory, compliable, consistently applied, and reasonably stable. He is not suggesting that a just society can never have any laws that deviate from these virtues—that is, laws that are retroactive, unclear, frequently-changed and so on. It is simply that these deviations are the exception, rather than the rule and that such exceptions are dependent on the bulk of laws possessing the relevant virtues.

Drawing on Hayek and Fuller, Cass sees the rule of law as involving 'principled predictability'.[25] He emphasizes the importance of:

1. predictability being based on rules;
2. sufficient clarity for predictability;

---

[21] Hayek, p. 154. Obviously, Hayek's notion of rape is outdated, but the example regarding childbirth—and the general idea—remains valid. [22] Hayek, p. 154.

[23] Raz, p. 209.

[24] LL Fuller, *The Morality of Law* (Yale University Press, New Haven; London, 1964) (1969) 39 *ff.*

[25] Cass writes: 'A critical aspect of the commitment to a rule of law...is the promise that the government's force will be brought to bear on individuals—especially in criminal proceedings where that force is at its most fearsome—only after fair warning'. (RA Cass, 'Judging: Norms and Incentives of Retrospective Decisionmaking' (1995) 75 *Boston University Law Review* 954.) 'Predictability allows adjustments of individual behaviour that increase societal well-being; increased predictability lowers costs associated with a decision' (Cass, at 960).

3. accessibility;

4. reasonableness and cost (clarity and accessibility are not free);

5. generality—so that each law covers many cases (which makes communication easier) and is framed neutrally rather than being directed at particular people.

Unlike some conservative writers on the rule of law (such as Geoffrey de Q Walker),[26] Cass' model neither elevates predictability above every other value, nor suggests that perfect predictability is possible. The point is that unpredictability in laws is resolved through resort to principled reasoning from legal rules—reflecting Raz's conception of law as a two-stage decision-making process and Dworkin's idea of law as integrity.

Joseph Raz is one of the most influential authors on the rule of law since Fuller. While identifying the problems in Hayek's view mentioned above, Raz still approves of the basic definition, which he characterizes as 'one of the clearest and most powerful formulations of the ideal of the rule of law'.[27] His own definition has two basic aspects: '(1) that people should be ruled by the law and obey it, and (2) that the law should be such that people will be able to be guided by it'.[28] The first is related to the second because unlike *conforming* to the law (which people may do just if they do not happen to break it), obeying the law requires that the *reason* for one's conforming is that one knows the requirements of the law. Thus, obeying the law requires that the law itself is capable of providing guidance.

According to Raz, 'most of the requirements which were associated with the rule of law before it came to signify all the virtues of the state can be derived from this one basic idea'.[29] He lists eight principles which he considers to be the most important of those derivable from the basic principle, but notes that there are many other derivable principles which 'depend for their validity or importance on the particular circumstances of different societies'.[30] These eight principles are as follows:

1. *All laws should be prospective, open and clear.* People cannot be guided by laws which do not meet these criteria.

2. *Laws should be relatively stable.* If laws are too frequently changed, people's knowledge of the law will be unreliable and difficult to maintain, making it hard for them to be guided by it.

3. *The making of particular laws (particular legal orders) should be guided by open, stable, clear and general rules.* This is an attempt to get around the problems of Hayek's too-general account without introducing an objectionable kind of particular legal order, which would make it different for people to be

[26] G de Q Walker, *The Rule of Law: Foundation of Constitutional Democracy* (University Press, Melbourne, 1988).   [27] Raz, p. 195.
[28] Raz, p. 198.   [29] Raz, p. 198.   [30] Raz, p. 198.

guided by the law due to the introduction of too much arbitrariness and flexibility.

4. *The independence of the judiciary must be guaranteed.* If the judiciary do not apply the law when adjudicating cases, then people cannot be properly guided by the law; the only way to ensure that judges will not be influenced by extraneous considerations is to make them independent.

5. *The principles of natural justice must be observed.* Principles such as the absence of bias and a fair hearing are required to ensure correct application of the law, which is essential to maintaining the capacity of the law to provide guidance.

6. *The courts should have review powers over the implementation of the other principles.* Raz thinks this power should be very limited—'merely to ensure conformity to the rule of law'—and again is designed to ensure that administrative or executive power is not abused.

7. *The courts should be easily accessible.* Since the courts are essential in maintaining the rule of law, their inaccessibility will mean that laws cannot be enforced, which will make it more difficult for people to be guided by their knowledge of the law.

8. *The discretion of the crime-preventing agencies should not be allowed to pervert the law.* This, again, is a requirement if the law is to be accurately applied, which is crucial to its capacity to provide guidance.[31]

The first three principles largely reflect Lon Fuller's views and concern the standards the law itself must meet if it is to effectively guide action.

The next five principles are directed to the 'legal machinery' to prevent it being distorted in ways that would undermine the first three standards. These principles set standards for the application and enforcement of law to ensure 'that it shall be capable of supervising conformity to the rule of law and provide effective remedies in cases of deviation from it'.[32]

Raz's theory is one of the most widely accepted and cited. As Walker concedes, all of the principles Raz sets out can be found mentioned in connection with the Rule of Law elsewhere.[33] Raz emphasized that this is a limited concept of the rule of law. For him, it is essentially a negative value insofar as it is directed at preventing some of the harms that could be done by those wielding power. It does not, however, eliminate all harms and might exacerbate others.

The rule of law, so conceived, makes law a more effective tool. Officials would enforce rules uniformly and those subject to them would modify their behaviour in the light of those rules (to realize the benefits it provided or avoid the harm it could do to them). This made the law more effective and, for most people, self-enforcing. In his famous analogy, the rule of law is good law in the same sense

---

[31] Raz, pp. 198–201.   [32] Raz, p. 202.   [33] Walker, p. 21.

as a knife is good. Whether harm results depends on what the law, like the knife, is used for.

This limited concept of the rule of law does not seek to incorporate the other Enlightenment values of democracy, citizenship and human rights.[34] It does not eschew these values but allows them to be defined more independently and their presence or absence to be determined more reliably. This does not mean that the other values cannot be embraced wholeheartedly. Rather, it means that there are a number of values for assessing the worth of a legal order of which the rule of law is one. The lack of one or more of the other values might well justify us in overthrowing a legal order that had the one virtue of exhibiting the rule of law. The lack of democracy, for example, will generally justify the replacing of that order with a democratic one—although a democracy with no rule of law may generate at least as much misery as an autocracy with the rule of law.

A good legal order needs more than one virtue. As Raz argues, it is better to separately identify the various virtues we would wish legal orders to demonstrate, rather than to roll them all into a single virtue. Theories that do not seek to incorporate other Enlightenment values we call, in Rawlsian fashion, 'thin theories' of the rule of law.[35] In contrast, theories that add other Enlightenment values we call 'thick theories' of the rule of law.

2.6 Broader definitions—'thick theories' of the Rule of Law

Not everyone is satisfied with such 'thin' theories. There is a genuine concern that it turns the Rule of Law into a purely formal matter: if there is a system of law to which everyone including the lawmakers is subject, then the Rule of Law prevails. As long as those in power are officially subject to the law, that regime is a true *Rechtsstaat*. This seems to concede that the Rule of Law exists in societies which are repressive, totalitarian or tyrannical, and in which gross violations of rights occur. For, as Jefferson wrote, 'law is often but the tyrant's will, and always so when it violates the rights of the individual'.[36] This conception of the Rule of Law would support the view of officials of the African dictatorship of Malawi, who assured Geoffrey Robertson that Malawi 'was a State which embodied the Rule of Law: the Constitution laid down that there shall be only one party, and there was'.[37] For some, the theory is not merely thin but emaciated.

More generally, many are uneasy with this formulation because quite draconian restrictions would be consistent with this kind of rule of law, as long as fair

---

[34] See chapter 7.

[35] John Rawls, *A Theory of Justice* (Harvard University Press, Massachusetts, 1971) 118–42. See also Michael Walzer, *Thick and Thin: Moral Argument at Home and Abroad* (Notre Dame University Press, Indiana, 1994). We first used this distinction in 'Reconceiving the Rule of Law for a Globalizing World', in S Zifcak (ed), *Reconceiving the Rule of Law* (Routledge, London, 2004).

[36] Letter to Isaac H Tiffany (1819).

[37] Geoffrey Robertson, *The Justice Game* (Vintage, London, 1999) 218.

warning is given. The sensitivity of most 'thin' theorists is illustrated by the
emphasis which some make that really draconian laws would not, in fact, get up in
the transparent conditions of the rule of law. Hayek admits that his theory—unlike
rivals based on natural law or human rights—would not invalidate draconian laws
worded in the proper form. However, followers of Fuller and Hayek will reply that
draconian laws are unlikely to be enacted if they must satisfy the set criteria of
publicity, simplicity, and generality. These concerns have tempted many to add
other desiderata to the lists of virtues found in Fuller or Raz including 'social,
economic, educational and cultural conditions',[38] legitimacy, accountability and
respect for human rights. Herein, we see a tendency to add many of the later
Enlightenment values (particularly democracy and rights) as well as some of the
institutional mechanisms thought to be most effective in realising those values, to
the minimalist early-Enlightenment value of the rule of law—turning the rule of
law into the rule of just law or the rule of justice.

The International Congress of Jurists is one of the 'thickest' definitions of Rule
of Law:

The Rule of Law is a convenient term to summarize a combination of ideals and practical
legal experience concerning which there is, over a wide part of the world, although in
embryonic and to some extent inarticulate form, a consensus of opinion among the legal
profession; two ideals underlie this conception of the Rule of Law. In the first place, it
implies without regard to the content of the law, that all power in the State should be
derived from and exercised in accordance with the law. Secondly, it assumes that the law
itself is based on respect for the supreme value of human personality.

The practical experiences of lawyers in many countries suggests that certain
principles, institutions and procedures are important safeguards of the ideals underlying
the Rule of Law. Lawyers do not however claim that such principles, institutions and
procedures are the only safeguards of these ideals, and they recognize that in different
countries different weight will be attached to particular principles, institutions and
procedures.

[The Rule of Law is therefore defined as]:

The principles, institutions and procedures, not always identical, but broadly similar,
which the experience and traditions of lawyers in different countries of the world, often
having themselves varying political structures and economic backgrounds, have shown to
be important to protect the individual from arbitrary government and to enable him to
enjoy the dignity of men.[39]

The ICJ later expanded this definition to include 'not only the recognition of
[the individual's] civil and political rights but also the establishment of the social,

---

[38] Clause 1 of the Committee of the International Congress of Jurists at New Delhi, 1959 cited in
Robertson, p. 211. Raz is critical of extending the doctrine of the Rule of Law to include such desiderata referring to it as a 'perversion'. He writes that the report of the committee 'goes on to mention or
refer to just about every political ideal which has found support in any part of the globe during the
post-war years' (Robertson, pp. 211, 210).

[39] International Commission of Jurists, *The Rule of Law in a Free Society* (ICJ, Geneva, 1959) 313.

economic, educational, and cultural conditions which are essential to the full development of his personality'.[40]

It seems *prima facie* hard to argue with these broader definitions, the 'extra' values being widely shared. If we can secure their acceptance from everyone who claims to believe in the rule of law by showing that they are necessarily inherent within the rule of law, then why not do so? Surely, this would spare us the need to expend political capital fighting these battles, later to secure values we thought we had already won? We think, however, that we should restrain ourselves from this temptation and opt for a narrower conception of the rule of law—a 'thin theory' of the rule of law.[41]

While we are not sure we would go so far as Raz in calling the ICJ definition as a 'perversion of the doctrine of the rule of law', he persuasively argues that:

. . . if the rule of law is the rule of the good law then to explain its nature is to propound a complete social philosophy. But if so the term lacks any useful function. We have no need to be converted to the rule of law just in order to discover that to believe in it is to believe that good should triumph'.[42]

In particular, the Rule of Law should not be confused with democracy. The Rule of Law was possibly the first 'Enlightenment' value applied to law and when it was first articulated, there were no democracies worthy of the name and none that would meet the criteria for admission to the Community of Democracies established in 2000 and which comprises just over 100 countries (a number that fluctuates for obvious reasons). Many non-democratic societies (pre-1832 England, Hong Kong, some Gulf Emirates) have upheld the Rule of Law, while some democracies (revolutionary France and Iran) have not. Although these two values often tend to support one another (so that states which are more democratic are also more likely to uphold the Rule of Law), they are clearly separate concepts, since they come into conflict (for example, in cases involving delegation of discretionary powers, judicial review of legislation, and emergency powers). Therefore, as Raz writes:

[The Rule of Law] is not to be confused with democracy, justice, equality (before the law or otherwise), human rights of any kind or respect for persons or for the dignity of man. A non-democratic legal system, based on the denial of human rights, on extensive poverty, on racial segregation, sexual inequalities and religious persecution may, in principle, conform to the requirements of the rule of law better than any of the legal systems of the more enlightened western democracies.[43]

[40] International Commission of Jurists, *The Rule of Law and Human Rights: Principles and Definitions* (International Commission of Jurists, Geneva, 1966) 9.

[41] John Rawls famously outlined 'thick' and 'thin' theories of 'the good' (*A Theory of Justice* (Harvard University Press, Massachusetts, 1971) 118–42). We are proposing a similar distinction for the Rule of Law. However, the reasons for thinning out the Rule of Law are not because of the controversiality of some of the other additions.   [42] Raz, p. 196.

[43] Raz, p. 196.

Geoffrey de Q Walker[44] is one who cites Raz's criticism of the ICJ definition with approval but finds the need to add more elements of his own. His own book shows the danger of a selective addition of particular political preferences being added to the Rule of Law. He seeks to add elements he believes are missing— including 'the requirement of an independent bar', 'generality', 'general congruence of the law with social values', 'a mechanism to ensure that laws remain broadly in line with public opinion', 'substantive laws against anarchy and private lawless-ness',[45] and more vaguely, 'a legal *Geist*—an attitude of legality'.[46]

As Walker outlines his 'Democratic Theory' of law, we see that his concerns with democracy include a reduction in the power of elected parliament and an emphasis on the more easily manipulated institutions of citizen initiated referenda and the popular recall of judges (something that sits uneasily with his attacks on what he claims to be a 'populist orientation of many judges in Britain and the Commonwealth').[47] The substantive laws he wants against private lawlessness concern the behaviour of unions (while including the extensive private ownership of firearms—dubbed 'the privatisation of crime prevention').[48] His insistence on generality is part of his concerns with progressive taxation (indeed, taxation itself which he calls the nationalization of the individual's income)[49] and inflation which he claims 'is a conscious act of policy on the part of government' by which it 'sets out to cheat and defraud the people'.[50]

We would agree with Walker that the Rule of Law 'is plainly the essential prerequisite of our whole legal, constitutional, and perhaps social, order.... [It] is not a complete formula for the good society, but there can be no good society without it'.[51] It is important that it is a set of principles that govern the debate over the content of law, not a means to privilege one side in that debate. He is as offended by the ICJ's inclusion of rights that he thinks interfere with private rights as others are offended by Walker's inclusion of his idiosyncratic agenda.

2.7 A preference for 'thin theories' of the Rule of Law

The dangers of contentious inclusions are one of the reasons for caution towards 'thick' theories of law. First, while most will find one or more 'thick' theories more attractive than thin theories, many positive claims may be made about this more limited sense of the rule of law:

- Citizens can plan for their lives because the behaviour of state officials is predictable. (However, planning requires much else besides—including the

---

[44] For a full review, see C Sampford, 'Review of Walker's The Rule of Law' (1989) 16 *Melbourne University Law Review* 174.

[45] Walker, p. 23. Walker does note, however, that the last two points may be implied by what Raz did include.   [46] Walker, pp. 24–41.

[47] Walker, p. 272.   [48] Walker, p. 393.   [49] Walker, p. 347.   [50] Walker, p. 349.

[51] Walker, pp. 41–2.

resources to carry out plans. Furthermore, there are other sources of power which may be exercised capriciously and unpredictably, most noticeably corporate and economic power.)

- The rule of law avoids a number of important procedural injustices and establishes a clear model of formal justice.

- As Raz argues, where rulers are prepared to be bound by their rules, it makes the law a more effective tool. Indeed, if the rulers do not tie the sanctions they apply to the rules they have established in advance, then people will be less likely to follow the rules that they apply.

- One of the most famous and impassioned defences of the rule of law was with respect to a deeply flawed legal regime—that of eighteenth century England. At that time, democracy, rights, substantive equality and other liberal democratic values were not only unsupported but their advocacy could also lead to prosecution. Nevertheless, EP Thomson praised the rule of law because the imposition of effective restraints on power and the defence of the citizen from power's 'all-intrusive claims' seemed to him 'an unqualified human good'.[52] While we would never elevate any value to an unqualified good (especially one that is essentially an 'instrumental' one), Thomson provides a good reason for this to be one of the virtues of law.

This limited concept of the rule of law does not seek to incorporate the other enlightenment values of democracy, citizenship and human rights. It does not eschew those other values but allows those values to be more precisely defined and their presence or otherwise more reliably determined. This does not mean that the other values cannot be embraced wholeheartedly—as we do. What it does mean is that there are a number of values for assessing the worth of a legal order of which the rule of law is one. The lack of one or more of the other values might well justify us in overthrowing a legal order that had the one virtue of exhibiting the rule of law. The lack of democracy will generally justify the replacing of that order with a democratic one—although a democracy with no rule of law may generate at least as much misery as an autocracy with the rule of law.

A good legal order needs more than one virtue. Raz's point is that it is better to identify separately the various virtues that we would wish legal orders to demonstrate rather than to roll them all into a single virtue.

We can understand why many would prefer a 'thick' theory of the rule of law to a 'thin' theory. The added values of democracy and rights are admirable and we fully endorse them. We also fully accept that the value of the rule of law is enhanced if the law is made democratically and with a desire to protect and further human rights (as rights and democracy are enhanced by the rule of law). The rule of law, democracy, rights (along with citizenship, liberty, equality and the natural environment in which all this takes place) are a package of enlightenment

---

[52] EP Thomson, *Whigs and Hunters: The Origin of the Black Act* (Penguin, London, 1990).

values which are compromised and sometimes negated in the absence of each other. Nevertheless, like Raz, we prefer to use a narrower concept of the rule of law—as one value among other values that is not determinative of action or preference. We would argue that a thin theory is preferable for reasons set out in an earlier essay:[53]

- One must be cautious about the 'imperialism of values'. If we view democracy, liberty, or the rule of law as good things, we are tempted to include most of the (political) things that the author considers to be good within the relevant concept.

- The different values lose their focus with a number of undesirable ideological consequences. Different, potentially conflicting values are incorporated into the one value. The most common conflation over the last 50 years is that of human rights and democracy. Political liberty is a prerequisite for democracy. However, the entrenchment of rights against democratic legislatures is a restriction of democracy. Some such entrenchment is, in this author's view, justified. But, it is justified as a restriction of democracy rather than as a part of over-expansive concept of democracy.[54]

- As some of the values added become controversial, it will weaken support for the concept of the rule of law.

- An expanded list is far less likely to fit within an overarching concept and central organizing idea such as those discussed in the previous section.

- The more we build positive values into law before it is called a law, the more difficulties we will have in overtly criticizing that law. The more positive values that must be respected before the rule of law is seen to exist, the more difficulty there will be in questioning it through the prism of other values.

Strategically, we like to unpack the package of enlightenment values for a number of reasons:[55]

- If separated conceptually, they can be understood more effectively.

- Many of them are subject to competing definitions and a variety of nuances and subtleties. If other values are included within the rule of law, then one cannot know whether the rule of law is in place unless one has settled the meaning of, say, 'democracy'. Those who adopt a different conception of

[53] C Sampford, 'Reconceiving the Rule of Law for a Globalizing World', in S Zifcak (ed), *Reconceiving the Rule of Law* (Routledge, London, 2004).

[54] *Contra* John Hart Ely who argues that certain types of judicial activism can be democratically 'representation-reinforcing' (*Democracy and Distrust: A Theory of Judicial Review* (Harvard University Press, Massachusetts, 1980)).

[55] This separate treatment is behind the 'Challenges of Globalisation' Series which Haig Parapan and Charles Sampford jointly edited for Routledge. There is a separate volume for each enlightenment value and the ways in which it is challenged by globalization and may be reconceived to meet those challenges.

democracy may deny the existence of the rule of law or may put off its application until the other conditions are met.

- The values can have independent worth (even if diminished worth—as EP Thompson's plea makes clear).
- It may not be possible to introduce all the relevant values simultaneously so that it appears as if no progress is being made and no praise can be given for that progress.

One of the potential reasons for preferring thick theories is the concern that fundamentally inadequate laws will receive the cachet and legitimacy of the word 'law' and be supported by 'rule of law' values. Only laws that reflect values such as 'democracy' and 'rights' should receive the honour of being called 'laws' and the legitimacy that word generates. For me, this is the right answer to an unnecessary question. Because a particular form of words can be identified as a 'law' does not mean that one has to be bound by it. One can never surrender one's conscience to any outside power. The fact that something is a law does not mean that it must be unequivocally obeyed. We are attracted to the inclinations of British positivists from Bentham onwards. If law is seen as arising out of social facts, then one can fix it as a phenomenon for praise or blame. If law has to meet certain criteria of justice before being called law, it is harder to criticize it.

2.8 The reach of the Rule of Law

We have previously drawn attention to the way that the twentieth century has extended the reach of the rule of law—with administrative law enforcing the rule of law on all members of the executive and requiring that all exercises of power have a legal basis, and corporate law and governance applying similar principles to corporations.[56] The latter reflects an aspect of the widespread appeal of the rule of law. When the concept was originally outlined, the greatest source of power was the sovereign state. Sovereigns claimed absolute and paramount power. They had just fought for supremacy over other sources of power within their territories: the church, the aristocracy, and foreign states.

However, this should not blind us (as it sometimes did Enlightenment thinkers) to other sources of power that can arbitrarily restrict our capacities to make and carry out life plans. One of the features of the last 300 years is the appreciation of these other sources of power and the belief that those who hold such power are responsible for its exercise and should not do so in an arbitrary fashion. Sometimes this has manifested itself in demands that the law extend into what might otherwise have been considered the 'private sphere'. However,

---

[56] Sampford 2004.

another manifestation lies in the demands of shareholders, employees and other 'stakeholders'—whose lives are affected by the decisions of large organizations—that those who make those decisions are bound by, and act within, rules set by those organizations.

The rule of law was first conceived as a principle about the use of state power within bounds set, prescribed, and predicted by law rather than for the purposes, or according to the whims, of the rulers and thereby removes one means by which state power is abused. However, similar arguments apply to wielders of other kinds of strong organizational power. It is important to appreciate that struggles for power between state and non-state institutions are present today as they were in the pre-Westphalian state when princes competed with feudal lords (temporal and spiritual). Corporations (the modern version of 'over-mighty subjects') contest for power with states and may seek to use the Rule of Law to weaken the State to create more space for their own arbitrary use of power. The Rule of Law suggests that law should rule that contest and take into account the behaviour of the powerful whether in or out of government.

2.9 Relevant elements of the Rule of Law

Not all of these debates about the rule of law are relevant to debates over retrospectivity. Prospectivity is a virtue in Fuller and other thin theories and retrospectivity is something that should occur either rarely (Fuller) or never at all (Walker).

One of the leitmotifs of the rule of law is guidance. This is one of the most central rationales for the rule of law from the Greeks to Raz and underlies several of the key rule of law virtues. All the theorists accept that the *sine qua none* of Rule of Law is that citizens must be able to use the law to guide their actions. Citizens act upon the basis of expectations created by the law, and, by and large, the law respects those expectations. In order to uphold such expectations and foster such reliance, rules need to be public, and possible to comply with. If they are clear, stable, consistent, and general, they are easier to understand and act on.

While the above virtues are seen as supporting the capacity of law to guide citizens, some kinds of laws are seen to undermine the capacity of law to guide citizens: vague laws, 'closed-class' laws, and retrospective laws. While the topic of retrospective laws is the subject of this book, the first two are often closely related to the problems of retrospectivity. However, as we will see here and for the rest of the book, there is room for disagreement about the extent to which such laws can be compatible with the rule of law.

1. *Vague or Subjective Laws*

   a) A law can be considered to be vague if reasonable people can interpret it in substantially different ways (leading to substantially different legal outcomes). Because such laws are confusing and misleading, they cannot provide effective guidance,[57] and therefore fall foul of the ideal of the Rule of Law.

b) Obviously, vagueness is a matter of degree, but the use in laws of words such as 'fair' or 'reasonable' are often supposed to be objectionably vague: Hayek claims that 'one could write a history of the decline of the Rule of Law . . . in terms of the progressive introduction of these vague formulas into legislation'.[58] Other potential examples of objectionable vagueness are laws banning 'offensive' or 'obscene' material, and some laws against sexual harassment or racial vilification.

c) Similarly, legislation delegating detail-fixing power is often objected to on the grounds of vagueness. Such 'detail-fixing' power can be delegated to the executive (for example, by means of 'Henry VIII' clauses such as 'if the Minister thinks fit . . .', by requiring the Attorney-General's fiat for prosecution, or by conferring power to grant waivers or exemptions); to the judiciary (enacting a mandatory provision in such broad terms that judges are required to guess its potential meaning); to the legislature itself (by requiring that all exercises of a granted power be tabled before, and potentially disallowed by, it); or even the individual (if a legal declaration is non-justiciable expressly, by tradition, or because the judiciary refuses to hold it enforceable, and the individual is left to decide between different interpretations of their legal duty). Regardless, such laws, it is claimed, lack the proper capacity to provide guidance.

2. *'Closed-class' laws*

a) 'Closed-class' laws are also referred to as one-off, non-uniform, targeted, particular, or singling-out enactments. These are enactments which define their categories in such a way that legislators can identify, with a fair degree of certainty, the individuals to whom the enactment's benefits or burdens will apply. This can be achieved either by direct naming of the class (Acts of Attainder, or Bills of Pains and Penalties in which individuals are declared guilty without a trial), or by targeting classes by use of language that is *prima facie* uniform and general (such as in Lon Fuller's example of a statute applying 'to all cities in the state which according to the last census had a population of more than 165 000 and less than 166 000').[59] These laws fail to conform to the Rule of Law because they fail on the criterion of generality, and also on the ability to provide guidance: there is nothing the named class can do to avoid the burdens conferred by the law.

3. *Retrospective laws*

a) Finally, the Rule of Law is supposed to be incompatible with retrospective laws. As Raz points out, 'one cannot be guided by a retroactive law',[60] and

---

[57] Raz, p. 199.   [58] Hayek, p. 78.
[59] Lon Fuller, *The Morality of Law* (rev. edn, Yale University Press, 1969) 47n.   [60] Raz, p. 198.

Fuller criticizes 'the abuse of retroactive legislation, which not only cannot itself guide action, but undercuts the integrity of rules prospective in effect, since it puts them under the threat of retrospective change'.[61]

The reasons for thinking these kinds of law to be incompatible with the Rule of Law seems fairly clear. And yet the matter is not so simple. Firstly, all of the three characteristics above can be a matter of degree, so it is not true that a given law will be either in conflict with the Rule of Law or not. We have already seen in Chapter 1 that retrospectivity is a continuum concept, so that laws can be more or less retrospective. This is also true of vague and closed-class laws. In the case of the latter, there are 'mixed' examples in which a statute applies to all, but not only, the members of a particular closed class (that is, that particular class is subject to the statute's benefits and burdens, but these are not limited to that class). There may also be statutes which do not declare guilt or specify a punishment, but which make it more difficult for a particular group to evade burdens (or avail themselves of benefits).

Similarly, vagueness is something which laws can exhibit to a greater or lesser extent. For example, a law against 'driving dangerously' is fairly vague, especially at the boundaries, even though it clearly includes some things (for example, drink driving) and excludes others (for example, driving with an anti-government sticker on one's car). Even laws which seem vague on their face (and may indeed have been so when enacted) may be very clear in practice. This may be because there is a wide consensus on community values (for example, on what is fair or reasonable) or because over the years there has developed an accepted judicial interpretation of the particular law.

Another problem with blanket prohibitions on these kinds of laws is that their occasional use, in fact, seems indispensable to a well-functioning legal system. The delegation of detail-fixing power is, to some extent, unavoidable. Particular legal orders may be used to introduce flexibility into a legal system.[62] Vagueness may be used to advantage in some cases: as Fuller writes, 'sometimes the best way to achieve clarity is to take advantage of, and to incorporate into the law, common sense standards of judgement that have grown up in the ordinary life lived outside legislative halls. . . . A specious clarity can be more damaging than an honest open-ended vagueness'.[63] And retrospectivity is not only (as we shall argue) sometimes a useful tool, it is also unavoidable to a certain extent: Fuller claims that any theory which endorses an absolute prohibition on retrospective law making is 'a theory that disregards completely the realities of creating and administering a legal system'.[64] For one thing, an absolute constitutional prohibition on *legislative* retrospectivity would require enforcement and interpretation through judicial decisions, which are themselves inherently retrospective.

[61] Fuller, p. 39.   [62] Raz, p. 200.   [63] Fuller, p. 64.   [64] Fuller, p. 116.

This recognizes the fact that the Rule of Law is first and foremost an ideal to which a body of law (what some might call a 'legal system')[65] may aspire, rather than as a standard which must be met by each individual enactment. The Rule of Law, as an ideal, is something that legal systems can be closer to, or farther from, realizing; a failure to conform even loosely to this ideal (for example, through routine use of vague, closed-class, or retrospective laws) means that a legal system fails to achieve even the minimum standards for the Rule of Law. But in this case, as Fuller points out, the system may fail to achieve the status of law at all: retrospective laws, for example, could not be effective unless in the context of a system of prospective laws that allowed for their enforcement. In this context, however, an individual retrospective enactment might have a useful role to play:

A system of law composed exclusively of retrospective rules could exist only as a grotesque conceit worthy of Lewis Carroll or Franz Kafka. Yet a retrospective 'curative' statute can perform a useful function in dealing with mishaps that may occur within a system of rules that are generally prospective.[66]

Thus a law that does not meet one of the desiderata set down by Fuller or Raz but which helps the legal 'system' provide more effective guidance may not only be defensible but preferable or even necessary.

At the same time, however, it should not be assumed that the Rule of Law is an appropriate standard of evaluation *only* for whole systems of laws, and should never be used to evaluate individual laws. With few exceptions, each individual retrospective, vague or closed-class law results in the system to which it belongs being further from the ideal. Some might argue, as Walker seems to,[67] that *any* departure from the ideal is unjustifiable, but we might all agree that being closer to the ideal is, *ceteris paribus*, better. And, insofar as conformity to the Rule of Law is desirable, an individual enactment which does not conform to the rule of law is, at least in that respect, a source of disvalue. The fact that an individual law fails to conform to the Rule of Law, then, is at least grounds for a presumption against it.

2.10 Criticisms of the Rule of Law

There is an assumption which tends to go unnoticed in much of the discussion of what is prohibited by the Rule of Law. This is that if a law is unjustified by the standards of the Rule of Law, then it is unjustified *tout court*. In other words, it is assumed that the Rule of Law has normative force as an appropriate standard

---

[65] For reasons set out in *The Disorder of Law* (Blackwell, 1989), we are reluctant to use the term 'legal system' because of the difficulties of centripetal forces in law that spoil attempts to systematize them on the basis of authority, content or function. However, given the wide use of the term by others writing in the area, we will use the term 'legal system' meaning a set of laws from one jurisdiction without implication that they are or can be systematized. [66] Fuller, p. 74.
[67] Walker, p. 321.

by which to judge (systems of) laws. If, however, the Rule of Law were itself problematic, then this assumption would be unwarranted. Thus, criticisms of the Rule of Law, if successful, would indicate that it may be no grounds for concern if a law (or system of laws) failed to conform to the ideal. For if the Rule of Law is not itself justified, then an incompatibility with it can hardly be used as grounds for arguing that some particular law (or system of laws) is unjustified. It would therefore be remiss not to consider the merits of objections to the Rule of Law.

One criticism of the Rule of Law is that it might prove to be an obstacle to governments wanting to pursue legitimate social goals. This potential problem has already been noted above. For example, governments might want to delegate broad discretionary powers to administrative bodies (such as anti-discrimination or mental health tribunals) which operate more cheaply, flexibly, and justly than traditional courts. Similarly, legislation targeting named individuals and groups may serve the public interest by achieving the government's intended aims (for instance, the neutralization of dangerous groups) without risking undesirable and unintended consequences which could result from general and open-ended laws.

Particularly relevant to this book is the potential social utility of retrospective legislation. One claimed example of this is the use of retrospective legislation by the Australian Commonwealth government in the 1980s against so-called 'bottom of the harbour' tax avoidance schemes. One benefit of such legislation was the ability to recoup large amounts of tax revenue from those who had engaged in such schemes. Another, more important, reason for *retrospective* legislation, however, is that it foreclosed a means by which those engaged in tax avoidance might otherwise be able to indefinitely evade paying their fair share of tax: namely, by engaging in one scheme, completing it, then moving on to another as soon as the first was (prospectively) made illegal. Another potential use of retrospective legislation is where there might otherwise be a temptation for people to engage in activities such as 'panic-clearing' between the announcement of the intention to make the law and its actual enactment.

The above criticism, then, suggests that the Rule of Law would go too far in prohibiting certain kinds of legislation which are, in fact, justified by their promotion of social good. A second criticism, however, claims that the Rule of Law does not go far enough: it stops short of achieving certain important social aims (namely, equality of rights).

A more radical version of this criticism sees the Rule of Law claimed to be inextricably linked to *inequality* of rights; the Rule of Law, in other words, serves only to entrench and maintain the power of the ruling class. Worse, it also provides a convenient disguise for the exercise of power, which prevents the disenfranchised from being able to effectively challenge it.

This criticism might take its starting point from an observation already made in connection with the Rule of Law: namely, that even laws which seem to be neutrally and generally worded can mask an unequal application of the law's benefits or burdens. The accusation here is that such disguised inequality is in fact systematic, and consistently works to the advantage of the ruling class. Thus, Mark Kelman argues that mere insistence on neutral and general laws 'seems legally naïve, unable to recognize the manipulability of language that permits us easily to create seemingly universal rules with utterly disparate, narrow impacts'.[68] And Anatole France memorably made the same point when he noted that 'the law, in its majestic equality, forbids the rich as well as the poor to sleep under bridges, to get in the streets, and to steal bread'.[69]

A more recent, Australian, example which might be used as evidence of this phenomenon is a law passed in the Northern Territory in the 1990s, which banned the consumption of alcohol within two kilometres of licensed premises. The Northern Territory government introduced the law on the grounds that it would reduce public drunkenness. However, it could be argued (as Amnesty International did) that the 'two-kilometre' law, in practice, singled out Aboriginal people, who were often denied access to licensed premises.[70]

If we take the more moderate (that is, the first two) of these criticisms, the complaint seems to be that the Rule of Law cannot be used as the sole standard of justification for a system of laws: there are important things (such as equal worth of liberty, and the promotion of social goods) to which the Rule of Law seems blind. The radical (third) criticism seems to suggest that the Rule of Law should not be considered as a normative standard at all: that is, the claim seems to be that we might be better off giving up entirely on the Rule of Law.

EP Thompson has convincingly rebutted the radical criticism. Thompson agrees that the Rule of Law can be used 'instrumentally as mediating and reinforcing existent class relations and, ideologically, as offering to these a legitimation'.[71] However, he points out that it is wrong to regard the Rule of Law as *nothing more* than this: he repeatedly emphasizes that this view fails to make a rather important distinction between the Rule of Law (however unjust in practice) and the mere arbitrary exercise of power outside of the law.[72] Although the Rule of Law may do little more than serve the interests of powerful groups, it is crucially different from the mere exercise of power in that it requires that those in power also submit to the authority of the law. Moreover, Thompson points out that in order to serve the function attributed to it by the critics—that is, the entrenchment of existing power relations—the Rule of Law must, at least, be *perceived* to be minimally just. For 'if the law is evidently partial and unjust, then it will mask nothing, legitimize nothing, contribute nothing to any class's hegemony'.[73]

More generally, if we take it that the function of the Rule of Law is to provide guidance, then the justification of the Rule of Law is just an outline of the desirability

[68] Mark G Kelman, *A Guide to Critical Legal Studies* (Harvard University Press, Massachusetts: 1987) 72.   [69] Anatole France, *The Red Lily*, 1894, Chapter 7.

[70] Gay Alcorn, 'Northern Territory: Australia's Final Frontier' (February 1995) *Independent Monthly* 48–9. See also Gay Alcorn, 'NT Minister Rejects Law Criticism by Amnesty', *Melbourne Age*, 12 February 1993.   [71] Thompson, p. 262.

[72] Thompson, p. 265.   [73] Thompson, p. 263.

or moral import of this feature. The Rule of Law allows citizens to know how the authority will respond to any given action of theirs, and—because they know that other citizens are similarly bound—any given action of their fellow citizens. This knowledge protects and enhances the agent's autonomy—their ability to act to fulfil their goals on the basis of reasonable expectations and through coordinated interaction with (or even just avoidance of) other citizens and the state. So the justification for Rule of Law can rest upon the fact that most moral systems value the sort of autonomous goal-directed action that Rule of Law seeks to protect. Furthermore, it can simply be pointed out that, without this ability to be guided on the basis of predictions and justifiable expectations, it is difficult to know what sort of society worthy of the name could exist at all. If this is so, then we might be tempted to conclude with Thompson that, while it is important to expose the inequalities which may be hidden within the law, 'the rule of law itself, the imposing of effective inhibitions upon power and the defence of the citizen from power's all-intrusive claims, seems to me to be an unqualified human good'.[74]

That the Rule of Law is an *unqualified* human good might seem to be, however, precisely what the more moderate criticisms are disputing. For these criticisms allege that there are some goods which the Rule of Law cannot secure—and some goods the promotion of which it actively hinders. Thus, the radical critics may be wrong in altogether dismissing the Rule of Law, but more moderate critics might be right in suggesting that the Rule of Law is not always a good thing: or, at least, if it is always a good thing taken by itself, it is not always good all things considered.

It might be argued, however, that those making this claim are guilty of a misapprehension which is, in fact, shared by many defenders of the Rule of Law. This misapprehension, Raz thinks, is 'one of the two main fallacies in the contemporary treatment of the doctrine of the rule of law: The assumption of its overriding importance'.[75] A more reasonable view might be that of the Rule of Law as one of a number of desirable qualities in a legal system: as Raz argues, 'conformity to the rule of law is a virtue but only one of the many virtues a legal system should possess'.[76]

This view of the Rule of Law allows both of the moderate criticisms to be defused to a certain extent. The criticism that the Rule of Law fails to ensure equal protection of rights (since it allows the making of some kinds of unjust law) can be countered by pointing out that adherence to the standard of the Rule of Law, while vitally important, is not the *only* standard by which we ought to measure laws. Other elements are also important, and other standards are also necessary to achieve an ideal system of laws. Although one necessary condition for fully justified law is conformity to the Rule of Law, it may not be a sufficient condition.

The idea of the Rule of Law as only one among many possible virtues of the law also allows a reply to the first criticism—namely, that the Rule of Law sometimes

[74] Thompson, p. 266.   [75] Raz, p. 195.   [76] Raz, p. 202.

prevents realization of important social goals. For if there are other values which the law ought to aspire to meet or promote, then it is possible that the need to promote these values might sometimes be more important than full (ideal) conformity with the Rule of Law. As Raz writes, 'though other things being equal, the greater the conformity [with the Rule of Law] the better—other things are rarely equal. A lesser degree of conformity is often to be preferred precisely because it helps realisation of other goals'.[77]

It might, therefore, sometimes be justifiable to contravene the principles of the Rule of Law in order to promote some other especially valuable goal. This means that retrospective laws, closed-class laws, or vague laws might sometimes be justified despite their incompatibility with the Rule of Law. Having said this, however, caution is in order. For although it might be justifiable *on occasion* to violate the precepts of the Rule of Law, it is almost certainly true that this cannot be done systematically or too frequently. Moreover, the Rule of Law is still *one* of the values—perhaps the most important value—to which the law ought to aspire. For both these reasons, the failure of a law to conform to the Rule of Law is a matter of some concern, and establishes a substantial presumption against it.

2.11 Conclusion

The importance of discussing the issues raised in this chapter should now be clear: in order to fruitfully consider the question of retrospectivity, we must have a clear idea not only of what the Rule of Law is, but also of its significance. Although there is, as we have seen, no universally accepted definition of the Rule of Law, it still seems that the various proposed definitions have enough in common for us to get a good idea of its meaning and of the range and contestability of some of its more commonly asserted elements. Moreover, it seems reasonable to conclude, from evaluation of the criticisms of the Rule of Law, that this concept has substantial normative force as a standard to which law should aspire. A certain degree of conformity to the Rule of Law seems to be a *necessary* condition for justification of a *system* of laws, and also has presumptive force with regard to individual enactments. However, full conformity to the ideal is probably not to be expected in practice, and there are other valuable goals which might sometimes justify diverging from the Rule of Law in some particular cases.

The moral of this chapter, then, is that it is a matter of concern if a particular law does not conform to the Rule of Law, but this is a concern that can be addressed. That is, a law is not automatically unjustified if it fails to conform to the Rule of Law. For there may be reasons to allow an individual departure from the Rule of Law ideal within a system which displays a substantial degree of conformity to it; or it may be that other valuable goals override the normative

---

[77] Raz, p. 210.

force of the Rule of Law in particular cases. Thus, even if we accept the claim that retrospectivity constitutes a failure to conform to the Rule of Law, this will not be sufficient justification for asserting that all retrospective laws are unjustified.

However, we wish in the remainder of this book to make a stronger argument. It is not just that retrospectivity might sometimes be justified in spite of its not living up to the ideal of the Rule of Law. We wish, in fact, to dispute the assumption that retrospectivity *does* always constitute a departure from the ideal of the Rule of Law. If this is true, then it is not *only* when competing goals are at stake that retrospective laws might be justified. Rather, retrospectivity might sometimes be able to be justified even within the context of the Rule of Law itself.

3

Arguments against retrospective laws

3.1 Introduction

In this chapter, we discuss common arguments against retrospective law. These fall into four broad categories: firstly, the claim that retrospective laws are not *laws* at all; secondly, the argument that retrospective laws are undemocratic; thirdly, the claim that retrospective laws violate human rights; and finally, the argument that retrospective laws violate the Rule of Law by undermining the capacity of the law to provide guidance and form the basis of reasonable expectations. Of these, the first is unconvincing, and the second, insofar as it is convincing, is an argument not against all retrospective law, but only retrospective law that violates certain conditions. The third argument, to be plausible, must be interpreted as the claim that it is unjust to disrupt the expectations which people have formed on the basis of existing law, and is, therefore, a version of the fourth argument.

This fourth argument is, in fact, the strongest argument against retrospective law, and supports a strong presumption in favour of prospectivity. However, we will show that the desirability of protecting expectations does not justify an absolute prohibition on retrospectivity and that all arguments against retrospectivity have flaws, weaknesses, and limitations. Examining those flaws and limitations provides an indication of when retrospectivity is justified.

3.2 First objection: retrospective laws are not laws at all

Perhaps the most extreme argument which can be made against retrospective laws is that they are not laws at all. This means that retrospective enactments do not fall under the power to 'make laws' which, in most Western societies, is granted to the legislature by the Constitution. Thus, Walker claims that:

... the constitutions establishing the state and federal legislatures grant them the power to 'make laws'. A retrospective enactment does not fall within any accepted definition of 'law', whether in antiquity or in modern times. ... It may be an 'Act', or something cognate to a bill of attainder or a bill or pains and penalties, or it may be accorded the *force* of law, but a 'law' it is not.[1]

[1] Geoffrey de Q Walker, *The Rule of Law: Foundation of Constitutional Democracy* (University Press, Melbourne, 1988) 322.

One might wonder whether this matters. Suppose that we grant that retrospective enactments are not laws; instead, we can invent a term, 'schlaws', which describes those enactments which have the force of law, and indeed are just like laws except that they fail to meet some necessary criterion for being laws. We might then ask whether the legislature has the power to make '*schlaws*', and whether retrospective 'schlaws' are justified. However, an opponent of retrospective legislation might argue that legislatures do not have any power not explicitly granted to them by the Constitution, so that they do not have the power to make 'schlaws'. We do not propose to pursue this point here, however, since there are other good arguments against the view that retrospective enactments are not laws.

In fact, it seems that the grounds for Walker's assertion are less than solid. Walker does not elaborate upon his claim that retrospective enactments do not fall under any accepted definition of law. In his citations supposedly supporting the claim, he refers to *Calder v. Bull*, in which Justice Chase opined that 'an ACT of the Legislature (for I cannot call it a law) contrary to the great first principles of the social compact, cannot be considered a rightful exercise of legislative authority'.[2] However, this is merely a restatement of the claim itself, rather than an argument for it. Another case cited by Walker is *Fletcher v. Peck*.[3] This case, while it does emphasize the prohibition on the passing of retrospective enactments in the US Constitution, does not state that such enactments are not laws, much less provide an argument to this effect.

The other reference Walker uses to support his claim is a section on the definition of 'law' in Julius Stone's book *Legal System and Lawyer's Reasonings*.[4] However, Stone's discussion, while it does survey and evaluate a number of proposed definitions of 'law', does not show that any of these definitions rule out the possibility of retrospective laws: that is, none of the proposed definitions of law seems obviously incompatible with retrospectivity. In any case, Stone himself eschews the task of giving necessary and sufficient conditions for law: he remarks that any proposed set of requirements 'cannot serve as more than an outline, or index, or table of contents, for an explication of those matters which require to be discussed for an understanding of "law". In particular, it cannot serve as a touchstone of whether a particular norm is a legal norm under a particular legal order'.[5] Stone's survey, therefore, fails to support the claim that retrospective enactments are not laws.

Elsewhere, Walker does refer to a number of historical sources to support his claim that retrospective laws do not fall under accepted definitions of law; these include Plato, Hobbes and Demosthenes.[6] The Plato citation apparently references the following section of *The Laws*:

In addition to [pleasure and pain, the individual] has opinions about the future, whose general name is 'expectations'.... Over and against all these we have 'calculation', by which

---

[2] *Calder v. Bull* (1798) 3 US 386 (Dall.) at Chase J.   [3] *Fletcher v. Peck* (1810) 10 US 87.
[4] Julius Stone, *Legal System and Lawyer's Reasonings* (Stanford University Press, California, 1968) 165–85.   [5] Stone, p. 183.
[6] Walker, p. 16.

we judge the relative merits of pleasure and pain, and when this is expressed as a public decision of a state, it receives the title 'law'.[7]

The reference to Hobbes' *Behemoth* more clearly applies to retrospective law:

For by disobeying Kings, we mean the disobeying of his laws, those his laws that were made before they were applied to any particular person; for the King. . . . yet he commands the people in general never but by a precedent law, and as a politic, not a natural person.[8]

It is interesting to note, however, that those arguments by Plato and Hobbes appear to rely upon something similar to the Austinian command theory of law.[9] If one accepts this conception (a view of laws, roughly, as sovereign orders backed by threats), then it does seem incoherent (as well as unfair) to make 'laws' threatening to punish someone for not having followed an order which was yet to be made. However, HLA Hart—amongst many others—has convincingly demonstrated the inadequacy of this theory of law.[10] Indeed, as we have seen, Walker himself rejects the 'conception of a supreme and independent sovereign habitually obeyed, on which the model rests'.[11] Most importantly, even those positivists who still see law in terms of 'ought' statements see these as addressed to *officials* (to guide their decisions), rather than to private individuals.[12] Such rules must be promulgated before the officials make their decisions, of course, but not necessarily before the citizen acts, even if the official's decision is in response to the citizen's act which predates the order.

Another theory of law which might be thought to support Walker's claim is that of Fuller already discussed in Chapter 2. Fuller includes the making of retrospective laws as one of the 'eight ways to fail to make law'.[13] He writes that in the 'attempt to . . . . [one of which is] the abuse of retroactive legislation, which not only cannot itself guide action, but undercuts the integrity of rules prospective in effect, since it puts them under the threat of retrospective change'.[14] Thus, according to Fuller, 'a total failure in any one of these eight directions does not simply result in a bad system of law; it results in something that is not properly called a legal system at all, except perhaps in the Pickwickian sense in which a void contract can still be said to be one kind of contract'.[15]

Lyons, for one, takes Fuller to be making the claim that retrospective claims do not count as laws: he interprets Fuller as saying 'that law is followable. To the

[7] Plato, *The Laws* 644, trans. Trevor J Saunders (Penguin, Harmondsworth, 1970) 73–4.

[8] Tomas Hobbes, *The Behemoth* (in *The English Works of Thomas Hobbes* (2nd edn, vol. 6, John Bohn, London and Scientia Verlag Aalen, Germany, 1966) [1840] 227).

[9] Plato: 'The laws' method will be partly persuasion and partly (when they have to deal with characters that defy persuasion) compulsion and chastisement', *The Laws* 718, p. 178; 'Every law is a command to do, or to forbear' (Hobbes, p. 226).

[10] HLA Hart, *The Concept of Law* (2nd edn, Oxford University Press, 1997) 26–78.

[11] Hart, p. 27.

[12] Hans Kelsen, *The Pure Theory of Law* (University of California Press, 1967) 14–15.

[13] Lon Fuller, *The Morality of Law* (rev. edn, Yale University Press, 1969) 35.

[14] Fuller, pp. 38–9.   [15] Fuller, p. 39.

extent it is not followable, it does not count as law'.[16] However, he then goes on to point out that 'that claim seems false. Retroactive laws which provide criminal sanctions for conduct performed prior to their enactment may be unjust, but they seem no less laws for that'.[17] In any case, Fuller, himself, would probably not dispute this claim: his argument is not that an individual retrospective enactment cannot properly be called a law, but rather an entire *system* of retrospective enactments could not be properly regarded as law (that is, as a legal system). According to Fuller, there will be no laws in an entirely retrospective system, and it may also be doubtful whether there will be any laws in a system where 'so free a use is made of retrospective legislation that no law is immune to change *ex post facto* if it suits the convenience of those in power'.[18] In this sense, an individual retrospective enactment in such a system could not properly be called a law. However, it does not follow from this that an individual retrospective enactment in a generally *prospective* legal system would fail to achieve the status of law. Indeed, Fuller writes that retrospective laws in such contexts may sometimes 'be essential to advance the cause of legality'.[19] Thus, the argument that retrospective laws are not really laws is unconvincing. The 'power to make laws' conferred on the legislature by the constitution will include the power to pass retrospective enactments, since these do count as laws. Arguments against retrospective laws must, therefore, be based on something other than the assertion that they are not laws.

3.3 Retrospective laws are undemocratic

In fact, there is another way of making the claim that legislatures which make retrospective law are exceeding their proper authority: namely, that retrospective laws are illegitimate, not because they are not laws, but rather because they contravene the principles of democracy. The claim, in short, is that democratic governments can legitimately govern only within a set time-frame—namely, that of the term(s) for which they are elected—and that retrospective law making exceeds this 'temporal mandate'. If this is true, then a legislature in a democratic society does not have the authority to make retrospective legislation, and retrospective law should therefore not be tolerated within a democracy.

   Julian N Eule, who points out that retrospective legislation shares relevant characteristics of entrenchment, makes this argument. Entrenchment is the attempt by one legislature to bind future legislatures, and obviously violates democratic principles:

Each election furnishes the electorate with an opportunity to provide new direction for its representatives. This process would be reduced to an exercise in futility were the newly elected representatives bound by the policy choice of a prior generation of voters.[20]

[16] David Lyons, *Ethics and the rule of law* (Cambridge University Press, 1984) 76.
[17] Lyons, p. 76.   [18] Fuller, p. 40.   [19] Fuller, p. 53.
[20] Julian N Eule, 'Temporal Limits on the Legislative mandate: Entrenchment and Retroactivity' (1987) 379 *American Bar Foundation Research Journal* 404–5.

And this goes for retrospectivity as well as entrenchment:

> . . . whereas entrenchment involves a legislature's effort to exercise power *subsequent to the expiration* of its temporal mandate, retroactivity entails a legislature's effort to exert power *prior to the acquisition* of its mandate.[21]

Eule points out that 'the voters do not delegate authority to rewrite history. Their earlier agents exercised legitimate authority when they enacted legislation. While such efforts may be repealed, this is not the same as retrospective eradication'.[22] A number of examples where governments have sought to exceed their temporal mandates show that such attempts are generally seen as illegitimate, and an abuse of legislative authority.

In Australia, at the Australian Labor Party's (ALP) 1977 Federal Conference, a motion was passed declaring that a later Labor government would repudiate any uranium export contracts signed by the Coalition government. This 'was, as the *Financial Review* reported at the time, a cheeky attempt to govern the country from Opposition'.[23] In particular, in attempting to ensure such contracts were not signed in the first place, the (then hypothetical) future Labor government was acting outside of its temporal mandate. By the same token, however, the Coalition government's attempts to make the contracts legally irrevocable amounted to an attempt at entrenchment, which is equally objectionable.[24] Another attempt to 'govern from opposition' is that of Victorian opposition (Liberal) leader Jeff Kennett. With the Victorian economy in recession, Premier Joan Kirner's Labor Government was deeply unpopular. The opposition Liberals threatened to block the budget unless the government resigned or called an election. To his great embarrassment Kennett was reminded by Prof Cheryl Saunders, a senior constitutional lawyer, that amendments to the Constitution enacted with bipartisan support while he was a member made this unconstitutional during the first three years of the semi-fixed four-year parliamentary terms.[25] The only way that an election could be called during the first three years was if the government lost a motion of confidence in the lower house. So, in 1991, Kennett threatened Labor MLAs that, if they did not cross the floor soon to force Kirner out of office, his future Liberal government would legislate to retrospectively remove those MLAs' superannuation entitlements. Kennett's threat drew widespread criticism, even from Liberal MPs and other conservative pundits, and earned him a contempt of Parliament charge.

Every mainstream paper editorialized against Kennett's attempt, calling it an affront to democracy, a threat to the Westminster system, and even a resort to 'lynch-mob politics'. The *Age* warned that Kennett risked a serious constitutional crisis and 'massive dislocation of the business affairs of the state'.[26]

---

[21] Eule, p. 427.   [22] Eule, p. 445.

[23] Peter Walsh, *Confessions of a Failed Former Finance Minister* (Random House, Sydney, 1995) 3.

[24] Colin Howard, *The Constitution, Power and Politics* (Fontana/Collins, Melbourne, 1980) 109.

[25] *Constitution Act 1975* (Vic) s 38.

[26] Peter Boyle, 'Vic Labor allowed to hang on—for now' (12 June 1991) 15 *Green Left Weekly* 5. Reprinted at URL <http://www.greenleft.org.au/back/1991/15/15p5.htm> 16 March 2005.

Mr Kennett backed down. However, one of his most controversial actions in an extremely controversial term as Premier was a very ambitious inner city freeway project. It widened and linked three existing freeways with a massive tunnel and a new bridge but in so doing converted the existing publicly owned freeways into privately owned toll ways. The contracts required the government to reduce the carrying capacity of parallel 'free' roads to protect the new owner's income. The contracts were 'commercial in confidence' forbidding that government or any future government revealing their contents and imposing what are said to be massive penalties for alteration or even the kind of publicity that would seem an essential element of transparency and accountability.

Despite the fury of the Labor opposition, the positions were reversed in 2004. The new Labor government promised a new outer suburban freeway which they promised would be toll free. Following their re-election in 2002, they went back on their promise (citing budgetary reasons in the form of a budget surplus under threat) and let a contract to an infrastructure company (ConnectEast). The Liberal Opposition leader, Robert Doyle, declared that his government would buy or otherwise cancel the contract. The chair of ConnectEast referred to 'binding contracts with democratically elected governments', and referred to 'sovereign risk' on the way to a $1.1 billion float of the new company.[27]

These examples seem to indicate that the temporal mandate argument is a strong one, and that it runs more strongly against attempts by later governments to undo earlier decisions than attempts of earlier governments to entrench them. This is not an easy issue. Mines and roads have long lives that are likely to encompass several temporal electoral mandates. Incoming governments cannot promise never to do anything that will upset the effects of earlier investments, and outgoing governments cannot promise what their successors will do or not do. However, threats to act in a future term to frustrate the actions of a current government, and attempts to ensure that incoming democratically elected governments have difficulty implementing changes of policies, are clearly unpopular and may cost elections.

These examples also seem to give some bite to the argument that legislatures should not exceed their temporal mandate. It seems that this argument, used against retrospectivity, has a certain amount of plausibility. However, as Eule himself points out, the notion of a temporal mandate does not rule out *all* retrospectivity. Indeed, it positively supports retrospectivity in some instances. In particular, Eule argues that the temporal mandate permits retrospectivity in the following circumstances:

1. Curative retrospective legislation: If the laws enacted by a previous legislature are flawed and do not succeed in doing what they were intended to do, it is legitimate for a later legislature to retrospectively enact curative legislation to correct the flaws and ensure that the legislation achieves its intended effect. In such

---

[27] David Broadbent, 'Wrong Way: No Going Back' (24 October 2004) *The Age*.

circumstances 'the current legislature is helping to give full effect to its predecessor's intent, it is not acting contrary to the majoritarian impulses that produced the earlier statutory scheme'.[28] Interestingly, it seems that this would justify some retrospective taxation legislation, particularly that targeted at tax-avoidance schemes: if the earlier legislature had never intended for such schemes to be exempt from taxation, the retrospective legislation is only giving full effect to the intent of the preceding government.

2. Short-term and intra-term retrospectivity: The democratic argument against retrospectivity is that the legislature exceeds the temporal limits of its mandate. This argument, therefore, does not apply to retrospective laws which are enacted *within* the term of a government: that is, those which are enacted at a particular time but which are deemed to take effect at an earlier date within the term of the current legislature. In addition, it will be permissible to make use of short-term retrospectivity in order to stop people from acting in undesirable ways based upon their knowledge that particular legislation is about to be enacted. For example, there is the possibility 'that those with "insider information" will seek to gain advantage from a lengthy legislative process', [29] or that, in the knowledge that a certain activity is about to be prohibited, people will attempt to undertake as much of it as possible in the time before this occurs.

3. Overturning judicial decisions: According to Eule, while retrospectively overturning decisions of the prior legislature is illegitimate, the same is not true of retrospective alteration to judicial decisions. This is because judge-made law does not have the stamp of democratic authority as the legislature does:

A legislative directive represents an expression of majoritarian will, an exercise of the people's mandate to which succeeding agents may, in part, be legitimately bound. When judges make law, we regard them as temporary stand-ins for the legislature. A democracy only tolerates such lawmaking on the understanding that it is conditional, theoretically subject to immediate overrule or alteration by legislative action.[30]

4. Democracy may require the retrospective alteration of judicial decisions:

. . . the effect of not doing so will be anti-democratic, since the judiciary is a 'non-majoritarian' element. A principle that reconciles democracy with judicial lawmaking by reliance on the conditional and subservient nature of these judge-made laws must embrace the right of retractive nullification at the hands of the people's representatives. Any other standard would condone judicial entrenchment. . . . When the earlier command originates with the courts, the scale must be tipped in favor of the overruling body.[31]

5. For issues upon which the previous legislature was silent: Another category of permissible retrospective law is where there is no previous legislation on the matter.

---

[28] Eule, p. 448.   [29] Eule, p. 456.   [30] Eule, p. 450.   [31] Eule, p. 451.

Here, the people have not registered an opinion which must be respected within the limits of the temporal mandate of the government; that is, there is no exercised authority to be respected.[32] Thus, Eule claims that 'the power of the legislature adversely to affect existing legal arrangements should be at its zenith when no prior legislative voice can be heard'.[33] However, the presumption that such retrospectivity is permissible may be rebutted in some circumstances: for example, if the lack of legislation was a deliberate decision on the part of the legislature, or is due to the earlier proposal and defeat of legislation.

6. To overcome obsolescence: Eule notes that older statutes may remain in force despite being divergent from current popular opinion, due to 'retentionist biases' in the system:

... although limitations imposed by the sovereign ordinarily restrict the temporal agent's power to revise retroactively, permitting compensation for 'retentionist biases' with this democracy argument against retrospectivity, which is not intended 'to develop restriction on retroactivity that entrench obsolescence'.[34]

Another category of arguably permissible retrospectivity, which is not discussed by Eule but seems to follow from some of his categories, may be that of retrospective laws made by a democratic government where the previous legislature was non-democratic. In this case, the previous government did not have a temporal mandate which extended until the advent of the democratic government. However, there may be a need for caution here: even though the government was not democratic, the laws enacted may still have reflected the will of the people and would, therefore, be worthy of respect. All things being equal, however, the democratic basis of a later law is a good reason to prefer it to a non-democratic earlier law.

Another circumstance in which retrospectivity is arguably permissible is where it can be shown that popular opinion supported such a law before the people were given the chance to show their support by voting for it. Consider, as a possible Australian example, that the Hawke Labor Government was elected in 1983 on the basis of a platform promising further retrospective legislation against bottom-of-the-harbour schemes. The argument given was that the previous Fraser Liberal Government had not done enough during its term to deal with the problem of tax avoidance, so it was necessary not only to stamp out the industry for the future (that is, within the temporal limits of its term of office) but also to recover tax from those who had avoided paying it in the past (outside the temporal limits of its terms of office). To the extent that this was an issue with voters (something which is admittedly very difficult to ascertain), the electorate can be assumed to have agreed that too little had been done to counter tax avoidance and that too many people had been allowed to evade their tax liabilities.

This could be countered by saying that the Liberal Party had passed some retrospective and some prospective legislation to deal with tax avoidance during

---

[32] Eule, p. 453.   [33] Eule, p. 458.   [34] Eule, p. 457.

its term of office and that they had made the relevant judgements was to what was required during its term of office. The complexity of the Eulian mandate is exposed with the counter that many Liberal members and supporters were serious tax avoiders, something that simultaneously undermined respect for the government and its supporters.[35]

For Eule, there are very many areas in which it is compatible with democracy to enact retrospective law. Indeed, this compatibility extends to retro*active* law. And when we take into account all forms of retrospectivity, it becomes even more apparent that the temporal mandate of a democratically elected legislature cannot serve as a basis for an absolute prohibition on retrospective legislation. For, as we have seen, retrospectivity is a matter of degree; it is, therefore, inevitable that one legislature will, to some extent, 'step on the toes' of the previous legislature. This problem is already recognized in the case of entrenchment, where it is accepted that any government cannot help but bind their successors in some ways (in particular, by narrowing down the range of options which are open to them). Moreover, to fail to allow any retrospective effect would, in fact, be to allow the entrenchment of the decisions of the previous legislature. As Eule notes:

... at some juncture, a prohibition against retroactive lawmaking becomes entrenching. When this point is reached, the scope of authority delegated by the people to their representatives clearly comprehends ... the power to legislate 'retroactively'.[36]

The argument that retrospective laws are undemocratic therefore fails to achieve anything close to a blanket prohibition on retrospective laws. For there are very many kinds of cases in which democratic principles do not conflict with retrospective law; indeed, in some cases, retrospective law may be necessary to *uphold* democratic principles. This objection might, therefore, be seen as more of a constraint or condition which retrospective laws ought to meet if they are to be legitimate within a democratic society.

One of the interesting aspects of Eule's arguments is that they run strongly against some retrospective rule making and not others. By basing an anti-retrospective argument on democratic mandate theory, it opens up the possibility that arguments against retrospectivity in some cases may be used as arguments *for* retrospectivity in others. One such potential case is suggested by Eule's arguments (but not raised by him) and is discussed in Chapter 5: namely, retrospective laws made by a democratic government to counter laws passed by an earlier repressive regime.[37] In such cases, there is no competing mandate. We will see several such arguments that run strongly against retrospective laws in most cases but support them in certain circumstances.

However, the strongest arguments for and against particular retrospective laws will rarely be those based on democracy. The strongest arguments are based on

---

[35] See discussion of retrospective taxation legislation in Chapter 4.   [36] Eule, p. 443.
[37] Also see discussion in Chapter 4 retrospective *Criminal War Crimes Act* and East Germany post-unification.

the Rule of Law, and the protection it provides to reasonable expectations by citizens that state power will be exercised in the way predicted in legislation. Such arguments may stand even if democratic considerations would allow a retrospective law.[38]

3.4 Retrospective laws violate human rights

One argument which might be used against retrospective laws (even those with a democratic mandate) is the claim that retrospectivity violates human rights. And indeed, as we saw in the introduction, a right to protection against retrospective law has been included in many statements of rights, including: the US Constitution (which prohibits both Congress and the States from passing '*ex post facto* laws' in Article I); [39] the French *Declaration of the Rights of Man and of the Citizen*; the *Canadian Charter of Rights and Freedoms*; the *New Zealand Bill of Rights Act*; and the UK *Bill of Rights Act*.

Most importantly, a prohibition on retrospective law has been included in a number of international human rights instruments, including: the *European Convention for the Protection of Human Rights and Fundamental Freedoms* 1950 (Article 7); the *Universal Declaration of Human Rights* 1948; and the *International Covenant on Civil and Political Rights* 1966. Article 15 of the ICCPR states:

> (1) No one shall be held guilty of any criminal offence on account of any act or omission which did not constitute a criminal offence, under national or international law, at the time when it was committed. Nor shall a heavier penalty be imposed than the one that was applicable when the criminal offence was committed. If, subsequent to the commission of the offence, provision is made by law for the imposition of a lighter penalty, the offender shall benefit thereby.

This rights-based objection is also the strongest reading that can be given to the claim that retrospectivity is procedurally unjust. The most plausible conception of procedural justice appears to be Hart's suggestion that justice is a matter of 'treating like cases alike',[40] or 'the application of any general rule to all of its instances'.[41] As Kramer notes, 'procedural justice ensures that official conduct in the administration of laws is no worse (and no better) than what is required by

---

[38] In this section, we have used the word democratic in its central sense that related to the contents of laws to the expressed wishes of the electorate and their representative. It is possible to use 'democracy' in a far looser way to refer to the whole package of liberal democratic principles that are commonly espoused by democratic states and which contribute to the effective functioning of democracy. However, as indicated in Chapter 2, the approach taken in this book is to follow Raz and see these values as a set of different virtues of law which are distinguishable and may sometimes conflict in theory and in practice—as is indicated in the above paragraph.   [39] Section 9(3) and Section 10(1).

[40] Lyons, p. 78.

[41] MH Kramer, 'Justice as Constancy' (1997) 16 *Law and Philosophy* 562.

the substantive standards of fairness in the laws themselves'.[42] Thus, the idea that retrospective laws are procedurally unjust amounts to the claim that subjecting an individual to a retrospective law is to fail to apply a legal rule to one of its instances.

At first blush, it is difficult to see how procedural justice would necessarily conflict with retrospective law. If the laws themselves are retrospective—or allow for retrospective application—then, it will not be a misapplication of the law to apply them retrospectively. Indeed, it might even be argued that retrospectivity *promotes* procedural justice by ensuring that all cases that come before the courts after the law is passed are treated in the same way. If, however, there is an explicit legal prohibition against retrospectivity, then to subject a person to retrospective law is a procedural injustice—and a violation of rights—because it involves a failure to apply a relevant legal rule; namely, the prohibition against retrospective application of laws.

This argument, however, is in fact a fairly weak one, for a number of reasons. Firstly, these prohibitions are generally understood to apply only to retrospective *criminal* laws. In the case of the ICCPR, this is made explicit. In the case of the US Constitution, the restriction of the *ex post facto* clause to criminal laws was affirmed in *Calder v. Bull* in 1798, and the courts have regularly refused since then to extend its application to civil or taxation law, despite attempts to draw analogies with criminal law.[43]

Secondly, the rule against retrospectivity can, like any rule of procedural justice, be overridden in certain circumstances, especially where it comes into conflict with procedural or substantive rules of equal or higher status respectively. In the case of the UK and New Zealand, the rule can be repealed by an ordinary legislative majority. And the ICCPR, after stating the rule against retrospective criminal laws, qualifies it by stating that:

(2) Nothing in this article shall prejudice the trial and punishment of any person for any act or omission, which at the time it was committed, was criminal according to the general principles of law recognized by the community of nations.[44]

Most importantly, however, the fact that retrospectivity is a matter of degree (and in any case does not have a universally agreed-upon definition) means that such prohibitions (and the rights they supposedly embody) may be indeterminate in any given case. As Fisch notes regarding the US Constitution:

Reliance on constitutionally based arguments is problematic... The Constitution does not define retroactivity; the parameters of any constitutional limitations are therefore

[42] Kramer, p. 566.

[43] Eule, p. 427. Also see discussion in Chapter 4 'Retrospective Criminal Legislation'.

[44] However, this statement, itself, implies that the general principles of law recognized by the community of nations are prior to the retrospective law. See discussion of this qualification in Chapter 4 'Retrospective Criminal Legislation'.

inherently ambiguous. Moreover, because application of a legal rule cannot be constrained within objective categories labelled 'retroactive' or 'nonretroactive', constitutional principles cannot definitively answer questions of legitimacy.[45]

Thus, if opponents of retrospectivity are to make an argument that retrospectivity violates rights, they will have to base this claim on something other than the idea that a rule against retrospectivity in constitutional guarantees or charters of rights make retrospective laws procedurally unjust. And this raises the question of what kind of justice is being discussed. There are several types of justice, and while retrospective laws are unjust in one sense, they may be just in another.

A retrospective law may, for example, further distributive justice by allocating resources more equitably. It may even be argued (though not by this author) that retrospective law is more useful for this purpose, since its redistributive effects can be certain while those of a prospective law may only be guessed at. In particular, it ensures that those who disingenuously avoided paying tax end up doing so. Retrospective law may also further retributive justice, by ensuring that society's approbation for certain kinds of action is expressed. A retrospective law may do this where a prospective law fails (due, for example, to a novel kind of wrongdoing, or because the law was poorly drafted).

The most plausible interpretation of the claim that retrospective law is substantively unjust, however, is that it involves a failure to respect the autonomy of individuals. The argument is that autonomy requires the ability to plan one's own life, and retrospective law impairs this ability, by introducing unexpected consequences to (or removing expected consequences from) past events, and thus disrupts the expectations people have formed on the basis of existing law and the actions they have taken in the expectation that the law that will be applied to determine the legal consequences of contemplated actions is the law standing at the time the action is taken. Thus, as autonomy is usually considered a fundamental human right, such interference with autonomy would be a violation of that right. This interpretation of the objection is reflected in Justice Toohey's comments in the case of *Polyukhovich v. Commonwealth* (to be discussed in Chapter 5):

All these general objections to retroactively applied criminal liability have their source in a fundamental notion of justice and fairness. They refer to the desire to ensure that individuals are reasonably free to maintain control of their lives by choosing to avoid conduct which will attract criminal sanctions; a choice made impossible if the conduct is assessed by rules made in the future.[46]

In fact, the claim that the law must provide guidance (and protect expectations formed on the basis of that guidance) is the most common objection

---

[45] Jill E Fisch, 'Retroactivity and Legal Change: An Equilibrium Approach' (1996–1997) 110 *Harvard Law Review* 1078–9.
[46] *Polyukhovich v. Commonwealth* (1991) 172 CLR 501 at 688.

to retrospective legislation. It is also the most powerful. Thus, Munzer writes that:

Retroactive lawmaking violates what is often called the rule of law, namely, an entitlement of persons to guide their behaviour by impartial rules that are publicly fixed in advance. This violation undermines human autonomy by hindering the ability of persons to form plans and carry them out with due regard for the rights of others.[47]

The injustice argument can, therefore, be seen as a way of formulating this claim: it is a requirement of justice that the law provide guidance, and refrain from disrupting reasonable expectations. The second more comprehensive version of this argument is formulated in terms of the Rule of Law, so it is this argument to which we will now turn.

3.5 Retrospective legislation and the rule of law

As we have just seen, the argument that retrospective law is unjust ultimately rests on the claim that retrospective law fails to provide guidance, and disrupts the expectations people have formed on the basis of existing law. That is, the objectionable nature of retrospective law is supposed to derive from its incompatibility with the Rule of Law. In this section, we discuss this supposed failure of retrospective law to provide guidance, and the reasons why this failure is thought to be problematic. One of these relates to considerations of justice, as mentioned above. However, other reasons include considerations of the purpose of law, or the supposedly undesirable social effects of a failure to provide guidance or respect expectations.

Before discussing this issue, however, it is worth mentioning another Rule-of-Law-based argument against retrospective law. This argument focuses not on the failure of retrospective law to provide guidance, but rather on the requirement of *generality* in the law. The claim is that retrospective law also violates this requirement: in other words, that retrospective law will have the features of a particular law or Bill of Attainder. Thus, Walker points out that 'when a statute is designed to act on a past event, it is possible to have a reasonably clear idea of who will be affected by it. This gives it the character of particular legislation analogous to a bill of attainder'.[48] And Munzer, in discussing retrospective criminal legislation, writes that 'though the new statute was framed in general terms, the legislature may have been moved to pass it because of the case at hand—raising the possibility of legislative abuse'.[49]

Interesting and novel though this claim is, it does not provide a good argument against the general application of retrospective legislation, even if we assume

---

[47] Stephen R Munzer, 'A Theory of Retroactive Legislation' (1982) 61(3) *Texas Law Review* 427.
[48] Walker, p. 316. [49] Munzer, p. 463.

(as we have been thus far) that the claim is limited to what other authors call retro*active* legislation. Firstly, as noted in Chapter 2, a well-functioning legal system will usually require a certain degree of departure from Rule-of-Law ideals. Moreover, like retrospectivity, the generality of a law can also be a matter of degree. Thus, while it will generally not be considered desirable to pass bills of attainder, the prohibition on non-general rules cannot be absolute.

In any case, it seems that it will be particularly unrealistic to disqualify laws on the basis merely that legislators *know* (let alone 'have a reasonably clear idea') who will be affected by it. For, while this will be true of much (though not all) retrospective legislation, it will also be true of some *prospective* legislation. With such prospective legislation, it will not be possible to determine *everyone* that will be affected by it; but since most retrospective legislation also operates for the future, this is true of retrospective law as well.

It seems that a more realistic standard for whether a failure of generality is problematic is whether or not it was *intended* to target particular (known) individuals. Such intentional targeting is rare. Although the legislators would be able to ascertain the particular individuals affected if they so wished, there is typically no consideration of who will fall under the terms of the law. In the only type of case in which this is always untrue (namely, judicial retrospectivity), it is precisely the *point* of the activity that those affected are known. If the judicial decision (which is inherently retrospective, especially where it overturns prior precedents) were not to be applied to the person(s) requesting adjudication of a legal dispute, then few would bother bringing such cases, and the laws themselves would become useless.[50]

Rather than phrasing the issue in terms of attainder, there is another way of expressing this weakening of generalization discerned by Walker and Munzer. In his *A Theory of Justice*, John Rawls introduced the idea that laws and social policy formed behind a 'veil of ignorance'—where legislators do not know, *inter alia*, their history, personal preferences and financial status—are bound to be fair.[51] That is, agents who are not sure of their ultimate place in society will legislate substantively superior laws to more knowledgeable agents. In particular, fine-grained discrimination targeting particular groups of people will not occur, for legislators behind the veil would never know whether they or those they love would be victimized by such legislation.

However, if the legislator happens to be aware of the identity of a particular individual who will fall under the reference of a new or newly amended law, then the veil of ignorance has been thinned. The legislator may not know who, in future, will come to be affected by the law, but as Walker and Munzer note, they can, in some cases, know quite precisely which individuals will be retrospectively

---

[50] See discussion in Chapter 5 'Judicial Retrospectivity'.

[51] John Rawls, *A Theory of Justice* (Belknap, Cambridge, 1971) 12. Even if one does not accept Rawls' argument in full as the basis of justice, most will accept that decisions reached behind the veil of ignorance as likely to be fair to the parties.

affected. This knowledge may potentially affect the crafting of the new law. Perhaps, the new law is not a better law at all, but is merely being introduced to target a particular person who is considered objectionable for some reason quite tangential to the new law. Alternatively perhaps, the level of punishment legislated might be crafted with an eye to the particular case and particular individual involved—this could be of particular concern if a law seeks to 'make an example' of an individual. In both cases, retrospectivity allows for a very fine-grained level of discrimination—targeting known groups or individuals—without the substantive content of the law itself containing anything other than the most general terms.

This 'thinning of the veil' also creates concerns with the trust the citizenry can have in the law. An individual convicted of some crime may proclaim the injustice of the relevant law for a variety of reasons, but if the law was fully prospective at least the individual, and the community at large, cannot reasonably suppose that the law was crafted specifically with them in mind. In the case of retrospective laws where the identity of the individual affected—and the reference class to which they belong—is well-known, it may be much more reasonable for a victim to suspect that they were specifically targeted.

While this feature of 'thinning the veil' clearly has deleterious consequences, it should be noted that it is only applicable to a very thin range of cases and should by no means be construed as a general argument against retrospective law *per se*. In most cases, the identity of the affected individuals is unknown to legislators and irrelevant to their considerations. However, it must be admitted that any retrospective law that is passed with the intention to target particular individuals is a serious abuse of power for the reasons noted above. In Chapter 4, we will consider a possible example of this occurrence in Australian law in the '*War Crimes case*'. In Chapter 5, we will argue that retrospective legislation can only be justified when legislators take a coherence-enhancing approach which seeks to make the law conform to general principles found in existing law rather than targeting individuals. In Chapter 6, we will consider some safeguards to protect the integrity of the legislative process and to reduce the likelihood of these and other abuses.

The only legitimate Rule of Law argument against the general practice of retrospective law is that the legal system ought to respect the expectations which people have formed on the basis of the existing law; and that the law should be such as to allow people to *form* expectations (that is, it should be capable of providing guidance). If retrospective law is incapable of fulfilling these requirements, and if law *always* ought to meet them, then this is an argument against retrospective law. But, as we can see, there are two questions to be asked here. The first is whether retrospective law always does fail to provide guidance or respect expectations. The second is what reason we have to think that the law ought always to play this role.

One obvious reason why retrospective law fails to meet these requirements is that retrospective laws, by their very nature, seem incapable of providing guidance. Thus, where the legal texts applied to an individual's action were created after the action, the text will not have created any expectation that could guide them. Indeed, they will often have formed a contrary expectation on the basis of the existing law; that is, they will have guided themselves by a law which is not then applied to their behaviour. Instead, what is applied is a law which it was impossible for them to guide themselves by, for it did not exist at the time the guidance was sought. But this shows us that there are in fact *two* ways in which retrospective laws fail to provide guidance or respect expectations: firstly, a retrospective law *itself* cannot provide guidance or form the basis of expectations; and secondly, retrospective laws undermine the ability of people to be guided by, or form expectations on the basis of, *other* laws, or the legal system as a whole.

The first of these claims, in fact, seems plainly true: it is indisputable that a retrospective law itself cannot offer guidance, or form the basis of expectations. The only sense in which such laws offer guidance is the trivial sense in which all laws tell courts and other legal officials what to do. But this is not the kind of guidance to which rule of law arguments are principally directed. As Honore writes in the course of an argument against 'individuators' (who seek to reformulate all legal rules in conduct-guiding form), 'any rule of law ... necessarily operates as a norm to a person whose duty it is to state, teach, apply, advise on, or decide the law. ... But these are not, I think, the act-situations that the individuator has in mind'.[52] Retrospective laws are not capable of providing guidance in the more substantive sense of guiding the conduct of those to whom the law will be applied.

It is debatable, however, whether we ought to accept the stronger claim that retrospective law undermines the capacity of *other* laws—or of the legal system in general—to provide guidance. Although this will sometimes be true, it is not always so. Firstly, the use of retrospective law (especially if confined to certain areas of law, under certain conditions) does not necessarily affect the guidance capacity of laws which are not subject to retrospective alteration; indeed, even laws which are subject to retrospective change are still capable of providing some guidance. And secondly, the use of retrospective law (or general acceptance of its use by the legislature) in a particular area of law can be a very important and useful source of guidance.

It seems fairly obvious that retrospective legislation does not undermine the guidance capacity of other laws which are outside the scope of retrospective change. Of course, it can be argued that the frequent and indiscriminate use of retrospective legislation will undermine the guidance of *all* laws, since people will not have any way of telling whether the law that now exists will be retrospectively altered; nor will they have any confidence that this is unlikely to happen. But this

---

[52] AM Honore, 'Real Laws', in PMS Hacker and J Raz (eds), *Law, Morality, and Society: Essays in Honour of HLA Hart* (Clarendon Press, Oxford, 1977) 105.

is not an argument against any and all retrospective law; rather, it is an argument against the too frequent and indiscriminate use of retrospective law. If the conditions under which retrospective law is acceptable within a legal system are themselves well known and strictly adhered to, there is no reason for people to expect or fear arbitrary and random retrospective change.

But what about laws in areas or situations in which retrospective change *does* occur? The existing law in this case does not seem to offer guidance, in that it does not allow people to form reasonable expectations of what legal consequences may be attached to their conduct in these areas. Even here, however, the case may be overstated. The guidance that such laws give may be fallible without being useless, just as weather reports are. In most cases, a law which is subject to retrospective change will not be altered in its entirety; rather, much of the existing law (including its underlying principles and justifications) will remain unchanged while some section of it is altered. And it may be possible to identify those sections which are most likely to be subject to retrospective change, and those which will, in all likelihood, remain the same.

This brings us to a second point concerning the guidance capacity of a system of laws containing retrospectivity. This is that the use of retrospective law (or the potential for its use) in a particular area of law and in particular circumstances may itself be an important and very desirable source of guidance. The guidance offered may be, for example, that people who attempt to exploit apparent loopholes or unintended effects of legislative regimes are likely to be penalized through retrospective alteration of the law. In such cases, the guidance offered by the use or acceptance of retrospective legislation is not so much a precise outline of how officials will understand and apply the law. Rather, the guidance it provides is a warning not to attempt to rely too closely on the details of existing law, especially where these details have effects that the legislature, in all likelihood, did not know about and did not intend. It sends the message that the tax scheme that seems too good to be true may be too good for the citizen, associated professionals and businesses, and too bad for the revenue, to stand.

Retrospective laws which close 'loopholes' and 'unexpected interpretations and consequences' reinforce the guidance of primary laws. Thus, the retrospective law does not itself provide guidance but assists other laws to provide guidance. 'Prospective retrospectivity' (that is, clear guidelines for retrospective rule making can generate an expectation that retrospective law will be applied in the future to prevent actions) is extremely important for this purpose. Indeed, this highlights an important feature of law: namely, that effects are usually produced through several laws interacting together. Laws are not usually applied singly, and therefore do not generate their effects (including that of guidance) singly.

What are we to make, then, of the claim that retrospective laws are not capable of providing guidance, and that they upset the expectations people have formed on the basis of existing law? We must agree that retrospective laws, alone, cannot offer guidance, or form the basis of expectations. It must also be admitted that retrospective laws can undermine the ability of other laws to provide guidance. However, this is not always the case: it is still possible for people to derive a great deal of guidance from a system of laws which contains—or allows for— retrospectivity. The clearer and more strictly observed are the conditions for allowable retrospectivity, the more capable the law is of providing guidance. Moreover, the use of retrospective laws—or the knowledge that they might be used—can itself provide guidance of a useful and socially desirable sort. For example, the good legal advisor will advise the client to give contentious activity a wide berth rather than seeking to rely on either legislation or case law that is subject to change or uncertainty. To use a classical metaphor, in such cases, the adviser does not plot a course between Scylla and Charybdis but advises the client to take the long way around Sicily.

Thus, the argument that retrospective law fails to provide guidance, and undermines the guidance of other laws, can be overstated. However, if it is a requirement that each and every law be capable of providing guidance, this would rule out *all* retrospective law. Even if the requirement is only that reasonable expectations formed on the basis of existing law must be respected, then this will rule out much retrospective law, including some examples of retrospective legislation that are generally seen as justified. If many actual uses of retrospective legislation are to be defended, then we must reject the idea that all laws must be capable of guiding behaviour. And indeed, this idea does seem to be faulty.

Firstly, it must be emphasized that the claim that all laws must be capable of guiding behaviour is a normative claim rather than a definitional one. This follows quite clearly from the fact, argued for in Chapter 3.2, that retrospective laws are laws, and the fact that retrospective laws are not capable of guiding behaviour, noted above. The claim is that all laws *ought* to be capable of guidance; that is, that they should meet the standard of the Rule of Law. This means not only that people be able to derive some guidance from the law, but that the expectations they form as a result of this guidance must be respected: that is, their reliance on the law must be protected. And there are three arguments which might be given in favour of this normative claim: firstly, that if a law could not guide conduct, it would fail to achieve the main purpose or point of law; secondly, that laws which cannot guide conduct are unjust; and thirdly, that some other desirable consequences (for example, encouraging respect for the law, or encouraging investment) require that laws be capable of providing guidance.

Guidance and the purpose of law

The first argument in support of the claim that laws must be capable of providing guidance is that this is the principal purpose of law, and that laws cannot be effective if they cannot provide guidance. This is the view of Raz, who writes that 'law is universally regarded as a special social method of regulating human behaviour by guiding it in various ways and directions'.[53] If this is what law *is*, then it clearly follows that law must be capable of guiding behaviour. And this, indeed, is what Raz takes as the basis for the Rule of Law.[54]

One counterargument against this view is that not all laws are intended to guide behaviour, or have this as their primary purpose. Indeed, laws which are 'directly normative' (to use Honoré's term) are only one subcategory of law. Honoré identifies five other kinds of law, which do not have the purpose of providing guidance:

1. *Existence* laws create, destroy, or provide for the existence or non-existence of entities.

2. *Rules of inference* provide how facts may or must or should preferably be proved and what inferences may or must or should preferably be drawn from evidence.

3. *Categorizing rules* explain how to translate actions, events, and other facts into the appropriate categories.

4. *Rules of scope* fix the scope of other rules.

5. *Position-specifying rules* set out the legal position of persons or things in terms of rights, liabilities, status and the like.[55]

Honoré goes on to claim that 'an exclusive preoccupation with the normative aspects of law, important as they are, is distorting. Besides guiding people's conduct laws sometimes protect them and sometimes subject them to deprivation'.[56]

As an example of such a law, consider the case of *Re a Solicitor's Clerk*, discussed in Chapter 1. As we saw, this was a law which allowed orders to be made prohibiting people convicted of larceny from being employed by a solicitor. It seems that the purpose of this law was not to guide the conduct of those convicted of larceny: that is, the function of the law was not to act as an instruction along the lines of 'if you have been convicted of larceny, you must not work for a solicitor'. It may not even have the (primary) function of instructing solicitors not to employ as clerks those who have been convicted of larceny. Rather, the point of the law is to protect the public from legal practitioners with a record of dishonesty (and perhaps to protect clients from the temptation of seeking dishonest lawyers who may fail in their duty to the court).

Similarly, consider a ban prohibiting people with particular medical conditions (for example, heart problems or epilepsy) from operating vehicles such as airplanes or trains. Such a law is not intended to provide guidance to people ('if you have a heart condition, you must not apply for a job as a train driver or airline pilot'). Rather, the function of the law is to ensure public safety. Thus, it is just not true that the purpose of all laws is the guidance of people's behaviour,

---

[53] J Raz, *The Concept of a Legal System: an introduction to the theory of legal system* (2nd edn, Clarendon Press, Oxford, 1980) 145.   [54] Raz, p. 98.

[55] Honoré, p. 112.   [56] Honoré, p. 116.

and the fact that retrospective laws do not do so is therefore not an argument against them.

At this point, however, it might be replied that a more sophisticated interpretation of the objection is possible. The version of the objection we have been considering thus far is that laws must be capable of guiding behaviour because the guidance of behaviour is their primary purpose. However, it might be conceded that laws are not all *intended* to guide behaviour, but still claimed that all laws must be *capable* of guiding behaviour. For it might be argued that *whatever* the purpose of a law, this purpose will only be achieved if the law is capable of guiding behaviour. Thus retrospective laws, since they are not capable of guidance, cannot achieve any purpose which a law might have.

Consider again the cases above, which, it was argued, are examples of laws intended to protect the public rather than guide behaviour. It seems that we can admit this, while also pointing out that these laws would not succeed in protecting the public unless they were *capable* of guiding people's behaviour. Suppose, for example, that people with heart conditions or epilepsy were, for some reason, not able to use the law as a guide: because the law was kept secret, or was extremely vague, for example, they were not guided by it to cease working as train drivers or pilots, and employers were not guided by it to refrain from employing people with such conditions. In this case, the law would not have the intended effect of protecting the public against the danger such people pose. By the same token, unless the prohibition on larcenous solicitor's clerks can provide some guidance (particularly, to solicitors thinking of employing such people), the public will not be protected against dishonest legal practitioners. At the very least, people who have been defrauded in such circumstances must be able to be guided by the law in order to know to pursue the compensatory justice allowed to them.

A similar objection applies to Honore's example, which is a law concerning the validity of wills: A will must be signed by the testator at the foot or end thereof or by some other person in his presence and by his direction.[57] Honore takes this rule not to be a normative one:

> . . . it simply states one of the conditions of the validity of a will . . . its main purpose is to ensure the authenticity of documents propounded as wills after the testator's death when he is no longer in a position to settle the matter. In this aspect the rule is a protective one, whose point it is to safeguard the interests of the intestate heirs, the beneficiaries under earlier wills, and the testator himself in his ultimate abode.[58]

However, this rule would clearly not be very effective if people could not use it for guidance, for example to ensure the validity of their own wills, or in deciding whether there is a basis for contesting the will.

Are there any examples of laws which can achieve their purpose (whatever it may be) without being capable of guiding behaviour? Or, are there some purposes which are achievable without guidance of behaviour? In fact, it seems that there

---

[57] Honore, p. 104.   [58] Honore, p. 106.

are. One such purpose of law may be distributive justice or revenue-raising: the main rationale for taxation laws, for example, is raising revenue for government purposes in an equitable manner, and it may also have the purpose of redistribution of wealth. This does not require that people be guided by the tax law in their financial conduct. Indeed, it seems that the law will often be more effective in achieving its purposes (that is, equitable revenue-raising) if people are *not* able to be guided by its loopholes in structuring their affairs so as to avoid or minimize the payment of tax.

Some laws which have the purpose of protecting the public may similarly achieve this purpose without being capable of guiding conduct. Take, for example, a law which states that those convicted of serious violent crimes may be incarcerated indefinitely following the expiry of their original jail term if they are deemed to be serious violent offenders who pose a continuing and grave risk to the community. The purpose of such a law is to protect the community from those who are judged to be highly likely to commit further violent crimes. And this purpose can be achieved even though the criminals were convicted before the law was passed and hence could not be guided by it.[59]

This raises a more general question about the guidance provided by laws that impose penalties. The threat of a penalty is intended to provide guidance to those contemplating such action—that is, to send the message 'don't do it!' The limitations on the penalties are not intended to provide guidance to those contemplating criminal actions. Consider our reaction if a convicted criminal was to say: 'I would never have committed this crime if I had known that I could have been put away for so long'. The natural reaction is not so much sympathy but a regret that we did not signal in advance the higher level of penalty required to be an effective deterrent. Not only are criminal sanctions intended to deter individuals from breaching the law, they are also an indication of how seriously the community considers the infraction (from the point of view of moral obloquy and/or threat to the community). Finally, criminal sanctions both order and guide judges on how they exercise their powers on behalf of the community.[60]

---

[59] See for example, the case of *Kansas v. Hendricks* (1997) 117 SCT 2072 discussed in Chapter 4 'Retrospective Criminal Legislation'. This is not to say that this author favours such laws, merely that the argument against them are not based on their retrospectivity. We would argue against such laws on the basis that one should not be incarcerated for crimes you might commit in the future. If this argument were rejected, we would draw a distinction between detention as a deliberate penalty for breach of prospective criminal law and detention for the protection of the public. The purpose of the former is to suspend some of the human rights of an individual (freedom of movement etc.) for a set period because of past conduct. Where the individual is held for the benefit of others, the conditions of detention should be such that human rights are limited to the very minimum and compensating benefits are provided wherever possible. This argument would apply to all forms of detention imposed on some for the benefit of others rather than the imposition of penalties for misconduct.

[60] Most systems have a mixture of fixed rules (about maximum sentences and, in some cases, minimum sentences), formal 'sentencing guidelines', and less formal case law based on sentencing appeals.

Another of Honore's examples seems similarly to show that laws can achieve their effects without providing guidance. This is his discussion of the *mens rea* rule:

Mens rea (intention, knowledge, or negligence) is presumed to be a constituent of every criminal offence.

Again, this rule does provide guidance to judges, juries and so on. But, as Honore writes, it 'is certainly not intended to guide the conduct of prospective criminals. They are not being advised to avoid criminal responsibility by doing wrongful acts without the appropriate intention or knowledge'.[61] Moreover, since such 'advice' would be unfollowable (the idea of having an intention to act wrongly without intention or knowledge being incoherent), it seems plausible to think that such a rule is not *capable* of providing guidance. But this rule can still have the intended effect, which is something like ensuring that only the morally culpable are punished for criminal offences.

Similarly, while most justifications for punishment focus on the importance of deterrence, many of these justifications also make allowances for the notion of 'desert'. In these more retributive theories of punishment, an offender should be punished if, and only if, they deserve punishment. On this view, one key reason for imposing a life-sentence for murder is to visit an appropriate punishment on offenders. In terms of such an aim, it is quite irrelevant whether or not a person was guided in their conduct by the knowledge that this would be a possible consequence of their behaviour. Thus, the law could be effective (in ensuring appropriate punishment for criminal offenders) even if would-be criminal offenders were not able to guide their conduct by it, or form expectations on the basis of it.

Another important example of non-normative laws are those which mandate that violently psychotic people can be locked away, or that sick people can be quarantined. In each case, there is no guidance to the individual involved. If an individual is contagious or psychotic to the relevant extent, there is nothing they can actively do, on the basis of the law's guidance, to avoid incarceration. Yet, we would not say that laws against the incarceration of psychotic or contagious individuals are, to that extent, not laws—or not justifiable laws. They serve a public welfare agenda. So, it is false that laws must always serve as a guide to behaviour.

A final example is a tort law, which is normative and may generally provide guidance but still serves a vital purpose when it is not guiding behaviour.[62] Much of tort law is about the allocation of losses arising out of the interaction of human beings in a complex society. Whether or not a loss has occurred in the past or in the future, it is a critical function of the law to determine where such losses will fall. Every development of case law in negligence involves some variation in the previously expected rules concerning the allocation of such losses. Reliance arguments by either plaintiffs or defendants may well be dubious ('I relied on x case to know that if I slipped and fell at work I would receive a big payout' or 'Past damages awards indicated that it was cheaper to pay out the relatives of the victims

---

[61] Honore, p. 104.   [62] Fisch, p. 1086.

than fix the petrol tank'). However, the allocation of losses through the law of torts has the effect of guiding future behaviour—encouraging us to either take care or take insurance and hopefully both.

This guidance is informed by the famous 'neighbour'[63] principle espoused in the classic case of *Donaghue v. Stevenson*. In economic terms, it conveys a warning: 'your actions have consequences for others. You should not attempt to externalise your costs and you should not rely on seeking to benefit yourself at the expense of others'. Where the costs are discovered to be more significant than previously thought, individuals should not be surprised if they are required to make good the damage to others that arises from their own actions. This is not to say that all such losses will be compensated. Some are ignored as a matter of principle, others because they are limited and because the transaction costs would be too high. Although it is an imperfect system, one of the most important functions of Tort law is to warn individuals not to pursue their own benefit at the expense of others.

This section has clearly rebutted any idea that all laws necessarily involve guidance and that retrospective laws cannot provide such guidance. This is not to deny the importance of guidance in the operation and effectiveness of law.

While guidance is not the only means that law employs to further the purposes for enacting it, it is a means that is almost always employed. Indeed, it is such a powerful means that one would look very critically at any law which did not seek to avail itself of this powerful tool. None of the arguments that we have raised suggest that it should not be used.

Guidance and justice

We return, then, to the objection that retrospective law is unjust because people are not able to be guided by it. Although the law may be able to achieve its purpose without guiding conduct, it is often argued that doing so would be a serious abuse of power. It ought, in other words, to be a moral constraint on the operation of the law that it not be applied in cases where people have not been able to be guided by it. This seems to be a widespread view: for example, Lyons writes that 'it is generally considered unjust to penalize a person for failing to follow a law it is impossible to follow. Fairness requires that a person have fair warning—the opportunity to know what is expected of her and to decide what to do in light of that knowledge'.[64] Later he reiterates this claim, saying that 'considerations of fairness and autonomy...argue against penalizing people for doing what they had no reason to believe would be punishable'.[65] Similarly, Woozley writes that while it is difficult to say what the claim of unfairness *means*, it is 'easier to say *why* it is unfair to hurt a man in this way, viz., because a man ought to (be able to) know what the rules or the game are by which he is bound before he is exposed to playing it; and he cannot know this if they have not been made up yet'.[66] And

---

[63] *Donoghue v. Stevenson* [1932] AC 562.   [64] Lyons, p. 75.   [65] Lyons, p. 201.
[66] AD Woozley, 'What Is Wrong With Retrospective Law?' (1968) 18(70) *The Philosophical Quarterly* 41.

Walker writes that 'the policy basis of the presumption against the *ex post facto* operation of statues is usually taken to be as stated in a well-known passage in *Maxwell on the Interpretation of Statutes*: 'Upon the presumption that the legislature does not intend what is unjust rests the leaning against giving certain statutes a retrospective operation'.[67]

One interesting reply to this claim, discussed by Woozley, is Kelsen's argument against the injustice of retrospective law based on the *ignorantia* principle. In short, since legal systems generally contain the principle that ignorance of the law does not excuse, why should we suppose that there is an excuse when the ignorance is due to a later law being retrospectively applied? Given that we have in our legal system the principle that ignorance of the law does not excuse, what is the difference between not knowing a law which is not there and not knowing a law which is there but which is so obscure or buried in time that it might as well not be there?[68]

However, as Woozley points out, this defence is unacceptable for two reasons. Firstly, it is not correct to describe as ignorance of the law a situation where someone does not know the content of a law because it has not yet been made. 'A necessary condition of my being ignorant of the law is that there should be a law to be ignorant of—and in the case in question there is not'.[69] So a retrospective law can be unjust even though it is not unjust to apply to someone a law of which they were ignorant.

Secondly, even if there were an analogy between retrospective law and ignorance of the law, Kelsen's argument would not necessarily hold up. This is because supporters of this argument are making an undefended assumption: namely, that the *ignorantia* principle itself is justified. It may be, however, that although the principle is common in legal systems, it is not justified or may only be justified with significant modification. Ignorance may only fail as an excuse where the government has made a reasonable attempt to communicate the relevant legal rule or that it was reasonably discoverable. This indicates a degree of reciprocity between the duty to communicate and the duty to find out. Thus, the general acceptance of the *ignorantia* principle would not be grounds for thinking that there ought to be general acceptance of retrospectivity. To the contrary: the unacceptability of retrospective legislation could potentially be used against the *ignorantia* principle. Moreover, the point may be made that it is precisely the prohibition on retrospectivity that makes the *ignorantia* principle acceptable: Walker writes that 'it is a condition for the fair operation of the rule that ignorance of the law is no excuse that legislation should be prospective'.[70] Thus, the *ignorantia* principle cannot be used to show that the lack of guidance of retrospective law is unjust.

What the *ignorantia* analogy does bring out, however, is the importance of remembering that not all expectations or guidance can or should be respected

---

[67] Walker, pp. 318–19.   [68] Woozley, p. 44.   [69] Woozley, p. 45.
[70] Walker, p. 316.

within the law. That is, the law will generally undertake to respect the guidance derived from (or expectations formed on the basis of) the law only if it meets certain conditions. As we have seen, the law will not respect expectations that are formed in ignorance of the law. Thus, for a start, only expectations that are actually based on the law are entitled to protection.

More substantive conditions which expectations must meet in order to trigger the presumption of legal protection may also be proposed. Thus, Munzer argues that the only expectations deserving of legal protection are those which are both rational and legitimate.[71] Expectations are *rational* when they meet two criteria:

1. That they be based on 'an appropriately accurate and detailed knowledge of the law'.

2. That there be 'some ratiocinative ability to make predictions on the basis of that knowledge'.[72]

Sometimes a third criterion will also be relevant: 'when expectations are layered, rational expectations will include ... some ability to replicate the expectations and reasoning of others ... [including] the ability to anticipate subsequent actions by officials that may upset initial expectations'.[73] And an expectation is *legitimate* when it is 'supported, first, by the underlying justifications of the laws inducing it, and second, by the fundamental principles embedded in the legal system itself'.[74]

Thus, retrospective legislation is not unjust if it only upsets expectations that are not rational or not legitimate (or both). If one misinterprets the law, or relies too heavily on a particular contentious interpretation where other interpretations are equally plausible, then one's expectations are not rational. Moreover, where layering occurs, and rationality requires a prediction that officials may later change the law, then relying on even a correct interpretation of existing law may not be rational. Similarly, if one relies on a loophole or unintended consequence of the law where this is inconsistent with the underlying purpose of the law, then one's expectations will be, according to Munzer, illegitimate. In none of these cases will one's expectations warrant the presumption of legal protection.

It can be argued that many instances of retrospective legislation only disrupt non-rational and non-legitimate expectations. Take taxation legislation, for example: retrospectively closing tax avoidance loopholes does not upset expectation, but it is not unjust, as it does not *legitimate* expectations. Indeed, it might also be argued that reliance on existing law in such situations is an *irrational* expectation.

Where retrospective rule making is either promised or threatened, an expectation that there will be no such rule-making is not so much rational as obstinate and foolhardy. The opponents of retrospectivity seek to rely on such an expectation to argue that the expectation should not be defeated. As argued in Chapter 5,

---

[71] Munzer, p. 429.   [72] Munzer, p. 431.   [73] Munzer, p. 431.
[74] Munzer, p. 432.

the solution is for governments to be very clear about their intentions to provide guidance as to the kind of circumstances where they will legislate retrospectively and to give fair warning of where reliance is risky given the unsettled state of existing legal texts.[75]

In fact, expectations—or *reliance* on existing law—may be unreasonable for a more general reason: namely, that an expectation that the law will never change is somewhat bizarre. Of course, the idea that reliance ought to be protected derives from the Rule of Law ideal of certainty. But something, which is often overlooked in debates about retrospectivity, is that absolute certainty is impossible, and indeed undesirable (since it would prevent a necessary degree of flexibility and capacity to adapt to changing circumstances). As Kaplow notes, the idea that we can expect the law to stay forever constant is 'a particularly perverse assumption given that laws change quite frequently, and often in predictable ways'.[76] Indeed, Graetz points out that reliance-based claims for protection are circular:

The argument asserts that people have a right to protection merely because either they now expect such protection or the expected such protection when they entered into a transaction; their expectations allegedly create a right and their asserted rights legitimate their expectations. Often this expectation-based argument amounts to nothing more than an assertion that the status quo should be shielded from normal legislative change—an odd claim since people surely expect legislative change.[77]

The idea that legal change is to be expected means that reliance on the existing state of the law is not reasonable (that is, it is neither rational nor legitimate). This is particularly true of areas of law—such as taxation law—where change is common, and is often either announced in advance or predictable on the basis of underlying legal principles.[78] And if reliance is not reasonable, then there is no basis for arguing that justice requires its protection.

It must be noted, however, that this argument does not extend to *all* cases of reliance. Firstly, just because the expectation-based argument for protection of reliance is circular, this does not show that reliance should never be protected. Kaplow argues that such an argument would itself be circular 'because the fact that legal change is expected does not imply that compensation is never appropriate in response to that change'. Furthermore, the knowledge that legal change will occur does not necessarily encompass knowledge of the nature of that change or, more critically, what areas of the law relevant to an individual are most at risk of change.[79] Some kinds of reliance *will* therefore be reasonable. The injustice of failing to protect reliance interests will, therefore, vary according to how predictable legal change is. And this may vary even within an area of law: Goode

---

[75] While this may mean that the law provides less effective guidance, this is not necessarily so.

[76] Louis Kaplow, 'An Economic Analysis of Legal Transitions' (1985–1986) 99 *Harvard Law Review* 509 at 522.

[77] Michael J Graetz, 'Retroactivity Revisited' (1984–1985) 98 *Harvard Law Review* 1820 at 1823.

[78] R Goode, 'Disappointed Expectations and Tax Reform' (1987) 40 *National Tax* Journal 159, p. 160.   [79] Kaplow, p. 525.

observes that 'some expectations of tax benefits are found to be so subjective and weakly based ... that they merit little public consideration. Other expectations are so firmly based that they are seldom questioned'.[80]

Whether an expectation of the law's not changing is reasonable or not will, therefore, depend upon the context. Jill Fisch offers an 'equilibrium theory' as a way of determining how reasonable it is to rely on existing law. She points out that legal contexts will tend to fall somewhere on a continuum between a 'stable' and 'unstable' equilibrium. There is a stable equilibrium:

... when the applicable legal rules are clear, have been promulgated by a higher legal authority, have persisted over time and in a variety of specific cases, and have not been widely criticized or questioned by lawmakers with comparable authority. The extent to which the government has attempted to induce reliance upon the legal status quo may also be relevant.[81]

In a stable equilibrium, it may be reasonable to expect the law to remain constant. In an unstable equilibrium, however, there is an 'inherent potential for change',[82] which means that the risk of legal change should be factored in by rational actors. Reliance on the existing state of the law in an unstable equilibrium is, therefore, unreasonable: it is both irrational (because not in line with the likelihood of legal change) and illegitimate (because not in line with the underlying purposes and principles of the law, which are presumably the goal of the legal change).[83]

Of course, because some legal contexts will be somewhere in between a stable and unstable equilibrium, the reasonableness of reliance will be a matter of degree. As Fisch points out, this is pleasingly congruent with the idea that retrospectivity is a matter of degree.[84] In general, then, we can say that greater degrees of retrospectivity are justifiable in inverse proportion to the reasonableness of reliance on existing law. The more likely legal change is in a given context, then the less compelling will be the arguments for protecting people from that change. It is not unjust to fail to protect people's reliance on the law where this reliance is irrational, illegitimate, or both. And it must be borne in mind that while legal certainty is *ceteris paribus* a desirable thing; absolute certainty in all legal contexts is neither possible nor desirable.

Thus, it can be argued that retrospective law is justifiable where the only upset expectations are those which are irrational and illegitimate. However, it might also be possible to go further, and argue that retrospective legislation is sometimes justifiable even when it upsets expectations that are both rational and legitimate. Although we can agree, then, that the failure to protect rational and legitimate expectations always amounts to a *prima facie* injustice, it does not always amount to an injustice, *all things considered*. Even if defeating rational and legitimate expectations is seen as 'playing unfairly', Woozley argues that:

... while it may be true that playing unfair is always bad, it does not follow that it is always wrong; and it will not be wrong in the case where, even if playing unfair is bad, playing fair

---

[80] Goode, p. 160.   [81] Fisch, p. 1102.   [82] Fisch, p. 1102.
[83] For discussion of this assumption, see Chapter 6.   [84] Fisch, p. 1103.

is even worse. It is a legitimate objection to a retrospective law that it is unfair to the innocent and even to the not-so-innocent who will suffer under it, but it is not on that account an overwhelming objection.[85]

For example, the demands of substantive justice may sometimes favour the use of retrospective law, even where this is a *pro tanto* injustice to the person to whom it is applied. This is the compelling justification laws enabling the retrospective prosecution of war crimes and human rights abuses, as discussed in Chapters 4 and 6. Justice Isaacs observed that 'what may seem unjust when regarded from the standpoint of one person affected may be absolutely just when a broad view is taken of all who are affected'.[86] Walker objects to this argument, saying that:

. . . the trouble with this formulation is that it can be used to justify anything. . . . If there is one thing the history of the twentieth century should have made clear to us, it is the depth of the human talent for rationalising wrong-doing . . . the Isaacs formulation may be just another way of saying that the end justifies the means.[87]

However unrealistic it may be not to take into account the human propensity for rationalizing wrongdoing (indeed for anything we may want to do or to happen), it would be even more unrealistic not to take into account the fact that different values can conflict. The only way to avoid this is if values are lexically ordered—a position held by few and incompatible with the position taken by Raz and endorsed by Walker that there are other values than the rule of law.[88] In any case, no set of laws can achieve absolute justice for all. No legal system can pursue perfect justice. And this is not just the case in situations where retrospective law is contemplated. Decisions like case management, for example, involve curtailing the pursuit of justice for one party so as to ensure resources are left over to secure some justice to everyone else.

When assessing the claim that overall considerations of justice can outweigh the *pro tanto* injustice of retrospective legislation, it is important to remember that there are various different kinds of justice.[89] One kind of justice which might justify the disruption of rational and legitimate expectations is that of distributive justice. If the effect of the tax laws, for example, is distributively unjust (that is, its benefits and burdens are not evenly spread across the members of society), then there may be an argument for disrupting expectations formed on the basis of that law, if doing so restores a just distribution. As Munzer points out:

if a given distribution is unjust, a prospective change may confirm or even aggravate the maldistribution. Since the general social and economic function of retroactive laws is to rearrange the social effects of earlier laws, retroactive legislation is at least a possible means to advance utility and to rectify or prevent injustice.[90]

---

[85] Woozley, p. 53.

[86] *George Hudson Limited v. Australian Timber Workers' Union* (1923) 32 CLR 413 at 434.

[87] Walker, p. 319.   [88] See section 2.6.

[89] See Brian Beaumont, 'Managing Litigation in the Federal Court', in Brian R Opeskin and Fiona Wheeler (eds), *The Australian Federal Judicial System* (Melbourne University Press, 2000) 166—citing *Sali v. SPC Ltd* (1993) 116 ALR 625.   [90] Munzer, p. 450.

This argument would apply in the case of retrospective taxation legislation in Australia, which sought to rectify a situation in which large-scale tax avoidance had caused an unequal distribution of tax burdens that was converting a progressive tax system into a savagely regressive one. Taxation laws seek to pursue distributive justice, while providing the government with enough funds to defend the country from attack, provide security for persons and for property, equality of opportunity and minimal social justice. Providing certain services to the community, or reducing the overall rate of taxation, might be seen as part of distributive justice. Distributing the burden of tax could also be seen as promoting distributive justice. But the ability of the legislature to pursue these goals could be threatened if too much revenue is lost through tax avoidance. Therefore, it might be permissible for the legislature to give higher priority to distributive justice in taxation than the justice of protecting the expectations of those who seek to avoid tax and reverse the distributional decisions reached through democratic processes.

Another kind of distributive justice which is relevant here is access to the legal system and to legal advice. Thus, Munzer points out that those with rational and legitimate expectations may have them precisely because they are able to afford better legal advice, and have better access to the legal system, than those whose expectations are not as rational or legitimate:

Given the conditions for rationality and legitimacy, the wealthy, the well-educated, and the well-counselled enjoy the best chance of having rational and legitimate expectations. Hence, to protect all and only those expectations may skew a distribution that initially satisfies some patterned principle of justice, and aggravate a distribution that violates such a principle.[91]

In this case, protecting rational and legitimate expectations might sometimes protect those who are already advantaged, and upsetting such expectations might sometimes level the playing field. Moreover, 'the targets of retroactive legislation are often better able than others to bear the disruption of their expectations'.[92]

Another important kind of justice is compensatory, remedial or retributive justice. So although we might accept Munzer's caveat that distributive arguments should not apply in the case of retrospective criminal legislation, it may not advance the cause of justice to prohibit *all* retrospective changes to criminal legislation. As Munzer writes, 'compensatory and retributive justice are also relevant. After all, the victim and the state have a stake in fair redress and punishment'.[93] Thus, considerations such as these may sometimes be powerful enough to justify disrupting even rational and legitimate expectations regarding the criminal law.

There are, in addition, other considerations which, while not of themselves considerations of justice, may justify imposing the *pro tanto* injustice of retrospective legislation in some cases. Firstly, there are considerations of utility and administrative efficiency: for example, 'if changes disadvantageous to defendants

---

[91] Munzer, p. 438.   [92] Munzer, p. 450.   [93] Munzer, p. 466.

were barred altogether, then at any given time multiple procedures would have to be followed'.[94] A similar point may be made about retrospective taxation legislation: by allowing only prospective amendments, legislators would be cutting off one head of a hydra only to see seven more grow in its place. It may be possible that through sheer exhaustive legislation, the legislature may hit upon and rule out every possible combination of tax avoidance or minimization schemes that can be devised. The price, however, will be a massively inflated statute book full of sections with numbers such as '25ZAC' and rules that make no sense unless one knows the historical details of the particular target, often a one-off, against which they were directed. If we are concerned about citizens knowing the law in any real sense, such a development is no less worrying than the legislature passing acts that retrospectively reinstate one interpretation over another of its previous statutes. Another consequence of this approach is that 'the legislature may have no practical alternative but to vest tax officials with more and more discretion', which could 'lead to tax laws capable, if unchecked, of great oppression'.[95]

Secondly, the use of retrospective legislation (or the threat of such use) could be extremely useful as a deterrent. As we will see in Chapter 4, the acceptance of retrospective legislation against exploitation of tax loopholes has been extremely effective (in fact, has been the only effective measure) in stamping out the tax avoidance industry in Australia.

Similarly, in Chapters 4 and 6, we argue that the acceptance of retrospective legislation allowing for punishment of war criminals might operate as a deterrent to those thinking of carrying out such acts in the future. And since the mere threat of use of retrospective legislation may not be sufficient to convince such people that it will be used, it will sometimes be necessary to actually punish some people under retrospective legislation in order to achieve the desired deterrent effect.

In summary, it is not always unjust to disrupt expectations, for they are not always rational or legitimate. Moreover, even when the individual's expectations are rational and legitimate, and it is therefore an injustice to that individual to disrupt them, there are sometimes justifications for doing so. Thus, the claim that we must always protect expectations because of the injustice of failing to do so cannot be used against all retrospective legislation. Although the desirability of protecting expectations will sometimes, perhaps very often, mean that retrospective law is unjustifiable—and that there is, therefore, a fairly heavy burden of proof on those seeking to justify retrospectivity—this does not mean that retrospectivity, as such, is unjustifiable under any circumstances. It may well be warranted to have retrospective laws that transgress, to some extent, rational and legitimate expectations. However, such laws may only be considered if we accept two caveats. First, we must recognize that all such laws may carry a certain

---

[94] Munzer, p. 466.
[95] *Federal Commissioner of Taxation v. Westraders Pty Ltd* (1980) 144 CLR 55 at 80.

pro tanto injustice that must be overcome by counter-veiling considerations. Second, we must acknowledge that we cannot have too many such laws, lest the ability of the overall system to provide guidance be genuinely impaired.

Other beneficial effects from protecting expectations

We have seen that an absolute requirement to protect expectations cannot be justified either on the basis of the purposes of law, or the injustice of disrupting expectations. Another argument, however, is that there are very valuable consequences realized by the protection of expectations within a legal system (and conversely, that extremely undesirable consequences will follow from the disruption of, or failure to protect, expectations). Thus, any benefits of an individual piece of retrospective legislation will never outweigh the general disbenefits of using it.

There are three main disbenefits which are imagined to follow from the failure to protect expectations. Firstly, it is claimed that regardless of the merits of any individual piece of retrospective legislation, allowing its use in even one, justified case will open the floodgates to a host of unjustified retrospectivity challenges. Secondly, it is alleged that if citizens know that retrospective change is possible and that they may be subjected to retrospective law, then they will lose respect for the law generally and no longer seek to be guided by it. Finally, it is claimed that retrospective taxation legislation, in particular, will discourage the kind of planning and investment that is most socially beneficial.

Clearly, these are empirical claims which can be assessed on the basis of actual states of affairs following the use of retrospective legislation. As retrospective legislation has been quite widely used both in Australia and elsewhere,[96] we should be able to see some of the deleterious effects if the above claims are true. Walker claims that such effects are apparent: the floodgates have long ago been flung open as a result of increasing acceptance of, and decreasing resistance to, retrospective legislation in even ordinary circumstances.[97] The claim is that the use of retrospective legislation in an emergency situation has caused the taboo against retrospectivity to be weakened. If a strong aversion to retrospective legislation is overcome even once, it becomes easier to overcome again, until legislators resort to retrospectivity at the drop of a hat. And this is undesirable because it will undermine the integrity of the legal system: we will slip further and further away from the ideal of the Rule of Law.

Although Walker seems to believe that these effects are evident, there is little evidence of it. Obviously, the Australian legal system does not perfectly conform to the ideal of the Rule of Law—for no actual legal system will. But it does not seem that the law in Australia has slipped so far from the ideal as to be a cause of concern for most; it certainly has not slipped to the point where it can no longer

---

[96] See Chapter 4.   [97] Walker, p. 318.

be considered 'law'. And neither is it plausible to suppose that the inevitable decline has not yet become apparent because of the recent advent of retrospective legislation: retrospectivity is hardly a new phenomenon. In any case, it can be argued that any such bad effects could have been avoided by clearly stating, and strictly adhering to, the conditions under which retrospective legislation should be used.

It is also worth noting that modern democracies have a variety of avenues available to circumscribe indiscriminate retrospective law making. As we will see in Chapter 4, this is very much the situation in Australia, where innocuous retrospective legislation is passed as a matter of course, but more problematic retrospectivity invites more scrutiny and controversy, and often fails hurdles— such as the Senate—put in place precisely to circumvent such unrestricted activities. Although as illustrated by examples in Chapter 4, democratic checks and balances sometimes fail to prevent the enactment of objectionable laws. However, there would appear to be no reason why we should expect retrospective legislation to 'open the floodgates' to legislative abuse of retrospectivity as a matter of course.

The second claim regarding retrospective law and the failure to protect expectations is that it will undermine respect for the law. For if people have no way of knowing what legal principles will be applied to their behaviour (as is the case where the existing law could be replaced by a retrospective law the substance of which they cannot know), they will see little point in trying to adhere to the existing law. And this will mean that the law becomes ineffective. For example, intentional tax measures designed to encourage certain kinds of investment may be ineffective where retrospective amendment is considered acceptable, because investors will not be able to rely on legal protection of their expectations.

In response to this objection, it must firstly be noted that even if one is uncertain what law will be applied to one's behaviour, it would not be reasonable, in most cases, to simply disregard all existing law. Obeying existing law may not guarantee an absence of unintended consequences, but it is still one's best bet for avoiding liability. As an analogy, obeying all of the road rules does not guarantee that one will never be in an accident; however, we would not consider it reasonable for people to completely disregard the road rules on the basis of this fact (even if their only reason for obeying them is to avoid accidents).

Of course, as the probability of an accident (even when obeying the road rules) goes up, it may become more rational for one to place less importance on the rules, and disobey them. Analogously, where retrospective laws become common and difficult to predict, it may no longer be much use to guide oneself by existing law. But insofar as this is true, it is an argument not against any and all retrospective legislation (or other legislation which necessarily disrupts expectations), but rather against too frequent and arbitrary use of retrospective legislation. As we have previously noted, what this argument shows is not that there should be a blanket prohibition on retrospectivity (or disruption of expectations), but rather that the use of legislation that upsets reasonable expectations should be carefully circumscribed, and the conditions under which it is justified be made publicly available.

In the case above, uncertainty regarding taxation legislation could be allayed by encouraging potential investors to consult the Australian Taxation Office (ATO) for a ruling (for example, by establishing avenues for easy, low-cost and effective communication) where they are in doubt as to the status of a planned scheme or transaction. Of course, this is unlikely to be foolproof: the legislature may be reluctant to guarantee that expectations formed on the basis of such rulings will *always* be protected, for officials might not always display probity and integrity in their rulings, and there is a potential for a conflict of interest.[98] However, it seems plausible to suppose that such factors may fall under the scope of the definition of 'layering of expectations' (discussed above), making at least some such expectations irrational. Moreover, it is hardly true that *all* financial expectations will be rendered uncertain by such considerations.

To this should be added the observation that, in some cases, a *failure* to legislate retrospectively may cause people to lose respect for the law. For example, during the 1970s and 1980s widespread and blatant tax avoidance by the most privileged members of Australian society caused resentment amongst ordinary taxpayers, directed against successive governments incapable or unwilling to take the necessary steps to stamp it out.[99]

With regard to taxation legislation, however, it might be argued that a related claim is true. This is that, where there is a threat that expectations will not be protected, investors will no longer see longer-term investments as a worthwhile risk. Unless investors have some assurance that the rules will not be changed to their detriment, they will play it safe, and will instead concentrate their energies on short-term ventures, or not invest at all. And this will have undesirable effects, leading to less-than-optimal levels of social wealth production.

The problem with this argument, however, should be clear from the discussion in Chapter 1. Even with a ban on retrospective legislation (that is, one which stops short of banning almost *all* legislation), it will be impossible to protect all such expectations. The only kinds of plans that could be fully protected against future legislative change are those that are completed over a short time-span. It is possible to give this kind of protection to a scheme that is completed in a day; but it is not possible to give such protection to a ten-year manufacturing or marketing strategy which may be of more benefit to the community. Thus, the adverse consequences of failure to protect these kinds of expectations are, to some extent, unavoidable in any workable legal system. And the problems with retrospective law making,

---

[98] See, for example, Mike Bannon, 'Draft ATO rulings offer immunity from penalties' (16 July 2000) *Canberra Times*; Toni O'Loughlin, 'Private tax rulings may be published' (26 July 2000) *Sydney Morning Herald*; Toni O'Loughlin, 'Secret rulings: PM defends department' (29 July 2000) *Sydney Morning Herald*; Jim Dickins, 'Fears of tax office corruption' (17 November 2000) *Courier Mail*; Allesandra Fabro, 'Tax Office flaws revealed' (17 November 2000) *Australian Financial Review*.

[99] See discussion in Chapter 4, 'Retrospective Taxation Law'.

insofar as they are related to *avoidable* uncertainty, will derive more from arbitrary and unpredictable legislative change. Once again, where retrospective legislation is made only under certain publicly known conditions, it need not jeopardize productive or long-term investment. Thus, the potential for sub-optimal wealth production does not justify the claim that expectations must always be protected. The most that these arguments tell us is that retrospective legislation is something which must be used with extreme caution, and which will only be justified if certain strict conditions are met.

3.6 Re-reading the expectations objection: unconscionable legislative conduct

Those familiar with Anglo-Australian concepts of equity might find something very familiar in the above reliance arguments. Equity emerged in England in the late middle ages to deal with some of the injustices of what was, even then, seen as an overly rigid system of Common Law. Equity was to be the 'conscience' of the law. The way that it dealt with such injustices was not to overturn common law but rather to issue injunctions as to how litigants were permitted to exercise their rights under the common law. The rights were not extinguished. However, the possessor of that right was estopped from asserting it because, given previous conduct of the individual concerned, it would be 'unconscionable'. Over the last 50 years, English and Australian judges have revived equity and expanded the categories of equitable relief. *High Trees* and *Walton's Stores*[100] established and refined the principle of promissory estoppel designed to avoid a classic (and, for the purposes of this book, highly relevant) example of unconscionable conduct. Where individuals or corporations give assurances as to their proposed actions and others rely on these assurances to their detriment, then the individual or corporation may be required to act in the way signalled if:

(1) the plaintiff assumed that a particular legal relationship existed or would exist between them;

(2) the defendant induced the plaintiff to adopt that assumption;

(3) the plaintiff acted in reliance on the assumption;

(4) the defendant knew or intended the plaintiff to do so;

(5) the plaintiff's action will occasion detriment if the assumption is not fulfilled;

(6) the defendant has failed to act to avoid that detriment.[101]

---

[100] *Central London Property Trust Ltd v. High Trees House Ltd* [1947] KB 30 and *Waltons Stores (Interstate) Ltd v. Maher* (1988) 164 CLR 387.

[101] *Waltons Stores (Interstate) Ltd v. Maher* at 428–429.

This is very much analogous to the reliance argument in the Rule of Law. The lawmaker (be it parliament or judge) passes laws which indicate the way that it will use its powers. Citizens do, and are expected to, modify their behaviour as a result. Lawmakers know this and intend it. Indeed, that is one of the major functions of law and the principal (and principled) way in which law attempts to achieve its effects. Putting it another way, the laws indicate the legal consequences of citizens' actions. Citizens choose how to act in the belief that the state will impose the legal consequences determined by the legal text discoverable at that time and not on other texts which were not in existence at the time of the relevant action. If the state were to change the texts which are applied to those actions in ways that cause detriment to the citizens, it could be accused of unconscionable legislative or judicial conduct (in the court of public opinion if not in an actual court of law). This approach is promising:

- it neatly and exactly captures the powerful Rule of Law arguments against retrospective lawmaking;

- it makes the Rule of Law a principle about the ethical use of power in the long term interests of the state and its citizens—or what EP Thompson calls the 'unqualified good' which is best achieved when the powerful flag in advance how they will use their power;[102]

- it also emphasizes the Rule of Law requirement of asymmetric responsibility of the powerful, in general, and the lawmakers, in particular (when the citizen has broken the law but the powerful are still bound by it).

This is not a coincidence. Although the basic idea of the Rule of Law can be found in antiquity and was riskily propounded by Coke, it emerged as part of the European enlightenment as the result of English writers such as John Locke. Locke appears influenced by equity in his thinking on the relationship between citizen and subject and the way it modified Hobbes' version of the social contract. Thus, the Rule of Law entered mainstream Western thinking influenced by equitable notions that have become incorporated into our ideas about law and the way it should operate in a well-ordered society.

Finn[103] emphasizes Locke's view that sovereigns held power on 'trust' to be exercised to the benefit of the people[104] and uses analogies from equity to unpack

---

[102] EP Thompson, p. 266.

[103] P Finn (1995) 'A Sovereign People, A Public Trust' in P Finn (ed) (1995) *Essays on Law and Government Volume 1 Principles and Values* (The Law Book Company) 5.

[104] This offers some advantages over traditional social contract theory which suffers from the fact that there is no actual contracting, no bargaining, and no superior law to govern the bargaining process. It is merely a device for considering what the terms of such a contract would be—something that leads to endless debate about the original terms of any such contract made between imaginary people and the conditions under which it might be changed by the real people who are supposedly subject to it. On the other hand, powers held on trust are rarely given by the beneficiaries and generally come from some other source. Two examples from Trust law that are particularly apposite

what this means. This book applies the equitable notion of 'unconscionability' to help understand our approach to retrospective rule making. Equity imposes responsibilities on the holders of power when they indicate how it will be exercised, and others act to their potential detriment, trusting that the power holder will keep to their word. The quasi-contract approach is a specific version of the larger social contract idea of particular relevance to retrospective rule making and the Rule of Law.

The suggestion is not that the Rule of Law is a precise equitable argument. Rather, this equitable approach provides a strong basis for our general and sometimes inchoate view that the passing of retrospective laws is generally wrong in an ethical or moral sense. However, it also provides insights into some of the reasons why retrospective law making will not always be morally wrong.

For example, the equitable notions of unconscionable contract do not indicate that we must always do what we say we are going to do—let alone be held to account for it. We are forced to live up to our undertakings and promises only when:

(a) others relied on those undertakings;

(b) we knew that they would rely on those undertakings and act to their detriment but encouraged them to do so rather than warning them.

This argument has some built-in limitations. The only persons who can claim to be aggrieved are those who actually relied on the undertaking. We saw earlier that the fact of reliance cannot be incorporated into a satisfactory definition of 'retrospective' rules. However, equitable notions are relevant when deciding what kinds of retrospective rules should be discouraged and who is entitled to argue that they should not be disadvantaged by the change. The issue is an important one: but it goes to justification and scope rather than definition. Of course, if a large and indeterminate number of persons may have relied on the law not being altered, this is a strong argument against retrospective rule making. However, where there are relatively small numbers who are likely to have relied on the law remaining the same, this may suggest that an alternative remedy may be compensation for those few who would have a legitimate grievance against the rule change. Where there is a serious issue as to the fact of reliance, the reasonableness of the reliance, and the legitimacy of the claim to have that reliance protected, such circumstances may provide a particularly good reason to follow the conditional compensation route rather than the purely prospective legislation course.

A second important limitation is found in other equitable doctrine. One of the most important equitable maxims is that those who come to equity must come with 'clean hands'. You can call the powerful to account and require them to live up to their undertakings. However, if you do seek to call them into account,

are trusts created by will (a direct correlation between 'will trusts' and power handed from sovereigns to the successors) or by unlawful taking (which creates a resultant trust on behalf of the rightful owner—offering a strong similarity to the forceful seizure of power on which all modern constitutions eventually rest).

your own behaviour will be considered. These nuances will help explain some of the common and generally tolerated forms of retrospective law making considered in the next chapter and some of the arguments in favour of some kinds of retrospective law making in Chapter 6.

3.7 Conclusion

This chapter has examined the main arguments used against retrospective rule making. Despite the stridency with which they are often put, none of these arguments are strong enough to justify an absolute prohibition on retrospectivity. Some of these arguments do, however, show that retrospective law will only be justified under very tightly circumscribed conditions—especially for retrospective criminal law. Of the arguments that have merit, most of them are related to the idea that the state should give as clear an indication in advance of the way that officials will use their power. In doing so, it provides guidance to citizens and other subjects of the law—something that allows citizens to modify their behaviour to take advantage of the opportunities lawmakers intentionally create and avoid behaviour lawmakers intentionally seek to discourage. If state officials exercise their powers as indicated by law, not only is this fair, just and equitable for the individuals involved but also makes the law more effective.

Such arguments do not support an absolute prohibition of retrospective laws. Indeed, they provide clear pointers to potential justifications of retrospectivity that would make such rule making acceptable, desirable, or even mandatory. The expectations argument points to the possibility of expectations that are irrational and/or illegitimate. The equity arguments point to the possibility of fair warning and the relevance of the conduct of those who seek to argue reliance.

As we will see in the next chapters, retrospectivity is a regular feature of legislative law making and an inextricable part of judicial law making.

4

Retrospective legislation

4.1 Introduction

The widespread antipathy to retrospectivity documented in the previous chapters might lead one to expect that actual retrospective laws are fairly rare. In fact, just the opposite is true: retrospective legislation is such a common occurrence that it would be impractical to survey all the instances of retrospective legislation across all jurisdictions that espouse the Rule of Law. We will provide Australian examples of retrospective legislation in a jurisdiction without a constitutional prohibition of *ex post facto* laws, extending an earlier study.[1] We will also include examples from the United States (the state with the oldest constitutional limitation on retrospective law-making, and the United Kingdom (one of the newest).

Our earlier study divided retrospective legislation into a number of categories and these will be retained. These categories are not meant as an exhaustive classification of possible types of retrospective legislation, nor should they be considered to be mutually exclusive but indicative of some of the varieties of retrospective law that are passed by actual legislatures:

1. Curative legislation: the largest and perhaps least controversial class of retrospective legislation can be further broken down into the subcategories of routine revision; restorative legislation; validating legislation; and the overturning of judicial decisions.

2. Beneficial legislation: since no one could have had an expectation that the benefit would be conferred upon them, these statutes are, in effect, the legislative equivalents of *ex gratia* payments and are seldom controversial.

3. Subordinate legislation: this category includes statutes explicitly conferring retrospective regulatory powers, as well as retrospective subordinate legislation.

---

[1] C Sampford and A Palmer, 'Retrospective Legislation in Australia' (1994) 22 *Federal Law Review* 217. The task of locating Commonwealth retrospective legislation is made far easier by the establishment in 1981 of the Senate Standing Committee for the Scrutiny of Bills (SSCSB), which reports to the Senate on Bills that 'trespass unduly on personal rights and liberties', including legislation which purports to have retrospective effect. See Senator Michael Tate, 'The Operation of the Australian Senate Standing Committee for the Scrutiny of Bills, 1981–1985', Australian Parliament, Parliamentary Paper No. 137 of 1985. In addition, there has been a practice, since, 1989, of including commencement dates in the Acts tables of the bound volumes of Commonwealth statutes.

4. Procedural statutes: courts generally treat procedural statutes in this category differently from non-procedural statutes, thus providing a rationale for examining them separately.

5. Retrospective criminal law.

6. Retrospective taxation law (anti-avoidance statutes).

7. Laws retrospective to the date of announcement ('legislation by press release'): legislation is deemed to have taken effect from the date of a Ministerial announcement of an intention to enact it.

The inclusion of different cases in particular categories is naturally a matter of interpretation, and is made more problematic when a Bill falls clearly into two or more of the given categories. For example, from the period 2000–04, we estimate that around twenty per cent of all Australian federal legislation, and Queensland state legislation—the Australian State with the strongest scrutiny of legislation committee—had some retrospective aspect. While various types of curative legislation are the most common forms of retrospectivity, most years in the last two decades provide examples of retrospective criminal, procedural or taxation legislation.

We will discuss these categories in an order which roughly indicates an increasing level of general controversy surrounding the retrospective legislation in question.

4.2 Curative legislation

Curative legislation is perhaps the least controversial, and most commonly used, type of retrospective legislation. It encompasses various types of statute, from the correction of typographical errors, to the overturning of a judicial decision or the validation of an unlawful administrative practice. Curative statutes are part of the complex interaction between legislation and administration in a modern state. The government introduces legislation to achieve certain policy or administrative goals, but sometimes the legislation fails to achieve those goals. The government may then decide to introduce further legislation to retrospectively cure the defects, thus ensuring not only that the goals will be achieved in the future, but that the goals are achieved from the outset. There are, in fact, several important subcategories of curative legislation.

Routine revision

Examples of routine revision include the correction of typographical errors,[2] changes consequent on previous amendments,[3] and the routine updating of

---

[2] For example, the *Racing (Amendment) Act 1989* (Vic) substituted the word 'section' for 'secton' in the Principal Act; the *Fisheries (Abalone Licence Charges) Amendment Act 1989* (Vic) substituted '5000' for '500' in the *Fisheries (Abalone Licence Charges) Act 1989* (Vic).

[3] For instance, the retrospective alteration of a reference to 'Family Benefit' to 'Family Allowance'.

statute law.[4] Sometimes the revisions carried out are of a slightly more significant nature, as, for instance, with the *National Parks (Amendment) Act 1989* (Vic), which varied the boundaries of a National Park. Sometimes the effect on individuals and their rights can be very significant. The Immigration and Asylum Appeals (Fast Track Procedure) (Amendment) Rules 2004 (UK) have retrospective effect to cure defective drafting in the original statutory instrument, the Immigration and Asylum Appeals (Fast Procedure) Rules 2003. The effect of the amendment was to ensure that the 'fast track' deportation procedure for failed asylum seekers also applied to a person detained at one of the designated Removal Centres accidentally omitted from the Schedule.

No doubt it would be desirable if typographical errors were never made; if the persons responsible for drafting major amendments to legislation could be aware of all the consequential amendments which would be necessary; and if routine changes were always made prospectively. Given the pressure under which parliamentary counsel and draftspersons operate, these goals are unlikely ever to be achieved, and this sort of retrospectivity might be seen as an inevitable by-product of the legislative process and of human fallibility. In many cases, the mistake will not have been noticed, let alone relied upon. Where it is noticed, it may be seen as a mistake. Rectifying the mistake will give effect to the intended purpose of the legislation, ensure that like cases are treated alike, ensure the workability of the legislation and will not arouse controversy.

Of course, for those who do not like the legislation, unworkability may be a virtue. If the government has sought to do the wrong thing and failed, then it will have to live with its mistake and will not be able to do the wrong thing until new legislation is introduced. However, for such people the problem is the legislation, not the retrospectivity. If you do not like fast tracking, then it is wrong to impose it on anyone rather than wrong to retrospectively impose it on those who were mistakenly made immune to it. Neither the legislature nor the courts can take the desirability of the legislation as a reason for not correcting clearly unintended drafting errors.

Restorative legislation

Restorative legislation is used where a legislative scheme has been unintentionally allowed to lapse, creating a sort of legislative lacuna. The cause of this happening is, no doubt, some degree of negligence on the part of the Department responsible for the legislation. Nevertheless, retrospective restoration of the relevant scheme or provision is often in the interests not only of the Department concerned, but also of the persons affected by it; that is, persons who may have relied on the scheme continuing.

---

[4] Such as where an Amending Act substitutes one year for another in the title of an Act referred to in the Principal Act.

This is most obviously the case where the effect of the lacuna is that a liability to tax or some other charge arises, or the right to some government payments ceases. In such cases, the government has either become entitled to revenue which it was never intended should be payable, or has ceased to be obliged to make a payment which the legislature always intended that it should make. In passing restorative legislation, the government will be foregoing revenue to which it has become legally entitled, or incurring expenditure which it was not obliged by law to make; but it will also be acting to ensure that people's expectations about these matters are respected. The *Customs Tariff (Coal Export Duty) Amendment Act 1989* (Cth), for example, restored an exemption from duty which had been allowed to lapse; duty would have been payable if the restoration of the exemption had not been retrospective.

On other occasions, changes to legislation may have unintended effects, perhaps creating an anomaly which may take some time to discover, and which might, in fact, be practically undiscoverable to the person affected. The *Customs Tariff Amendment Act 1986* (Cth), for instance, restored duty-free entry to certain parts used in the construction or modification of bountiable vessels; the parts had lost their duty-free status as an unintended result of amendments to some customs by-laws.

An example of the retrospective imposition of an obligation to make a payment was the extension of the Commonwealth Export Market Development Grant Scheme; the scheme lapsed on 1 July 1982 but was retrospectively restored and prospectively renewed by the *Export Market Development Grants Amendment Act 1982* (Cth).

Where the effect of the lapse of the scheme is that liability to tax ceases, then it is clearly not in the interests of the person affected that the liability be retrospectively restored. For example, the *Tobacco Charge (No 1) Amendment Act 1986* (Cth), *Tobacco Charge (No 2) Amendment Act 1986* (Cth), and *Tobacco Charge (No 3) Amendment Act 1986* (Cth), re-established legal rates of charge from the date on which the previous rates had expired; the new rates were the same as the old.

The *Sea Fishing Grants (Charges) Act 2000* (UK) retrospectively ensures the validity of charges levied by the Sea Fish Industry Authority and its predecessor between 1972 and 1996. The legislative charges funded grants made available to fishermen for the construction, improvement and safety of their vessels. The Act was passed because of concerns about whether the Minister had authority to levy the charges. However, there had been no complaints by the individuals affected by the charge. Those who received the grants signed the conditions of approval for their payment, which referred to the deduction of the charge from the overall grant.[5] It cannot generally be said that the retrospective restoration of

---

[5] House of Commons Standing Committee, Sea Fishing Grants (Charges) Bill, 14 March 2000, Session 1999–2000; and comments by 'The Public Whip', Sea Fishing Grants (Charges) Bill, 22 May 2000, Division No 203 available at <http://www.publicwhip/org/uk/division/php?date= 2000-05-22&number=203>.

the liability will upset the expectations of persons acting in reliance on the law, who would probably remain unaware that the legislation had lapsed. And if they were aware, such persons would probably realize that it was due to a mistake rather than to a change in government policy. Therefore, it would be unreasonable for reliance to be placed on the emergence of the relevant lacuna.

Validating legislation

Validating legislation is passed where someone, usually the executive arm of government, has acted in reliance on an erroneous view of the law, which action the retrospective statute is intended to validate. Thus, this sub-category includes statutes designed to overcome more significant legislative defects than those considered in the routine revision category; often there are complicating factors such as a person's reliance on the defective scheme. However, provided that no new (that is, unexpected) obligations are imposed on anyone, there is little that can be objected to in the retrospective curing of the defect. Indeed, here reliance on the existing state of the law is an argument *for* retrospectivity, because the executive and others relied on what turned out to be a mistaken interpretation of the law.

In these instances, it would be perverse not to perfect that law given that people have been led into error by the government. The retrospective legislation is concerned with making the law conform to that which people acting in purported reliance on the law believed to be the case. Failure to cure the defect and validate those actions in these circumstances could diminish respect for the law rather than support it. Sometimes, the fact that the person's view of the law was erroneous comes to light as a result of a judicial decision; such cases are considered separately below. The legislation concerned is used to make the law retrospectively conform to that which the person acting in purported reliance on it believed it to be, and to thus validate any actions taken by that person. Although the validation of those actions may detrimentally affect an individual's actual legal rights, it is very seldom that it will defeat expectations as to rights and liberties.

There are many reasons why retrospective validating legislation may be thought necessary. First, regulations may have been beyond power: the *Transport and Communications Legislation Amendment Act 1989* (Cth) allowed for the making of retrospective regulations which were necessary to validate routine telex and zonal changes dating back to 1980.[6]

Secondly, technical requirements may not have been observed. For example, the *Quarantine (Validation of Fees) Act 1985* (Cth) was necessary because the Department had failed to table certain notices in Parliament; and the *Food (Validation) Act 1990* (Vic) removed doubts about the validity of the Food

---

[6] See Australia, 'First to Twenty-First Reports of 198', *Parliamentary Paper No 466 of 1989*, SSCSB, Australian Parliament, p. 73.

Standards Code and the Food Standards Regulations 1987 which had arisen as a result of the failure to table in Parliament certain materials adopted in the Code.

In some cases, ambiguities, lacunae and technical mistakes in the law come to the fore in a court case. Even when a judgment comes down on the side of the executive's interpretation of the law, it may be considered wise to retrospectively enshrine the judgment in law—so as to remove altogether the problematic section of law. In the next section, we will consider the way in which the executive can act to overturn judicial decisions, but the executive can also stamp such rulings with its official imprimatur. A recent example of this was the *WorkCover Queensland Amendment Act 2002* (Qld). In *Tanks v. WorkCover Queensland*,[7] the Qld Court of Appeals, while interpreting the law in line with the views of the government, conceded that the relevant law was not entirely clear. The government, in turn, legislated to clarify the law in line with the decision by inserting a new section 252A(1) which declared that nothing in the Act 'affects or has ever affected' the commencement of a limitation period in respect of actions for personal injury provided for in the *Limitations of Actions Act 1974* (Qld). The Scrutiny of Legislation Committee (Qld) accepted this retrospective ambit, noting that this declaration 'does not alter the current state of the law, but merely states it more expressly'.[8]

A similar situation occurred in the *Plant Protection Amendment Act 2004* (Qld). In response to an outbreak of citrus canker outbreak, the Department of Primary Industries and Fisheries exercised its powers under the *Plant Protection Act 1989* (Qld) to control the disease. However, the affected property owner brought applications before the Supreme Court for an injunction. The Supreme Court found in favour of the government. In the previous WorkCover example, the enshrining of the judicial interpretation in legislation was to remove an ambiguity in law that opened up the possibility of an undesirable outcome: the unintended affect on statutory provisions determining limitations of actions for personal injury. However, in the citrus canker example, it was the very act of filing the injunction that the government wished to foreclose—regardless of whether the court could be relied upon to favour the government's intention. The government argued that it needed to be able to 'take necessary and timely action to prevent, control and eradicate a serious pest'.[9] The public benefit in preventing delays to the implementation of emergency disease control measures affecting an important industry was considered to outweigh any right land-owners might ordinarily possess to protect their property interests through recourse to the courts.

---

[7] (2001) QCA 103.

[8] Scrutiny of Legislation Committee (Queensland), Alert Digest 11, Queensland Parliament, 26 November 2002, p. 35. Also see Queensland, *Hansard*, 27 November 2002, p. 4869 (comments by V Lester that the change ensures 'consistency between legislation and judicial decision making').

[9] See Queensland, *Hansard*, 1 September 2004, pp. 2222–3 (comments by Hon NI Cunningham).

Thirdly, a question mark may hang over the validity of a piece of legislation. Perhaps the best example of this is the *Constitution (Supreme Court) Act 1989* (Vic). Section 18 of the *Constitution Act 1975* (Vic) provides that an absolute majority of the Parliament is necessary for the enactment of Bills which, among other things, repeal, alter or vary provisions in the *Constitution Act* which deal with local government or the Supreme Court's jurisdiction. Because of this section, doubts arose as to the validity of certain legislation enacted between 1 December 1975 and 1 July 1989, and, in particular, as to the validity of the *Retail Tenancies Act 1986* and the *Planning and Environment Act 1986*. The *Constitution (Supreme Court) Act* barred challenges to the validity of any legislation passed in the period in question, or of anything done under such legislation, on the ground that section 18 was not followed. On its face, the Act was procedural; but because it prevented any challenge to the potentially unconstitutional Acts, it effectively validated them.[10]

Sometimes, there may simply never have been a statutory warrant for what was done. This may have been because of some oversight as, for example, with the *Chicken Meat Research Amendment Act 1984* (Cth); the Principal Act contained no provision stating what was to happen to penalties for the late payment of a levy, but since 1969 they had been paid into the Chicken Meat Research Trust Account. The defect in the original legislation was essentially a failure by the legislature to provide the necessary direction to the executive. Issuing that direction retrospectively did not contradict any individual's expectations, because any doubt was not over whether the penalties were valid, only over where they should be paid. The only issue was the power of the relevant executive body to deal with the penalties once collected.

The *Transport and Other Legislation Amendment Act 2004* (Qld) was concerned with the statutory validation of subordinate legislation. Certain subordinate legislation, concerning speed zones in Marine Parks, had been gazetted but not actually presented to Parliament in order to allow for the possibility of parliamentary disallowance. The relevant Department had mistakenly thought this process was not required for this type of subordinate legislation. The subordinate legislation was retrospectively validated by the Act in order to make sure that previous actions taken under the law could not be challenged or disputed.[11]

As the above examples show, legislation validating defects is usually commonsense and unproblematic, and therefore does not provoke much opposition. However, it should be borne in mind that government officials may take too far the idea of 'validating defects': it is probably wise to be wary of officials' conviction that the law should be changed to reflect their views rather than that their views should be changed to conform to the law. For example, one criticism of the *Plant*

---

[10] For further discussion, see R Lombardi and S Martin, 'Acts Without Power?' (1991) 65 *Law Institute Journal* 75.

[11] See Queensland, 'Transport and Other Legislation Amendment Bill Second Reading', *Hansard*, 13 May 2004, p. 1005.

Protection Amendment Act 2004 (Qld), discussed above, was that it removed the right of affected property owners to challenge and seek review of decisions made by the Department of Primary Industries and Fisheries to destroy (without compensation) valuable plants and material as part of an emergency fruit disease eradication program.[12] There is therefore some potential for injustice to be done by laws which are intended to validate defects.

One example of this is curative legislation which is made in order to prevent persons from receiving benefits which it was never intended they should receive. For instance, certain amendments made by *the Social Security Amendment Act 1988* (Cth) prevented 'double dipping' by a person who has received or is eligible to receive payments under *the Social Security Act 1947* (Cth) but who has also received statutory compensation or damages at common law.[13] While the amendments were undoubtedly necessary to ensure that the intention behind the legislation was effective, they may also have caused considerable injustice to persons who acted in accordance with advice that they were eligible for the relevant payments.

An example of such a case is *Re Krzywak*.[14] In this case, the Administrative Appeals Tribunal (AAT) noted that the applicant, after receiving incorrect legal advice that the compensation would not affect her benefit payment, had then continued to receive those payments. Accordingly, much of her common law compensation payment had been used to pay off debts, and she was now without savings or income. It is difficult to characterize the nature of the applicant's expectation that she was entitled to receive benefits. It was illegitimate in the sense that it was contrary to the intention behind the legislation, but that intention was perhaps not easily discoverable, while the initial continuance of benefits would have provided some rational basis for her expectation. The expectations in this case were certainly at least as legitimate as those of tax avoiders who took advantage of provisions whose effect was similarly contrary to the intention behind the legislation; indeed, they were probably more so since there is no evidence that the party in this case had looked for such a provision to exploit. It is interesting, however, that there was little political opposition to this particular piece of retro-spective legislation, compared to the furore typically generated by retrospective tax legislation discussed later in this chapter.

A more controversial example of Australian validating legislation, however, is the *Excise Tariff Amendment Act 1990* (Cth), which retrospectively validated the classification and rate of an excise duty which had been collected for nearly a decade and which was in the process of being challenged before the AAT.[15]

---

[12] Queensland, *Hansard*, 1 September 2004, p. 2223 (comments by Ms Lee Long).

[13] This was, in fact, the second attempt to close this loophole. The first was *the Social Security and Veterans' Entitlements Amendment Act (No 2) 1987* (Cth), the partial failure of this attempt was exposed by the Administrative Appeals Tribunal in *Re Tallon and Secretary, DSS* (1988) 8 AAR 348.

[14] *Re Krzywak and Secretary, DSS* (1988) 9 AAR 275.

[15] See 'Government's Action Sets Dangerous Precedent for Taxpayers' (1990) 25 *Taxation in Australia* 546; and Australia, *Seventh Report of 1990*, SSCSB, 7 November 1990, Australian Parliament, p. 116.

The Minister of Small Business and Customs, in a letter to the Senate Standing Committee for the Scrutiny of Bills (SSCSB), acknowledged that 'the excise paid at the "old oil" rate, while in accordance with the legislative intention and the producers' understanding of their liability, in fact exceeded that payable under the law'.[16] On 1 March 1990, BHP decided to challenge the relevant determinations by seeking a refund of excise. When the Collector of Customs refused the refund, BHP commenced proceedings in the AAT. It seems that $30 million was at stake (with a similar amount for Esso). The legislation was passed when the case was part heard, and hence closed off the argument being put by BHP. The Minister, however, claimed that the amendments might 'properly be characterized as curative, and merely effecting a correction of a technical defect' and argued that failure to have made the amendments would have resulted in a 'windfall' gain to the two producers affected.[17]

BHP's version of events was, however, slightly different. The company claimed that it had always believed that the oil should have been classified as 'new oil', but that it was 'constrained by officials' determinations, over the years, to accept their version'.[18] The company noted that the original determination was incorrect because it applied the wrong test, and that subsequent legislative amendments in 1994 did not validate any earlier decisions which might have been incorrect. BHP denied that its seeming lack of protest should be construed as acceptance of the determination and argued that if anyone had had a windfall it was consolidated revenue.[19]

In some ways, this case seems analogous to legislation which retrospectively validates the collection of fees. However, there are major differences. Most importantly, it seems arguable that there was no technical mistake in the original Acts, but simply a misinterpretation of them by the Minister. In addition, the producers had challenged the determinations (albeit belatedly) and the legislation deliberately pre-empted the outcome of the proceedings. It seems from these facts that BHP must, at some stage, have developed an expectation that the higher rate of duty was not payable and that the company's expectations were, by the Minister's own admission, in accordance with the law. BHP's expectation could therefore be classed as legitimate.

On the other hand, it can be argued that BHP must always have known that the government regarded the higher duty as payable. The decision by the government retrospectively to ensure that it was payable cannot, therefore, have

---

[16] Australia, SSCSB (1990), p. 116.

[17] The US Supreme Court has similarly drawn a distinction between 'a bare attempt of the legislature retroactively to create liabilities for transactions ... and the case of a curative statute aptly designed to remedy mistakes and defects in the administration of government', holding that the power to pass the latter kind of statute 'is necessary that government may not be defeated by omissions or inaccuracies in the exercise of functions necessary to its administration'. See *Graham v. Goodcell* (1930) 282 US 409, 429–30; 75 Law Ed 415 at 440–41.

[18] Australia, *Seventh Report of 1990*, SSCSB, Commonwealth Parliament, 7 November 1990, p. 118.

[19] Australia, SSCSB (1990), pp. 124–5.

surprised BHP. Indeed, it might have been rational to assume that the government would do so if challenged. Whatever BHP's expectations, it was clear that the government had different expectations. Indeed, the government would, at least, have passed new prospective legislation earlier if it had known of the possibility that it may have been misinterpreting the Act. Furthermore, BHP would presumably have taken the higher payments into account when working out production costs: the fact that the company continued to produce the oil, presumably, indicates that it remained profitable to do so. It seems to us, therefore, that no great injustice was done to BHP by the retrospective validation of the duty.

Probably the most controversial recent piece of retrospectively validating Australian legislation is the *Border Protection (Validation and Enforcement Powers) Act 2001*. As we note in the introduction to this book, this Act retrospectively validated—to the point of decriminalizing—any and all actions taken by agents of the executive *vis-à-vis* the interception of the *MV Tampa* by the Australian Defence Force on 28 August 2001 and the removal of 433 asylum seekers from Australian territorial waters.

The legality of the interception and subsequent detention of the rescuees was challenged in the Federal Court where (on appeal) a majority of the Full Federal Court reversed North J's decision at first instance and accepted that the government of a sovereign nation possessed a broad 'executive prerogative' to expel unauthorized entrants, and to detain them for that purpose, even in times of peace.[20] This was despite the fact that there was a comprehensive statutory regime in place for the processing of unauthorized arrivals, and there was no valid reason why the procedures established by statute were not followed by the executive (other than the invalid one of thereby preventing the boat-people from accessing the statutory right to apply for protection visas).[21]

Notwithstanding this ruling in its favour, the government in its second attempt successfully legislated to validate its action through the *Border Protection (Validation and Enforcement Powers) Act 2001* (Cth) which formed part of an administrative package of Acts popularly referred to as the 'Pacific Solution'.[22] This Act explicitly validates the majority decision—to the point of inserting a new section 7(a) in the *Migration Act 1958* (Cth) which stipulates that 'the existence of statutory powers under this Act does not prevent the exercise of any

[20] *Ruddock v. Vadarlis* (2001) 183 ALR 1.

[21] Note Black CJ's dissent in which he observed that the provisions of the *Migration Act 1958* (Cth) and *Border Protection Legislation Amendment Act 1999* (Cth) 'provide a comprehensive regime for the control of Australia's border and territorial waters and regulation of the right to detain'. His Honour observed that the statutory regime could have applied to the rescued people and (as the government acknowledged in evidence) had the executive 'not taken a view' that it did not wish to apply the Act it would have done so. (*Ruddock v. Vadarlis* (2001) 183 ALR 1 at 18.)

[22] The first Border Protection Bill 2001 failed in the Senate. The legislative framework for the 'Pacific Solution' consists of the following statutes: *Migration Amendment (Excision from Migration Zone) Act 2001; Migration Amendment (Excision from Migration Zone) (Consequential Provisions) Act 2001; Migration Legislation Amendment (Judicial Review) Act 2001; Migration Legislation Amendment Act (No 1) 2001; Migration Legislation Amendment Act (No 6) 2001; Border Protection (Validation and Enforcement Powers) Act 2001.*

executive power of the Commonwealth to protect Australia's borders, including, where necessary, by ejecting persons who have crossed those borders'. In other words, this section has the curious effect of stamping an ostensibly pre-existing extra-statutory executive prerogative with statutory validation.

Those concerned over the government's use of extra-statutory action in such matters might well consider that—to the extent that such acts can be validated by retrospective legislation—so much the worse for any justification of retrospective legislation. Indeed, while this book is mounting a case for the justification of many different types of retrospective legislation, it is not the author's position that all recently passed retrospective legislation is justified. It could be argued that this process of pursuing retrospective validation still attenuates executive power in an important way. When considering whether to respond to a situation (possibly an emergency) in an extra-statutory manner, the executive must consider whether their actions in this case are such as will be able to be validated by future legislation. In other words, they must consider the normal democratic obstacles that prevent Bills becoming laws.

This is a much stricter curtailment of executive action than the aforementioned 'executive prerogative'. The prerogative allows for extra-statutory actions relating to sovereignty and national security, but seemingly places very few substantive restrictions on the type of actions justified, or in which particular instances extra-statutory action should be utilized. As Justice French in his majority judgment admitted, the court was able to determine as a matter of law whether or not the government had the relevant power, but 'not whether it was exercised wisely and well'.[23] In contrast, the process of retrospective validation of extra-statutory actions may occur over a much broader range of issues, but is restricted both in the type of action taken and in which particular cases it should happen, by the hurdles that must be passed before the retrospectively validating Bill becomes law. This process constitutes a much more rigorous and democratic test of when and how governments may act in an extra-statutory manner. However, the Border Protection Act's eventual passage through both Houses of Parliament with minimal (and suppressed) debate is also an example of government possessing the numbers on the floor of parliament and exploiting a weak opposition to prevent these checks and balances being effective.[24]

[23] *Ruddock v. Vadarlis* (2001) 183 ALR 1 at 55.
[24] The government failed to respond in Parliament to the SSCSB's Alert Digest No 13 of 20 September 2001, which queried, amongst other things, why the powers and immunities were not subject to a sunset clause, why the retrospective validation was expressed so widely and whether the retrospectively validated actions must have complied with internal regulatory guidelines as to conduct by those exercising them. The Australian Labor Party was worried about the looming Federal Election and did not want to be perceived as 'soft' on border protection issues; thus it declared its support for the measure. The government also imposed a guillotine to suppress debate by the Democrats and Greens in the Senate. See Senate Official Hansard No 13, Thursday 20 September 2001, Commonwealth Parliament, pp. 27469, 27693, 27732; and also Wednesday 26 September 2001, p. 27936. (Senator Bartlett's comment that '[g]iven that we are passing retrospective legislation, it is probably appropriate that we pass a retrospective guillotine as well'.)

Given the fact that the government's action was subsequently validated by the federal court, the substantive provisions of the Act did not create a retrospective change in the actual rights and interests of individuals. The government could argue that they thought they had the power to act as they did; were aware that there were alternative interpretations of the prerogative that could lead to a challenge; and sought to clarify the position at the earliest opportunity. However, an alternative view is that the usual response to a situation of legal uncertainty is to choose a course of action whose legality is not in doubt and that a very pressing case has to be made for violent action to restrict human rights. Finally, we have already commented in the introduction that the case never reached the High Court and that the full Federal Court majority judgments give sufficient weight to the asylum seeker rights under both international and Australian law. If the purpose of the legislation were to deter future 'boat people', then prospective legislation would have been sufficient.

The government could argue that the refugees had no legitimate expectations of entering Australia so that no rights were being defeated. However, this ignored their rights under the UN convention on refugees and Australian law that still recognized their rights once they did enter Australia as they had done. It also ignored the rights of sea-going vessels to protect themselves against what would otherwise be piracy. It could be argued that it is important that soldiers know that their orders are lawful. The best way to ensure that is not to give orders that could be potentially unlawful. Given the fact that the government did not have control of the Senate, introducing retrospective legislation is an insufficient protection for the soldiers involved. It should also be pointed out that members of the government that gave orders to commit unlawful acts of violence would also be liable so that the retrospective legislation was potentially to protect the government from criminal prosecution for acts already committed—something that raises considerable potential conflict of interest issues. In the end, the legislation was passed after four judges had heard the matter and split 2:2—with the government fortunate that the two in favour were hearing the appeal.

A further Australian example of legislation that could only tenuously be described as validating—since it is difficult to define precisely what the Act is validating—is the *Natural Resources and Other Legislation Amendment Act 2004* (Qld). This legislation changed the circumstances under which the Department of Natural Resources was required to provide valuations to local councils. Given that the councils pay for this service, it might be thought that it would not be entirely fair to alter such legislation without consultation or notice.[25] Far worse, however, was that the legislation had the effect of covering the government's statutory obligations for the previous year, during which—due to industrial action—very few valuations were actually performed.

---

[25] See Queensland, 'Question to Minister for Local Government and Planning', *Hansard*, 11 May 2004, p. 793.

Effectively the government retrospectively legislated in order to at once *ex post facto* change its commitments for the last year and simultaneously foreclose the possibility of legal action arising from (what would presumably otherwise have been) a breach of statutory obligation by the Department.[26] This allowed it impunity in billing local councils for hundreds of thousands of dollars for a service the Department did not perform yet which was relied upon by councils for setting rates. It is also worth noting that—perhaps because of the timing of the parliamentary debates, the date of the Bill's ascension and the timing of the reports of the Queensland Scrutiny of Legislation Committee—the Bill did not draw any criticism, comment, or enquiry from the Committee regarding this retrospective application.

Overturning judicial decisions

Legislation to overturn a judicial decision can occur where the executive's reliance on an erroneous view of the law has been successfully challenged in the courts; the legislation is intended to give statutory validation to the executive's originally erroneous view (but not usually to validate the specifically impugned actions). Therefore, it is, in many ways, a subset of validating legislation, in that the usual reason for enacting legislation to overturn a judicial decision is to make the law conform to that which the executive always believed it to be. Had the *Tampa* appeal gone the other way and the Senate dropped its opposition,[27] the *Tampa* legislation would have fallen into this category. The distinguishing feature of the statutes included in this category, however, is the realization that an erroneous view of the law was relied upon due to a court's interpretation of the statutory provision concerned. That a court was involved points to another distinguishing feature: at least one person was aware of what eventuated as the correct view of the law. What is more, that person demonstrated their reliance on this view in a particularly expensive way: by taking the matter to court and making the executive follow a judicial decision rather than on its own erroneous view.

Therefore, it seems unsporting, at the least, to deprive this person of a hard won victory in the courts. A classic example from the United Kingdom is the *War Damages Act 1965* which overturned the decision of the House of Lords in *Burmah Oil v. Lord Advocate*[28] to award compensation for the wartime destruction of oil installations. Sheena McMurtrie comments that:

A recent example from the United States which also seems to fall into this category is the *Victim Allocution Clarification Act* 1997 which amended title 18 of the United States Code to *prevent* a United States district court from ordering any victim of a criminal offence excluded from the initial trial of a defendant on the basis that the victim may

---

[26] See Logan City Council, 'Anger at Valuation Role Fee', Wednesday, 23 June 2004, at <http://www.logan.qld.gov.au/LCC/logan/news/NewsArchive.htm>.
[27] This is a highly unlikely scenario.   [28] [1965] AC 75.

during the subsequent sentencing hearing make a statement or testify as to the effect of the offence on the victim and the victim's family. The amendment was stated to apply to all cases pending on the date of the Act's enactment. One such pending case was the Oklahoma City bombing case, in which Judge Matsch of the District Court had already ruled that due to the unique circumstances of the case the families of victims and survivors had to be excluded from the trial proceedings if they were to give crime impact testimony at the sentencing phase in order to reduce the risk of prejudice to the defendant.

Some of the bill's sponsors argued for the reversal of the ruling on appeal and introduced the legislation after they failed.[29]

In this category of retrospective legislation, there is often the concern that winning the case made the litigant(s) known to the government, so that a newly drafted law, however generally worded, in fact constitutes a direct attack upon that individual, along the lines discussed in Chapter 3, where fine-grained discrimination can occur when the veil of ignorance is diminished. In recognition of this, such legislation usually includes some kind of savings provision which protects the litigant from losing the fruits of their victory, and so that the new legislation does not appear vindictive or otherwise contrary to the Rule of Law. Thus, applications lodged or actions taken under the original legislation up until the date of the facts in the relevant court decision are commonly exempted from the operation of the retrospective legislation.

A typical example is provided by the *Superannuation Legislation Amendment Act 1986* (Cth), which gave retrospective validity to the Commissioner for Superannuation's interpretation of a section in the *Superannuation Act 1976* allowing the Commissioner to issue a certificate stating that, due to a condition specified in the certificate, a person 'is not likely' to continue as an eligible employee until retirement. The purpose of this section was to allow the payment of reduced benefits to an employee who retired on the grounds of invalidity where the Commissioner was of the opinion that the invalidity was caused or substantially contributed to by a condition specified in the certificate. The Commissioner had always interpreted the 'is not likely' test as meaning 'there is a real risk'. In *Re Bewley*, however, the AAT held that the test actually meant 'more probable than not'.[30] Any AAT decision, made before the date of Assent, to set aside the Commissioner's decision to issue a certificate, was saved.

An example of overturning judicial decisions that involves several interesting retrospective issues occurred in the *Property Agents and Motor Dealers Amendment Act 2002* (Qld). Two years earlier, the original Act had established a claim fund with the intention of compensating consumers for losses due to fraud by licensed real estate agents or by people masquerading as such.[31] However, the courts interpreted the Act to include compensation for fraud by 'marketeers', who—while

---

[29] See House of Representatives Committee on the Judiciary, Report 105-028 (105th Congress) available at <http://judiciary.house.gov/legislativereports.aspx>.

[30] *Re Bewley and Commissioner for Superannuation* (1985) 8 ALD 293.

[31] *Property Agents and Motor Dealers Act 2000* (Qld).

they never claimed to be licensed real estate agents—nevertheless were deemed to fulfil a similar role.[32] The amendment proposed by the new Act aimed to overturn this interpretation and explicitly stated that fraud by 'marketeers' would not be compensated by the fund. The amendment clearly had retrospective effect insofar as it changed and, in most cases, denied compensation that could arise from long-past acts of fraud. Indeed, the opposition cited figures that 540 pending claims would be affected. Political argument over the act centred on a variety of themes, including whether or not the new rule was better at all (that is, if it was appropriate to compensate real estate fraud, then why should 'marketeer' fraud not be similarly compensated?),[33] and also about whether reliance on the law as it stood should be upheld.

The government argued that there was no legitimate expectation that it should compensate people for what it claimed was, essentially, a bad investment decision, while the opposition contended that very point; 'We are not just dealing here with something that people could unreasonably expect'.[34] As we will see in Chapter 6, reliance claims do not have their typical force when applied to actions that the individual did not intend at all—for instance, it is highly unlikely that any individual relied on the likelihood of compensation when they set about being defrauded. However, a stronger reliance argument may be able to be made for the 540 individuals who were already involved in the legal process to claim compensation and had begun to structure their affairs accordingly.

The *Criminal Procedure (Amendment) Scotland Act 2002* was passed by the Scottish Parliament as 'emergency legislation' to restore the law to that which was thought to apply before the Court of Criminal Appeal ruling in *Reynolds v. Procurator Fiscal, Linlithgow*.[35] The Court ruled that where an arrest warrant is granted at an intermediate diet[36] because an accused has failed to present, the court must formally cancel the original date set for the trial diet. The accepted practice adopted by courts since the introduction of intermediate diets in 1980 was that the trial diet was automatically cancelled without any formal recording of the cancellation. The effect of the ruling was to render courts incompetent to hear further proceedings, affecting around 7000 pending cases and an unknown number of concluded cases. The Justice Minister commented that the Act 'simply restores the position to that which was thought to apply before the Appeal Court ruling by making clear that the issue of an arrest warrant does automatically cancel the trial diet'.[37]

---

[32] Queensland, 'Second Reading Speech', *Hansard*, 26 November 2002, p. 4737.

[33] Queensland, *Hansard*, 26 November 2002, p. 5351.

[34] Queensland, *Hansard*, 26 November 2002, p. 5350.

[35] Appeal No 1858/00, 14 Februrary 2002, Court of Criminal Appeal (High Court of Justiciary) *available at* <http://www.scotcourts.gov.uk/opinions/1858_00.html>.

[36] 'Diet' is a hearing set by the Scottish Sheriff and District courts in criminal summary cases to ascertain whether the case is likely to proceed to trial on a date assigned.

[37] See 'News Release: Emergency Legislation Introduced', 27/02/2002 available at <http://www.scotland.gov.uk/News/Releases/2002/02/1170>.

Although the *Criminal Procedure (Amendment) Scotland Act* is retrospective, it is unlikely to contravene the prohibition against retrospective criminal legislation in article 7 of the European Convention on Human Rights (ECHR) as enshrined in domestic legislation by the *Human Rights Act 1998* (UK)[38] because 'it creates no crime that did not previously exist; secondly, it constitutes no extension of the jurisdiction of the court'.[39] The legislation was justified on the basis that it prevented the Scottish court system from being thrown into disarray and removed the potential that defendants otherwise guilty of criminal offences would be acquitted on what was effectively a technical or procedural ground. However, there is a strong argument that these justifications for the retrospective nature of the legislation are insufficient to meet the 'compelling grounds of the general interest' exception to the protections contained in Article 6 of the ECHR upholding the rule of law and the right to a fair trial. The three objections are that most of the summary cases affected by the *Reynolds* ruling involved minor offences; most sentences for the concluded cases had already been served and, except for time-barred statutory offences, the Crown, in most cases, would have been able to re-introduce proceedings against any defendant whose appeal based on the decision in *Reynolds* was successful.[40]

By way of concluding comment on curative legislation: in general, persons adversely affected by curative legislation will not be able to claim that they acted in reliance on the defective legislation, and were consequently surprised by the curing of the defects. In most cases, the persons affected will, like the draftsperson of the defective legislation or the legislature which enacted it, have been unaware of these defects. Indeed, they may have organized their affairs in reliance on what the legislature intended the law to be, rather than on what the law was later interpreted to be. In such cases, the reliance argument would actually work in favour of a retrospective statute, since without it, people's reasonable (albeit erroneous) expectations might be defeated. The exception to this is where a person was aware—or believed—that the view of the law being applied by the executive was erroneous and challenged that view in the courts; however, in such cases, curative legislation usually contains a savings provision to protect their reliance interests.

4.3 Beneficial legislation

Obviously, those on whom a law confers a benefit, retrospectively or otherwise, voice few objections. Nor does anyone object when the government voluntarily imposes some disadvantage upon itself or its statutory authorities. The fact that

---

[38] The *Scotland Act 1998* (s 29) provides that an Act of the Scottish Parliament may not include provisions which are incompatible with Convention rights, as defined in the Human Rights Act.

[39] This was the argument used in debates over the validity of a previous Act passed by the Westminster Parliament with similar effect: the *Criminal Procedure (Intermediate Diets) (Scotland) Act 1998*. See House of Commons Hansard Debates, 2 April 1998, column 1473.

[40] David Leighton, 'No Compelling Grounds for Retrospective Legislation' (2002) *Journal of the Law Society of Scotland* 20 available at <http://www.journalonline.co.uk>.

these statutes rarely create controversy may mean that people are generally unaware that retrospective statutes can be beneficial; yet such statutes are actually quite frequent and have become increasingly more so in recent years. Indeed, some of the examples of curative legislation above can perhaps be classed as instances of beneficial retrospectivity. However, the statutes discussed in this section can be distinguished from those in the previous section, because they are purely beneficial: they are, in effect, the statutory equivalents of *ex gratia* payments, in the sense that the persons receiving the benefits would have had no expectation that the benefit would be conferred. An example is the greater consumer protections enshrined in the Consumer Credit Bill 2005 (UK) with the retrospective application of the Bill's new unfair relationship test, enabling consumers to challenge unfair practices and contract terms in court. The Finance and Leasing Association commented adversely on the retrospective application of the provisions creating uncertainty and the potential impact on the United Kingdom's £235 billion per year securitization market. However, the government response was that: 'Many credit agreements run for a considerable length of time. Without a retrospective dimension to the Bill, too many people will be left uncovered by the protection that it offers'.[41] The Joint Committee on Human Rights reported that the application of the unfair credit relationship provisions to existing agreements created no significant risk of incompatibility with the principle of legal certainty in Article 1 of the ECHR: 'the very purpose of Acts of Parliament is to alter the existing legal situation and this will often involve altering existing rights for the future'.[42]

The government's response to industry criticism of the Consumer Credit Bill was somewhat confused because the number of people benefiting from any law could be increased if it were made retrospective. However, to the extent that others lose out, this merely increases the extent to which the law affects others adversely. However, despite this flaw in the government's reasoning, three points can be made. First, governments are reminded that in drafting such legislation they should not only listen to those who claim to lose from retrospective legislation but look to who may benefit from it. Secondly, the fact that contracts may continue into the future and may purport to regulate the relationships between citizens for a long time means that it is not unreasonable for legislation to prospectively alter the future relationship and it is not clear that this change is truly retrospective merely because the relationship started in the past. This, in essence, was the conclusion reached by the Joint Committee on Human Rights. There is broad social acceptance of governments legislating to change family law, employment law, contract and company law in ways that affect the future relationships between those who have commenced those relationships in the past. Third, in this example, the

---

[41] House of Commons Hansard Debates, 14 July 2005, vol. 436 part 34, column 1015.
[42] UK Joint Committee on Human Rights, *Scrutiny: Seventh Progress Report*, Fifteenth Report of Session 2004–5, p. 8.

alleged disruptive effects to the economy or a particular industry can only be substantial if the number of unfair contracts were substantial. If the industry were to claim the latter, then it indicts itself and provides a justification for major remedial action.

Benefits conferred by retrospective legislation may take a number of other forms. First, the legislature may decide to forgo revenue to which it is legally entitled. For example, the *Taxation Laws Amendment Act (No 5) 1990* (Cth) retrospectively widened the capital gains tax exemption for homes purchased as principal places of residence. Another example of a retrospective exemption occurred in the *Community Ambulance Cover Amendment Act 2004* (Qld). The Queensland Government's ambulance tax on electricity accounts impacted on people in a number of unforeseen and inequitable ways, resulting in the imposition of multiple levies upon the one residence/owner. For instance, some domestic premises were taxed twice merely because they had an additional electricity connection for a stand-alone hot-water system. The amending legislation exempted such premises from having to pay the tax twice, and the exemptions were backdated in order to give statutory backing to informal exemptions that had previously been put in place by the government in response to public outcry over the defects of the original Act.[43]

Secondly, the legislature may confer a benefit by retrospectively conferring a right to payments or allowances. For example, the *Veterans' Affairs Legislation Amendment Act 1989* (Cth) backdated certain pension increases. The benefit conferred, however, may be non-financial or only indirectly financial. An example of such legislation is the extension of the period of validity for drivers' licences issued under the *Motor Car Act 1958* (Vic) from twelve months to three years. Notably, the subject of the benefit need not be a citizen of the country—or indeed an individual at all. Retrospective legislation such as the Customs Tariff Amendment Bill (No 1) 2003 (Cth) was justified on the basis that it benefited the newly formed country of East Timor.

Most of these acts are obviously unproblematic; they can be justified as readily as any other prospective (or retrospective) legislation. However, it would be a mistake to assume that such legislation is always and completely unproblematic, and we would caution against ignoring them completely when discussing retrospective legislation. For some, beneficial legislation may have non-beneficial side effects. In particular, any government payment reduces the options for other initiatives. Every dollar foregone in a 'beneficial' retrospective statute is a dollar that is unavailable for welfare payments, infrastructure or tax cuts. Public Choice theorists should be particularly careful as this is an area where lobbyists may plead for favours for their constituencies without any possibility of wider public benefit.[44] Moreover, being retrospective, the law cannot offer citizens an incentive

---

[43] Queensland, *Hansard*, 5 October 2004, p. 2669.
[44] See James M Buchanan and Gordon Tullock, *The Calculus of Consent: Logical Foundations of Constitutional Democracy* (University of Michigan Press, 1962).

for future good behaviour—thus wasting a potentially costly benefit. Thus, beneficial retrospective legislation should be carefully judged in the same way as non-beneficial retrospective legislation: by the normal standards of justice and equity as to its content, with reliance arguments (both positive and negative) being considered.

4.4 Subordinate legislation

Legislatures are generally wary of retrospective subordinate legislation; its potential significance means that they mostly prefer retrospective legislation to be principal legislation and may, like the Commonwealth of Australia, legislate to that effect. Section 48(2) of the *Acts Interpretation Act* states:

Regulations shall not be expressed to take effect from a date before the date of notification in any case where, if the regulations so took effect: the rights of a person (other than the Commonwealth or an authority of the Commonwealth) existing at the date of notification, would be affected in a manner prejudicial to that person; or liabilities would be imposed on any person (other than the Commonwealth or an authority of the Commonwealth) in respect of anything done or omitted to be done before the date of notification; and where, in any regulations, any provision is made in contravention of this subsection, that provision has no effect.

The Australian Senate Standing Committee on Regulations and Ordinances is not concerned so much with regulatory powers as with the regulations themselves. The SSCRO is required to recommend to the Senate the disallowance of any retrospective legislative instrument which is not accompanied by the relevant Minister's explicit assurance that no individual apart from the Commonwealth will be deleteriously affected.[45] This gives the Committee considerable power to ensure that only the most uncontentious legislation is ever passed.

Analogous legislative restrictions on retrospective subordinate instruments do not apply to the Parliament of the United Kingdom. Statutory instruments are subject to 'parliamentary approval' only in the sense that they are 'laid before Parliament'. Despite scrutiny by the House of Commons Standing Committee on Delegated Legislation, the Joint Committee on Statutory Instruments and, perhaps, the Joint Committee on Human Rights, subordinate legislation will automatically become law after a short period as objections will rarely sway the government of the day. Of course, many retrospective statutory instruments may be curative or beneficial in nature. Examples include the Local Government Pension Scheme (Amendment) Regulations 2005 which revoked previous regulations with retrospective effect to ensure continued solvency of a pension scheme; and the Duration of Copyright and Rights in Performances Regulations 1995 (UK)

---

[45] See, for example, Australia, Standing Committee on Regulations and Ordinances, '109th Report', Senate, October 2000, p. 13.

which harmonized the length of copyright protection for existing works irrespective of when they were created to bring UK law in line with the European Council Directive on Term of Protection of Copyright 1993.[46]

However, more controversial is the *Extradition Act 2003* (Designation of Part 2 Territories) Order 2003 (Statutory Instrument 20003/3334), which came into force 1 January 2004 and has the effect of ratifying the controversial Extradition Treaty between the United Kingdom and the United States with retrospective criminal consequences. The treaty removes the requirement on the United States to provide *prima facie* evidence when requesting the extradition of people from the United Kingdom (but not the United Kingdom's obligation to satisfy the constitutional 'probable cause' requirement when seeking the extradition of United States nationals). The statutory instrument has retrospective criminal consequences because its effect is to remove the right of British citizens facing more than a year in jail to argue that there is no *prima facie* evidence linking them to the offence. Article 22(1) of the Treaty covers offences committed before its entry into force. It is now possible that the United States will be successful in a new extradition application, despite a failed earlier attempt based on insufficient evidence, even in cases automatically leading to the imposition of the death penalty.[47] Implementing the treaty through a statutory instrument rather than primary legislation enabled the British government to avoid normal parliamentary debate in both Houses.[48]

Of course the real problem with this measure is the nature of the power (its potential for abuse and arbitrary application) rather than its retrospective nature *per se*. However, there is also a strong argument that individuals previously subject to a failed extradition procedure because of a judicial determination of insufficient evidence should be able to rely on the finality of this decision and not be subject to a further attempt at extradition based on a lower evidentiary standard.

4.5 Procedural legislation

It is a normal presumption of statutory interpretation that, absent clear intention to the contrary, statutes do not have retrospective operation. But procedural statutes are generally applied retrospectively to all actions or proceedings that are

---

[46] See 'Frequently Asked Questions about Copyright', Technical Advisory Service for Images, available at <http://www.tasi.ac.uk/advice/managing/copyright-faq.html>; and 'Intellectual Property Rights: Overview of Intellectual Property by the JISC Legal Information Service available at <http://www.jisclegal.ac.uk/ipr/IntellectualProperty>.

[47] An example is the case of Algerian Pilot Lofti Raissi wanted by the United States on dubious FBI evidence for alleged hijacking. The United States still regards him as a 'suspect' despite no clear evidence which resulted in the UK refusing an extradition request: see Statewatch report available at <http://www.statewatch.org/news/2003/jul/25ukus/htm> and report by 'Cage Prisoners' available at <http://www.cageprisoners.com/prisoners.php?id+1329>.

[48] See David Hencke, 'Bunkett offers US easier extradition of Britons', *The Guardian*, 15 December 2003 and Statewatch News 'UK applies new simplified extradition procedures to USA and over a hundred other countries', 4 January 2004, available at <http://www.statewatch.org/news/2004/jan/06extradition.htm>.

not complete at the time of enactment, no matter when the right to the action accrued. The reason courts prefer to apply procedural statutes retrospectively is no doubt to avoid the complications that would result if they had to apply different procedural rules according to when the action accrued or was instituted. This is generally considered acceptable:

No suitor has any vested interest in the course of procedure, nor any right to complain, if during the litigation the procedure is changed, provided, of course, that no injustice is done.[49]

In other words, where procedural changes are concerned, courts assume that rights are not affected, making it no injustice to apply the changes to all pending cases. However, as the above statement makes clear, this presumption is rebuttable. If injustice *would* be occasioned by the application of a procedural change to an existing action, the change should not be applied.

Therefore, there is considered to be a dichotomy between procedural rules (changes to which are presumed not to give rise to injustice), and substantive rights (which, as we saw in Chapter 3, it is presumed unjust to trespass upon). Justice Fullegar in *Maxwell v. Murphy*[50] described this distinction as between 'statutes which create or modify or abolish substantive rights or liabilities on the one hand, and statutes which deal with the pursuit of remedies on the other hand'. But he went on to note that the distinction 'has not unnaturally been criticized on the grounds that it does not represent a logical dichotomy'... if one traces any substantive right back far enough, it will be found 'secreted in the interstices of procedure'.[51] Thus, the distinction is not a clear one, and this may give rise to controversy over procedural legislation, especially in the criminal sphere.[52]

There are several types of legislation which fall under the category of procedural legislation, including statutes of limitations, rights of subrogation and new remedies or penalties.

Statutes of limitation

As far as the courts are concerned, statutes of limitation are presumed to be procedural, but the presumption is rebuttable.[53] In particular, 'statutes which enable a person to enforce a cause of action which was then barred, or provide a bar to an existing cause of action by abridging the time for its institution, could hardly be described as merely procedural'.[54]

An example of such legislation is the *Taxation Administration Amendment (Recovery of Tax Debt) Act 1986* (Cth), which was passed in order to overcome the

---

[49] *Republic of Costa Rica v. Erlanger* (1876) 3 Ch D 62 at 69 per Mellis LJ; quoted by Dixon CJ in *Maxwell v. Murphy* (1957) 96 CLR 261 at 267. [50] Ibid, at 285.

[51] *Maxwell v. Murphy* (1957) 96 CLR 261at 285.

[52] Sheena McMurtrie argues that the procedural/substantive distinction is 'merely a weapon that the courts can use' in their dislike of retrospective legislation. See McMurtrie (1992) at 142.

[53] Ibid, at 286–91 per Fullegar J. [54] Ibid, at 278 per Williams J.

effect of the decision of the Queensland Supreme Court in *Deputy Commissioner of Taxation v. Moorebank Pty Ltd*.[55] Prior to that decision, the ATO had always assumed that taxation debts could, by virtue of Crown prerogative, be recovered at any time. In *Moorebank*, however, it was held that the relevant State or Territory limitation periods apply to such debts as they do for private citizens. The Deputy Commissioner appealed to the High Court; meanwhile, this Act was passed to provide that the relevant limitation period would apply, not from the date when the action accrued, but from the date when there were finalized all proceedings arising out of any objections to the assessment of the debt. These provisions applied to all actions for taxation debt, whether they accrued before or after the commencement of the section, other than those which had been determined before the introduction of the Bill on the basis that a limitation period applied.

Whether this extension of the limitation period could be described as procedural would depend upon whether the statute revived any actions which would otherwise have been statute-barred, or whether it simply allowed extra time for the issuing of proceedings in respect of actions which had not yet been barred. Even if it did revive certain actions, however, it is doubtful that any unfairness was caused. The law that was finally applied was indeed the law that was discoverable at the time the taxpayer (T) acted. T cannot have relied on a lack of action being taken before it was time barred and was not disadvantaged because the action was in fact taken during a retrospectively extended limitation period. The only basis for an argument that T was disadvantaged was if, after the limitation period ran out and before the Bill to retrospectively extend the limitation period was enacted, and T relying on his freedom from tax, invested in an asset that would have to be sold at a loss to pay the tax debt. However, this would not be a reason against the retrospective legislation. It is merely a reason to provide T with the opportunity to make a case to court that the hardship of selling such assets should allow a reduction in, or deferral of, the liability.[56] The ATO could still only recover the amount of tax which had been payable before the expiration of the limitation period, while no taxpayer would be 'ambushed' by an unexpected tax liability. It was on essentially the same ground that the US Supreme Court held that a statute retrospectively allowing the collection of tax debts that had become statute-barred did not breach the due process clause of the US Constitution.[57] Ultimately, however, the High Court upheld the Deputy Commissioner's appeal, thus rendering the Act unnecessary.[58]

---

[55] (1986) 70 ALR 357.

[56] Legislatures may well decide against such provisions as they are rare and complicated. It could be argued that most investments in capitalist economies are profitable most of the time and few would suffer from the retrospective change. In addition, a government that allowed a reduced payment because of losses on such investments that would not have taken place except for the delay in collecting tax should also seek to capture the windfall gains of most investments made because of such delays.   [57] *Graham v. Goodcel* (1930) 282 US 409 at 430; 75 Law Ed 415 at 440.

[58] *Deputy Federal Commissioner of Taxation v. Moorebank Pty Ltd* (1988) 165 CLR 55.

In 1995 the United States Supreme Court in *Plaut v. Spendthrift Farm*[59] struck down as unconstitutional section 27A(b) of the *Securities Exchange Act* of 1934, which provided for the reinstatement of any action alleging fraud and deceit in the sale of stock commenced prior to the Supreme Court's ruling in *Lampf v. Gilbertson*,[60] that such an action was, in fact, time-barred. The *Lampf* decision applied new legislation reducing the limitations period applicable to private actions for securities fraud retroactively, with the effect of dismissing cases that had been within time when they were filed. However, the Court in *Plaut* held that section 27A(b) did not merely have a remedial procedural effect but violated the Constitution's separation of powers by requiring federal courts to reopen final judgments entered before the provision's enactment.

Rights of subrogation

Rights of subrogation (which can arise by agreement, or by operation of law) give one person the right to pursue another's legal claim as if it were that person's own. For example, a Victorian statute, the *Legal Profession Practice (Amendment) Act 1989*, applied where the innocent employer of a defalcating (that is, embezzling) solicitor had paid compensation to the solicitor's victim. Section 12 gave the employer a right of subrogation to the victim's normal claim against the Solicitor's Guarantee Fund (SGF)—a right that already existed when the defalcating and the compensating solicitors were partners. The conferral of this right was backdated to 6 November 1986.[61] Exercising the right would, in turn, give the SGF a right of subrogation on the part of the fund against the defalcating solicitor.

A defalcating employee solicitor might, perhaps, argue that it was unfair that they could be sued as a result of someone exercising a right of subrogation that did not exist when the embezzlement occurred. But such a solicitor could not argue that he or she was being sued for something that was not actionable at the time or that the legal consequences of his defalcation were other than those discoverable at the time. Indeed, ensuring that the person who was ultimately liable for the cost of compensation was the person who had caused the loss probably advanced the cause of justice. It also provided an extra way for the victims to receive the compensation they deserved (but not a right to be compensated twice). Accordingly, those who bore the new burden were entitled to ensure that the burden was no greater than providing a more prompt and certain remedy for the victims.

---

[59] 514 US 211 (1995).   [60] 501 US 350 (1991).

[61] This was not the date of an earlier amendment, nor was the provision mentioned in the Parliamentary debates on the Bill, so its significance can only be guessed at. But, it is, at least, plausible that Parliament fixed that date so as to give a right of action to a specific compensating solicitor.

New remedies or penalties

On several occasions, courts have ruled that statutes that give the judiciary new powers to grant a remedy, or to make an order, are procedural.[62] The conclusion that all statutes concerning new remedies or penalties are procedural is debatable, since a novel remedy or order could drastically alter the outcome of particular litigation. The issue is even more controversial when the penalty for a criminal offence is increased: the cases are divided as to whether the penalty to be imposed on a convicted person is that which existed at the time of the offence, or that which exists at the date of conviction.[63]

An example from Australia is the *Crimes Legislation Amendment Act 1989* (Cth). The relevant sections dealt with penalties for persons convicted of narcotics offences under the *Customs Act 1901* (Cth). The pecuniary penalty that can be imposed under the Principal Act is calculated by reference to the benefit the person derived from engaging in the drugs trade. One of the 1989 amendments allowed the court to 'lift the corporate veil' in making this calculation, and to treat as the defendant's any property under that person's 'effective control'.[64] The amendment applied to proceedings instituted before the commencement of the amending Act where the hearings had not yet begun. It did not, therefore, increase the maximum penalty that existed at the time of the offence, but rather increased the likelihood that the penalty imposed would accurately reflect the benefit a person had derived from involvement in the narcotics trade.

A related amendment allowed the court to order that a pecuniary penalty could be satisfied from property that it considered to be under the defendant's effective control. Such an order could be sought and made at any time after the hearing at which the pecuniary penalty was imposed, including where the person against whom the order was sought had been tried, convicted and sentenced before the commencement of the amending Act.[65] Again, this would not mean that a heavier penalty could be imposed, but only that it would be more likely that the penalty already imposed would actually be recovered. The only expectations which might have been defeated by this legislation would be an expectation by a person accused or convicted of trafficking in narcotics that they would be able to retain some of the profits of this activity by hiding them behind a corporate veil. Such an expectation is illegitimate. It is clearly not based on the underlying purposes of the law. Indeed, it is based on an attempt to avoid the penalty the law had clearly intended to impose. Supporting such expectations would undermine the law.

Other procedural cases arise similar to the case of the Solicitor's Clerk discussed in Chapter 2, where the status or character of the person considered relevant for

---

[62] See *Minister for Home and Territories v. Smith* (1924) 35 CLR 120; *Realty Development & Mortgage Co Ltd v. Londish* (1967) 87 WN (Pt 1) (NSW) 92; and *Re Hassell, ex parte Pride* (1984) 52 ALR 181. All of these are summarized in Dennis C Pearce and RS Geddes, *Statutory Interpretation in Australia* (Butterworths, 1988) 190.   [63] Pearce and Geddes, pp. 171–2.
[64] Section 243C.   [65] Section 21.

their obtaining a job or licence take into account previous actions of that person. This occurred most recently in the *Transport and Other Legislation Amendment Act 2004* (Qld) which prevents people convicted of child sex offences from holding a public bus licence. The Department of Transport found that 38 current drivers were disqualified on this basis and announced that 'letters have been sent notifying the drivers that they are ineligible to hold driver's authorisations and their driver's authorisation licence has been cancelled. There is no appeal against this decision'.[66]

Retrospective changes to the assessment of civil liability for negligent acts occurred in the *Civil Liability Act 2003* (Qld). Apart from certain special provisions the Act was taken to have commenced on 2 December 2002; the legislation contains detailed provisions curtailing common law personal injury claims. Any pending litigation claims, and future claims arising from earlier incidents, were caught within its ambit. The Act limits both the types of actions that give rise to a negligence claim and the amount of damages that can be awarded by the courts. The Queensland Government in the Act's Explanatory Memoranda claimed that the impact of increasing litigation and open-ended payouts on insurance premiums constituted a compelling reason for the retrospectivity.

As noted above, some types of retrospective procedural legislation border on making changes to criminal law. For instance, the *Child Protection (Offender Reporting) Act 2004* (Qld) imposed a variety of new and substantially increased requirements for offenders previously sentenced—and indeed released. Such requirements involved having to personally report regularly to police stations, to advise of travel plans and club memberships and, on occasions, be fingerprinted and photographed. For the more serious crimes, the length of reporting period is the life of the offender. Another act with similar requirements was the earlier *Sexual Offences (Protection of Children) Amendment Act 2002* (Qld). The Scrutiny of Legislation Committee (Qld) noted the evident concerns with this sort of legislation: namely that it involved 'a retrospective change which, though not technically "punishment" ... nevertheless represents a substantial imposition on an offender'.[67] An explicit *substantive* change which retrospectively altered the legal punishment accruing from an act not only after the incident or after the initial sentencing but, in fact, after the completion of sentencing would be highlighted as a serious and presumably quite controversial example of retrospective legislation; yet Acts, such as this one, involve—through retrospective *procedural* amendments—ultimately similar effects.

In the United States, the Supreme Court in *Landgraf v. USI Film Products*[68] has considered this issue as part of an examination of the principles to be applied

---

[66] Queensland, 'Comments by Mr Lucas', *Hansard*, 20 July 2004, p. 258. Another recent example is the *Workplace Relations Amendments (Codifying Contempt Offences) Act 2004* (Cth) which retrospectively excludes from a trade union any individual found guilty of a violent crime.

[67] Queensland, 'Scrutiny of Legislation Committee (Qld): Alert Digest 11', 26 November 2002, p. 22.   [68] (1994) 511 US 244.

in considering the extent to which legislation should be construed as retrospective in operation. The Court held that *Civil Rights Act 1991* which added compensatory and punitive damages to the remedies available to victims of intentional discrimination did not apply retroactively to actions challenging discrimination acts that occurred before the passage of the Act. This issue had been left unresolved by Congress, leading to confusion in the lower courts.[69] The Court held that the punitive damages clauses shared key characteristics of criminal sanctions and would raise a serious question under the *ex post facto* clause if retroactively imposed. The Court also found that the compensatory damages provision conferred a new right to monetary relief and substantially increased the liability of employers for harms. However, Justice Blackmun in dissent characterized the effect of the provisions as procedural and would have allowed the statute to operate retrospectively:

At no time within the last generation has an employer had a vested right to engage in or to permit sexual harassment; "there is no such thing as a vested right to do wrong" ... Section 102 of the Act expands the remedies available for acts of intentional discrimination, but does not alter the scope of the employee's basic right to be free from discrimination or the employer's corresponding legal duty. There is nothing unjust about holding an employer responsible for injuries caused by conduct that has been illegal for almost 30 years.[70]

The Landgraf Court ruled that the traditional presumption against legislative retrospectivity in the absence of clear Congressional intent is triggered when the statute would 'impair rights a party possessed when he acted, increase a party's liability for past conduct, or impose new duties with respect to transactions already completed'.[71] Subsequent courts have confirmed that this formulation of categories triggering the presumption is non-exclusive; it 'does not purport to define the outer limit of impermissible retroactivity'.[72] The *Landgraf* Court held that new statutes are to be applied to pending cases, even in the absence of specific legislative intent, when a court is considering granting injunctive relief; when the statute addresses a court's jurisdiction, *or when the statute changes procedural rules*.[73] Two subsequent cases, *Ins v. St Cyr*[74] and *Austria v. Altmann*,[75] have considered the application of the *Landgraf* principles to the *Illegal Immigration Reform and Immigrant Responsibility Act 1996* (IIRIRA) and the *Federal Sovereign Immunities Act 1976* (FSIA) respectively. In *Ins v. St Cyr* the Supreme Court held in a 5:4 opinion that the IIRIRA's removal of the Attorney-General's discretion to

[69] See Scott M Pearson, 'Canons, Presumptions and Manifest Injustice: Retroactivity of the Civil Rights Act of 1991' (1993) 3 *Southern California Interdisciplinary Law Journal* 461.
[70] Legal Information Institute Supreme Court Collection available at <http://straylight.law.cornell.edu/supct/html/92-757.ZS.html>. [71] (1994) 511 US 244 at 273.
[72] *Hughes Aircraft Company v. United States* 520 US 939 (1997) at <http://laws.findlaw.com/us/520/939.html>.
[73] (1994) 511 US 244 at 273–9, emphasis added. See discussion of this case and of legislative retrospectivity in the US in Jill E Fisch, 'Retroactivity and Legal Change: An Equilibrium Approach', (1997) 110 *Harvard Law Review* 1055 at 1063–66; 1091–94. [74] 533 US 289 (2001).
[75] 124 S Ct 2240 (2004).

waive deportation of permanent residents who had been convicted of criminal offences did not have retrospective effect. There was no clear indication that Congress intended the Act to have retroactive effect and the Court thus undertook a *Landgraf* analysis to 'determine whether IIRIRA attaches new legal consequences to events completed before its enactment, a judgment informed and guided by considerations of fair notice, reasonable reliance, and settled expectations'.[76] The defendant had agreed to plead guilty to a drug offence in a plea bargain arrangement on the clear understanding that there was a strong likelihood that the discretion to waive deportation would be exercised in his favour; the Court observed that the retrospective denial of the possibility of discretionary relief offended against the *Landgraf* guidelines.

In the *Altmann* case, which concerned a claim against Austria for restitution for the expropriation of valuable artwork from a Jewish home during the Nazi era, the United States Supreme Court held that the FSIA, which allows civil suits against foreign states if the sovereign was not entitled to immunity under the Act or protected by an international agreement, was intended to have retrospective effect by Congress. The Court held that the unique subject matter of the Act (clarifying the application of sovereign immunity) meant that it did not clearly fit into the retroactive harm categories under a Landgraf analysis, and further that substantive rights were not impaired because sovereign immunity 'has always been a gesture of comity and not an absolute right'.[77] Academic commentary also supports the conclusion that the 'FSIA only opens US courts to pre-existing claims against foreign states and does not increase liabilities or impose new duties... while the FSIA may appear to affect substantive rights by creating jurisdiction where none otherwise existed, the FSIA only affects substantive rights incidentally'.[78]

We would argue that the Landgraf approach to statutory interpretation is desirable as it calls for an examination of the specific effects of the legislative change before the new rule can be invalidated; and recognizes that the increase in sanctions argument against retrospectivity is usually not a good one because of the deterrence justification underlying the initial creation of the offence. If the offender argues that they would not have broken the law if they had known that the penalty would have been so high, this would, in fact, seem to justify the retrospective imposition of the new sanction. If the law recognizes this kind of reliance, it makes law breaking more, not less, likely. Of course, most of the effectiveness of the new sanction is through affecting future behaviour rather than punishing past behaviour. Nevertheless, that imposition of the higher sanction at the earliest opportunity reminds people of this. It also reminds people not to treat the criminal law as a Benthamite bargain.

---

[76] 533 US 289 (2001) at 291.   [77] 124 S Ct 2240 (2004) at 2252.
[78] Seanna C Balfe, 'Case Comments: International Law—Retroactive Application of Foreign Sovereign Immunities Act Allows Claims for Pre-Enactment Conduct—Austria v. Altmann, 124 S Ct 2240 (2004)' (2005) 28 *Suffolk Transnational Law Review* 359 at 365–6.

However, there are limits to this argument; and there is potential for abuse of the category of retrospective procedural amendments imposing altered conditions of punishment. In the next category, that of retrospective criminal law, we examine the recent development in United States jurisprudence of such distinctions between substantive/procedural and criminal/civil legislative amendments as a means of overcoming the otherwise broad prohibition of retrospective criminal laws contained in the *ex post facto* clause of the United States Constitution.[79]

In the United Kingdom, Part 10 of the *Criminal Justice Act 2003* removes the protection of the double jeopardy rule for individuals acquitted of a broad range of criminal offences, with retrospective effect, when the Court of Appeal is satisfied that there is new and compelling evidence.[80] 'Compelling' evidence is defined as reliable, substantial and, 'in the context of the outstanding issues, it appears highly probative of the case against the acquitted person'.[81] The provisions have been heavily criticized by the National Council for Civil Liberties on broad due process grounds (degradation of the principle of finality and diminished chance of a fair trial) as well as the potential for the retrospective targeting of particular individuals:

The qualifying offences (those offences for which a retrial is possible) are set down in schedule 4. A total of 29 offences are listed (as well as conspiracy to commit any of these 29 offences). The offences include robbery, drugs trafficking and "seizing or exercising control of the Channel Tunnel system". There does not seem to be any logic or pattern to the offences that have been selected. We are left with the impression that the government has decided on a list of defendants who, in their opinion, should have their cases retried and produced a list of offences to accommodate them. This list is far more extensive than the one originally suggested . . . which limited the qualifying offences to murder, rape, manslaughter and armed robbery.[82]

In Australia, the most controversial recent example of procedural legislation at the Commonwealth level is the *Migration Amendment (Excision from Migration Zone) Act 2001* (Cth). This Act was retrospective in order to cover the 'boat-people' brought to Christmas Island (in Australian waters) by the *Tampa* (whose

---

[79] See section on retrospective criminal legislation below.

[80] See Robert L Weinberg, 'England is Abandoning the Fifth Amendment Rights that it Bequeathed to the United States', 29 AUG Champion 50. In Australia, the draft Criminal Appeal Amendment (Double Jeopardy) Bill 2003 (NSW) is modelled upon the UK version and also has retrospective effect although it is yet to be presented to the New South Wales Parliament although other states are largely unsupportive of analogous legislation despite the controversial Queensland case of Raymond John Carroll, who was acquitted on appeal for the murder of an infant (*Carroll v. R* (1985) 19 A Crim R 410) and subsequent attempts to obtain a conviction for perjury failed all the way to the High Court based on the application of the double jeopardy rule: *R v. Carroll, ex parte AG* [2001] QCA 394; *R v. Carroll* (2003) ALR 1. See discussion of double jeopardy by the University of NSW Council for Civil Liberties at <http://www.nswccl.org.au/unswccl/issues/double%20jeopardy.php>.

[81] *Criminal Justice Act 2003* (UK) s 78.

[82] National Council for Civil Liberties, 'Liberty's briefing on the Criminal Justice Bill for the House of Lords', June 2003, available at University of NSW Council for Civil Liberties website <http://www.nswccl.org.au/unswccl/issues/double%20jeopardy.php>.

acrimonious history was outlined earlier in this chapter) as well as arrivals at a similar date on other outlying islands. The Act altered the migration zones around Australia by creating the categories of 'excised offshore places', with the effect that the 'offshore entry persons' were not able to apply for protection visas under the *Migration Act 1958* (Cth), and could effectively be denied status as refugees. The Act's excision of Australian territory for migration purposes only has been scathingly referred to as creating:

legal fictions... unacceptable from the perspective of the rule of law. The Alice in Wonderland contortion and the extent to which the legislation strains to call a spade a sea anchor, or anything other than what it is, will... take its toll on the credibility of the laws enacted in haste.[83]

The retrospectivity of this legislation is of particular concern because it arguably falls under the feature of attainder and 'thinning the veil' discussed in Chapter 3. The Democrats and Greens argued in the Senate that the Act was 'purely a device to allow the government and the Department of Immigration and Multicultural Affairs to achieve their long-term objective of exempting their refugee status determination processes from proper review'.[84] The question to consider is whether this change in Migration Zones was enacted because it was deemed to be a better law, or whether the law functioned with fine-grained discrimination by targeting a group of people whose status was deemed objectionable to the executive.

The Democrats and the Greens strongly objected to what they saw as the racial and discriminatory aspects of the entire 'Pacific Solution' legislative package. They asked if a boatload or planeload of white Zimbabweans would have been treated in the same way.[85] If the government would have acted differently in such a case, the legislation might be seen to exemplify the fears of Munzer and Walker— retrospectivity allowing fine-grained discrimination while masquerading as generalized legislation.[86] Against this, it could be argued that the original *Migration*

[83] Kim Rubenstein, 'Citizenship, Sovereignty and Migration: Australia's Exclusive Approach to Membership of the Community', paper presented to seminar 'Boundless Plains to Share? Australia's Response to the MV Tampa Asylum Seekers', Institute for Comparative and International Law, University of Melbourne, 11 October 2001, p. 9.

[84] Australia, *Hansard*, Senate, 24 September 2001, Commonwealth Parliament, p. 27695 (Comments by Senator Bartlett). As with the Border Protection Act, the Democrats and Greens proposed various amendments which were rejected by the government, including removing the Henry VIII clause enabling subsequent additions to the definition of 'excised offshore areas' to be made by regulation; limiting the period of mandatory detention in an excised offshore place to 14 days; and introducing a sunset clause to limit the Act's lifespan.

[85] See Australia, *Hansard*, Senate, 20 September 2001, p. 27710 (Senator Bourne); and 25 September 2001, p. 27822 (Senator Ridgeway comments that more than 80 per cent of Afghan or Iraqi asylum seekers who have come to Australia have been accepted as genuine refugees under the statutory migration regime).

[86] Geoffrey de Q Walker, *The Rule of Law: Foundation of Constitutional Democracy* (Melbourne University Press, Melbourne, 1988) 316; and Stephen R Munzer 'A Theory of Retroactive Legislation' (1982) 61(3) *Texas Law Review* 463.

Act was, itself, designed to limit the number of people able to apply for Australian protection-visas by stipulating that Australia's migration zone applied only to the low-water line of Australia's territories, and not, as one might intuitively suppose, all the area over which Australia holds sovereignty.[87] By increasing the hurdles involved before any person may apply for a visa, the Act, presumably, intended to limit the number (and possibly type) of people who Australia is obliged to process in accordance with its international obligations.[88] One of the possible justifications for such a limitation may be that it allows the government the capacity to create an effective response to the criminal activity of people-smuggling.[89] If this is a plausible construal of the intention of the initial legislation, then it might be argued—against the above concerns—that the amendment was merely an extension of, or improved mechanism towards furthering, the general intention behind the original Act.

4.6 Retrospective criminal legislation

Australian examples

Retrospective criminal legislation is one of the rarest forms of retrospective legislation and is one of the most controversial. However, it has so far withstood challenge in Australian courts. Despite Justice Kirby's view that '[it] is a departure from fundamental principle to create new legal offences with retrospective effect',[90] the High Court has never questioned that the Commonwealth and States have the power to enact retrospective laws—even criminal laws—in principal legislation. In the two most prominent cases—*Kable*[91] and *Polyukhovich*[92]—the High Court held that the Parliament's power to enact retrospective laws included not only civil remedies and criminal laws declaratory of the common law, but also criminal laws creating new criminal offences or

---

[87] Indeed, it could be argued that the original *Migration Act* was a 'cynical attempt' to avoid international refugee obligations created by the 1951 Refugee Convention. Centre for Comparative Constitutional Studies and the Institute for Comparative and International Law, 'International Law and the Tampa Affair: A Legal Twilight Zone', Centre for Comparative Constitutional Studies and the Institute for Comparative and International Law, The University of Melbourne, 11 October 2001, p. 5.   [88] Ibid, p. 5.

[89] This objective was stated in the Explanatory Memorandum to the Migration Legislation Amendment (Further Border Protection Measures) Bill 2001 (Cth) which sought to retrospectively extend the number of 'excised offshore areas' to almost 3000 islands after the Senate disallowed regulations to the same effect made under the *Migration Amendment (Excision from Migration Zone) Act* amendments to the *Migration Act*. This Act failed in the Senate—the Federal Election had since been held and the Australian Labor Party, safely returned to opposition, felt free to finally oppose the government's immigration policy.

[90] *Lipohar v. The Queen* (1999) 200 CLR 485 at 543 (per Kirby J).

[91] *Kable v. Director of Public Prosecutions (NSW)* (1996) 189 CLR 51.

[92] *Polyukhovich v. The Commonwealth* (1991) 172 CLR 501 ('The War Crimes Act Case'). This case is discussed in detail below in the section 'War Crimes Legislation'.

extending the scope of extraterritoriality for Australian courts to have jurisdiction over them.[93]

The case of *Kable v. Director of Public Prosecutions (NSW)*[94] challenged the validity of the *Community Protection Act 1994* (NSW). This Act was passed in order to authorize the making of a detention order against Kable who was at the time serving a prison sentence for the manslaughter of his wife. There was a concern that he would pose a danger to members of the wife's family upon his release. The Act allowed for an order to be made for the detention of a specified person in prison for a specified period if the New South Wales Supreme Court was satisfied that 'the person is more likely than not to commit a serious act of violence and that it was appropriate, for the protection of a particular person or the community generally' that the person be held in custody.[95] However, the Act also specified that 'the object of this Act is to protect the community by providing for the preventive detention . . . of Gregory Wayne Kable . . . This Act authorizes the making of a detention order against Gregory Wayne Kable and does not authorize the making of a detention order against any other person'.[96]

Kable's challenge to this order in the Court of Appeal was unsuccessful; however, his appeal to the High Court resulted in the Act being declared unconstitutional. The reason for this ruling, however, was not the retrospective nature of the law. Rather, it was the fact that the legislation effectively directed the courts to rule a particular way in cases involving a named individual. This was taken to transgress the strict constitutional separation between legislative and judicial power. Because the New South Wales Supreme Court exercises federal judicial power, legislation could not require the Court to exercise what was an executive function; inconsistent with the separation of powers contained in section 71 of the Commonwealth Constitution. In the words of Justice Gummow, this would render the judiciary little more than 'an arm of the executive which implements the will of the legislature'.[97] However, the Court reiterated that 'no non-territorial restraints upon parliamentary supremacy arise from the nature of a power to make laws for peace, order (or welfare), and good government or from the notion that there are fundamental rights which must prevail against the will of the legislature'.[98]

A more recent example is the *Criminal Code Amendment (Offences Against Australians) Act 2002* (Cth). The Act criminalized offences occurring against Australians in foreign countries and the Bill was backdated in order to cover recent terrorist bombings in Bali—similar in many ways to the war crimes

---

[93] Indeed, prior to these cases, retrospective criminal laws had been upheld in *R v. Kidman* (1915) 20 CLR 425 and *Millner v. Raith* (1942) 66 CLR 1—although it should be noted that both cases involved wartime measures. See Greg Taylor, 'Retrospective Criminal Punishment under the German and Australian Constitutions' (2000) 33(2) *University of New South Wales Law Journal* 196 at 203.   [94] (1996) 189 CLR 51.

[95] *Community Protection Act 1994* (NSW) s 5(1).   [96] Ibid, s 3.

[97] *Kable v. Director of Prosecutions (NSW)* (1996) 189 CLR 51 at 134.

[98] *Ibid* at 66 per Brennan CJ; at 76 per Dawson J; at 121 per McHugh J.

legislation discussed below, where the egregiously malicious nature of the crimes, involving the mass-murder of innocent people, provided the justification for the retrospective nature of the law. The SSCSB[99] endorsed the reasons given in the Explanatory Memoranda; 'the conduct which is being criminalised—causing death or serious bodily injury—is conduct which is universally known to be conduct which is criminal in nature'.[100] As such, these laws are not so much creating a retrospective offence but creating a new institutional mechanism for prosecuting them. Notably, the Explanatory Memoranda also drew a distinction between such criminal actions and merely regulatory offences, 'which may target conduct not widely perceived as criminal, but the conduct is criminalised to achieve a particular outcome'.[101]

The main concern with retrospective criminal law is not usually retrospective changes to the benefit of the accused, but rather retrospective legislation that increases the legal punishment that follows from some act. However, the *International Transfer of Prisoners Amendment Act 2004* (Cth) arguably falls into the former category. It altered Australian law to allow the transfer back to Australia of Australian citizens detained at Guantanamo Bay who may subsequently be convicted, found guilty and sentenced to imprisonment by a military commission of the United States of America. The Act was explicitly retrospective in allowing for the Australian incarceration of prisoners whether they were tried at Guantanamo Bay either before or after the enactment date. Even without this explicit retrospectivity however, the Act still would have been functionally retrospective—for even future convictions from Guantanamo Bay would, in all likelihood, stem from actions committed well before this Act became part of Australian law (that is, convictions might stem from actions taken in the war in Afghanistan).

It is not entirely clear which category such retrospectivity should reside in—or what justifications for it proved most compelling. In a sense, it is clearly retrospective criminal legislation; the act effectively authorizes Australia to punish individuals over whom it may otherwise have held minimal jurisdiction. However, it might be contended that the act was fundamentally curative—it amends the *International Transfer of Prisoners Act 1997* to include under the definition of a 'transfer country' areas under the control or jurisdiction of such a country (thus catering for the idiosyncratic status of Guantanamo Bay), and also includes provision for sentencing by military tribunals as well as courts. Such changes do not seem anathema to the intention of the original legislation but simply bring within its ambit the unique circumstances of the military detention (often without trial) and (possible subsequent) conviction of foreign nationals by the United States following the Afghanistan and Iraqi invasions and the 'September 11' bombings. A third possibility is, however, that the retrospectivity is fundamentally for the benefit of the convicted party. Without such legislation, any convicted individual

---

[99] Australia, SSCSB, *Alert Digest 15*, 4 December 2002, p. 6.
[100] Criminal Code Amendment (Offences Against Australians) Bill 2002, Explanatory Memorandum, p. 3.   [101] Ibid, p. 3.

may have to serve their time in a military prison either in the United States or in Guantanamo Bay itself.

United Kingdom examples

Despite the dominance of parliamentary sovereignty in the United Kingdom and the relative weakness of separation of powers doctrine because of the absence of a written constitution, United Kingdom courts looked upon retrospective criminal legislation with strong disdain long before the coming into effect of the *Human Rights Act 1998* enshrining Article 7 of the ECHR into domestic law. For example, the House of Lords in *R v. Home Secretary, ex parte Pierson*[102] held that the Home Secretary's power under section 29 of the *Crime (Sentences) Act 1997* to decide the 'tariff' or period of detention to be served before consideration for parole for prisoners convicted of murder could not be increased retrospectively without reasoned justification. The interpretation of the prohibition against retrospective criminal legislation in Article 7(1) of the ECHR has not been without difficulty:

No one shall be held guilty of any criminal offence on account of any act or omission which did not constitute a criminal offence under national or international law at the time when it was committed. Nor shall a heavier penalty be imposed than the one that was applicable at the time the criminal offence was committed.

In *Welch v. UK*,[103] the European Court of Human Rights held that the *Drug Trafficking Offences Act 1986* imposed a retrospective 'penalty' because it authorized the confiscation of property from those convicted of drug trafficking offences even in respect of property not directly related to the offence. The confiscation order had been obtained after separate civil proceedings and applied to property obtained during the previous six years before the drug trafficking conviction. The Court in *Welch* gave much more weight to the nature and purpose of the Act, the procedures involved in implementing it and its severity than to the characterization of the confiscation order as 'civil' rather than 'criminal' in nature.

As Simon Atrill observes, 'the purposes for which measures are characterised by domestic law rarely have anything to do with the concerns sought to be addressed by Article 7'.[104] Atrill further notes that the fact that a judge shaped the confiscation order to the particular circumstances of the individual suggested that the order was a penalty. However, mandatory sex offender registration legislation[105] and orders preventing sex offenders from working with children[106] have been judicially characterized as not constituting a penalty on the basis that the former

---

[102] [1998] AC 539.   [103] (1995) 20 EHRR 247.

[104] Simon Atrill (2003) 'Cleaning up the Lords: Are the Proposed Reforms of the House of Lords ECHR-Compliant?' available at <http://www.dca.gov.uk/consult/hdref/responses/h1008.pdf>.

[105] *Adamson v. UK* (1999) 28 EHRR CD 209.   [106] *R v. Field* [2003] 1 WLR 882.

was simply an automatic and straightforward requirement to register with the police and the latter did not necessarily require a criminal conviction.[107] These examples would also satisfy the balancing test suggested in *Coeme v. Belgium*[108] when the Court is considering whether domestic legislation infringes Article 7:

Having regard to the aim of the Convention, which is to protect rights that are practical and effective, it may also take into consideration the need to preserve a balance between the general interest and the fundamental rights of individuals and the notions currently prevailing in democratic States.

A controversial proposal in 2003 to retrospectively bar peers jailed for twelve months or more from their right to sit in the House of Lords, after the sentencing of Jeffrey Archer to a prison term for perjury, was never enacted. The provision was contained within the House of Lords Reform Bill, which was not proceeded with when the Lords made it clear that they would not pass the Bill which otherwise dealt with removing remaining hereditary peers in the House of Lords and setting up a statutory appointments commission.[109] The provision was made retrospective specifically to eject Jeffrey Archer and thus had some similarities with a Bill of Attainder but would also have targeted Lord Montagu of Beaulieu, who was convicted 50 years ago for an 'offence' of homosexuality.[110] Atrill concludes that the legislation, if enacted, would probably not have contravened Article 7 for two reasons. First, the disqualification of peers would not be viewed as a criminal 'penalty' according to current case law:

On one view, the disqualification of a peer is a severe punishment: it involves deprivation of a title akin to a property rights, as well as an occupation and such a disqualification would have considerable force as a declaration that the person is unfit for public office. In reply to each of these arguments it may be said that titles are privileges, deprivation of this honorary position leaves open all other types of employment (indeed, many peerages are granted as a result of exceptional success in other spheres) and the declaration of unsuitability for office pales in comparison to the stigma attached to a conviction for a serious criminal offence.[111]

More fundamentally, the House of Lords Reform Bill concerned a question of qualification for a public position rather than punishment for an offence. Public offices are not privileges but are filled on the basis that the holding of such office is of benefit to the public. Although the public benefit of the House of Lords may be debatable today, the argument is that a house of review with the ability to block legislation for six months that is not controlled by the government provides a check on government error. The public have a right that the government not exclude such members capriciously. However, it does not do so capriciously in

[107] Atrill (2003).   [108] [2000] ECHR 249.
[109] See Department for Constitutional Affairs, 'The House of Lords Frequently Asked Questions', April 2004 available at <http://www.dca.gov.uk/constitution/holref/lordsfaq2004.htm>.
[110] Philip Johnston, 'The Retrospective Law that will Hound Archer out of the House', 19/09/2003 available at <http://www.telegraph.co.uk.news>.   [111] Atrill (2003).

introducing qualifications and disqualifications for the right to sit in future. In this case, the criteria for disqualification were to be the same as for the House of Commons and similar to those in most Houses of Parliament in many other jurisdictions.

A recent example of legislation which may offend Article 7 of the ECHR is the Serious Organised Crime and Police Bill 2005 which makes demonstration in the vicinity of Parliament without authorization a criminal offence. Clause 132 confers the power upon police officers at a demonstration to impose further conditions and vary existing conditions 'on the spot' relating to the prior authorization of the demonstration by the Commissioner. The proposed Bill also affects freedom of expression and freedom of peaceful assembly under Articles 10 and 11 of the ECHR.[112]

United States examples

In the United States, challenges to criminal legislation based purely on its retrospectivity (that is, it violates the *ex post facto* clause of the United States Constitution) have had mixed success. The consensus seems to be that this is partly because the Supreme Court has 'struggled with developing an accurate test to determine whether a law is *ex post facto*'[113] and partly because, in particularly notorious instances of child sexual abuse arousing community outrage, courts have been willing to acquiesce with legislatures to water-down constitutional protections of individual rights.[114] Cases such as *Kansas v. Hendricks*[115] (US Supreme Court); *Doe v. Poritz*[116] (New Jersey Supreme Court); and *State ex rel Olivieri v. State*[117] (Louisiana Supreme Court) have thus endorsed the relevant legislature's characterization of its enactment as procedural or civil (rather than substantive or criminal), effectively by-passing the *ex post facto* clause and the categories of laws that fall within its ambit as defined in the 100-year-old case of *Calder v. Bull*:

1st. Every law that makes an action done before the passing of the law, and which was innocent when done, criminal; and punishes such action. 2d. Every law that aggravates a crime, or makes it greater than it was, when committed. 3d Every law that changes the punishment, and inflicts a greater punishment, than the law annexed to the crime, when committed. 4th. Every law that alters the legal rules of evidence, and receives less, or

---

[112] UK Parliament, Joint Committee on Human Rights, *Scrutiny: Fourth Progress Report*, Eighth Report of Session 2004–5.

[113] Lori N Sabin, 'Doe v. Poritz, A Constitutional Yield to an Angry Society' (1996) 32 *Californian Western Law Review* 331 at 342. We do not propose to undertake a detailed analysis of (the often conflicting) US authorities for the purpose of this chapter.

[114] Sabin, ibid, cf Julie E Hebert, 'State Ex Rel Oliveri v. State: The Scarlet Letter of Protection— A Constitutional Analysis of Louisiana's Megan's Law Statutes' (2002) 48 *Loyola Law Review* 327.

[115] (1997) 117 S Ct 2072 discussed in Wayne A Logan, 'The Ex Post Facto Clause and the Jurisprudence of Punishment (US Supreme Court rules against ex post facto clause) (1998) 35 *American Criminal Law Review* 1261.   [116] (1995) 662 A.2d 367.

[117] (2001) 779 So 2d 735; and *Hutchinson v. Louisiana*, 122 S Ct 208 (2001). Discussed in Julie E Hebert, ibid.

different, testimony, than the law required at the time of the commission of the offence, in order to convict the offender. All these, and similar laws, are manifestly unjust and oppressive.[118]

For example, in *Kansas v. Hendricks* the United States Supreme Court upheld a law allowing for indefinite civil confinement, analogous to involuntary confinement for mental illness, of a 60-year-old child sex abuser who was then serving a prison term for his offences and was soon to be eligible for parole. The majority held that the law did not impose 'punishment' because its object was expressed to be 'the long-term care and treatment' of persons such as Hendricks (despite the fact that the State of Kansas had made no attempt to treat or rehabilitate him during his prison term and he did not suffer from any recognized category of 'mental illness'). The Court characterized the punishment question as, first of all, a question of statutory construction (the law was described as a civil commitment procedure and was not found in the Kansas Criminal Code); further the purpose and effect of the Act was not punitive because the requirement that an individual be 'convicted or charged with a sexually violent offence' was merely evidentiary (to demonstrate that a 'mental abnormality' existed or to support a finding of further dangerousness).

The mere fact that the statute in *Hendricks* imposed involuntary restraint did not, in the majority's opinion, make it punitive because restricting the freedom of the 'dangerously mentally ill' was a legitimate governmental objective and a finding of 'mental illness' was not a prerequisite for involuntary civil confinement in any case. (Suffering from a 'personality disorder' was held to be sufficient to meet due process concerns.) Finally, even presuming that Hendricks was treatable, the statute was constitutional if treatment was only a possible 'ancillary purpose'; if he was not treatable confinement was still constitutional because to conclude otherwise 'would obligate a State to release certain confined individuals who were both mentally ill and dangerous simply because they could not be successfully treated for their afflictions'.[119] This reasoning may be contrasted with the strong dissenting judgment of four justices, who looked at the practical effect of the statute on Hendricks and the fact that Kansas had taken no practical steps to provide Hendricks with treatment; this indicated that the legislature did not view treatment as an important objective and that the statute was not 'simply an effort to commit Hendricks civilly, but rather an effort to inflict further punishment upon him'.[120]

The cases of *Doe v. Poritz* and *State ex rel Olivieri v. State* concerned the validity of so-called 'Megan's Laws' passed by state legislatures requiring convicted sex offenders to not only register with the police after release from prison but also mandating community notification of their whereabouts (including requiring the

---

[118] (1798) 3 US 386 at 390.
[119] Logan, analysing *Kansas v. Hendricks* (1997) 117 S Ct 2072 at 2084–5.
[120] (1997) 117 S Ct 2072 at 2088.

offender to publish his photo in the local newspaper accompanied by the offender's name, address, and crime and in some cases to display a car bumper sticker and to wear labelled clothing). Failure to comply with these provisions was itself a criminal offence. In both cases, the state supreme courts upheld the validity of the legislation, holding in effect that the scheme was regulatory in nature (providing conditions upon which the defendant may be released on probation) and remedial in intent (the protection of the public from sex offenders). The courts also noted that if a disability was imposed not to punish but to achieve some other legitimate purpose, it would not be considered penal for the purposes of the *ex post facto* clause. Further, if the statute did not apply to sex offenders convicted prior to the scheme's enactment, the law's effectiveness would be compromised.[121]

Whilst this analysis seems to be a valid characterization of the registration requirements, the notification requirements go beyond this and clearly constitute a form of punishment in the form of public humiliation. In both cases, the courts failed to give sufficient weight to the *effect* of the laws on the individual. In particular, such factors as whether the sanction involves a positive disability/restraint; whether its operation will promote traditional aims of punishment (retribution and deterrence); whether it has historically been regarded as punishment (visions of the medieval 'pillory and stock' come to mind); and whether it seems excessive in relation to the alternative (non-punitive) purpose of the law.[122] The fact that the US Courts tend to aid and abet extra judicial vigilante punishment of the convicted felon is similarly ignored.

However, the recent Supreme Court decisions of *Carmell v. Texas*[123] and *Stogner v. California*[124] seem to signal a return to a bright-line interpretation of the *ex post facto* clause upholding constitutional protection of individual rights. In *Carmell* the Court invalidated a Texas statute of criminal procedure in trials against sexual offenders for offences committed prior to the 1995 amendment of the statute on the basis that this retrospectively altered the sufficiency of evidence required for a conviction (the fourth ground of invalidity set out in *Calder v. Bull*). The Court in *Stogner* struck down the retrospective extension of a statute of limitations which would have allowed the re-opening of cases of child sexual molestation time-barred decades ago. The Court ruled that the statute fell within the second category of invalidity in *Calder v. Bull* (a law that aggravates a crime, or makes it greater than it was, when committed) as well as the fourth category (the court holding that a law may fall within more than one of the invalid categories).[125]

---

[121] See discussion in Sabin, esp. pp. 343–5; and Hebert, esp. pp. 333–5; 343–7.

[122] These factors were enumerated in *Kennedy v. Mendoza-Martinez* (1963) 372 US 144 at 168–9. See Sabin, at 345–6.

[123] (2000) 534 US 957 discussed in Danielle Kitson, 'It's an Ex Post Facto Fact: Supreme Court Misapplies the Ex Post Facto Clause to Criminal Procedure' (2001) 91 *Journal of Criminal Law and Criminology* 429.   [124] (2003) 539 US No 01-1757.

[125] *Stogner v. California* (2003) 539 US 607 at 615.

The court in *Stogner* explicitly took account of the defendant's reliance interests, noting that he lacked notice that he might be prosecuted and was unaware of any need to preserve evidence of innocence, and this was exacerbated by the problems with 'recovered' memory and witness recollections and was the very justification for the enactment of a statute of limitations in such cases and the reason why retrospective withdrawal of the limitations period would be unfair. And despite the state's interest in prosecuting child abuse cases, 'a constitutional principle must apply not only in child abuse cases, but in every criminal case'.[126]

Reliance interests were also important to the United States District Court for Columbia in deciding the case of *United States of America v. Zayd Hassan Abd Al-Latif.*[127] The defendant successfully obtained an order barring the government from seeking the death penalty pursuant to 'a judicially-fashioned amalgam' of the *Anti-Hijacking Act 1974* and the *Federal Death Penalty Act 1994* for homicides committed prior to the coming into effect of the latter statute. Applying *Landgraf*, the Court observed that 'considerations such as fair notice, reasonable reliance and settled expectations offer sound guidance' in considering whether the legislation attaches new consequences to acts committed prior to the statute's effective date. The Court refused to find a Congressional implied intent to legislate retroactively in the absence of express intention because the result would be a statute violating the *ex post facto* clause (the third and fourth *Calder* prohibitions), contrary to the presumption that Congress intends statutes to be constitutional. According to the District Court, it 'would be a fiction to describe the statute as merely "procedural" because it not only created new sentencing procedures but the new substantive offence of aggravated murder'. The Court distinguished between a 'clearly procedural' statutory change of simply altering the methods employed in determining whether the death penalty was to be imposed and the substantive change in the quantum of punishment wrought by the FDPA in altering the very conditions under which the death sentence was available. Finally, the Court referred to comments by the United States Court of Appeals for the District of Columbia in *Warren v. United States Parole Commission*[128] in considering the operation of the *Calder* categories:

The elements of fair notice and reasonable reliance are closely associated with another basis for the *ex post facto* proscription. Because an *ex post facto* law fails to provide fair warning, it cannot serve the core purpose of the criminal law, to regulate behaviour by threatening unpleasant consequences should an individual commit a harmful act. Obviously, when a law is enacted after the fact, the time for threat has already passed.

Stogner's characterization of criminal legislation as contravening the *ex post facto* clause when it 'inflict[s] a punishment upon a person where that person was

---

[126] *Stogner v. California* (2003) 539 US 607 at 631–2.

[127] United States District Court for the District of Columbia, Criminal No 91-504-03 (2003). Available at <http://www.dcd.uscourts.gov/91cr504.pdf>.

[128] 659 F2d 183 at 188 (1981); cert denied 455 US 950 (1982).

not, by law, liable to that punishment', potentially invalidates some of the notorious provisions of the *USA Patriot Act 2001*.[129] This statute retrospectively expands the definition of 'terrorist', 'terrorist activity' and 'material support' to authorize the conviction and deportation of individuals under various criminal and immigration statutes even when, for example, that person made a donation a decade ago for the humanitarian activities of a group not previously designated as terrorist in any published government list.[130] Examples of excesses under this legislation include the government seeking the deportation of two long-term permanent residents for having provided 'material support' to a 'terrorist organisation' by distributing PLO magazines in the 1980s, when it was lawful to do so; and the conviction of the Executive Director of Benevolence International Foundation for providing boots, tents, uniforms and an ambulance to units of the Bosnian army defending itself against the Bosnian-Serb army.[131]

Although the Patriot Act is yet to be challenged under the *ex post facto* clause, the ban on providing 'expert advice or assistance' to terrorist groups has been held by a US District judge to contravene the First and Fifth Amendments and to be 'unconstitutionally vague'.[132] The Patriot Act is yet another example of retrospective legislation successfully challenged on non-retrospective ancillary constitutional grounds. This points to a deep problem with the current pejorative conceptualization of retrospectivity which this book hopes to remedy, wherein retrospective legislation is commonly passed until some proposed legislation is judged objectionable on some other grounds, upon which time its retrospectivity is held up as an indefeasible argument against its validity.

4.7 War crimes legislation

Australia and the United Kingdom have both enacted legislation to allow for the prosecution of war crimes committed in Europe during World War II: the *War Crimes Amendment Act 1988* (Cth) and the *War Crimes Act 1991* respectively.

---

[129] *Uniting and Strengthening America by Providing Appropriate Tools Required to Intercept and Obstruct Terrorism Act of 2001* (USA Patriot Act), 107 Pub L No 56, 115 Stat 272 (2001).

[130] For detailed analysis of the Patriot Act see Shirin Sinnar, 'Patriotic or Unconstitutional? The Mandatory Detention of Aliens Under the USA Patriot Act' (2003) 55(4) *Stanford Law School* 1419; Daniel Kanstroom, 'Criminalizing the Undocumented: Ironic Boundaries of the Post-September 11th Pale of Law' (2004) 29(4) *North Carolina Journal of International Law and Commercial Regulation* 639, esp. at 647–8 (pointing to the blurring of legal categories of citizen/non-citizen and civil/criminal in immigration law, resulting in 'a new system of maximizing prosecurial discretion and minimizing individual rights').

[131] These examples are highlighted by the Bill of Rights Defense Committee in their 'Companion Guide to the Department of Justice's Report from the Field: The USA Patriot Act at Work', available at http://www.bordc.org/companion and by Professor David Cole's testimony to the US Senate Committee on the Judiciary, available at <http://www.bordc.org/companion>.

[132] See *Humanitarian Law Project v. Ashcroft* 352 F.3d 382 (9th Cir 2003); *Humanitarian Law Project v. Ashcroft*, No CV-03-6107, 2004 US Dist Lexis 926 (CD Cal Jan 22, 2004).

The United States possesses no equivalent legislation because of concerns about contravention of the *ex post facto* clause, although some members of Congress attempted to include a provision in the *War Crimes Act 1996* making the Act retroactive to the Vietnam War.[133]

In Australia, the only individual brought to trial under this legislation has been Ivan Polyukhovich; two other defendants were acquitted during the committal stage. In *Polyukhovich v. Commonwealth*,[134] Polyukhovich challenged the legislation, partly on the grounds of its retrospective operation. It was alleged that making criminal previously non-criminal conduct constituted an invalid attempt by Parliament to usurp the judicial power of the Commonwealth.

The majority judges (Chief Justice Mason, Justices Dawson, Toohey, and McHugh) agreed with this in part, noting that a Bill of attainder or retrospective law which found persons guilty would constitute trial by legislature (that is, usurpation of judicial power). However, they argued that the War Crimes Act was not an example of such a law because, although retrospective, it defined the offence in general terms and did not direct the court to convict named individuals:

The application of the doctrine depends upon the legislature adjudging the guilt of a specific individual or specific individuals or imposing punishment upon them. If, for some reason, an *ex post facto* law did not amount to a Bill of attainder, yet adjudged persons guilty of a crime or imposed punishment upon them, it could amount to trial by legislature and a usurpation of judicial power. But if the law, though retrospective in operation, leaves it to the courts to determine whether the person charged has engaged in the conduct complained of and whether that conduct is an infringement of the rule prescribed, there is no interference with the exercise of judicial power.[135] ... An *ex post facto* law ... not being a bill of attainder ... simply does not amount to trial by legislature. It leaves for determination by the court the issues which would arise for determination under a prospective law.[136]

Polyukhovich, therefore, drew a distinction between laws that name specific individuals (which are unconstitutional as usurping judicial power) and laws that prescribe conduct in general, but retrospective, terms (which are valid since they preserve the judiciary's prerogative of applying them to particular individuals). The *War Crimes Amendment Act 1988* did not designate specific individuals either by name or characteristic; rather, it focused upon conduct, and did not foreclose a determination of either guilt or innocence. The task before the court— to determine whether, during World War II, the defendant engaged in conduct defined by the Act as war crimes—was the same, irrespective of whether the Act was passed in 1989, 1929, or 1889. Nothing in the definition of the punishable conduct made it inevitable that those individuals would be the ones convicted,

---

[133] See Ted Sampley, 'United States War Crimes Policy is Duplicity of the Worst Kind', September 1997, available at <http://www.11thcavnam.com/main/united_states_war_crimes_policy_.htm>.

[134] *Polyukhovich v. Commonwealth* (1991) 172 CLR 501 ('The War Crimes Act Case').

[135] Ibid at 32 per Mason CJ.   [136] Ibid at 39–40 per Mason CJ.

nor was there any evidence that Parliament had defined the offences in such a way as to catch those individuals and only those individuals.[137]

After the *War Crimes Case*, the consensus by the majority of the Australian High Court is, therefore, that retrospective criminal law is not unconstitutional provided that it does not also have the characteristics of a Bill of attainder. In the United Kingdom, a challenge to the *War Crimes Act 1991* (UK) was upheld by the European Court of Human Rights in *Sawoniuk v. United Kingdom*.[138] Sawoniuk, a retired British Rail ticket collector, was found guilty of murder on two counts under the War Crimes Act.[139] Sawoniuk's challenge was based on Article 6 of the ECHR (right to a fair hearing) rather than Article 7 with the Court rejecting his argument that the time between the alleged acts and the trial was of such length that, combined with the nature of the evidence against the applicant (the prosecution's cases depended almost entirely upon the evidence of two witnesses who were at the time aged 13 and 20 respectively), he was unable to defend himself sufficiently to receive a fair trial. Akin to the reasoning in *Polyukhovich*, the Court noted that the Convention does not impose any time-limit in respect of war crime prosecutions. The prosecution had to satisfy the requisite burden of proof and the jury was left to decide for itself whether the evidence dating back to events in 1943 was credible and reliable.

Article 7(2) of the ECHR provides an exception to the general prohibition against criminal retrospectivity in Article 7(1):

This article shall not prejudice the trial and punishment of any person for any act or omission which, at the time when it was committed, was criminal according to the general principles of law recognised by civilised nations.

An equivalent provision exists in the prohibition against retrospective criminal offences in Article 15 of the International Convenant on Civil and Political Rights:

i. No one shall be held guilty of any criminal offence on account of any act or omission which did not constitute a criminal offence, under national or international law, at the time when it was committed. Nor shall a heavier penalty be imposed than the one that was applicable at the time when the criminal offence was committed. If, subsequent to the commission of the offence, provision is made by law for the imposition of a lighter penalty, the offender shall benefit thereby.

ii. Nothing in this article shall prejudice the trial and punishment of any person for any act or omission which, at the time when it was committed, was criminal according to the general principles of law recognized by the community of nations.

[137] The dissenting judges, Deane J and Gaudron J, argued that the Act made a finding of guilt inevitable even though it did not name the actual persons to be punished. Their Honours' reasoning has been much criticized: see, for example, Taylor, pp. 205–7.
[138] ECHR, Application No 63716/00, 29 May 2001.
[139] *R v. Sawoniuk* [2000] 2 CAR 220.

Both the Australian and UK war crime statutes would seem to fall within the second exception. There are a few laws that might seem to fit within the first. Although this exception generally refers only to the retrospective application of a lighter penalty than that which existed at the time of the commission of the offence, the beneficial principle would also presumably apply if a person would benefit from the application of a retrospectively created offence. This was arguably the case with the *Extradition Act 1988* (Cth), which allowed for certain Australian citizens to be prosecuted within Australia, rather than extradited beyond its borders. Effectively, this Act extended Australian criminal laws to conduct occurring outside the Commonwealth, making it similar in operation to the *War Crimes Amendment Act 1988* (Cth). The reason for giving the section a retrospective operation was to enable Australia to refuse extradition on the basis of citizenship from the time the legislation commenced. Otherwise as the Attorney-General explained:

Australia would, unless it was to create a haven for Australian criminals, in practical terms be unable to refuse to extradite on the basis of citizenship alone any citizen accused of an offence committed abroad before the commencement date. Thus the benefit of the section would not fall on Australian citizens for some years.[140]

Most Australian residents would rather be tried and punished in Australia than be extradited to another country. First, Australia does not impose the death penalty; secondly, prison conditions may be better in Australia than in many of the countries whose extradition requests the Attorney-General is likely to refuse; thirdly, it will be easier to maintain contact with family and friends during a period of imprisonment.

However, under some circumstances, the retrospective criminalization in Australia of the person's conduct will not be beneficial: for example, if the Attorney-General would have refused the extradition request even without the ability to prosecute the person under Australian law.

In relation to the *Extradition Act 1988* (Cth) however, it is difficult to make a case against the prosecution of a person based upon their reliance on the previously existing state of the law. It is possible that a person might have moved or returned to Australia in reliance on a belief that extradition was, for whatever reason, unlikely; in other words, to take advantage of the 'haven' referred to by the Attorney-General. But this is a different matter from saying that the person chose to avoid conduct which would attract criminal sanctions. What was chosen was, rather, a course of conduct—namely, returning to Australia—which made it unlikely that the criminal sanctions they had already attracted in a foreign jurisdiction would be enforced. It is debatable whether such expectations meet the criteria for being deserving of protection.

The War Crimes Act appears to fall within Article 1SII of the ICCPR for the reasons noted by Dawson J noted in *Polyukhovich*: 'war crimes of the kind created

---

[140] Australia, 'Letter to SSCSB', reproduced in *SSCSB Eleventh to Eighteenth Reports of 1987* (Parliamentary Paper No 442 of 1987), p. 112.

by the Act could not, in any civilised community, have been described as blameless conduct merely because of the absence of proscription by law'.[141] It may be objected that the exception provided by the ICCPR for 'any act or omission which, at the time when it was committed, was criminal according to the general principles of law recognized by the community of nations' is vague, and vague laws themselves (especially when criminal punishment is at stake) offend the Rule of Law ideal. Indeed, Article 1SII of the ICCPR may be compared to the German Criminal Code, enacted by the Nazi government, which stated that 'whoever commits an act which...deserves punishment according to the principles of criminal law and to the sound feelings of the people, will be punished'.[142] There are important differences between these two principles. The Nazi article is framed in normative terms and asks judges to decide what is 'deserved' and what feelings are 'sound'. The ICCPR's test, however, is a factual question: have all or almost all of the nations around the world acknowledged this principle?

Even those countries whose Constitution contains an express and, on its face, absolute and unequivocal prohibition of retrospective legislation, such as Germany, recognize that there may be circumstances where the admittedly strong arguments against retrospective criminal laws are not always sufficient reasons for avoiding retrospectivity. Germany recognizes an unwritten 'natural law' exception for cases such as war crimes, based on the principle that the demands of substantive justice sometimes override the formal requirements of justice embodied in the general prohibition against retrospective criminal laws.[143] This has allowed the prosecution of former soldiers in the East German regime who were instructed by their superiors to shoot unarmed civilians trying to flee over the Berlin Wall to West Germany.[144] Defendants have been unable to rely on arguments that they were acting lawfully according to the legal regime that existed at the time in East Germany: the Federal Constitutional Court ruled, in effect, that the German Constitution requires that the previous laws being relied on for protection were enacted by a legislature bound to respect basic human rights, the Rule of Law and democratic parliamentary checks and balances. 'When such laws or practices require the perpetuation of gross injustice, it cannot be assumed that there is a firm basis for the citizen's reliance on their lack of amenability to retrospective change'.[145]

Many countries' Constitutions incorporate a rule copied from the ICCPR, or another similar law. Australia's does not; nor does it incorporate customary international law. It does, however, to some degree, incorporate international law indirectly. One of the Commonwealth's most often-invoked powers is its authority to make laws with respect to 'External Affairs'.[146] This requires in most

---

[141] *Polyukhovich v. Commonwealth* (1991) 172 CLR 501 at 643.

[142] *Reichsgesetzblatt* (1935) I Article 1. (Cited in Sheldon Glueck, *The Nuremberg Trial and Aggressive War* (Knopf, New York, 1946) 73.)   [143] See detailed discussion in Taylor, at 217–21.

[144] *Streletz v. Germany* (2001) 33 EHRR 363.   [145] Taylor, at 218.

[146] Commonwealth Constitution, s 51 (xxix).

(though not all) cases that such laws be made to implement a treaty, and that they conform closely to the terms of the treaty. The *War Crimes Amendment Act 1988* (Cth) defines punishable war crimes by reference to the domestic law in force in Australia at the time the acts were committed, rather than by reference to international law. As Toohey J noted:

Conduct constituting such an offence under the Act was conduct which attracted the sanctions of criminal laws generally, not just the censure of moral codes. In those circumstances, it cannot be said that an individual is caused detriment to which he or she would not have been subject at the time of the conduct, or that he or she had 'no cause to abstain' from that conduct.[147]

We would argue that rather than 'trumpeting rare cases' as exceptions to the general rule, we should analyse more precisely when reliance, and, qualitatively, what type of reliance should be protected when assessing when the prohibition against retrospective criminal law should apply.

Even if the War Crimes Amendment Act 1988 was not an exception to the right (under the ICCPR) to protection from retrospective criminal law, it could be argued that retrospective law in such circumstances actually promotes the cause of human rights overall. First, those who might otherwise engage in torture or persecution may be deterred from doing so by the threat that their actions could be retrospectively criminalized years (or decades) later. The prospect of a return to democratic rule, and the precedent created by the Nuremberg Trials (as well as recent *ad hoc* tribunals for the former Yugoslavia and Rwanda and the prosecution of former East German border guards, Argentinean torturers and Chilean dictators)[148] might well discourage an individual from joining in such crimes, even if authorized to do so by the laws in force at the time.

Some might see this potential deterrence as too small a gain in return for what they consider an erosion of the Rule of Law and the application of a modern day 'Bill of Attainder'. The latter argument raised by the dissenters in *Polyukhovich* is based on the fact that the war crimes statutes are limited in temporal and geographical scope (to actions in Europe during the Second World War) and were enacted after investigations had been made into allegations against specific individuals.[149] However, in cases such as those which we have been considering, while there might be an erosion of the authority of the *domestic* laws under which the human rights abuses were carried out, the rule of *international* law (which attempts to protect human rights) is furthered. International law may intervene to provide clear guidance (even if the abuse of human rights is legal according to domestic law) because the domestic laws in question are unlikely to have rated very highly in their conformity to the Rule of Law in any case. Indeed, Taylor observes that Australia might itself be in breach of its international obligations

---

[147] *Polyukhovich v. Commonwealth* (1991) 172 CLR 501 at 691.   [148] See Chapter 5.
[149] See McMurtrie (1992) at 146–7 who discusses this argument in detail.

if it is unable to (retrospectively) prosecute perpetrators of acts that are crimes under international law.[150]

4.8 Retrospective taxation law

As mentioned in the previous section, the most controversial use of retrospective legislation in Australia, the United Kingdom and the United States in the last three decades has involved neither war crimes nor terrorism but taxation. It is possible to distinguish between two types of retrospective taxation legislation. The first 'imposes a tax charge on income earned, gains realised or transactions concluded at a time before the legislation was enacted' when that income, gain or transaction would have otherwise not been taxed or been subject to a lower rate of tax. The second type which has been called 'quasi-retrospective legislation' is where 'legislation imposes a tax charge on income or a gain realised after the date when the legislation enters into force, but that income or gain arises from transactions entered into (or at least commenced) before the legislation'.[151] Although anti-avoidance statutes may take both forms, the courts are more tolerant of this second form of retrospective taxation as the argument against retrospectivity based on the reliance interests and settled expectations of taxpayers is weaker.

Australian tax avoidance schemes and the legislative response

Successive Australian governments have resorted to retrospective taxation laws because, by the late 1970s, widespread tax avoidance was causing billions of dollars in lost revenue. This was caused by a combination of political indifference, complex legislation, lax administration, a 'pro-taxpayer' High Court, the marketing of tax minimization schemes and the lack of acceptance of an ethical obligation to pay tax among many in business and the professions.

Curran schemes

In *Curran's case*,[152] the taxpayer purchased 200 shares in a private company for $186,000 (figures rounded for convenience). As principal shareholder, he then caused a dividend of $191,000 to be paid in the form of 191,000 bonus shares. These dividends were not assessable as income, because section 44(2) of the *Income Tax Assessment Act 1936* (Cth) recognized that a bonus issue of shares represented, not a realization of income, but simply a further subdivision of the shareholder's interest.

---

[150] Taylor, at 207.

[151] Phillip Baker, 'Retrospective Tax Legislation and the European Convention on Human Rights' (2005) 1 *British Tax Review* 1 at fn 1.

[152] *Curran v. Federal Commissioner of Taxation* (1973) 131 CLR 409.

The taxpayer then sold the 191,200 shares for $188,000, making a profit of $2000 on the entire transaction. But he claimed that, to determine his profit/loss figure, he should be allowed to deduct not only the cost of purchasing the original shares, but the par value of the bonus shares (that is, $191,000). In other words, he wanted to claim that the bonus shares, *which had cost him nothing*, should for tax purposes be deemed to have cost him $191,000. Amazingly, the High Court (Chief Justice Barwick, Justices Menzies and Gibbs, with Justice Stephen dissenting) agreed. The transaction, therefore, gave rise to a tax loss of $189,000, but the effect was that, through issuing bonus shares, an actual profit on an investment in shares could be converted into a paper loss, for tax purposes, of whatever magnitude the taxpayer desired. Liability to pay tax could, in this way, be eliminated for years in advance.

Despite the protestations of opponents of the anti-*Curran* legislation, it is difficult to see any substantive injustice in denying a taxpayer the right to claim a cost which they had never actually incurred (although they might have lost money through fees paid to the schemes' promoters). Indeed, it is highly doubtful that the participants' expectations of being allowed to keep their gains were either rational or legitimate; in which case, such expectations were not deserving of protection.

First, as regards rationality, the then Treasurer specifically announced on 1 December 1974—less than one month after the High Court decided *Curran*—that the judgment would be reversed by statute. The 1977 Budget speech gave a more general warning about blatant avoidance schemes[153]; and the anti-*Curran* legislation was made retrospective to this date. Given that some promoters of *Curran* schemes offered money-back guarantees if such schemes were retrospectively prohibited, many participants must have been aware of the threat of retrospective legislation.[154] As the Australian Taxpayers' Association newsletter at the time commented, 'people "doing *Curran*" knew the risks'.[155]

As regards legitimacy, it is hard to see *Curran's* case as consistent with the underlying justifications for the system of deductions established by the *Income Tax Assessment Act*. Despite this, however, many in the Liberal Government were anxious about the use of retrospective legislation, and to assuage their concerns, its supporters emphasized that this was to be a unique exercise. Anti-*Curran* laws were a one-off response to a one-off problem; a problem that in future would be solved by better drafting of prospective laws. Secure in that expectation, the Australian tax avoidance industry flourished during the 1970s and 1980s.

Bottom-of-the-harbour schemes

Although *Curran* schemes were blatant in that their sole intent was to avoid tax, they did not, at least, involve any outright criminality. 'Bottom-of the harbour'

---

[153] Australia, *Hansard*, House of Representatives, 1977, vol. 106, p. 54.

[154] See Treasurer Howard, 'Second Reading Speech', *Hansard*, Australian Commonwealth, House of Representatives, 1978, vol. 108, p. 1245.

[155] 'Editorial' (1978) 8 *Taxpayer* 99 (Australian Taxpayers Association).

evasion was of an entirely different character. Stripping untaxed profits from companies so as to leave the vendor free of any liability to pay tax (and the ultimate purchaser unable to pay it) required more than just a clever lawyer or accountant; it often also required links to organized crime, and determination to deliberately flout company and tax laws. Of course, the vendors involved claimed that they knew nothing about what had happened to a company after they sold it, and were therefore not responsible for its failure to pay tax; this has been said to have involved 'the largest single case of mass wilful blindness known'.[156]

The Commonwealth Parliament did not respond to the bottom-of-the-harbour 'schemes' until late 1980, when it passed the *Crimes (Taxation Offences) Act*, making it a criminal offence for a person to be party to arrangements designed to render a company or trustee incapable of meeting its taxation obligations. Although the legal profession vehemently condemned this introduction of criminal penalties into taxation law, it is credited with bringing the bottom-of-the-harbour industry to a sudden halt.[157] On 25 July 1982, the then Treasurer John Howard announced that legislation would be introduced to recover tax evaded through bottom-of-the-harbour schemes.[158] In the end, the legislation regime enacted imposed on vendor shareholders a tax liability equal to the amount of tax owed by the company that had been stripped.[159]

Following the 1983 Federal election, the new Hawke Labor Government promised very bluntly to stamp out the tax avoidance industry once and for all, justifying the use of retrospective legislation 'to ensure that tax sought to be avoided under any blatant tax avoidance scheme that comes to light during our term of office will be collected, irrespective of when the scheme was entered into'.[160] True to its word, the new Government first sought to enact further bottom-of-the-harbour legislation in order to recover, among other things, personal tax on a sold company's undistributed profits but these Bills were repeatedly blocked by the Senate.

Undaunted, on 9 October 1984, the Government introduced the Trust Recoupment Tax Assessment Bill to deal with the practice known as trust income stripping.[161] The original draft would have applied to all trusts entered into for tax avoidance purposes on or after 1 July 1980, but the Senate amended this date to 12 May 1982—the day when former Treasurer Howard had given a clear and unambiguous warning about the practice. The effect of this Liberal Opposition

---

[156] Arie Freiberg, 'Ripples from the Bottom of the Harbour: Some Social Ramifications of Taxation Fraud' (1988) 12 *Criminal Law Journal* 136 at 143.   [157] Freiberg (1988), at 160.

[158] Announcement repr. in ICF Spry QC, 'Retrospective Legislation for Company Tax' (1982) 11 *Australian Tax Review* 152.

[159] The later date was the commencement date for the *Crimes (Taxation Offences) Act 1980*. See The *Taxation (Unpaid Company Tax) Assessment Act 1982*, the *Taxation (Unpaid Company Tax— Promoters) Act 1982*, the *Taxation (Unpaid Company Tax—Vendors) Act 1982*, and the *Taxation (Unpaid Company Tax—Consequential Amendments) Act 1982*.

[160] Finance Minister John Dawkins, Press Release: 'Retrospective Legislation Against Tax Avoidance' (28 April 1983), reprinted in (1983) 17 *Taxation in Australia* 1006–7.

[161] This Bill lapsed when Parliament was dissolved for the December 1984 election, but was reintroduced on 22 February 1985.

amendment, then, was to convert a fully classically retrospective law into 'legislation by press release' (see below). The Finance Minister, Senator Walsh, described the difference between the Government's and the Opposition's views as being that:

... the Government has said that if it is discovered that people have been plundering the public purse they will be required to pay the money back no matter when they did it. [The Opposition] has said that if it is discovered that people are plundering the public purse they will be told: 'Those who plundered the purse yesterday and earlier can keep the money and those who plunder today and thereafter will have to pay it back'.[162]

It seems likely that the precedent created by the preceding Coalition Government's own legislation, together with the Labor Government's determination to ensure that tax avoidance schemes would never succeed, played an important part in eventually ending large-scale tax avoidance. Its demise was also helped along by changing community perceptions; by aggressive tactics on the Australian Tax Office's part, making tax avoidance a potentially expensive risk; by the new anti-avoidance provisions in Part IVA of the *Income Tax Assessment Act 1936* (Cth); and by changing judicial approaches to interpreting tax legislation. Quite possibly, in the long term the last was the most important. However in all of these attitudinal changes, one can see the pivotal role played by the retrospective legislation and the public debates about it.

Of course, a policy cannot be judged solely by its success. The tax-avoidance industry was defeated, but did the end justify the means? A writer's choice of metaphors used to answer this question often casts more light on the writer's own beliefs than on the merits of the debate. On the one hand, the use of military metaphors makes retrospectivity seem eminently reasonable:

For years a battle of manoeuvre has been waged between the legislature and those who are minded to throw the burden of taxation off their shoulders on to those of their fellow subjects. In that battle the legislature has often been worsted by the skill, determination and resourcefulness of its opponents ... It would not shock us in the least to find that the legislature has determined to put an end to the struggle by imposing the severest of penalties.

It scarcely lies in the mouth of the taxpayer who plays with fire to complain of burnt fingers.... The fact that the section has to some extent a retroactive effect appears to us of no importance when it is realized that the legislation is a move in a long and fiercely contested battle with individuals who well understand the rigour of the contest.[163]

On the other hand, describing the contest between government and taxpayer in terms of a game makes a legislative resort to retrospectivity sound like cheating, or like kicking the board over out of pique at losing under the existing rules:

It is suggested that there is an important distinction between either or both sides taking advantage of the existing rules, on the one hand, and one side not letting the other know what the rules are, on the other.[164]

---

[162] Australia, *Hansard*, Senate, 1985, vol. 107, p. 608.
[163] *Lord Howard de Walden v. Inland Revenue Commissioners* [1942] 1 KB 389 at 397–98 per Lord Greene MR.
[164] Harry Reicher, 'Legislation by Press Release' (1978) 7 *Australian Tax Review* 32.

As we have seen, the expectations of *Curran*-type tax avoiders were neither rational nor legitimate, and the expectations of bottom-of-the-harbour avoiders were, at least, not legitimate. Therefore, the arguments about the injustice of retrospective legislation do not apply in this case. Moreover, there are strong arguments in support of such retrospective tax measures: for example, that they are necessary in order to avoid enormous loss of revenue, to uphold the institution of taxation, or to ensure that the taxation system is fair and equitable. The government holds itself out as taxing income on a progressive scale. The tax avoidance industry was attempting to make the income scale regressive. The government was keeping its word.

The last decade

During the 1990s, the increasing acceptance of retrospectivity as a legislative tool to protect the Commonwealth Government's revenue base resulted in the enactment of such measures as the *Taxation Laws Amendment (Trust Loss and Other Deductions) Act 1997*, which had the effect of preventing the selling of trust losses to others so that only those who actually incurred the loss should be entitled to deduct that loss against income, with retrospective effect from 6 May 1995.[165] More subtle cases include the *New Business Tax System (Capital Allowances) Act 2001* (Cth) which had retrospective application in order to foreclose a 'potential' tax-avoidance loophole allowing taxpayers to divide up a single expensive capital outlay into multiple components, thereby receiving an immediate deduction for the purchase of 'low-cost assets' rather than the depreciation which would otherwise apply over a number of years.

United Kingdom examples

An interesting example of retrospective taxation amendment in the United Kingdom which manages to combine an anti-avoidance objective and the protection of the reasonable reliance interests of a small number of taxpayers is the 1988 insertion of sections 112(4) and (5) into the ICTA following the High Court decision in *Padmore v. CIR*.[166] The Court, in this case, had upheld the validity of Double Taxation Agreements used to avoid paying tax on overseas profits. Taxpayers had formed artificial partnerships with partners resident in the UK arguing that the provisions of the Double Taxation Agreement between the UK and the country where the partnership was managed and controlled prevented the UK from assessing their shares of the profit because the partnership was an enterprise of the other country. The new section of the Act was stated as 'intended to do no more than restore the previous general understanding of the ability of the

---

[165] This measure was not without controversy, largely because of the lengthy period that had elapsed between the press release and the enactment of legislation. See Australia, *Work of the Scrutiny of Bills Committee During the 38th Parliament*, 1997, chapter 2, Senate Committees; and Australia, *Economics Legislation Committee*, Senate, 13 November 1997, E 75. [166] 62 TC 352.

United Kingdom to charge tax on its own residents'. The section is deemed to have retrospective effect for all taxpayers *except* the successful litigant in Padmore and a small number of additional taxpayers for whom Padmore was a test case. The Inland Revenue department had notified the latter that their cases would be assessed in accordance with the Padmore decision.[167] It can be argued that this legislation protected the reliance interests of those few taxpayers who could be said to have reasonably relied on the High Court's interpretation of the law in Padmore whilst also protecting the general public interest in stamping out a specific tax avoidance scheme.

United Kingdom taxpayers have had limited success in both domestic courts and the European Court of Human Rights challenging the constitutionality of retrospective taxation measures based on Article 1 of the First Protocol to the European Convention which states:

Every natural or legal person is entitled to the peaceful enjoyment of his possessions. No one shall be deprived of his possessions except in the public interest and subject to the conditions provided for by law and by the general principles of international law.

The preceding provisions shall not, however, in any way impair the right of a State to enforce such laws as it deems necessary to control the use of property in accordance with the general interest or to secure the payment of taxes or other contributions or penalties.

In the early case of *A, B, C and D v. United Kingdom*,[168] the Commission of Human Rights upheld the validity of retrospective legislation targeting commodity future trading[169] against a complaint by four solicitors who had entered into trading partnership agreements with the objective of offsetting the trading loss against their earnings as solicitors. The Commission recognized the adverse effect of taxation measures with retrospective effect in terms of producing uncertainty amongst taxpayers and preventing the taxpayer's affairs from being restructured to minimize the taxation consequences, as is sometimes possible with prospective legislation. However, the provision was deemed to be compatible with the Convention because the government was able to demonstrate that the only way in which this form of contrived and secretive tax avoidance scheme could be defeated was through the enactment of retrospective legislation. The Commission concluded that the retrospective provision was not excessive because there was a reasonable relationship of proportionality between the means employed and the aim sought to be realized by the provision.

In *National and Provincial Building Society v. UK*,[170] the ECHR upheld the validity of legislation reinstating the validity of tax provisions after they had been invalidated by the House of Lords in *Woolwich Building Society v. Inland Revenue*

---

[167] See discussion at HM Revenue and Customs 'INTM163130—UK residents with foreign income or gains: income arising abroad' available at <http://www.hmrc.gov.uk/manuals/ithmanual/html/ITH1600/17_0039_ITH1660.htm>.

[168] Application No 8531/79; (1981) 23 DR 203.   [169] Finance Act 1978, s 31.

[170] (1998) 25 EHRR 127.

Commissioners.[171] Building societies other than the successful appellant were affected by the legislation and had claimed restitution of about 72 million pounds for interference with possession under Article 1 of Protocol 1. The ECHR held that there was an obvious public interest in securing the payment of taxes and that the applicants could not establish that they had a legitimate expectation that the government would not enact validating legislation with retrospective effect. Thus, the balance between protecting the appellant's Convention rights and protecting the general public interest was not upset. The Court further rejected the claim that the applicants had been discriminated against compared to the position of the Woolwich Building Society, noting that Woolwich alone showed its readiness to bear the costs and risks of litigation all the way to the House of Lords. Even if the other building societies were in a similar position to Woolwich, the decision to exclude Woolwich from the retroactive effect of the legislative provision was reasonably and objectively justified given that Woolwich had secured a final judgment in its favour and Parliament, understandably, did not want to interfere with this judgment.[172]

A stronger argument on the basis of Article 1 of Protocol 1 could be mounted in relation to the introduction of a pre-owned assets charge (POAC) in section 84 and Schedule 15 of the *Finance Act 2004.* The annual charge applies to those who occupy or benefit from assets that they have previously owned—primarily targeting assets derived from gifts and contributions. The provisions are designed to defeat the avoidance of inheritance tax through Double Trust Schemes created to remove the family home from a person's taxable estate, whilst allowing that person to continue to reside in it. The history of anti-avoidance and regulatory response in this area has a very familiar ring:

The Inland Revenue challenged the avoidance schemes validity in the courts. It lost. It changed the legislation. More schemes appeared, the Revenue suffered more defeats in the courts and more IHT leaked out of the Treasury.[173]

However, the scope of this legislation (affecting not just participants in contrived anti-avoidance schemes but anyone who has made a non-commercial disposal of an asset since 1986 and 'reserved an interest or benefit') means that it also targets otherwise legitimate inheritance tax planning. Affected taxpayers must either decide to leave the scheme in place and pay an annual income tax charge (in the case of land as if the taxpayer had received market rent for the occupation of the land or, for other assets, a tax charge based on official interest rates) or make an election prior to 31 January 2007 to bring the property back within the scope

---

[171] [1993] AC 70; *Finance Act 1986*, s 47.

[172] See commentary on this case by the Association of Chartered Certified Accountants at <http://www.accaglobal.com/publications/ipi/8/24542>; and 'Case Comment: Invalid Tax Provisions—Woolwich Case—Claims to Restitution—Retrospective Legislation' (1998) 2 *European Human Rights Review* 236.

[173] 'The pre-owned assets charge' available at <http://www.legal500.com/devs/uk/sl/uksl_056.htm>.

of inheritance tax. Furthermore, many taxpayers will be unable to dismantle earlier transactions, particularly as the financial consequences will be 'a capital gains tax charge and possibly a stamp duty charge at 4 per cent and without any specific concession from the Revenue'.[174] For these reasons, the legislation is arguably a disproportionate response to the stated objective of eliminating a specific tax avoidance scheme.[175]

United States examples

In 1993, one of Bill Clinton's first measures as incoming President was to enact the *Omnibus Budget Reconciliation Act* (OBRA). The Act contained two controversial provisions; the first, increasing the income tax rates for both corporations and certain categories of wealthy individuals; and the second, increasing estate and gift taxes.[176] Both provisions were expressed to have retrospective effect to 1 January 1993, over seven months before the Act was passed. The Act was expressed to have as its objective the reduction of the federal budget deficit; the use of *retrospective* taxation merely to raise revenue rather than to target anti-avoidance caused considerable outcry and some members of Congress unsuccessfully sought to pass subsequent legislation to repeal the provisions.[177] A court challenge to the estate and gift taxes provision based on the due process, detrimental reliance and notice test espoused by the Court of Appeals in *Carlton v. United States*,[178] discussed below, was dismissed by the Supreme Court.[179] However, there was little doubt that detrimental reliance on the prior tax law had occurred as an essential part of estate tax planning; moreover, the taxpayers had no actual or constructive notice of the retroactive rate increases, particularly as the provisions reached back to the last three weeks of the George Bush (Senior) presidency and the specific provisions were not announced by the Clinton administration until 3 April. Academic commentary also supports the conclusion that these provisions were constitutionally problematic.[180]

In relation to taxation legislation, the United States Supreme Court has narrowly construed the traditional constitutional protections against retrospectivity and

---

[174] Daniel Feingold, 'Double Trusts Schemes and the New Pre-Owned Assets Income Tax' available at http://www.taxationweb.co.uk/taxlaw/article.php?id=13.

[175] Ibid. Also see John Wray, 'Pre-Owned Assets Income Tax Charge', available at Gordons Cranswick website <http://www.gordonscranswick.co.uk/Legal_Updates/articles/2004/ jpw-17-06-04-01.htm>.

[176] See detailed discussion in Andrew G Schultz, 'Graveyard Robbery in the Omnibus Budget Reconciliation Act of 1993: A Modern Look at the Constitutionality of Retroactive Taxes' (1994) 27 *John Marshall Law Review* 775.

[177] 'To repeal the retroactive application of the income, estate, and gift tax rates made by the budget reconciliation act and reduce administrative expenses for agencies by $3,000,000,000 for each of the fiscal years 1994, 1995, and 1996, H.R. 3250, introduced 10/07/1993, House of Representatives, available at <http://thomas.loc/gov/egi-bin/bdquery/z?d103:h.r.03250>.

[178] 972 F2d 1051 (9th Cir 1991).

[179] *NationsBank of Texas v. United States of America*, 01-1584, Monday 7 October 2002 (certiorari denied).   [180] Schultz (1994) p. 16.

has been deferential to state and federal government judgments about the justifications for such legislation, so long as it can be broadly supported by a legitimate public purpose furthered by rational means. Commentators have often remarked that the Supreme Court has not overturned a retroactive taxation statute since the 1930s, with taxpayers unsuccessfully mounting challenges based on the Contract Clause, the Direct Taxation Clause, and the Equal Protection Clause in addition to the Due Process Clause.[181] Although the Due Process Clause provides the most promising avenue for a constitutional challenge, the Supreme Court's departure from earlier case law in *Carlton v. United States*[182] practically removed the importance of the traditional detrimental reliance and notice analysis in establishing constitutional violation in favour of a rational means test.

In *Carlton* the Supreme Court unanimously upheld a retrospective amendment to the *Tax Reform Act 1986* which removed an estate tax deduction previously available to estates that made a 'qualified sale' to an Employee Stock-Ownership Plan (ESOP). Congress had originally created the tax deduction to encourage people to sell shares in a company to the ESOP. To obtain the benefit of that deduction, the executor of an estate sold stock to an ESOP at a loss. The retrospective repeal caused the estate more than $600,000 and was characterized as an example of 'bait and switch taxation'. The Supreme Court's narrow inquiry focused on whether Congress's purpose in enacting the statute served a legitimate public purpose or was illegitimate or arbitrary; and whether the statute established only a short period of retroactivity. In relation to the first question, the Court relied on the legislature's characterization of the legislation as curative (to correct a defect in the original legislation that would have created significant revenue loss). However, one commentator observes that 'the Court's classification of Congress' action being one of curing a mistake leads to a very slippery slope... Unfortunately, the distinction between an unintended benefit and a repudiated policy judgment is generally difficult to draw'.[183]

In respect of the second question, the Court approved of the fact that the retroactive effect of the legislation was only just longer than a year, with Justice O'Connor commenting that a longer period of retrospectivity would raise serious constitutional questions.[184] In subsequent cases, courts have applied this temporal limitation inconsistently. For example, in *Montana RailLink v. United States*[185] tax legislation with a four-year retrospective period was upheld with the Court stating that *Carlton* requires only that the period of retrospectivity bear a 'rational relation to underlying legislative purpose'. However, in *Rivers v. State of South*

---

[181] See Ronald Z Domsky, 'Retroactive Taxation: United States v Carlton—The Taxpayer Loses Again!' (1995) 16 *Northern Illinois University Law Review* 77.

[182] 512 US 26 (1994). For case analysis see Laura Ricciardi, 'The Aftermath of United States v Carlton: Taxpayers will have to pay for Congress's Mistakes' (1996) 40 *New York Law School Law Review* 599.

[183] Ronald Z Domsky, 'Retroactive Taxation: United States v Carlton—The Taxpayer Loses Again' (1995) 16 *Northern Illinois University Law Review* 77 at 86–7.

[184] 512 US 26 (1994) at 38.   [185] 76 F3d 991 (9th Cir 1996).

Carolina[186] the retrospective removal of a state capital gains tax refund with a retrospective period of up to three years was held to violate the due process clause under both the state and federal constitution:

At some point, however, the government's interest in meeting its revenue requirements must yield to taxpayers' interest in finality regarding tax liabilities and credits. That point has been reached in this case.[187]

In *Carlton*, the Supreme Court discounted the importance of lack of actual or constructive notice and detrimental reliance in challenging retrospective taxation on due process grounds. In the process, the Supreme Court overturned the Court of Appeal's decision in favour of the taxpayer which, according to the Supreme Court, had been based on earlier case law[188] 'during an era characterized by exacting review of economic legislation under an approach that has long since been discarded'.[189] All members of the Court accepted that it was sufficient to satisfy the Due Process Clause that the 1987 amendment was supported by a legitimate legislative purpose furthered by rational means, with Blackmun J commenting that 'Tax legislation is not a promise, and a taxpayer has no vested right in the Internal Revenue Code'.[190] However, this reasoning has been severely criticized on the doctrinal basis. In applying to retrospective taxation legislation a broad rational means test applicable to prospective laws, the factors of notice and reliance unique to due process retrospectivity analysis were ignored. Nor does it reflect the facts of the case in that the taxpayer was effectively penalized for responding to the government's inducement to increase employee stock ownership by offering tax deductions:

Under this scheme the government attained its objectives while not only removing the deduction *ex post facto*, but also by leaving the estate in a worse position than it would have been in had the government never offered the deduction. Here, both the government and the ESOP benefited from the 'bait and switch' taxation whereas the estate suffered a loss of more than half a million dollars.[191]

4.9 Legislation by press release

One form of retrospective legislation that has been much used since the late 1970s is derisively known as 'legislation by press release', in which Ministers announce that the law will be changed, and that those changes will be backdated to the date of that announcement. The legislation thus has a date of commencement earlier than the day it receives royal assent. Despite being attacked from

---

[186] Sup Ct South Carolina, Opinion No 24682, 2 September 1997, available at <http://www.law/sc.edu/opinions/24682.htm>.   [187] Ibid.
[188] See in particular *Welch v. Henry* 305 US 134 (1938).
[189] 512 US 26 (1994) at 34 per Blackmun J.   [190] Ibid at 33.
[191] Ricciardi (1996) at 14.

many quarters,[192] the practice is specifically designed to answer the major objection to retrospectivity. It does not undermine guidance or expectations, since no reasonable person would rely on a law remaining the same when the Minister has specifically said that it will be changed.

In Australia, the practice of legislation by press release has been used by a variety of Commonwealth Departments, for example in relation to foreign takeovers and to prevent the Northern Territory Government from putting Crown land out of the reach of aboriginal land claims.[193] A recent example from the United Kingdom is the Commons Bill 2005 (not enacted at time of writing) which contains provisions prohibiting the severance of common land rights from the property to which rights are attached in order to protect the environment from overgrazing and inappropriate development. The provisions are expressed to come into force retrospectively from the date of the Bill's publication on 28 June 2005 in order to prevent a rush of opportunistic severance of common rights prior to enactment.[194]

The most frequent users of legislation by press release, however, have undoubtedly been taxation authorities. Where tax avoidance is concerned, the rationale for allowing a statute, regulation or ruling to be retrospective to the date of its announcement is obvious: legislation takes time to draft, and if the executive is unable to announce the immediate closure of the 'avenue' being exploited, the avenue will turn into a freeway. There is also a long-standing convention that, where changes to taxation laws are announced in the Budget speech or in similar statements, they may—indeed, should—be made retrospective to the date of announcement, to prevent tax-payers from taking advantage of any foreknowledge provided by the statement.[195] This convention extends to situations where the Parliament has enacted legislation permitting the responsible Minister to announce changes which can then be subsequently validated by legislation. For instance, the *Excise Act 1901* (Cth) permits the Minister to alter excise tariffs by tabling an excise tariff proposal in Parliament; the proposal must then be validated by legislation within twelve months.[196]

---

[192] See, for example, Australia, 'Annual Report 1986–7 SSCSB', *Parliamentary Paper No 443 of 1987*, pp. 11–17; Sir Anthony Mason, 'The State of the Australian Judicature' (1989) *Law Institute Journal* 977; Law Council of Australia, 'Legislation by Media Release', Media Release of 18 July 1988; Law Council of Australia, 'Submission on Legislation by Media Release', attachment to Media Release of 18 July 1988; Law Council of Australia, 'Views of Taxation Commissioner Condemned', Media Release of 5 October 1988. Australia, *Work of the Committee During the 38th Parliament*, SSCSB, 1997 Chapter 2, p. 10, available at <http://www.aph.gov.au/senate/committee/scrutiny/work38/report/c02.htm>.

[193] See C. Sampford and A. Palmer, 'Retrospective Legislation in Australia' (1994) 22 *Federal Law Review* 217.

[194] See 'Common land, town and village greens and the Commons Bill', Defra, 2005, available at <http://www.defra/gov.uk/wildlife-countryside/issues/common/legislation/commons-bill>.

[195] Australia, *Annual Report 1986–87*, SSCSB, Parliamentary Paper No 443 of 1987, p. 13.

[196] *Excise Act 1901*, s 114. The *Customs Act 1901* contains a similar provision. Commonwealth statutes falling within this convention include the *Bass Strait Freight Adjustment Levy Amendment Act 1985*, the *Customs Tariff Amendment Act 1985*, the *Excise Tariff Amendment Act 1985*, the *Customs Tariff Amendment Act 1986*, and the *Excise Tariff Amendment Act 1986*.

Objections to legislation by press release include a lack of precision; the under-mining of Parliament, respect for the law and the Rule of Law; and excessive delay. In the United States, the *Taxpayer Bill of Rights Number 2* (1996) offers some temporal protection to taxpayers by providing that any temporary, proposed, or final Internal Revenue Service regulation may not apply to any taxable period ending before the earliest of two dates: the date the regulation is published in the Federal Register or the publication date of 'any notice substantially describing the expected contents of any temporary, proposed or final regulation'. Furthermore, the effective date of a final regulation cannot be any earlier than the date it was published in the Final Register in temporary form. However, regulations to prevent taxation abuse and regulations to correct 'procedural defects' in prior regulations are excluded from the above requirements.[197]

Despite the numerous objections to legislation by press release, governments have generally been prepared to pass tax Bills backdated to the announcement that foreshadowed the Bills' policy. This may indicate the beginning of an extension of the Budget convention to statements made at any time of the year; this could be defended on the ground that the tax system is so complex that it requires fine-tuning throughout the year, not just at Budget time. Alternatively, Parliament's non-rejection of such Bills may be evidence of how far the practice has under-mined the independence and authority of Parliament. Faced with a *fait accompli*, and the very fact that citizens will have acted in reliance on the Ministerial announcement, Parliament may have little choice but to cave in.

Lack of precision in ministerial announcements

One objection is that the eventual Bill is generally not made available until well after the press release:

Persons such as lawyers and accountants who must advise their clients on the law are compelled to study the terms of the press release in an attempt to ascertain what the law is ... one press release may be modified by subsequent press releases before the Minister's announcement is translated into law. The legislation when introduced may differ in signif-icant details from the terms of the announcement.[198]

However, this generally overstates the difficulty. In most cases, the lawyer's advice is simple—'do not touch that tax scheme and do not go near anything similar'. While lawyers would like to be able to give their clients very precise advice, this is not always possible; for example, the meaning of existing legislation may be unclear and a common law precedent may be under doubt. In any unsettled or unclear area of law, the good lawyer will advise caution. Certainly the government should give as much guidance as possible and as early as possible.

[197] Public Law 104-168-July 30, 1996 (H.R. 2337), Title XI—Relief from Retroactive Application of Treasury Department Regulations, s 1101. The Bill is available at <http://www.unclefed.com>.
[198] Australia, *Annual Report 1986–87*, SSCSB, Parliamentary Paper No 443 of 1987, p. 12.

In the United Kingdom, a criticism of the press-release announcement of anti-avoidance provisions relating to employee securities, tax arbitrage and financial avoidance, which were to be contained in the Finance Bill 2005, was that their scope and operation was not 'sufficiently clear', running counter to the European Court of Justice judgment in *Stichting Goed Woenen*.[199] The ECJ held that a Community measure may 'exceptionally' have retrospective effect 'where the purpose to be achieved so demands and where the legitimate expectations of those concerned are duly respected'. It further stated that in assessing whether the legitimate expectations of taxpayers were respected, 'the procedures for dissemination of information normally used by the Member State which adopted it and the circumstances of the case must be taken into account'. However, the Court held that it was for national courts and not the ECJ to determine 'whether those documents were sufficiently clear to enable an economic operator ... to understand the consequences of the legislative amendment proposed for the transactions it carries out'. The conclusion to be drawn from this case is that legislation by press release is acceptable provided that it is clear and is communicated in a manner appropriate for the country and in line with its normal practices.

Furthermore, expectations formed by taking a literalist as opposed to a purposive approach to interpreting a press release, particularly one heralding an anti-avoidance taxation measure, are probably not rational. In Australia, persons may request a private ruling from the Australian Tax Office when they have some genuine doubt as to whether the transaction they wish to enter will be covered by tax legislation foreshadowed in a press release. In the United Kingdom, there is a similar procedure of 'post-transaction rulings' and the provision of information and guidance as to HM Revenue and Customs' interpretation of the law in situations of genuine uncertainty.[200] The Internal Revenue Service in the United States offers taxpayers a system of private letter rulings, determination letters and information letters which will 'not generally be revoked or modified retroactively'.[201]

Taxpayers who chose not to avail themselves of these procedures may in fact be motivated by the desire to exploit a loophole which they believe tax officials have overlooked. This was certainly the Australian Government's defence of the *Taxation Laws Amendment Act 1987*. It argued that 'those who sought to rely on a narrow interpretation of the announcement deliberately took a risk that the foreshadowed Bill might not be as complete in its outlawing of a tax avoidance

---

[199] C-376/02 (17 April 2005). The eventual bill that was passed, the *Finance Act (No 2) 2005* omitted many of the anti-avoidance provisions of the original Finance Bill 2005 due to the calling of the UK general election and the dissolution of Parliament. The government has announced its intention to re-introduce the provisions at a later stage. Lawrence Graham 'Finance Bill 2005' available at Legal500.com at <http://www.legal500.com/devs/uk/ct/ukct-280.htm>.

[200] See 'Information and Advice', Code of Practice 10, HM Revenue and Customs (UK) available at <http://www.hmrc.gov.uk/pdfs/cop10.pdf>.

[201] See IRS Revenue Procedure 1997-1-Letter rulings, determination letters, and information letters available at Uncle Fed's Tax Board website <http://www.unclefed/com/Tax-Bulls/1997/Rp97-1.pdf>.

practice as would obviously be necessary'[202] and warned that the chief effect of the Senate's eventual removal of those provisions that went beyond the announcement was to 'confer an unwarranted benefit on a small group of eagle-eyed tax accountants and their clients who deliberately tried to frustrate the intention of the Treasurer's announcement'.[203] The ATO noted that it had received very few enquiries about the Bill, and suggested that this was because 'people had seen a loophole in the announcement and did not really want to have that drawn to attention'.[204]

Undermining Parliament, respect for the law and the Rule of Law

Some strongly object that 'legislation by press release . . . involves a usurpation of the Parliament's legislative power by the Executive'.[205] The Australian SSCSB has, itself, argued that the practice of making statutes retrospective to the date of their announcement:

. . . treats the passage of the necessary retrospective legislation 'ratifying' the announcement as a pure formality. It places the Parliament in the invidious position of either agreeing to the legislation without significant amendment or bearing the odium of over-turning arrangements which many people may have made in reliance on the Ministerial announcement.[206]

In the tax avoidance cases, this is not really a problem because the taxpayer will generally not rely on either the existing law (which is under risk of change) or the new law (which no one can be sure will pass) but seek to avoid legal regulation entirely. However, where a citizen or corporation seeks to rely on the proposed new legislation before it is passed and acts in ways that remain legally forbidden until and unless the retrospective legislation is passed, Parliament may be faced with and uncomfortable dilemma. For example, on 27 November 1986, the Minister announced the Australian Government's intention to replace the 'two-station' rule limiting ownership of commercial television licences with a '75 per cent reach' rule, with new legislation to be backdated to the date of this announcement. The *Broadcasting (Ownership and Control) Act 1987* (Cth) eventually passed; however, not before a '60 per cent reach' rule was substituted. It was obvious that this change to the rules would lead to drastic changes in the ownership and control

---

[202] *Reports on the Sales Tax (Exemptions and Classifications) Amendment Bill (No 2) 1986* and *Taxation Laws Amendment Bill (No 5) 1986* (Parliamentary Paper No 137 of 1987, at para. 3.13).

[203] Minister Cohen, *Hansard*, House of Representatives, 1987, vol. 155, p. 3950.

[204] *Reports on the Sales Tax (Exemptions and Classifications) Amendment Bill*, at para. 3.14.

[205] Law Council of Australia, 'Legislation by Media Release' Media Release of 18 July 1988. See also Australia, *Annual Report 1986–87*, SSCBS, Parliamentary Paper No 443 of 1987, pp. 12–13; Sir Anthony Mason, 'The State of the Australian Judicature' (1989) *Law Institute Journal* at 977.

[206] Australia, *Annual Report 1986–87*, SSCSB, Parliamentary Paper No 443 of 1987, p. 12. See also Australia, Work of the Committee During the 38th Parliament, SSCSB, chapter 23, p.10, available at <http://www.aph.gov.au/senate/committee/scrutiny/work38/report/c02.htm>.

of the Australian media. But the Minister's announcement effectively precluded Senate debate. With the 'two-station' rule effectively suspended by Executive fiat, those seeking to buy licences acted at once on the basis of that Minister's declaration that the 'two-station' rule would be retrospectively repealed as from the date of announcement. By the time the Bill was introduced into Parliament, media ownership patterns now largely conformed to the rule which had been announced, rather than to the law as it stood. Parliament's options were either to ratify the policy change, or to reject it and so force some of the new owners to divest themselves of their acquisitions.

Another objection to 'legislation by press release' is one of the arguments made against retrospective law in general: namely, that it undermines the respect of citizens for the law because '[p]eople are expected to comply, not with the law as it stands, but with what the Executive says that the law will be declared to be at some future time . . . These procedures encourage people to act on the footing that the existing law is irrelevant'.[207]

This gives further credence to the argument that although the Executive's use of 'legislation by press release' may serve the valid purpose of discouraging reliance on pre-existing inadequate/unsettled law, we should be alert to the dangers of encouraging reliance on yet-to-be enacted laws by the same means.

The undermining of Parliament and respect for the law objections to legislation by press release both fall within the umbrella 'Rule of Law' critique of retrospective legislation.[208] We have already noted that the reason why retrospective laws, in general, are seen to contravene the Rule of Law is that the law should be capable of guiding the behaviour of citizens. But as long as the announcement foreshadowing changes to the law is specific and clear, the delay between announcement and enactment is not too great, and the legislation which is eventually enacted conforms to the announcement, there is no reason why the announcement should not be capable of guiding the behaviour of citizens until the legislation is introduced. The Rule of Law criticism applies, in other words, not to the practice as a whole but to isolated instances of it (or certain ways of carrying it out) where the above requirements are not met.

Excessive delay

The problem with excessive delay is that it creates a degree of uncertainty about whether the legislation will ever be introduced, and therefore about the substantive law that will eventually govern the transactions concerned.

The solution is to impose a reasonable time limit within which the Bill should be introduced. The Australian Senate seeks to impose a six-month rule, which on its face is entirely reasonable but in practice may not be sufficient because of

---

[207] Mason (1989) at 977.
[208] Law Council of Australia, 'Views of Taxation Commissioner Condemned', Media Release of 5 October 1988.

unforeseen circumstances.[209] One example was given by the SSCSB in relation to the *Taxation Laws Amendment Act (No 2) 1997.* The Government had first announced its intention to change the law in a press release dated 6 December 1995; a general election was called on 27 January 1996 and the new Government was sworn in on 11 March 1996. The amendments were re-announced in a press release of 25 June 1996 and on 31 July 1996 the release of draft legislation was announced. In other words, the six-month rule was exceeded by eight weeks but this could be 'attributed to the 14 weeks between the announcement by the previous Government on 6 December 1995 and the swearing in of the [new] Government on 11 March 1996'.[210]

The Senate has shown it is prepared to take action in the case of what it (reasonably) deems to be excessive delay. The *Taxation Laws Amendment Act (No 4) 1988* was foreshadowed by an announcement on 4 February 1985 that non-cash business benefits would be taxed. When the Bill was introduced three-and-a-half years later, the Senate amended the Bill to take effect from the date of introduction.

Improved taxation practice

The Australian Taxation Office has recently released guidelines for the administrative treatment of retrospective legislation which clarify when departures from the usual principle that taxpayers should apply the law existing at the time of lodging their income tax returns may be appropriate.[211] These guidelines seek to address the compliance costs and uncertainty caused by taxation legislation by press release, reducing the need for individual taxpayers to resort to private rulings to clarify their legal obligations. In general, the Commissioner may specifically advise taxpayers to meet their obligations by anticipating the effects of a proposed change to the law. Alternatively, where details of the new law are unsettled and there is no existing law covering the topic, the Commissioner may inform taxpayers that the ATO will not be seeking to enforce compliance with the existing law subject to the outcome of the proposed amendments.

The Commissioner is to take into account the following factors in determining whether a departure from applying the existing law at the time of lodgement is justified:

(a) the taxpayers affected can be identified;

(b) the likelihood of Parliamentary passage of the change is high and imminent;

(c) the change is revenue neutral or risks to revenue are extremely low;

---

[209] Senate Resolution of 8 November 1988 reproduced in Australia, *Work of the Committee During the 38th Parliament,* SSCSB, 1997 Chapter 2, pp. 10–11, available at <http://www.aph.gov.au/senate/committee/scrutiny/work38/report/c02.htm>.   [210] Ibid, p. 11.

[211] Australian Taxation Office, *Administrative Treatment of Retrospective Legislation* (1994), available at <http://www.ato.gov.au/taxprofessionals/content.asp?doc=/content/45130.htm>.

(d) the change reflects current community practice;

(e) using the existing law (that is, not anticipating the change) would undermine the community's confidence in the tax system; and

(f) it would not be a proper use of resources (both the Tax Office's and taxpayers) to require taxpayers to apply the existing law and then amend their returns once the proposed change is enacted.[212]

The ATO describes the rationale for a 'risk management approach' to administration of retrospective tax laws as being '[w]here the Government has announced a policy change, it is reasonable that a taxpayer may expect that the change has effect immediately and organize their business accordingly'.[213] Thus the ATO will not penalize taxpayers who have exercised reasonable care (either by following the existing law or following ATO advice to anticipate a change in the law) and will give taxpayers a reasonable time to put their affairs in order following enactment of the new law.

Many of the scenarios described in the guidelines are applicable to legislation by press release. For example, where 'a broad government announcement of intent has been made, but there is not yet sufficient detail to allow the Tax Office to provide appropriate practical guidance' and a taxpayer lodges a return making their 'best reasonable efforts to anticipate announcements', no tax shortfall penalties will apply when a later revision is required because of the effect of retrospective legislative change.[214] Likewise, a taxpayer who has acted reasonably to anticipate a legislative change which never eventuates, and who is thus liable to an amendment increasing their tax liability, will be publicly advised by the ATO that this is the case and will be granted a 'reasonable time' to lodge amendments and/or make payment.[215] Thus, in relation to taxation measures, the guidelines minimize damage to reliance expectations caused by such factors peculiar to legislation by press release as lack of detail and uncertainty as to whether the proposed changes will eventually be given force of law.

In the United Kingdom, accountants, lawyers and professional bodies are arguing for the introduction of a General Anti-Avoidance Rule and a pre-transaction ruling system (as opposed to the more limited post-transaction ruling system that currently exists) to provide more certainty and 'reduce the ever more complex anti-avoidance provisions [which are] denying the average taxpayer the ability to self-assess'.[216] The Institute of Chartered Accounts of Scotland in a recent report on retrospective legislation and tax simplification comments that:

There has to be a balance between the legitimate interests of the authorities in protecting tax revenues and the rights of taxpayers. The rights of taxpayers include legal certainty so anti-avoidance that works solely by creating uncertainty would appear to be contrary to fundamental EU legal principles. The uncertainty created by threatening retrospective

---

[212] Ibid, p. 1.   [213] Ibid, p. 1.   [214] Ibid, p. 4.   [215] Ibid, p. 5.
[216] See Institute of Chartered Accountants of Scotland, 'Simplification: Is it Time for a GAAR' (2005) available at <www.icas.org.uk>.

legislation, which has an effect back to the date of a press announcement, is a most unwelcome development . . . The Government itself has recognized that legislation targeted at specific avoidance schemes or arrangements may stop the scheme for the future but remain vulnerable to yet further avoidance schemes, constructed to find a way round the letter of the law. Experience has shown that the Office of Parliamentary Counsel finds it very difficult to draft legislation which is sufficiently well focused to affect only those practicing avoidance. If we have now reached the situation where the Government is introducing, with retrospective effect, legislation that is adversely affecting genuine commercial transactions whose sole or main purpose does not have any objective of tax avoidance, it is time to consider whether another process would make more sense.[217]

We would agree with this argument that the ever-increasing willingness of legislatures in all jurisdictions to resort to retrospective taxation measures with minimal parliamentary debate and justified analysis of consequences is a cause of great concern. Whilst recognizing that protecting tax revenue is a relevant interest, the war over avoidance is, itself, damaging to predictability. Reasonable reliance and alternative suggestions, such as a system of rulings, have greater merit in that they increase the possibility of taxpayer reliance on the law.

4.10 Conclusion

As the discussion in this chapter makes clear, retrospective legislation is quite common despite the negative light in which it is usually viewed. Although the least problematic kinds of retrospective law are obviously the most common, there have been examples even of the sorts of retrospectivity which are normally considered most objectionable (that is, retrospective criminal law).

It should be evident that not all of the uses of retrospective law considered here, however, are justifiable. Although many are unproblematic, others raise important issues, and some seem to represent an abuse of legislative authority. In order to prevent such abuses without also precluding the ability to make retrospective legislation where it is genuinely justified, it is important to be clear about the circumstances under which a positive argument exists in favour of retrospective law. However, before tackling that issue in Chapter 5, we should turn to the most common and least controversial forms of retrospective law-making—that practised by judges. The principles which justify judicial retrospectivity provide useful guides for when, and especially how, retrospective law-making should be pursued.

---

[217] 'Simplification: Is it Time for a GAAR' (2005) available at <www.icas.org.uk>.

5
Retrospective judicial law-making[1]

5.1 Introduction: Different conceptions of judging and the role of reliance

Justice Holmes once famously wrote that 'Judicial decisions have had retrospective operation for near a thousand years'. In doing so, he dismissed the Blackstonian formalist view of law which was that a change in a court's ruling implied 'not that the law is changed, but it was always the same as expounded by the later decision, and that the former decision was not, and never had been, the law, and is overruled for that very reason'.[2] He recognized that the judging process as inherently retrospective in the sense that it involves judges 'looking back at the acts of the parties who have brought their conflict before the court' as well as looking at their 'own previous acts and to reflect upon the significance of those prior acts of judgment in order to determine the outcome of the present case'.[3] With the rejection of the declaratory theory of law (the conception of the common law as existing independently of judicial decisions, with the judge's role to declare what the underlying law was according to established rules and precedents), the concept of judicial *law-making* was explicitly recognized and the categorical separation of previous old judicial rules from new rules was rendered impossible. This, in turn, created the problems of what law to apply (old or new) to the parties before the initial (law-changing) court and other courts and, in making these decisions, how to account for parties' reliance on previous law at the time of their action/transaction.

Including judicial retrospectivity in an overview of retrospective legislation shows not only how widespread retrospectivity is, but also how necessary it is. The principles which limit judicial retrospectivity also provide a useful general guide for when retrospective law-making (including legislation) is legitimate. And yet judicial retroactivity is arguably more complicated and can be distinguished from legislative retroactivity because judicial decisions operate on three sources of

---

[1] See C Sampford and A Palmer, 'Judicial Retrospectivity' (1995) 4 *Griffith Law Review* 170; some of the arguments and early case law are drawn from this article.
[2] K Roosevelt III, 'A Little Theory is a Dangerous Thing: The Myth of Adjudicative Retroactivity' (1999) 31 *Connecticut Law Review* 1075. Although Holmes' conception of law was essentially formalist, he rejected a merely mechanical jurisprudence. See Ronald A Cass, 'Judging, Norms and Incentives of Retrospective Decision-Making' (1995) 75 *Boston University Law Review* 941 at 942.
[3] Jeffrey Malkan, 'Retrospective Justification' (1990) 6 *Touro Law Review* 213 at 213.

law: the common law, statutes and the constitution.[4] Moreover, judicial retrospectivity is more likely to have retrospective effects than legislation, which are usually prospective in operation and effect.[5]

We have already noted that the primary argument against retrospectivity is the reliance citizens may reasonably place upon their expectations that the laws to be applied to their action/transaction will be the same as those applicable at the time of the action/transaction. Perhaps, the most celebrated attack on judicial retrospectivity was by Ronald Dworkin, who rejected Hart's theory of law because it appeared to entail a retrospective legislative role for the judiciary in so-called 'hard cases'.[6] Dworkin argued that judges do not exercise discretion to choose a new rule but find the rule which has the best fit with 'the best constructive interpretation of the community's legal practice', consisting of other rules and principles. Dworkin raised reliance to the pinnacle of his political philosophy—rights. There would be, in theory, only one right answer, and the party that would benefit from this best fit rule had a legitimate expectation that the right answer would be applied (a 'right to win').

For Dworkin, even in those cases where the court consciously, explicitly and formally overruled an earlier case, there would be no retrospectivity. The overruled case simply did not fit because it was inconsistent with higher principles already present within the law. However, the Dworkinian model does not adequately account for reliance expectations in cases where the decision is not simply to extend an existing rule or distinguish it, but is one that abrogates an existing rule or overrules an earlier decision. Whether or not the new decision fitted the law better than the previously accepted rule, it is likely to defeat reasonable reliance upon the older 'ill-fitting', but at the same time apparently authoritative, rule.

Of course it could be argued that the retrospectivity objection has little relevance to 'hard cases' because these are, by definition, situations in which there is uncertainty in the law and hence reliance cannot be reasonable. In such cases, it may be argued that the dispute could not be resolved without the retrospective application of the new rule, and that the uncertainty makes it difficult for anyone to mount the most powerful argument against retrospectivity—that they had relied upon the law to their detriment.[7] However, judges respect the difficulty this creates for citizens trying to arrange their affairs, taking reliance seriously and attempting to be relatively predictable. They generally avoid overruling earlier decisions of their own and try to achieve a degree of consistency in their

---

   [4] See Roosevelt, at 1076.
   [5] See Cass, at 957, who notes the difficulty with maintaining a rigid retrospective-prospective distinction.
   [6] Ronald Dworkin, *Taking Rights Seriously* (Duckworth, London, 1987) 81–130 ('Hard Cases'); HLA Hart, *The Concept of Law* (Clarendon Press, Oxford, 1961) 128. This is discussed in greater detail in Sampford and Palmer.
   [7] Chapter 7 considers the issue of whether post-modernist assertions of legal indeterminacy destroy reliance and the rule of law.

interpretations. They respect decisions by appellate courts and try to avoid a permanent state of legal flux and resort to appeals.

Although judges only attempt to achieve these ends, and their degree of success is debatable, they are engaging with recent jurisprudential debates and theories of adjudication that consider the nature and limits of judicial power and what constitutes good decision-making. On the one hand, there is the traditionalist/ strict legalism argument that 'judicial activism' (or the creation of 'new' rules in 'hard cases' based on recourse to not only legal authority/precedent but also broader legal principles and policy, including human rights and international conventions)[8] amounts to retrospective judicial legislation, contrary to the rule of law and an impermissible intrusion into legislative and executive functions.[9] In response, there has been the rejection of the declaratory argument that judges should merely apply and never make the law, and the suggestion of some sort of 'happy medium' based on 'judicial creativity within constraints' or careful judicial consideration of 'when and why a new legal rule should be expressed by a judge; when restraint is called for in the judicial decision; and, when a new rule is justi-fied'.[10] The traditionalist conception of judging emphasizes systemic constraints whereas the other stresses judicial autonomy within reasonable bounds.[11] It is important to note that even the most strident supporters of judicial creativity are not advocating the abandonment of reliance expectations as a factor to consider in deciding whether to overrule a previous ruling by the court.

In summary, it would appear that we are being offered two versions of the func-tion of the judge and the judicial system. The declaratory paradigm (including Dworkin's conceptualization) stipulates that the judge in making a decision may only pay attention to the current established legal corpus, in the form of, for instance, common laws, statutes and the Constitution. It is assumed that in each case there is a legally right answer provided by this corpus and that this answer is able to be known by a given judge. The argument for the declaratory paradigm is threefold. First, it is unjust to retrospectively evaluate past actions on the basis of newly formed laws. Second, it is harmful to the Rule of Law to do so. Third, judicial law-making dissolves the division of powers between the legislature and the judiciary; and in democracies, judicial law-making does not have the democratic mandate which justifies legislation.

The activism paradigm leaves room in the judgment for strictly non-legal issues—including those of logic or rationality, notions of justice and fairness, and beliefs about public harm and benefit that can come from the judgment. It leaves open precisely how much room should be made for these issues, but generally

---

[8] See generally W Lacey 'Judicial Discretion and Human Rights: Expanding the Role of International Law in the Domestic Sphere' (2004) 5 *Melbourne Journal of International Law* 108.

[9] See Justice JD Heydon 'Judicial Activism and the Death of the Rule of Law' (2003) 23 *Australian Bar Review* 1; and in response Justice M Kirby, 'Judicial Activism? A Riposte to the Counter-Reformation' (2004) 24 *Australian Bar Review* 1. Also see Frank Carrigan, 'A Blast from the Past: The Resurgence of Legal Formalism' [2003] *Melbourne University Law Review* 163.

[10] See Kirby, at 1.   [11] See Cass, at 942.

accepts large constraints on when such considerations should be allowed involvement in the judicial decision-making process. There are four arguments for the activist paradigm. First, it is at the very least an unsubstantiated and contingent presumption—and at worst naïve and idealist—to claim that there is always one legally right answer to all cases, and that this can be known by any given judge. If this idealistic presumption is rejected, then the judge must appeal to some method of determining judgments in hard cases, and it seems that appealing, in a predictable and systematic way, to notions of rationality, justice and social harmfulness are reasonable ways out of this impasse.

Second, while it may be unjust to retrospectively evaluate past actions on the basis of a newly formed rule, this violation of justice only has *pro tanto* force— there may be other morally salient considerations of justice, fairness and social harm that vastly outweigh it in any given instance. For the declaratory paradigm demands that even patently unjust applications of a particular law must be enforced. So it is important to note that the declaratory paradigm does not rest on the moral belief that *Fiat Justitia, ruat caelum*. Rather, it is adherence to the much less plausible (and less poetic) proposition that 'the legally right judgment must be made, though the heavens fall and justice not be done'.

Third, leaving no room for considerations of the potential harm of adhering to the legally right answer itself deeply undermines the Rule of Law. In cases where myriad agents have acted in good faith on past precedents fixed by a judgment now believed to be mistaken, there is no room in the declaratory paradigm for giving these expectations any consideration whatsoever. But if the citizenry are aware that any new judgment, coming without warning, could conceivably illegalize a lifetime of actions performed with full respect and well-informed knowledge of the law, then the amount the citizenry's actions can be guided by the law is significantly diminished.

Fourth, while it is true that in judicial activism there is some dissolution of the distinction between the legislature and the judiciary, this dissolution need only be very slight. The legislature still has the final say in the creation of all new laws, and may use with impunity its power to overrule judicial activism in those cases where the executive feels this is required. Thus, while judicial activism allows the judiciary to play a role in the creation of laws, it ultimately cedes the final decision to the legislature.

For these reasons, the declaratory paradigm is untenable. Judges do alter the law through clarification and overruling inconsistent rules and in doing so they use contestable propositions of law, general political theory and their understanding of the effects of earlier decisions. Given the obvious parallels between these processes (with its necessarily retrospective application) and retrospective legislation, we might expect that the principles judges use to determine when and how they will engage in judicial law-making may have relevance to the ways in which retrospective legislation should be circumscribed.

Clearly, when courts abrogate an existing rule of law, this has the closest similarities to a legislative process. For example, in the High Court of Australia decision of *Trident General Insurance Co Ltd v. McNiece Bros Pty Ltd*,[12] it was held that a third party, who was not a party to the insurance contract in question, but who fell within the class of persons expressed to be insured by the contract, was indemnified by the insurance contract and could insist on its performance. The decision makes inroads into the doctrine of privity of contract and to the requirement that consideration must move from the promisee. Justice Mason and Chief Justice Wilson stated that it was 'the responsibility of the Court to reconsider in appropriate cases common law rules which operate unsatisfactorily and unjustly'.[13] To deny the plaintiff the opportunity to enforce the contract would have been unjust because it would fail to give effect to the common intention of all the parties; and the plaintiff almost certainly would have relied on the (erroneous) belief that the insurance contract provided it with a benefit. Given that the defendant had received consideration for the promise to provide the benefit, justice favoured ensuring that the expectation was not defeated.

However, although philosophers and judges alike recognize the importance of reliance, there is always a strong, simple, contrary argument that the new rule is simply a better rule. According to von Savigny, 'a new law is always enacted in the persuasion that it is better than the former one. Its efficacy, therefore, must be extended as far as possible, in order to communicate the expected improvement in the widest sphere'.[14] Justice McHugh of the Australian High Court stated that the alternative to allowing the retrospective application of new rules is that 'the court should maintain and apply an unjust or inefficient rule'.[15] While this evaluation of the original rule does not undermine the argument for reliance, it is also the case that reliance on a rule around which judicial storm clouds are gathering may not be entirely rational. Lord Devlin's 'warnings of unsettled weather' which reduce the likelihood of later judge-made change coming 'out of blue sky', spring to mind.[16]

Thus we may conclude, as we do with legislative retrospectivity, that reliance arguments are important but they will vary in strength, depending on how uncertain the judicial and legal climate was and what alternatives were available to those who acted on an assumption of no change. And judicial retrospectivity need not be particularly worrisome (and particularly, need not have any significant adverse

---

[12] *Trident General Insurance Co Ltd v. McNiece Bros Pty Ltd* (1988) 165 CLR 107.

[13] Ibid, at 123.

[14] FC von Savigny, *Private International Law, and the Retrospective Operation of Statutes* (T. and T. C., Edinburgh, 1869) 344.

[15] Hon Mr Justice M McHugh, 'The Law-Making Function of the Judicial Process—Part II' (1988) 62 ALJ 116 at 124; and J Bell, *Policy Arguments in Judicial Decisions* (Oxford University Press, Oxford, 1983) 234.

[16] Lord Devlin, *The Judge* (Oxford University Press, Oxford, 1979) 11; approvingly quoted by McHugh at 124.

effects on people's reliance on the law) provided that the courts' exercise of the power to overrule themselves is exercised in a reasoned and principled manner set out as much as possible in advance so that citizens can appreciate the potential for change in the law. However, this proviso will not always be met, giving real cause for concern. In *R v. Shipuri*,[17] Lord Bridge used *dicta* to wonder if he might be prepared at some future date, having overruled an earlier decision in *Shipuri*, to then in turn overrule *Shipuri* and reaffirm the earlier decisions. Were such indiscriminate overruling to become commonplace, we might expect a diminution in the Rule of Law. At the same time, however, it is arguable that parties should not discount the possibility of a court later reaffirming an earlier decision that had been subsequently overruled.

Hodder summarizes the following themes invoked by those in favour of 'judicial creativity':

1. It is wrong for the court to perpetuate past errors.
2. It is right to modify the law to reflect changes in society.
3. It is right to reverse earlier decisions that may (now) be seen to be contrary to principle.
4. It is right to modify common law rules, made by judges, to bring them into conformity with contemporary notions of justice and human rights (especially where such rights have a quasi constitutional status).[18]

However, the traditional rule of law arguments by those concerned to preserve the role of precedent in 'deciding cases according to law' are as follows:

1. It is wrong to proceed on the basis that the judges of a final court of appeal are not themselves bound by established law.
2. It is wrong, and productive of undesirable uncertainty, for judges to decide the law is one thing on one date but another thing on a later date.
3. It is wrong, and damages judicial legitimacy, if a change to the law is a result of the accident of the membership of the court on the particular occasion.
4. It is wrong to encourage litigants to pursue a claim on the basis that a latter court might form a different outcome to that pronounced earlier.
5. The consequences and desirability of a change in the law will require accumulation of a range of information and advice, and balancing of competing social forces, properly undertaken through legislative processes, not the judicial process.[19]

What, then, are the principles by which courts have overruled an earlier decision and how have they been applied?

---

[17] *R v. Shipur* [1987] 1 AC 1 at 23.
[18] Jack Hodder, 'Departure from "Wrong" Precedents by Final Appellate Courts: Disagreeing with Professor Harris' [2003] *New Zealand Law Review* 161 at 176.   [19] Hodder, at 176–7.

5.2 Overruling: Broad constraining principles in the House of Lords, High Court of Australia and the United States Supreme Court

The overruling by a court of its own earlier decision, like retrospective legislation, clearly involves issues of retrospective rule making and its potential effect on those who rely on the decisions overruled. Harris identifies four general principles constraining the House of Lords in exercising the power to overrule its own earlier decisions.[20] The first is what he calls the 'No-New-Reasons Principle': where a legal question is finely balanced between two equally tenable views, a court should not second-guess, because they will be unable to deny that a later court might wish to third-guess. New reasons may arise where there is evidence of the legislature's intention, which was not introduced in the earlier case. If the case turned on questions of doctrine, new reasons may arise where some principles were over-looked[21] or if new principles have emerged in earlier cases. If the decision turned on the consequences of the competing alternatives, a new reason may arise from the emergence of unforeseen or unforeseeable consequences of the earlier decision.[22]

The second principle applies where there has been justified reliance on the previous decision. For example, the House of Lords will take into account 'the danger of disturbing retrospectively the basis on which contracts, settlements of property and fiscal arrangements have been entered into and also the especial need for certainty as to the criminal law'.[23] This principle of justified reliance is obviously most relevant to the issue of retrospectivity.

The third constraining principle Harris terms 'Comity with the Legislature'. This is the idea that a court ought not to overturn a decision if the legislature appears to have acted on the assumption that the decision represents the law, and in particular, has evinced an intention that the decision ought to remain the law. He states that the most convincing evidence is where the Parliament has rejected, or failed to adopt, the recommendation of a law reform agency that the rule be changed.

The fourth and final constraining principle is that of 'mootness'; the principle that a court should not embark on the review of rules which do not bear directly on the issue in the case at hand.

Harris subsequently argued for a relaxing of these principles so that 'merely wrong' precedents of final appellate Courts should be subject to a presumption in

---

[20] JW Harris, 'Towards Principles of Overruling—When Should a Final Court of Appeal Second Guess' (1990) 10 *Oxford Journal of Legal Studies* 135.

[21] Gaurdon J's dissent in *Jones v. The Commonwealth* (1987) 61 ALJR 348 at 349–50 was based on this reason. This case is discussed below.

[22] An example being the difficulties for judge and jury resulting from the rule in *Viro v. R* (1978) 141 CLR 88, discussed below.

[23] *Practice Statement (HL: Judicial Precedent)* [1966] 1 WLR 1234.

favour of reversal, which might be rebutted by 'overriding *stare decisis* values'.[24] He suggested that this presumption should apply where judges hold the view that the decision is 'merely wrong' on the basis of ideals of justice or human rights considerations but are unable to draw upon the usual grounds for departing from precedent such as the existence of a distinguishable circumstances, the earlier decision overlooked a material factor, the earlier decision proved to be unworkable, or new arguments were not put to the earlier court.

Against this, Hodder argues that this model fails to give enough weight to the general presumption against judicial law-making; in particular with the risk that a 'right' answer may become 'wrong' because of a changed composition on the bench with different opinions as to a 'more just' outcome.[25] However, Harris's discussion of relevant case law suggests he was aware of this risk.[26] His model involves a presumption in favour of reversal tempered by *stare decisis* considerations is one approach to the acknowledged need for appellate courts to more clearly and openly enunciate principles in deciding whether or not to overrule in 'hard cases'. Whereas Harris favours judicial creativity within bounds, Hodder puts a higher premium on stability; although, he too recognizes that there may be circumstances in which 'compelling reasons of logic and public benefit' justify the overruling of an earlier decision.[27]

Excessive retrospective judicial law-making is kept in check by the judicial obligation to give and publish reasons; to sit in public; the potential of review and overruling of judgments by appellate courts; and judicial consideration of how those who may have relied on earlier statements of the law by courts should be treated. For example, the *Practice Statement (HL: Judicial Precedent)* states that their Lordships are free to depart from earlier decisions when it is 'right to do so'.[28] The only caveat that appears on the face of the Practice Statement is that, when considering overruling an earlier decision, their Lordships should be mindful of the possible adverse (retrospective) impact of the new decision on, for instance, existing contracts entered into in reliance on the earlier decision. In short, this possible adverse impact is a relevant public policy consideration that, in appropriate circumstances, might stay their Lordships' hand from overruling an earlier decision. Thus, although the House of Lords considers itself as having the power to overrule its own earlier decisions, it states that it will only do so under certain conditions: namely, (a) that the earlier decision was wrong; (b) that the particular proposition advanced for the court's consideration in the present case represents an advance and benefit for the law as a whole; and (c) that there is

---

[24] JW Harris, 'Final Appellate Courts Overruling Their Own "Wrong" Precedents: The Ongoing Search for Principle' (2002) 118 LQR 408.   [25] Hodder, at 176–7.

[26] Hodder notes that Harris discusses the Privy Council case of *Lewis v. Attorney-General of Jamaica* [2001] 2 AC 50 at 89–90 in which Lord Hoffmann in dissent discusses the inadequacy of changing judicial personnel as a ground for departing from previous governing decisions. See Hodder, at 173.   [27] Hodder, at 184.

[28] *Practice Statement (HL: Judicial Precedent)* [1966] 1 WLR 1234.

little or no likelihood that the court will later reaffirm its earlier decision.[29] This approach suggests that the moving force is a clear, firm and stable view that the new rule is 'better' tempered with a respect for reliance interests.

The High Court of Australia also takes itself to have the power to overrule its own earlier decisions, and has exercised this discretion from at least 1914.[30] However, the Court will not be persuaded to overrule an earlier decision just because the earlier case now appears to have been wrongly decided. Rather, other public policy factors must also apply. In *John v. Commissioner of Taxation*[31] the High Court identified the following four matters that justified the overruling of an earlier decision, the fourth of which is concerned with reliance:

1. If the earlier decision was not based on a principle carefully worked out in a significant succession of cases.

2. If there were differences in the reasoning of the majority judges.

3. If the earlier decision had achieved no useful result and had in fact caused considerable inconvenience.

4. If the earlier decision had not been independently acted upon in a way which militated against its reconsideration.

The first two matters indicate that the decisions are less anchored in existing law and consistent with other legal rules. The third refers to consistency of purpose and effect, and the final one reflects reliance concerns. The Court explicitly acknowledged that people had acted on its earlier overruled decision in *Curran v. Commissioner of Taxation*[32] during the period 1974 to 1978 (before *Curran* was reversed by statute) in a way which militated against its reconsideration. However, the High Court held that its fundamental duty was to give effect to the intention behind the statute (an attitude that would, if taken by the Barwick court, have largely prevented the problems of tax avoidance and the need for retrospective legislation and legislation by press release). Arguably, there was no real injustice in this case because the affected tax-payers did not rely on the Curran interpretation to their detriment, but had hoped to generate very large paper losses for taxation purposes from transactions that, in fact, cost them no more than the schemes promoter's fees. The court's concern should not be that the taxpayer loses a benefit to which (as subsequently realized) he was never entitled: the concern should be that the tax-payer should not suffer because of the court's temporary 'error' in interpretation.

In the High Court of Australia, the latest judicial statement of general principles appears in the majority judgment delivered by Kirby J in *Brodie v. Singleton*

---

[29] Ibid. The High Court of Australia takes a parallel position regarding its power to overrule its own earlier decisions. See discussion of High Court cases in this section, below.

[30] *Tramways Case* (1914) 18 CLR 54.

[31] *John v. Commissioner of Taxation* (1989) 166 CLR 417 at 438–9.

[32] *Curran v. Commissioner of Taxation* (1974) 131 CLR 409.

Shire Council.[33] His Honour describes four considerations supporting changes to the common law, despite the effect this has on the rights of parties and others:

1. The common law must be compatible with the Constitution so that '[c]onsiderations of inconvenience, the existence of longstanding authority and cost must bend to the *Constitution's* requirements'.

2. Where previous decisions have significantly altered the direction of the common law, particularly where influenced by fundamental civil rights, the Court must 'follow through the "logical consequences" of the previous shift in law' in subsequent cases.

3. The High Court's function is to 'contribute to the simplification of legal concepts, replacing categories with principles that will permit a more coherent and efficient application of the common law', particularly where the law is anachronistic, contrary to principles of equality or subject to 'defects occasioning confusion, uncertainty or injustice'.

4. While acknowledging the primary role and responsibility of the legislature, the Court also has a responsibility to 'repair clearly demonstrated defects of judge-made law'.

The first consideration emphasizes the differential authority of the sources of law and the last is a clear 'better rule' argument. The middle two involve giving judge-made law greater coherence and consistency. The last two grounds for overruling are the more controversial.[34] However, Kirby J tempers this analysis with a consideration of those factors which might persuade a given court to leave legal change up to the legislature, including the extent to which there is long-standing authority for the rule, the scope and implications of any change including social, economic and political impact and the fact that legislatures unlike the judiciary can effect change after 'notice to the public, appropriate debate and an opportunity for expert advice'.[35] The last two points indicate a degree of flexibility available to legislatures—the ability to halt new legislation until sufficient information has been gathered and the ability to determine the degree to which the legislation is prospective. His Honour acknowledges that the decision to either retrospectively alter the common law or reaffirm past authority is 'not susceptible to a mechanical solution' but a balancing act depending on the circumstances of the case:

[T]he greater the apparent affront to justice and the more confused, anachronistic and unprincipled the current law appears to be, the more likely is it that a judge with authority to do so will eventually feel obliged to attempt a re-expression of the law. On the other

---

[33] *Brodie v. Singleton Shire Council* (2001) 206 CLR 512 (discussed below). All quotes are found at 593.

[34] Kirby J goes so far as to assert that courts cannot be expected to 'indefinitely ignore' such defects where legislatures have had defects drawn to their attention and failed to act: (2001) 206 CLR 512 at 594.   [35] Ibid, at 595–6.

hand, the greater the antiquity of the rule, the larger the implications of change, the more interests that are affected and the closer the occasions of legislative attention, the less likely will it be that the judge will feel authorized to disturb past authority.[36]

The United States Supreme Court also takes itself to have the power to overrule its own decisions and its justices are in fact more likely to give candid and detailed consideration to the problems inherent in overruling and to policy considerations than their English and Australian colleagues. Some explain this by citing a more collegial and flexible nature of the United States Supreme Court, with a written decision arrived at in advance after debate and discussion between justices as opposed to the usual practice in England and Australia of individual judgments arrived at separately.[37] It seems that the United States Supreme Court considers the doctrine of *stare decisis* to be more 'a rule of thumb than an iron-fisted command' and, particularly in constitutional cases, will reconsider a precedent simply because it believes the prior case to have been incorrectly decided.[38] This traditionally relaxed approach to *stare decisis* in constitutional cases may reflect the difficulty of amending the Constitution, or the more politicized nature of the Court (the influence of voting and opinion coalitions within the Court),[39] which makes the court the only effective mechanism for change.[40]

However, common law precedents enjoy a much stronger presumption of correctness, with Eskridge suggesting that the United States Supreme Court will engage in the following tripartite analysis of common law precedent, with the precedent only overruled when each question is 'answered in the affirmative':

(1) Informated by criticism of the precedent and its reasoning by commentators, lower court judges, and the Court's own opinions, can the Court now say with confidence that the precedent was wrongly decided? (2) Is the precedent not just wrong, but also pernicious, detracting from overall national policies? (3) Do the policy problems engendered by the rule outweigh the potential unfairness to private persons and the uncertainty for the other rules based upon the challenged rule, which will occur if the precedent is overturned?[41]

---

[36] Ibid, at 596.

[37] See for further discussion Richard P Caldarone 'Precedent in Operation: A Comparison of the Judicial House of Lords and the United States Supreme Court' (2004) *Public Law* 759; and 'Charnock—Overruling as a speech act' (no author) available at <trinity.dit.unitn.it/ipra2005/uploads/Charnock_Overruling.doc>.

[38] William N Eskridge Jr 'Overruling Statutory Precedents' (1988) 76 *Georgetown Law Journal* 1363.

[39] '[t]he first and most obvious factor affecting the Court's decision to overrule a precedent is the ideological compatibility of the court with the precedent.' James F Spriggs II and Thomas G Hansford 'Explaining the Overruling of US Supreme Court Precedent', available from University of California Center for the Study of Law and Society Jursprudence and Social Policy Program at <http://repositories.edlib.org.csls.lss/9>.

[40] This argumenet originated with Justice Louis Brandeis in his famous dissent in *Burnet v. Coronado Oil and Gas Co* 285 US 393 at 406–7 (1932), in which he stated 'in cases involving the Federal Constitution, where correction through legislative action is practically impossible, this Court has often overruled its prior decisions.'   [41] Eskridge (1988) at 1388.

Like the House of Lords and the Australian High Court, the United States Supreme Court will also give special treatment to its statutory precedents, based on the traditional arguments that first, statutory amendment is for the legislature not the judiciary; second, the lack of legislative intervention to counter the judicial precedent governing interpretation of the statute is assumed to indicate legislative approval or at least acquiescence in the *status quo*; and third, a contrary interpretation will upset private parties settled expectations, conduct and business arrangements made in reliance on the authority of the precedent.[42] However, also on a par with the House of Lords and the Australian High Court, Eskridge observes that despite the theoretical objections to revisiting statutory precedents, the United States Supreme Court will overrule or at least significantly modify statutory precedents using two methods:

(1) not completely admitting what it is doing, or

(2) by reference to three 'exceptions': (a) if the Court's original discussion of the issues is procedurally unsatisfactory; (b) if the statute is generally worded and has not been the subject of extensive legislative tinkering; and/or (c) if subsequent legislative developments have undercut the rationale of the decision and private parties have not extensively relied on it.[43]

The following three sections of this chapter will consider actual examples of superior courts overruling their own precedent from the House of Lords, the Australian High Court and the United States Supreme Court respectively.

5.3 House of Lords examples

Until the adoption of the Practice Statement in 1966, the House of Lords had considered itself bound by Lord Halsbury's ruling in the 1898 *London Tramways* case that 'a decision of this House once given upon a point of law is conclusive upon this House afterwards, and that it is impossible to raise that question again as if it were *res integra* and could be reargued.'[44] The Law Lords had sought to ameliorate the harshness of this rule by distinguishing cases on the facts; subject to the following limitation: distinguishing two legal situations not only consists in finding their factual variants, but also requires that these differences are such as to justify the rejection of a precedent which is *a priori* binding. Accordingly, the process of distinguishing cannot always set aside an unfair or absurd precedent and, where abusively used, it denatures and complicates the content of legal rules.[45]

---

[42] Eskridge (1988) at 1366–7. The second argument, as pointed out elsewhere in this chapter, is particularly problematic as it assumes too much from legislative inaction.

[43] Paraphrasing Eskridge (1988) at 1367; 1384.

[44] *London Tramways v. London City Council* [1898] AC 375 at 380.   [45] Rorive, at 331.

Paterson extracts the following normative criteria or guidelines for overruling espoused by Lord Reid in a series of early cases[46] which continue to enjoy varying degrees of support from the Law Lords:

1. The freedom granted by the 1966 Practice Statement ought to be exercised sparingly.

2. A decision ought not to be overruled if to do so would upset the legitimate expectations of people who have entered into contracts or settlements or otherwise regulated their affairs in reliance on the validity of that decision.

3. A decision concerning questions of construction of statutes or other documents ought not to be overruled except in rare and exceptional cases.[47]

4. (a) A decision ought not to be overruled if it would be impracticable for the Lords to foresee the consequences of departing from it.

5. (b) A decision ought not to be overruled if to do so would involve a change that ought to be part of a comprehensive reform of the law. Such changes are best done 'by legislation following on a wide survey of the whole field'.

6. In the interests of certainty, a decision ought not to be overruled merely because the Law Lords consider that it was wrongly decided. There must be some additional reasons to justify such a step.

7. A decision ought to be overruled if it causes such great uncertainty in practice that the parties' advisers are unable to give any clear indication as to what the courts will hold the law to be.

8. A decision ought to be overruled if in relation to some broad issue or principle it is no longer considered just or in keeping with contemporary social conditions or modern conceptions of public policy.[48]

Principles 2, 3, 5 and 6 are related to the reliance arguments that are so central to debates about retrospectivity. Principle 4 reflects a recognition that the legislature is the primary organ for changing the law but principle 7 recognizes that this does not absolve the Courts from their responsibility to update the Common Law.

A commonly-cited example of a case judicially-recognized as falling within the terms of the Practice Statement is *Miliangos v. George Frank (Textiles) Ltd*[49] in which the House of Lords effectively overruled its earlier holding in *United Railways of the Havana and Regla Warehouses Ltd*[50] that courts cannot give judgment for payment of a sum in a foreign currency. Lord Wilberforce explicitly referred to the Practice Statement and held that to depart from *United Railways*

---

[46] See especially *Jones v. Secretary of State for Social Services* [1972] AC 944, 966.

[47] See generally G Maher, 'Statutory Interpretation and Overruling in the House of Lords' (1981) *Statute Law Review* 85.

[48] A A Paterson, 'Lord Reid's Unnoticed Legacy—A Jurisprudence of Overruling' (1981) 1 *Oxford Journal of Legal Studies* 375 at 375–6. Paterson notes that the sixth criterion of overruling cases which cause great uncertainty has received less support.   [49] [1975] 3 All ER 801.

[50] [1960] 2 All ER 332.

'would not involve undue practical difficulties, that a new and more satisfactory rule is capable of being stated' and that to change the rule would 'avoid injustice in the present case' and 'enable the law to keep in step with commercial needs and with the majority of other countries facing similar problems.'[51]

An additional (eighth) criterion referred to by Paterson which appears in the Practice Statement but was not the basis of Lord Reid's reasoning in the subsequent decade is 'the expectation that a decision in criminal law ought to be overruled only in exceptional circumstances, in view of the especial need for certainty in criminal law.'[52] Thus in *C v. Director of Public Prosecutions*[53] the House of Lords refused to abolish the blanket common law presumption that a child between the age of 10 and 14 is incapable of commiting a crime, rebuttable only by clear positive evidence that the child knew that his or her act was seriously wrong, with evidence of the acts amounting to the offence itself being sufficient to rebut the presumption. All Law Lords acknowledged 'the anomalies and even absurdities' the presumption produced but held that it was for Parliament and not the courts to review the law as it stood. Lord Lowry in setting out the following guidelines for judicial legislation referred to Lord Lloyd's leading judgment in *R v. Clegg*[54] (in which the House of Lords refused to create a new qualified defence of using excessive force in self-defence or to prevent crime/effect lawful arrest, available to a soldier or police officer acting in the course of his duty, to reduce what would otherwise be murder to manslaughter): (1) if the solution is doubtful, the judges should beware of imposing their own remedy; (2) caution should prevail if Parliament has rejected opportunities of clearing up a known difficulty or has legislated while leaving the difficulty untouched; (3) disputed matters of social policy are less suitable areas for judicial intervention than purely legal problems; (4) fundamental legal doctrines should not be lightly set aside; (5) judges should not make a change unless they can achieve finality and certainty.[55] In this formulation, reliance was not a primary consideration. In the unlikely event that a child under 14 relied on the blanket presumption that they could not commit a crime, the child would be disproving that which was presumed.

However, in *R v. Howe*[56] the House of Lords overruled *Lynch v. DPP for Northern Ireland*[57] and held that the defence of duress was not available to a person charged with murder whether as principle in the first degree (the actual killer) or as principle in the second degree (the aider and abettor).[58] The House of

---

[51] [1975] 3 All ER 801 at 812 per Lord Wilberforce.

[52] Ibid, at 380–1, noting that Lord Reid commented (somewhat ironically given the outcome in that case) on the particular need for certainty in the criminal law in *DPP v. Shaw* [1962] AC 220 at 281–2.

[53] [1995] 2 All ER 43.   [54] [1995] 1 All ER 334.   [55] [1995] 2 All ER 43 at 52.

[56] [1987] 1 All ER 771.   [57] [1975] 1 All ER 913.

[58] In *R v. Gotts* [1992] 1 All ER 832 the House of Lords approved of the Court of Appeal below following dicta of Lord Griffiths in *R v. Howe* that a defence of duress should also not be available on a charge of attempted murder: 'It was always pure chance that the attempted murderer was not a murderer and the fact that the attempt failed to kill should not make any difference to the defences available to the accused' [1992] 1 All ER 832 at 832.

Lords noted that the weight of authority 'dating back to Hale and Blackstone' was that duress was not available to a defendant accused of murder (despite a lack of clear precedent one way or another) and added that 'the right course in the instant appeal is to restore the law to the condition in which it was almost universally thought to be prior to Lynch's case.'[59]

Lord Hailsham stated that principle and public policy dictated that those charged with murder (as opposed to the lesser crime of manslaughter) be deprived of the defence of duress and implied that this alone was sufficient to justify the overruling of *Lynch*: 'the overriding objects of the criminal law must be to protect innocent lives and to set a standard of conduct which ordinary men and women are expected to observe if they are to avoid criminal responsibility.'[60] This highlights the reliance of those whom the Criminal Law is intended to protect which is stronger than the reliance that might be placed for someone who might have killed in reliance of the defence.

The cases of *R v. Shivpuri*[61] and *R v. G*[62] are rare examples of the House of Lords overruling its previous decisions despite the fact that the relevant precedents concerned the application of the criminal law *and* statutory interpretation. In *Shivpuri* the House of Lords overturned *Anderton v. Ryan*[63] as to the correct construction of s 1(1) of the *Criminal Attempts Act 1981*, resulting in the conviction of Mr Shivpuri for attempting to commit the offence of being knowingly concerned with dealing with prohibited drugs. Although Shivpuri in fact believed that he was carrying a prohibited substance, the material found in his possession was subsequently analysed as harmless vegetable matter. The decision in *Anderton* was only a year old. Lord Bridge, who had been in the majority in *Anderton* asked: 'Is it permissible to depart from precedent under the 1966 Practice Statement...notwithstanding the especial need for certainty in the criminal law?' He concluded that it was, particularly as there was no valid ground upon which the court could simply distinguish the prior precedent:

Firstly, I am undeterred by the consideration that the decision in *Anderton v. Ryan* was so recent. The 1966 Practice Statement is an effective abandonment of our pretension to infallibility. If a serious error embodied in a decision of this House has distorted the law, the sooner it is corrected the better. Secondly, I cannot see how, in the very nature of the case, anyone could have acted in reliance on the law as propounded in *Anderton v. Ryan* in the belief that he was acting innocently and now find that, after all, he is to be held to have committed a criminal offence.[64]

In *R v. G*[65] the House of Lords overruled *R v. Caldwell*[66] as to the correct interpretation of the term 'reckless' in section 1 of the *Criminal Damage Act 1971*. In that case, Lord Diplock had formulated a model direction to the jury which the trial judge in *R v. G* felt bound to follow despite expressing unease that under the

---

[59] [1987] 1 All ER 771 at 778.   [60] Ibid at 778.   [61] [1986] 2 All ER 334.
[62] [2004] 1 AC 1034.   [63] [1985] 2 All ER 355.   [64] [1986] 2 All ER 334 at 345.
[65] [2004] 1 AC 1034.   [66] [1982] AC 341.

Caldwell direction 'the ordinary, reasonable bystander' is an adult and that no allowance was made for the youth of the boys or their lack of maturity (the case before the House concerned two children who had lit fires under a wheelie bin not forseeing the possibility that the fire might spread to nearby buildings). The risk of potential injustice and sustained academic criticism of *Caldwell* outweighed such factors as the age of the precedent (relevant to the second criterion), the need for certainty in the law, and the fact that the case concerned a question of statutory interpretation of a criminal law which had been recently re-enacted unchanged despite recommendations to do so. Interestingly enough, there would be no reliance arguments either by the defendants (for whom such argument would be logically impossible) or the victims (whose ability to recover insurance would not have been affected either way).

Shivpuri and *R v. G* may be contrasted with *McDonnell v. Congregation of Christian Brothers Trustees and Others*,[67] in which the House of Lords refused to overrule or distinguish its earlier decision in *Arnold v. Central Electricity Board*.[68] The case turned on the statutory interpretation of a series of Limitation Acts affecting claims for damages for negligence in situations where plaintiffs did not become aware, at the time of suffering injury or before the expiry of the limitation period, of their injury or its link with the conduct of another (the facts concerned the sexual abuse of institutionalized children). Lord Bingham commented:

I would accept that a different conclusion might have been reached by the House in *Arnold*... The decision has been the subject of measured but penetrating criticism... It is arguably anomalous to treat six-year and three-year claims differently, since if a cause of action expires before a plaintiff can reasonably be aware of it the potential injustice is as great in the one case as in the other. But *Arnold* was a unanimous decision of the House which has now stood for 16 years. It may doubtless have been relied on and applied to defeat other claims. Parliament could, if it wished, have reversed the decision, but has not done so. The decision is not plainly wrong, even if one were inclined to disagree with it, and the House has made plain that 'it requires much more than doubts as to the correctness of [a considered majority opinion of the ultimate tribunal] to justify departing from it'... Sympathy for the possible injustice suffered by the appellant must be tempered by recognition of the almost impossible task the respondents would face in seeking to resist a claim of this kind after the lapse of half a century.[69]

The deciding factor against overruling precedent in this case seems to have been the subject-matter of the claim. Although the case did not strictly involve the criminal law, in the House of Lords opinion, the risk of injustice to defendants in seeking to defend themselves against a negligence claim for sexual abuse (that would otherwise have been time-barred according to an accepted interpretation of the law) outweighed the risk of injustice to the plaintiff.

However, this reasoning is clearly open to criticism on grounds of both principle and logic: potential evidentiary problems faced by defendants should not have

---

[67] [2004] 1 All ER 641.   [68] [1988] AC 228.   [69] [2004] 1 All ER 641 at 654.

prevented an alleged victim of child sexual abuse from having his claim determined in court, particularly when adhering to the statutory interpretation in *Arnold* led to the anomalous result of some plaintiff's actions being time-barred and others not in remarkably similar circumstances. The argument by Lord Bingham that 'Parliament could, if it wished, have reversed the decision, but has not done so' is also open to the obvious objection that parliamentary failure to act is simply a normal part of political life and should in no way be characterized as approval for the *status quo* without further investigation.[70]

The second and third guidelines extracted from the Practice Statement, weighing against retrospective overruling of precedent on the basis of both upsetting legitimate expectations of people who have acted in reliance on the pre-existing law, and on the basis of a new/different statutory interpretation, may be seen at work together in the reasoning of the House of Lords in the recent case of *Jindal Iron and Steel Co Ltd v. Islamic Solidarity Shipping Co Jordan Inc (The Jordan II)*.[71] The House of Lords refused to overrule *GH Renton and Co v. Palmyra Trading Corporation's*[72] interpretation of Article III rule 2 of the Hague Rules ('... the carrier shall properly and carefully load, handle, stow, carry, keep, care for and discharge the goods carried'). *Renton* had approved of earlier dicta of Lord Devlin that a purposive rather than literal interpretation of Art III rule 2 was called for to allow the responsibility for cargo work to be transferred contractually. In other words the rule did not override freedom of contract to allocate responsibility for loading and unloading cargo to another party but merely compelled carriers to exercise these functions carefully when they in fact performed them. The Court of Appeal below had found that the contract of carriage had effectively transferred responsibility for loading and discharge from the owners of the ship to the appellant and the receivers of the cargo.

In the House of Lords judgment was delivered by Lord Steyn who declined to overrule *Renton* on reliance grounds:

> ... the rule in Renton has stood for almost 50 years. It is probable that an enormous number of transactions have taken place on the assumption that Renton represents the law. Moreover, it seems likely that there are many open transactions, not yet finalized by judgment, arbitration award or settlement, which were concluded in reliance on the rule in Renton. Against this background, Counsel for cargo owners invited the House to rule that Renton was wrongly decided. Even if exceptionally a prospective overruling of a decision of the House could be permitted, it would be of no use to cargo owners ... Cargo owners ask the House not to regard the impact of past transactions as a factor of significance and to decide retrospectively that Renton was wrongly decided in 1957. Against this background an observation in *Vallejo v. Wheeler* (1774) 1 Cowp 143 is apposite. Lord Mansfield

---

[70] See Lord Reid and Lord Diplock in *R v. Knuller (Publishing, etc) Ltd* [1973] AC 435 at 455 and 480, noted by Maher (1981), at 90.

[71] [2005] 1 Lloyd's Rep 57; [2005] 1 All ER 175. The case is discussed by Timothy Young 'Precedent and travaux preparatoires: The Jordan II' available at <http://www.jus.uio.no/nifs/seminar/disposisjoner/Tim%20Young.doc>.   [72] [1956] 2 Lloyd's Rep 379.

observed (at 153) that: In all mercantile transactions the great object should be certainty: and therefore, it is of more consequence that a rule should be certain, than whether the rule is established one way or the other. Because speculators in trade then know what ground to go upon... That is, of course, not to say that the House might not be persuaded under the Practice Statement to depart from an earlier decision where that decision has been demonstrated to work unsatisfactorily in the market place and to produce manifestly unjust results... But, in a case such as the present, if that high threshold requirement is not satisfied, it would not be proper to reverse the earlier decision.[73]

If the law clearly allocates liability to one party, then they know the risks and can generally take action to insure against it, price the risk and take it or seek to pass the risk on to the other party for a negotiated fee. If the court changes the allocation of risk set out by previous interpretations, merchants, manufacturers and bankers may well be exposed to risks they could not reasonably expect while those who insured against the risk have wasted their money. Such an approach will run into difficulties where there is disparate bargaining power but the abuse of such market power is generally best left to specific legislation (such as Fair Trading Acts) or the requirements of equity than changing common law rules in an unpredictable way.

This is not to say that the House of Lords will never overrule its pervious interpretations, even in commercial cases. In *National Westminster Bank v. Spectrum Plus Ltd*[74] commercial lenders had relied on a decision of a lower court in *Siebe Gorman and Co Ltd v. Barclays Bank*[75] to the effect that a charge over present and future book debts, expressed to be a fixed charge, where the book debts were placed in an account with the lender but the borrower was free to draw on the account for its business purposes, as indeed constituting a fixed charge in law. This gave the lending bank priority over other creditors whose security was only in the form of a floating charge in the event of the borrower's insolvency. However, the House of Lords in overruling *Siebe Gorman* held that such a charge was in fact merely a floating charge because the asset subject to the charge was not finally appropriated as a security for the payment of the debt until the occurrence of a future event. The charger was left free to use the charged asset and to remove it from the security. Lord Hope commented:

It is hard to think of an area of the law where the need for certainty is more important than that which your Lordships are concerned in this case. The commercial life of this country depends to a large extent on the reliability of the security arrangements that are entered into between debtors and their creditors... [but] the fact is that [*Siebe Gorman*] was a decision that was taken at first instance, and it has now been conclusively demonstrated that the construction which he [Slade J] placed on the debenture was wrong. This is not one of those cases where there are respectable arguments either way. With regret, the conclusion has to be that it is not possible to defend the decision on any rational basis. It is

---

73 [2005] 1 All ER 175 at 183–184.
74 [2005] UKHL 41 <http://www.bailii.org/uk/cases/UKHL/2005/41.html>.
75 [1979] 2 Lloyd's Rep 142.

not enough to say that it has stood for more than 25 years. The fact is that, like any other first instance decision, it was always open to correction . . . Those who relied upon it must be taken to have been aware of this . . .[76]

However, they are still prepared to adopt a new interpretation where the previous interpretation is 'plainly incorrect'. In *Cave v. Robinson Jarvis and Rolf*[77] the House of Lords overruled an earlier interpretation of section 32 of the *Limitation Act* 1980 in *Brocklesby v. Armitage and Guest*[78] which would have deprived the defendants in a negligence claim of a limitation defence when they were in fact unaware that they were committing a breach of duty.

The coming into force of the *Human Rights Act 1998* (UK) on 2 October 2000 and the House of Lord's increased willingness to interpret legislation in light of changing public policy are both factors which have led to a relaxation of the court's extreme reluctance to overturn statutory interpretation precedents.[79] Section 3 of the Human Rights Act provides that: 'So far as it is possible to do so, primary legislation and subordinate legislation must be read and given effect in a way which is compatible with the Convention rights', without affecting the validity, continuing operation or enforcement of any incompatible legislation. Lord Nicholls in *Wilson v. First Country Trust Ltd (No 2)* commented that:

Section 3 is retrospective in the sense that, expressly, it applies to legislation whenever enacted. Thus section 3 may have the effect of changing the interpretation and effect of legislation already in force. An interpretation appropriate before the Act came into force may have to be reconsidered and revised in post-Act proceedings.[80]

The House of Lords has often struggled to reach a compromise between paying due deference to the original intention of Parliament in enacting the relevant legislation and its duty under section 3 to interpret the legislation so as to uphold Convention rights 'so far as it is possible to do so.' In *Wilson*, Lord Nicholls who gave the leading judgment for the House of Lords invoked the presumption against retrospective operation and the narrower presumption against interference with vested interests to justify the proposition that section 3 will not generally apply to causes of action accruing before the Human Rights Act came into force. He identified the correct approach for the courts to take as one of identifying the intention of Parliament in respect of the relevant legislation in accordance with Staughton LJ's statement in *Secretary of State for Social Security v. Tunnicliffe*:

. . . the true principle is that Parliament is presumed not to have intended to alter the law applicable to past events and transactions in a manner which is unfair to those concerned in them, unless a contrary intention appears. It is not simply a question of classifying an enactment as retrospective or not retrospective. Rather it may well be a matter of

---

[76] *National Westminster Bank v. Spectrum Plus Ltd* [2005] UKHL 41 <http://www.bailii.org/uk/cases/UKHL/2005/41.html>.   [77] [2003] 1 AC 384.

[78] [2002] 1 WLR 598.

[79] See Keir Starmer, '*Two Years of the Human Rights Act*' (2003) 1 *European Human Rights Law Review* 14.   [80] [2004] 1 AC 816 at 831.

degree—the greater the unfairness, the more it is to be expected that Parliament will make it clear if that is intended.[81]

The court in *Wilson* held that section 3 did not apply to the relevant provisions of the *Consumer Credit Act 1974* as it could not have been Parliament's intention to alter the existing rights and obligations of the parties to a contract so as to deprive the claimant of the consumer credit protections she acquired when entering into the contract in 1999. Lord Nicholls was careful to emphasize that this conclusion did not mean that section 3 could never apply to pre-Act events; for example, 'different considerations apply to post-Act criminal trials in respect of pre-Act happenings' because it could not be said that the prosecution had an accrued or vested right as such.

In *Ghaidan v. Godin-Mendoza*[82] the House of Lords accepted the defendant's argument that section 3 of the Human Rights Act required the court to read paragraph 2 of the *Rent Act 1977* in a way so that it includes couples in a stable homosexual relationship as well as couples in a stable heterosexual relationship. Lord Nicholls again gave the leading judgment and reaffirmed that the compatibility of legislation with Convention rights falls to be assessed when the issue arises for determination, not at the date when the legislation was enacted or came into force.[83] He noted that the court will accord Parliament a 'discretionary area of judgment' when reviewing legislation under the Human Rights Act, and 'the court will reach a different conclusion from the legislature only when it is apparent that the legislature has attached insufficient importance to a person's Convention rights'.[84]

Lord Nicholls reiterated that the readiness of the court to depart from the view of the legislature depends upon the subject matter of the legislation and of the complaint (his Lordship commented that housing policy was a field where the court will be less ready to intervene because it is Parliament's role to balance competing interests of tenants and landlords based on social and economic policy). Lord Steyn also approved of 'the obvious proposition that inherent in the use of the word "possible" in section 3(1) is the idea that there is a Rubicon which courts may not cross.'[85]

For example, in *Bellinger v. Bellinger*[86] (a man who underwent sex-change treatment and surgery sought to come within the definition of 'female' for the purposes of the *Matrimonial Causes Act 1973*) and *R v. Her Majesty's Commissioners of Inland Revenue, ex parte Wilkinson*[87] (a widower sought to come within the definition of 'widow' in section 262 of the *Income and Corporation Taxes Act 1988* for the purpose of entitlement to a bereavement allowance) the House of Lords refused to read legislation in a Convention-compliant way on the basis that to do

---

[81] [1991] 2 All ER 712 at 724.   [82] [2004] 3 All ER 411.
[83] [2004] 3 All ER 411 at 422.   [84] [2004] 3 All ER 411 at 420.
[85] [2004] 3 All ER 411 at 428.   [86] [2003] 2 AC 467.
[87] [2005] UKHL 30 <http://www.bailii.org/uk/cases/UKHL/2005/30.html>.

so would give the relevant statutory provisions a meaning entirely inconsistent with Parliament's intention, would be a judicial usurpation of Parliament's role and would have broad public policy ramifications.

However, the House of Lords in *Ghaidan* held that the discriminating distinction drawn between the position of heterosexual and homosexual couples by virtue of the omission of the latter from succession rights to an assured tenancy in the Rent Act was not justifiable and fell outside the 'discretionary area' granted to Parliament. The court held that the application of section 3 to the Rent Act had the effect that paragraph 2 should be read and given effect to as though the survivor of such a homosexual couple were the surviving spouse of the original tenant, even though the language of the paragraph ('as his or her wife or husband') plainly and unambiguously referred exclusively to heterosexual couples:

Section 3 may require a court to depart from the unambiguous meaning the legislation would otherwise bear... that is, depart from the intention of the Parliament which enacted the legislation... the intention of Parliament in enacting section 3 was that, to an extent bounded only by what is 'possible', a court can modify the meaning, and hence the effect, of primary and secondary legislation. Parliament, however, cannot have intended that in the discharge of this extended interpretative function the courts should adopt a meaning inconsistent with a fundamental feature of legislation. That would be to cross the constitutional boundary section 3 seeks to demarcate and preserve. Parliament has retained the right to enact legislation in terms which are not Convention-compliant. The meaning imported by application of section 3 must be compatible with the underlying thrust of the legislation being construed. Words implied must... 'go with the grain of the legislation'. Nor can Parliament have intended that section 3 should require courts to make decisions for which they are not equipped. There may be several ways of making a provision Convention-compliant, and the choice may involve issues calling for legislative deliberation.[88]

In *R v. Her Majesty's Commissioners of Inland Revenue* Lord Hoffmann underlined the reasons why the courts may need to update precedent, even precedents of statutory interpretation along the lines of the Practice Statement's seventh principle:

It may have come as a surprise to the members of the Parliament which in 1988 enacted the statute construed in the *Ghaidan* case that the relationship to which they were referring could include homosexual relationships. In that sense the construction may have been contrary to the "intention of Parliament". But that is not normally what one means by the intention of Parliament. One means the interpretation which the reasonable reader would give to the statute read against its background, including, now, an assumption that it was not intended to be incompatible with Convention rights.[89]

---

[88] [2004] 3 All ER 411 at 423–424. Also see *R v. A (No 2)* [2002] 1 AC 45 in which the House of Lords read the implied words 'evidence or questioning which is required to secure a fair trial under Art 6 of the Convention should not be treated as inadmissible' into s 41 of the *Youth Justice and Criminal Evidence Act 1999* (an unambiguous statututory provision) so as to modify the 'rape shield' prohibition of the defendant giving evidence/cross-examining about the sexual behaviour of the complainant, except with leave of the court.

[89] [2005] UKHL 30 <http://www.bailii.org/uk/cases/UKHL/2005/30.html>.

5.4 Australian High Court examples

The Australian High Court's role of final arbiter of the meaning of Australia's written constitution means that it may depart from previous authority in the following circumstances:

... the Court will re-examine a decision if it involves a question of 'vital constitutional importance' and is 'manifestly wrong'. Errors in constitutional interpretation are not remediable by the legislature, and the Court's approach to constitutional matters is not necessarily the same as in matters concerning the common law or statutes.[90]

However, in the *Second Territorial Senators Case*,[91] Stephen J stated that the power to overrule a previous decision should be exercised by the High Court only 'after the most careful scrutiny of the precedent authority in question and after a full consideration of what may be the consequences of doing so'. Similarly, the Court in *Jones v. The Commonwealth*[92] stressed that the power to overrule should be exercised with great caution; the court by a six to one majority declined to reconsider its then recent decision in *Hilton v. Wells*,[93] a controversial 3 : 2 split decision in which the court declared constitutionally valid provisions of the *Telecommunications (Interception) Act 1979* (Cth) which conferred the power to issue warrants for telephone intercepts on Federal Court judges. In this case, factors against the exercise of the power were the fact that the decision was a very recent one at the time the High Court in *Jones* was asked to re-consider it, and amendments had been made to the statute which had been interpreted in the decision, so that the authority of the earlier decision would be confined to that period before the making of the amendments. The fact that the earlier decision in *Hilton v. Wells* was solely one of statutory interpretation provided a further reason for declining to overrule it. However, one would have thought that the newness of a decision should be seen as a matter making the exercise of the overruling power more likely, given that the decision would not have had time to create long-acquired vested interests.

Boeddu and Haigh in their review of constitutional overrulings by the High Court observe that having sound, clearly enunciated principles for overruling are perhaps more important in constitutional cases given that the effects of constitutional rulings are more permanent than in ordinary litigation (citizens can only hope to change the Constitution by referendum or litigate a new case and hope the court will arrive at a different conclusion despite the principle of *stare decisis*). Furthermore, reconsidering constitutional decisions gives the High Court significant power over other branches of government and so should not be treated

---

[90] *Lange v. Australian Broadcasting Corporation* (1997) 189 CLR 520 at 554. Noted in Andrew Lynch, 'Dissent: The Rewards and Risks of Judicial Disagreement in the High Court of Australia' [2003] *Melbourne University Law Review* 724 at 762.

[91] *Second Territorial Senators Case* (1977) 139 CLR 585 at 602.

[92] *Jones v. The Commonwealth* (1987) 61 ALJR 348.

[93] *Hilton v. Wells* (1985) 157 CLR 57.

as simply part of general judicial decision-making.[94] The above pronouncements by the Court in the *Second Territorial Senators Case* and in *Jones* indicate that the Court will only decide to overrule after consideration of the constitutional and governmental consequences of so doing, even if the previous authority relied upon is considered to be incorrect.

However, apart from the general factors set out in *John*, which are applicable in all overruling cases, the High Court has, to date, avoided any clear and explicit statement of principles for overruling in constitutional cases other than consideration of correctness of a precedent (the 'manifestly wrong' and 'of vital constitutional importance' basis for overruling). The High Court has considered a variety of other factors on an *ad hoc*, case-by-case basis. Boeddu and Haigh discern the following main factors from the constitutional case law: the effect on individual rights, the extent of governmental reliance on settled constitutional law, possible public inconvenience and public perception. They note that the High Court has tended to hide its reasoning behind the (inconsistently applied) doctrine of *stare decisis*, which strikes 'with all the predictability of a lightning bolt'.[95] The authors argue that judicial statements that *stare decisis* is less relevant in certain circumstances indicate the implicit factoring into decision-making of these other considerations. Boeddu and Haigh recommend that the High Court explicitly acknowledge and develop a two-stage test based upon firstly whether a decision is considered to be correct according to the Constitution, and secondly, if not, whether it should be overruled, with the second stage taking into account the practical and public policy factors mentioned above.[96]

The High Court seems to give greater weight to 'financial reliance' than to other types of legislative and executive reliance in deciding whether or not to overrule constitutional precedents. In *HC Sleigh Ltd v. South Australia*,[97] Jacobs J stated the Court needed to be 'convinced' of the decision's wrongfulness *and* its causing of 'social, economic or political consequences' before it could disturb the 'delicate' fiscal arrangements of States relying on settled constitutional interpretations. And the High Court's repeated refusal in the licence fee cases,[98] spanning three decades, to review its earlier decision in *Dennis Hotels Pty Ltd v. Victoria*, was consistently based on argument that the States had arranged their financial affairs in reliance on the constitutionality of licence fees where the fee for the licensee was calculated on the value of alcohol or tobacco purchased over a fiscal period prior to

---

[94] Gian Boeddu and Richard Haigh, 'Terms of Convenience: Examining Constitutional Overrulings by the High Court' (2003) *Federal Law Review* 167.

[95] Boeddu and Haigh, at 187, citing Henry Monaghan, 'Our Perfect Constitution' (1981) 56 *New York University Law Review* 353 at 390.   [96] Boeddu and Haigh, at 187.

[97] *HC Sleigh Ltd v. South Australia* (1977) 136 CLR 475 at 513.

[98] *Dennis Hotels Pty Ltd v. Victoria* (1960) 104 CLR 529; *Dickenson's Arcade Pty Ltd v. Tasmania* (1974) 130 CLR 177; *Evda Nominees Pty Ltd v. Victoria* (1984) 154 CLR 311; *Gosford Meats Pty Ltd v. New South Wales* (1985) 155 CLR 368; *Philip Morris Ltd v. Commissioner of Business Franchises* (1989) 167 CLR 399; and *Capital Duplicators Pty Ltd v. Australian Capital Territory (No 2)* (1993) 178 CLR 465.

the time that the licence applied.[99] It was not until 1997 that the High Court in *Ha v. New South Wales*[100] finally decided that it was time to reinstate the paramountcy of the 'maintenance of constitutional principle' over the states' 'reliance on revenue from a constitutionally unsound source'.[101]

In constitutional overrulings, other types of legislative and executive reliance have not been given as much weight as fiscal reliance. Boeddu and Haigh suggest this is because it is more inappropriate for the Court to find legislative and executive reliance outweighing considerations which are otherwise in favour of overruling. At a practical level, it is harder to ascertain the extent of this type of reliance and to calculate how much weight to give to it. Where the effect of overruling is to disallow existing legislation or nullify executive actions, case law indicates these consequences must be taken into account by the Court but they will not prevent the overruling of an otherwise incorrect decision.[102] In *Re Wakim*,[103] the overruling of *Gould v. Brown*[104] by the High Court meant that a useful legislative scheme of cooperative state and federal cross-vesting of court jurisdiction was invalidated. Although the scheme itself was not enacted in reliance upon the validity of the earlier decision, members of the Court acknowledged the adverse effects of rendering the scheme unconstitutional and the inconvenience it would cause the legislature.[105]

In *Newcrest Mining (WA) Limited v. Commonwealth*,[106] the majority of the High Court disapproved of *Teori Tau*,[107] in which it was held that the right to just terms guaranteed by section 51(xxxi) of the Constitution, did not apply to property acquisitions carried out under the section 122 territory power. Justice Kirby in his majority judgment emphatically 'reject[ed] the suggestion that the Court's response to an application to reopen past authority is controlled by the reliance which the Executive Governments... have placed upon past authority. There can be no estoppel against the Constitution'.[108]

---

99 These cases are discussed in Boeddu and Haigh, at 176–8. It was not until 1997 that the High Court finally found the courage to reinstate the paramountcy of the 'maintenance of constitutional principle' over the states' reliance on revenue from a 'constitutionally unsound source': *Ha v. New South Wales* (1997) 189 CLR 465 at 503.

100 *Ha v. New South Wales* (1997) 189 CLR 465 at 503.   101 Boeddu and Haigh, at 181–2.

102 Boeddu and Haigh, at 180.   103 *Re Wakim* (1999) 198 CLR 511.

104 *Gould v. Brown* (1998) 193 CLR 346.

105 See especially Kirby J in dissent: *Gould v. Brown* (1999) 198 CLR 511 at 603.

106 *Newcrest Mining (WA) Limited v. Commonwealth* (1997) 190 CLR 513.

107 *Teori Tau v. Commonwealth* (1969) 119 CLR 564.

108 *Newcrest Mining (WA) Limited v. Commonwealth* (1997) 190 CLR 513 at 646–7. See discussion in Boeddu and Haigh, ibid at 179–80. Cf *Durham Holdings v. State of New South Wales* (2001) 205 CLR 399 in which the High Court declined to overrule previous authority and ruled that there was no constitutional restriction upon the legislative power of state parliaments that required them to provide just or adequate compensation for the acquisition of property. Kirby J at 426 stated that: 'An application by this Court of its settled rule is fatal to the applicant... the present application would not afford a suitable vehicle to permit the re-argument of such a large proposition' and at 428 that 'the rejection by the electors [in a 1988 Constitutional Referendum] of a proposed amendment to the federal Constitution [which would have invalided the NSW legislation at issue in this case]... suggests a reason for special caution when this Court is invited, but twelve years later, effectively to impose on the Constitution of the State a requirement which the electors, given the chance, declined to adopt'.

This can be contrasted with Chief Justice Brennan's dissent:

If [Teori Tau] is not adhered to, the powers of territorial legislatures with respect to the compulsory acquisition of property are denied. There is a further and powerful consideration which tells against the reopening of *Teori Tau* ... numerous property transactions have taken place in the course of the Territories' development. If the [section 122] power does not support compulsory acquisitions, any grant or transfer of property that involved a compulsory acquisition is exposed to uncertainty if not invalidity. No validation of such a transaction could be effected by a retrospective payment of compensation; the legal consequence of any invalidity would simply be that the grant or transfer must be taken never to have occurred. That would produce consequences of unforeseen and unforeseeable difficulty.[109]

The majority's response to this argument was that even if these were the likely consequences of not adhering to *Teori Tau*, they 'would be a reason for hesitation to depart from established authority and for *requiring convincing argument* to reach the alternative view' but 'they could not provide a reason for withholding the meaning which the [Constitutional] text required'.[110] This is a clear indication that the High Court will require evidence of genuine reliance on precedent before taking such reliance into account as a factor in considering whether or not to overrule. In *Hospital Contribution Fund (No 1)*,[111] the court pointed out that the only action taken by the States in relying on precedents were their attempts to negate the effect of the precedents and this was considered to be evidence of a lack of reliance, or, as Boeddu and Haigh argue, a kind of negative reliance.[112]

In the landmark decision of *Mabo v. Queensland (No. 2)*,[113] in which the High Court rejected the doctrine of *terra nullius* as part of the common law of Australia, Brennan J referred to *Jones v. The Commonwealth*[114] in the course of his judgment.[115] His Honour stated that the Court was 'even more reluctant to depart from earlier decisions of its own' than to depart from English precedent, where the consequence would be to 'fracture the skeleton of principle which gives the body of our law its shape and internal consistency'.[116] Justice Brennan argued that the Court was not free to adopt rules that accorded with contemporary values and human rights if their adoption would 'fracture' this 'skeleton of principle'. However, where the rule seriously offended modern values and rights and international standards, it was legitimate for the Court to determine whether the rule should be preserved. In answering this question, the Court should not only assess whether the rule was an essential doctrine of the legal system, but also weigh the benefits to be gained by the overturning of the rule against the potential for

---

[109] Ibid, at 544–5 per Brennan CJ.
[110] Ibid, at 651–2 per Kirby J, emphasis added. Kirby J points to 'several instances where the holding of the Court has obliged significant rearrangements and readjustments in the rights and duties of those affected by its decisions. This is no more than the application of the rule of law in the constitutional context'. [111] *Hospital Contribution Fund (No 1)* (1982) 150 CLR 49 at 58.
[112] See discussion in Boeddu and Haigh, at 180. [113] (1992) 175 CLR 1.
[114] *Jones v. The Commonwealth* (1987) 71 ALR 497.
[115] *Mabo v. Queensland (No 2)* (1992) 175 CLR 1 at 30. [116] (1992) 175 CLR 1 at 29.

community uncertainty and disturbance.[117] His Honour held that the theory that an inhabited colony could still be *terra nullius* because of the 'primitive' nature of its indigenous people, used to deprive indigenous people of title to their land, could no longer underpin the common law. It was based on discriminatory and racist assumptions about Aboriginal and Torres Strait Islander people that did not accord with the known facts—even from the early days of the colony's settlement—about Australian indigenous cultures. Nor would it 'fracture a skeletal principle of our legal system' for the common law to recognize the land rights of indigenous people, as: 'it is not a corollary of the Crown's acquisition of a radical title to land in an occupied territory that the Crown acquired absolute beneficial ownership of that land to the exclusion of the indigenous inhabitants.'[118]

Nevertheless, reliance was offered as a reason for declining to overrule an earlier decision in *Geelong Harbour Trust Commissioners v. Gibbs, Bright and Co*,[119] *Queensland v. The Commonwealth*,[120] and *Zecevic v. DPP*.[121] In the first of these cases, which concerned the question of whether a statute imposed strict liability on those who damage port facilities, the fact that commercial transactions may have been entered into on the basis that the impugned decision, *Townsville Harbour Board v. Scottish Shire Line Ltd*,[122] represented the law was important. The second case concerned the question of whether the Commonwealth Constitution permitted the Parliament to grant representation in the Senate to the Australian Territories. A majority of judges (4:3) decided the question in the affirmative in *Western Australia v. The Commonwealth*.[123] Four of the judges in Queensland thought that the decision in Western Australia had been wrong, but only two of these judges (Barwick CJ and Justice Aickin) were prepared to overrule it. The other two judges (Gibbs and Stephen JJ) thought that the decision should not be overruled because:

To reverse the decision now would be to defeat the expectations of the people of the Territories that they would be represented . . . by senators entitled to vote—expectations that were no less understandable because in my view they were constitutionally erroneous, and that were encouraged by the decision of this court.[124]

However, a much stronger reason was that the changed composition of the court appeared to be the only reason for the changed majority on the substantive

---

[117] (1992) 175 CLR 1 at 30.   [118] (1992) 175 CLR 1 at 48.
[119] *Geelong Harbour Trust Commissioners v. Gibbs, Bright and Co* (1970) 122 CLR 504.
[120] *Queensland v. The Commonwealth* (1978) 139 CLR 585.
[121] *Zecevic v. DPP* (1987) 162 CLR 645.
[122] *Townsville Harbour Board v. Scottish Shire Line Ltd* (1914) 18 CLR 306.
[123] *Western Australia v. The Commonwealth* (1975) 134 CLR 201.
[124] *Queensland v. The Commonwealth* (1978) 139 CLR 585 at 600 per Gibbs J; at 603–4 per Stephen J; and for a contrary view at 630 per Aickin J. The case is remarkable for the fact that the majority views on the two issues in the case did not produce the outcome that would be logically entailed by those views. Four Justices thought the first case was wrongly decided and at least four thought it appropriate to overrule in cases such as this (Barwick, Aickin, Murphy and Jacobs JJ). However, because part of the majority on the second point were in the minority on the first, the logical conclusion from the two majority held views did not prevail.

issue. The High Court was clearly discouraging the re-opening of recently decided questions on such a basis. If this were not discouraged, it might invite further litigation and, even more dangerously, encourage governments to take into account the views of aspiring appointees to the bench in relation to recently decided cases.[125]

In *Zecevic v. DPP*,[126] the High Court discarded the test for self-defence which it had, itself, enunciated in *Viro v. R*.[127] The *Viro* formulation of the defence was so complicated that it had caused great problems for judges directing juries. The difference between the new and old tests turned on the effect of a finding by the jury that the amount of force used by the accused, albeit in self-defence, was excessive. According to *Viro*, such a finding implied a verdict of manslaughter; according to *Zecevic*, such a finding would result in a verdict of murder (providing no other defence, such as provocation, was made out).[128] Justice Deane dissented on the grounds that there might be people awaiting trial who had relied on *Viro's* case, in the sense of having made admissions or confessions which they would not have made if the law had been as formulated in *Zecevic*. This is a legitimate concern. However, it could be addressed in a far less drastic way by determining that any such admissions or confessions reached in the course of such a trial could be withheld from the jury.

Pfeiffer v. Rogerson[129] and *Regie National des Usines Renault SA v. Zhang*[130] are recent common law examples of the category of overruling previous decisions which are controversial and have plunged the law into confusion.[131] The effect of these two decisions was to reject the *Phillips v. Eyre* double actionability rule in intra-national torts and to prescribe the *lex loci delicti* (law of the place where the event took place) as the common law choice of law rule, rather than the *lex fori* (law of the forum). Previous decisions of the High Court[132] had led to forum shopping and had resulted in limitation defences, and limitations on the assessment of damages, being treated as procedural and governed by the law of the forum. Although these cases can be treated as instances of the High Court exercising its discretion to overrule incorrect precedent, they were not without controversy. Commentators raised the spectre of judicial activism in their analysis of the majority's decision in *Pfeiffer* that section 118 of the Constitution, which requires that full faith and credit be given to the 'laws, the public Acts and records and

---

[125] Cf. Keyzer who argues that changes in court composition may be the most reliable indicator that constitutional change is likely: Patrick Keyzer, 'When Is an Issue of "Vital Constitutional Importance"? Principles Which Guide the Reconsideration of Constitutional Decisions in the High Court of Australia' (1999) 2 *Constitutional Law and Policy Review* 13 at 18.

[126] *Zecevic v. DPP* (1987) 162 CLR 645.   [127] *Viro v. R* (1978) 141 CLR 88.

[128] See 'Current Topics' (1987) 61 ALJ 759 and Harris (1990), at 149.

[129] *Pfeiffer v. Rogerson* (2000) 203 CLR 503.

[130] *Regie National des Usines Renault SA v. Zhang* (2002) 210 CLR 491.

[131] See discussion in A Mason 'Legislative and Judicial Law-Making: Can We Locate an Identifiable Boundary?' (2003) 24 *Adelaide Law Review* 15 at 31.

[132] *McKain v. RW Miller Co Ltd* (1991) 174 CLR 1; and *Stevens v. Head* (1993) 176 CLR 433.

the judicial proceedings of every state', operated as a choice of law provision in its own right.[133]

In the criminal law case of *R v. L*,[134] the High Court held that, even if the proposition that marriage involved the irrevocable consent of the wife to sexual intercourse with the husband was established by common law authorities, the Court 'would be justified in refusing to accept a notion that is so out of keeping with the view that society now takes of the relationship between the parties to a marriage'.[135]

The High Court has considered that retrospective alteration of laws affecting criminal liability should rarely, if ever, be attempted by the judiciary.[136] Justice Kirby has warned against 'impos[ing] by judicial fiat new penal liabilities which go beyond those that clearly applied at the time when it is alleged that the offence was permitted'.[137] In *Wong v. R*[138] the High Court set aside the sentencing order imposed by the New South Wales Court of Criminal Appeal in relation to the convictions of two persons for drug importation on the basis that the Court had wrongly issued a table of prescriptive judicial sentencing 'guidelines' in the course of its deliberations, which were addressed to lower courts as though departures from the guidelines would be evidence of error by a sentencing judge. Whilst judicial sentencing guidelines were not, *per se*, invalid when they served the useful function of replacing informal judicial means of ensuring consistency in sentencing with a publicly declared standard, in *Wong*, the majority held that the guidelines had exceeded this permissible usage and had effectively created judicial subsets of a legislatively defined offence (by attributing most importance to the amount (weight) of the narcotic found). The guidelines set a higher benchmark of punishment than that prescribed by the relevant legislation, or at the very least distracted the Court from a full consideration of all of the other relevant matters that would ordinarily have been given weight in determining the correct sentence, and were thus invalid.[139] This finding, together with the fact that the guidelines were likely to influence the sentencing decisions of future courts because of their prescriptive and prospective nature, also led the High Court to strongly suggest (without explicitly deciding) that they were unconstitutional (beyond judicial power).[140]

---

[133] See HA Amankwah, 'Judicial Legislation: A New Phase? John Pfeiffer Pty Ltd v. Rogerson [2000] HCA 36' 7 JCULR 254.

[134] *R v. L* (1991) 174 CLR 379.

[135] Ibid, at 390 per Mason CJ, Deane and Toohey JJ. The High Court referred to *R v. R (rape marital exemption)* [1991] 2 All ER 257 in which the House of Lords had also abolished a husband's common law immunity from criminal liability for raping his wife.

[136] *Brodie v. Singleton Shire Council* (2001) 206 CLR 512 at 596 per Kirby J, referring to *Lipohar v. R* (1999) 200 CLR 485 at 561–2.   [137] *Lipohar v. R* (1999) 200 CLR 485 at 543.

[138] *Wong v. R* (2001) 207 CLR 584.

[139] Ibid, at 614–16 per Gaudron, Gummow and Hayne JJ; at 618, 621, 624, 631–2 per Kirby J.

[140] Ibid, at 613–14 per Gaudron, Gummow and Hayne JJ; at 635–8 per Kirby J; at 642 per Callinan J.

Justice Toohey has described the basis for the objection to retroactive criminal liability in Hayekian terms as 'the desire to ensure that individuals are reasonably free to maintain control of their lives by choosing to avoid conduct which will attract criminal sanctions'.[141] However, he qualifies this principle by stating:

Where... the alleged moral transgression is extremely grave, where evidence of that transgression is particularly cogent or where the moral transgression is closely analogous to, but does not for some technical reason amount to, legal transgression, there is a strong argument that the public interest in seeing the transgressors called to justice outweighs the need of society to protect an individual from prosecution on the basis that a law did not exist at the time of the conduct.[142]

According to this analysis, in the case of *R v. L* there are two bases for overcoming the retrospectivity objection: the conduct of the husband was undoubtedly a moral transgression which was closely analogous to the legal definition of rape; and the public interest in punishing his moral transgression outweighed his right to protection. In other words, there was a clash of rights: the wife's right to bodily integrity prevailed. In addition, the reliance argument is weak as it is unlikely that the husband actually acted in reliance on this defence, although it is certainly possible that he was aware that there was no such thing, in the eyes of the law, as rape within marriage. If he was so aware, his reliance on the existing rule seems to make his actions more, rather than less, morally reprehensible because of the premeditation. His expectation that he would avoid criminal sanctions would be rational, but without moral force.

These cases all seem to be examples of litigants asking the High Court to depart from previous decisions in circumstances where social and economic values and conditions have changed and the legislature has been inactive.

A further example of this trend, *Brodie v. Singleton Shire Council*,[143] relating to the liability of councils for defects in roads and footpaths, practically illustrates the problems of parties' reliance on pre-existing common law rules and the financial consequences of defeated expectations. This case by a narrow 4:3 margin overturned the common law 'highway rule' with its distinction, long-since abolished by legislation in England but not in Australia, between 'non-feasance' and 'misfeasance'. Under the old rule, developed last century when the tort of negligence had not been disentangled from that of nuisance,[144] if a defect developed in a highway by reason of wear and tear, the growth of tree roots, effluxion of time or in any way other than the positive act of the local council, the council was not liable for damage which the hole caused to road-users.

The High Court's decision had retrospective effect beyond the particular plaintiff in this case. If local council's insurance policies were based upon the settled

---

[141] *Polyukhovich v. Commonwealth* (1991) 172 CLR 501 at 688.   [142] Ibid, at 689.
[143] *Brodie v. Singleton Shire Council* (2001) 206 CLR 512. See discussion by Heydon, at 19.
[144] See discussion in joint majority judgment of Gaudron, McHugh and Gummow JJ: (2001) 206 CLR 512 at 568.

common law distinction, the overturning of this distinction exposed them to 'wide past uninsured liabilities in relation to any injury caused by non-feasance in the preceding three years which could now be sued for'.[145] Furthermore,

... If a change of that type had been effected by parliament, not only would councils have been given prior notice so as to enable insurance adjustments and the effecting of changes in their systems for detecting and repairing faults in roads, but State governments, or the Federal Government, would have been able to make financial arrangements with councils to enable them to meet the new responsibilities created by the widened liability.[146]

However, Kirby J considered that the extent of this burden upon local statutory authorities was exaggerated, as the only change was to substitute an anomalous immunity with a duty to take reasonable care in accordance with the ordinary principles governing the tort of negligence. Litigants would still have to establish a failure to take reasonable care by the relevant statutory authority, and, depending on the circumstances of the case, a duty of care may be 'unwarranted in the evidence concerning the resources and obligations of the authority, the steps it has taken to discharge its functions and the alternative priorities faced by it'.[147] Justices Gaudron, McHugh and Gummow considered that the financial costs of the change in law could be balanced against the costs of retaining the rule, observing that the old distinctions encouraged litigation and lead to 'expenditure of public moneys in defending struggles over elusive, abstract distinctions with no root in principle'.[148]

The majority of the Court held that the highway rule 'discredits the Australian legal system' and the doctrine of *stare decisis* could not be relied upon because the inconsistent case law based on the pre-existing rule 'neither promotes the predictability of judicial decision nor facilitates the giving of advice to settle or avoid litigation'.[149] This case seems to be another example of the High Court responding to legislative inaction. One of the arguments relied upon by the minority in their refusal to overrule the highway rule was the fact that the New South Wales Parliament had not responded to Law Reform Commission recommendations for legislative reform, rather it had legislatively endorsed the common law rule in 1993 by granting to the newly-created Roads and Traffic Authority (RTA) 'the immunities of a roads authority'.[150]

Whilst Kirby J acknowledged that in considering whether to overrule 'it is relevant to consider whether the legislature has overlooked the defects in the law

---

[145] Heydon, at 19.   [146] Heydon, at 19.

[147] (2001) 206 CLR 512 at 601 per Kirby J. Indeed, this was the decision the Court reached in reviewing the facts in *Ghantous v. Hawkesbury City Council* according to the ordinary rules of negligence. This case was heard together with *Brodie v. Singleton Shire Council* in considering whether to grant special leave to appeal. The High Court held that the Hawkesbury City Council could not be held responsible for subsidence in a pathway which allegedly caused Mrs Ghantous to fall: no breach of duty of care could be established as the gradual deterioration with everyday use and wear and tear of a pathway was unpredictable and largely out of control of the Council. See (2001) 206 CLR 512 at 605–6 per Kirby J.   [148] Ibid, at 549.

[149] Ibid, at 560–1 per Gaudron, McHugh and Gummow JJ.

[150] *Roads Act 1993* (NSW), s 65. See (2001) 206 CLR 512 at 537 per Gleeson CJ.

in question or whether it has intervened, but withheld change',[151] the majority concluded the Court was overruling a common law immunity applied anomalously to one form of statutory authority, not an immunity that Parliament had expressly enacted. The reference to an 'assumed' but 'undefined immunity' in the legislation could not be construed as legislative enactment of the highway rule; the 1993 legislation simply placed the RTA in the same position in which the case law placed councils with respect to public roads, but that case law 'then was and had been for a long period in a state of flux'.[152] In addition, judicial abolition of the common law rule did not change the fact that:

[i]t will always be open to the Parliament...to confer a special immunity on highway authorities...if this were done now it would enjoy at least two advantages. It might be expected to define with greater precision and certainty the scope of any such immunity and any exceptions to it. And such immunity would then rest on the authority of elected representatives, not on an anomalous and dubious judge-made rule whose deficiencies are so manifest.[153]

5.5 United States Supreme Court examples

It has been said that the United States Supreme Court 'rarely overturns decisions in explicit terms, preferring instead to squeeze the life from them'.[154] However, compared to the British and Australian approach, the United States Supreme Court is more likely to overrule its own precedent, and to do so explicitly,[155] even when the only thing that has changed is the numbers on the court. This is particularly common with constitutional precedents, with two commonly-cited examples being *Garcia v. San Antonio Transit Authority*[156] and *Payne v. Tennessee*.[157]

In *Garcia v. San Antonio Transit Authority*, the United States Supreme Court held by a 5:4 vote that states are not constitutionally immune from federal regulation of 'areas of traditional governmental functions', upholding the validity of federal laws governing the minimum wages of state employees under the Commerce Clause. The Court overruled *National League of Cities v. Usery*,[158] itself a 5:4 decision which had in turn overruled *Maryland v. Wirtz*.[159] In realigning itself with the reasoning in *Maryland*, the United States Supreme Court in *Garcia*

---

[151] (2001) 206 CLR 512 at 596 per Kirby J.

[152] Ibid, at 571 per Gaudron, McHugh and Gummow JJ; at 602 per Kirby J.

[153] Ibid, at 602 per Kirby J. Indeed, Justice Heydon notes this is precisely what the New South Wales parliament subsequently announced it would do: see Heydon, at 20.

[154] H Ball, *Judicial Craftmanship or Fiat* (Greenwood Press, Connecticut, 1978) 15 cited in Paterson (1981), at 389. A useful resource is 'Supreme Court Decisions Overruled by Subsequent Decision' available at <http://www.gpoaccess.gov/constitution/html/scourt.html>.

[155] See Caldarone (2004) at 767 who notes that in comparison with the United States, researchers have found the House of Lords to be more 'restrained and constrained', with the UK's system of precedent being described as the 'extreme...of legal formalism' across a wide range of common-law and codelaw countries. [156] 469 US 528 (1985).

[157] 501 US 808 (1991). [158] 426 US 833 (1976). [159] 392 US 183 (1968).

completed 'a double reversal of constitutional doctrine within twenty years, with the dissent calling for a third turnabout'.[160] The majority opinion was delivered by Blackmun J who noted that *National League of Cities* had been decided 'by a sharply divided vote' and that the Court had given no explanation of how 'traditional' state government functions could be distinguished from 'non-traditional' ones, leaving subsequent courts struggling to identify a traditional function. He concluded that *National League of Cities* was 'unsound in principle' and 'unworkable in practice' because 'it inevitably invites an unelected federal judiciary to make decisions about which state policies it favors and which ones it dislikes.'[161]

The minority opinion, penned by Justice Powell, complained that '[t]here have been few cases . . . in which the principle of stare decisis and the rationale of recent decisions were ignored as abruptly as we now witness'[162] calling this a case of 'precipitous' overruling of a case in which Blackmun J had been part of the majority.[163] Nonetheless, Frickey argues that the majority's decision can still be justified according to normal principles of overruling:

A common pattern in the overruling of precedent involves initial attempts to apply the decision properly, followed by a frank recognition that the precedent is unworkable or inconsistent with the decisions that have followed it . . . it is difficult to conceive of this overruling as "precipitous", since several decisions since *National League of Cities* have been in tension with the basic rationale of that precedent. When Justice Powell's reliance on *stare decisis* is analyzed in that light, it becomes apparent that *Garcia* was less an affront to *stare decisis* than was the overruling of *Maryland v. Wirtz* in *National League of Cities*—an overruling that, unlike *Garcia*, was caused by major changes in the composition of the Court and was not nearly so predictable based on prior decision.[164]

However, *Payne v. Tennessee* is much more difficult to justify according to general principles of constitutional overruling. The Supreme Court in a 6:3 decision explicitly overruled its two recently decided decisions, *Booth v. Maryland*[165] and *South Carolina v. Gathers*,[166] and held that victim impact evidence relating to the personal characteristics of the victim and the emotional impact of the crimes on the victim's family presented to the jury in the sentencing phase of a capital (death penalty) case was not prohibited by the Eighth Amendment. The majority in *Payne* did not rely on traditional justifications for overruling but asserted merely that the previous precedents were wrong and were to be granted less weight because they were decided by 5:4 votes and were constitutional cases.

Chief Justice Rehnquist delivered the opinion of the Court, arguing that *stare decisis* is 'a principle of policy and not a mechanical formula of adherence to the

---

160 James C Rehnquist, 'The Power that Shall be Vested in a Precedent: Stare Decisis, the Constitution and the Supreme Court' (1986) 66 *Boston University Law Review* 345 at 345.
161 469 US 528 at 530, 545 (1985).   162 469 US 528 at 558 (1985).
163 469 US 528 at 559, 562 (1985).
164 Philip P Frickey, 'A Further Comment on Stare Decisis and the Overruling of National League of Cities' (1985) 2 *Constitutional Commentary* 341 at 345.   165 482 US 496 (1987).
166 490 US 805 (1989).

latest decision' and that this is particularly so in constitutional cases where 'correction through legislative action is practically impossible'.[167] He asserted that reliance interests were of less weight in constitutional cases than in cases affecting property and contract rights, particularly where the precedent merely involved procedural and evidentiary rules. Chief Justice Rehnquist concluded that because *Booth* and *Garners* were decided 'by the narrowest of margins, over spirited dissents challenging the basic underpinnings of those decisions', they were not to be given significant precedential weight. To the contrary, 'they were wrongly decided and should be, and now are, overruled'.[168]

Justice Scalia went even further in his disparagement of the doctrine of *stare decisis*, rejecting Justice Marshall's dissenting argument that overruling Booth and Garner demands some 'special justification' beyond the conviction that the rule is wrong and stating that *stare decisis* was merely a doctrine of 'administrative convenience' and 'the application to judicial precedents of a more general principle that the settled practices and expectations of a democratic society should generally not be disturbed by the courts'. Justice Scalia argued that a decision of the Supreme Court announcing a new rule, even if no precedent exists or no overruling is involved, should be treated with the same caution as explicit overruling, and that it was '*Booth*, and not today's decision, that compromised the fundamental values underlying the doctrine of stare decisis'.[169]

However, the three dissenting Justices (Marshall, Blackmun and Stevens) vigorously attacked the majority's discarding of 'fidelity to precedent' as this was fundamental to 'a society governed by the rule of law'. Justice Marshall pointed out that none of the traditional justifications for overruling precedent were present: subsequent changes in the law; the need to bring a decision in line with newly discovered facts; or evidence that the precedent undermined coherency or consistency in the law. He argued that adherence to precedent had a higher value than merely protecting reliance interests as it allowed the judiciary to be viewed as impartial and reasoned in its judgments, a consideration even more important in constitutional than property and contract cases. Justice Marshall warned that the majority's opinion encouraged the state as well as future courts to ignore, undermine or overrule with impunity existing 5:4 Supreme Court decisions, listing those 'endangered precedents' now subject to the majority's new criteria for overruling in a footnote and commenting that 'the continued vitality of literally scores of decisions must be understood to depend on nothing more than the proclivities of the individuals who now comprise a majority of this Court'.

Justice Marshall claimed that: 'Power, not reason, is the new currency of this Court's decisionmaking... Neither the law nor the facts supporting *Booth* and *Garners* underwent any change in the last four years. Only the personnel of this Court did'.[170]

---

[167] 501 US 808 (1991) at 828.   [168] 501 US 808 (1991) at 829–830.

[169] 501 US 808 (1991) at 834–835.

[170] 501 US 808 (1991) per Marshall J at 844. This is a reference to Justice Kennedy's and Justice Souter's replacement of (respectively) Justice Powell and Justice Brennan in the interim period between *Booth* and *Garners* and the decision in *Payne*.

Academic critiques of *Payne* and in particular the Rehnquist/Scalia argument of the reduced precedential effect of 5:4 decisions that have as their subject matter constitutional issues or were recently decided, without one of the traditional justifications for overruling being present, have also been strident.[171] It is argued that: 'Under Chief Justice Rehnquist's view in *Payne*, stare decisis would indeed be a truism: a precedent would deserve continuing support when it has continuing support from the current members of the Court.'[172] In constitutional cases, Justices Rehnquist and Scalia both use 'the wrongness characterization as a rhetorical device to undercut the authority of the initial decisionmaker', allowing the current court to 'privilege its view of the right over the view of a predecessor court'.[173] The emphasis on 'vote-counting' by these Justices also undermines certainty as to the future of a 5:4 decision. Finally, Rehnquist and Scalia's discounting of the importance of reliance in constitutional cases is too sweeping:

[T]he argument that constitutional cases are deserving of a weakened precedential effect fails in certain contexts. First, giving reduced weight to constitutional precedents detracts from the goal of certainty. Second, because most constitutional cases involve a governmental relationship, either with another branch of the government or with individual citizens, overruling constitutional cases can detract from the stability of governmental relations. Finally constitutional decisions may also result in reliance, either on the part of individuals or governmental entities.[174]

The radical implications of *Payne v. Tennessee* for overruling in constitutional cases appear to have been limited by the Supreme Court's decision a year later in *Planned Parenthood v. Casey*.[175] The joint majority opinion of Justices O'Connor,

---

[171] See in particular Andrew M Jacobs 'God Save This Postmodern Court: The Death of Necessity and the Transformation of the Supreme Court's Overruling Rhetoric' (1995) 63 *University of Cincinnati Law Review* 1119. The Rennquist/Scalia argument that recent decisions of the Supreme Court without a clear majority consensus are of 'questionable precedential value' was re-employed in *Seminole Tribe of Florida v. Florida* 517 US 44 (1996) which overruled *Pennsylvania v. Union Gas Co* 491 US 1 (1989), prompting Justice Stevens in dissent to comment that 'In a rather novel rejection of the doctrine of *stare decisis* the Court today demeans that holding by repeatedly describing it as a "plurality decision" because Justice White did not deem it necessary to set forth the reasons for his vote . . . far more significant than the "plurality" character of the three opinions supporting the holding in *Union Gas* is the fact that the issue . . . has been squarely addressed by a total of 13 Justices, 8 of whom cast their votes with the so-called "plurality".' 517 US 44 (1996) at 94 per Stevens J. Interestingly, Justice Stevens explicitly refused to accept *Seminole Tribe* as controlling precedent in *Kimel v. Florida Board of Regents* 139 F3d 1426 (2000), commenting that: 'I remain convinced that Union Gas was correctly decided and that the decision of five Justices in Seminole Tribe to overrule that case was profoundly misguided . . . by its own repeated overruling of earlier precedent, the majority has itself discounted the importance of *stare decisis* in this area of law.' See Michael H Gottesman, 'Recent Supreme Court Decisions Affecting Congress' Ability to Redress Employment Discrimination' p. 39, available at Citizen's Commission on Civil Rights website <http://www.cccr.org>.
[172] Amy L Padden, 'Overruling Decisions in the Supreme Court: The Role of a Decision's Vote, Age, and Subject Matter in the Application of Stare Decisis after Payne v. Tennessee' (1994) 82 Georgetown Law Journal 1689.
[173] Jill E Fisch, 'The Implications of Transition Theory for Stare Decisis' (2003) 13 *Journal of Contemporary Legal Issues* 93 at 101–2.   [174] Padden (1994) at 1716.
[175] 505 US 833, 112 S Ct 2791 (1992).

Kennedy and Souter, joined in part by Justice Stevens, espoused a 'special justification' approach to overruling, even in constitutional cases, and gave the following examples of 'prudential and pragmatic considerations designed to test the consistency of overruling a prior decision with the ideal of the rule of law, and to gauge the respective costs of reaffirming and overruling a prior case':

[W]e may ask whether the rule has proven to be intolerable simply in defying practical workability; whether the rule is subject to a kind of reliance that would lend a special hardship to the consequences of overruling and add inequity to the cost of repudiation; whether related principles of law have so far developed as to have left the old rule no more than a remnant of abandoned doctrine; or whether facts have so changed, or come to be seen so differently, as to have robbed the old rule of significant application or justification.[176]

The majority gave as an example of changed facts or perceptions of facts the Supreme Court's famous decision in *Brown v. Board of Education*[177] overruling the 1896 holding in *Plessy v. Ferguson*[178] that legislatively-mandated racial segregation was not a denial of equal protection in contravention of the Fourteenth Amendment. The *Casey* majority commented that 'it was clear by 1954 that legally sanctioned segregation had just such an effect'.[179]

A further example of changed facts or perceptions of facts is *Lawrence v. Texas*[180] in which the Supreme Court in 2003 overruled its 1986 decision in *Bowers v. Hardwick*[181] and struck down a Texas state law criminalizing homosexual sodomy on the basis that it prevented freely consenting adults from engaging in private conduct in the exercise of their liberty under the Due Process Clause of the Fourteenth Amendment.[182] Delivering the 6:3 decision, Kennedy J stated that: 'When homosexual conduct is made criminal by the law of the State, that declaration in and of itself is an invitation to subject homosexual persons to discrimination both in the public and private spheres'.[183] He concluded that the decision in *Bowers* had not created 'individual or societal reliance . . . of the sort that could counsel against overturning its holding once there are compelling reasons to do so' and that the 'compelling reason' was that the decision in *Bowers* failed 'to appreciate the extent of the liberty at stake':

To say that the issue in *Bowers* was simply the right to engage in certain sexual conduct demeans the claim the individual put forward . . . the statutes do seek to control a personal relationship that, whether or not entitled to formal recognition in the law, is within the liberty of persons to choose without being punished as criminals.[184]

---

[176] 112 S Ct 2791 (1992) at 2808–9 (caselaw omitted).   [177] 347 US 483 (1954).
[178] 163 US 537 (1896).   [179] 112 S Ct 2791 (1992) at 2813.
[180] 539 US 558 (2003). Another example based on interpreting the Eighth Amendment in terms of 'evolving standards of decency' so as to prohibit the imposition of the death penalty on the mentally retarded is *Atkins v. Virginia* 536 US 304 (2002).   [181] 478 US 186 (1986).
[182] See Kenji Yoshino 'Can the Supreme Court Change its Mind', *New York Times*, 5 December 2002.   [183] 539 US 558 (2003) at 571.
[184] 539 US 558 (2003) at 563.

An example of the unworkability of the precedent combined with doctrinal change in law rendering the precedent inconsistent with more recent decisions is *Agostini v. Felton*[185] in which the Court overruled its earlier decisions in *Aguilar v. Felton*[186] and *School District of Grand Rapids v. Ball*[187] because they could no longer be reconciled with the Court's subsequent Establishment Clause jurisprudence. Because of intervening case law, placing public school teachers on parochial school campuses to provide remedial education did not *as a matter of law* inevitably necessitate an excessive entanglement of church and state or have the impermissible effect of advancing religion through indoctrination. The majority held that:

> The *stare decisis* doctrine does not preclude this Court from recognizing the change in its law and overruling *Aguilar* and those portions of *Ball* that are inconsistent with its more recent decisions. Moreover, in light of the Court's conclusion that *Aguilar* would be decided differently under current Establishment Clause law, adherence to that decision would undoubtedly work a 'manifest injustice', such that the law of the case doctrine does not apply.[188]

In *Casey*, the majority examined in turn each of the 'special justifications' for overruling (the unworkability of the precedent, doctrinal change or changed facts and circumstances) said to be required in addition to the mere conviction that a precedent is wrong and reaffirmed *Roe v. Wade's*[189] holding that a woman's decision to terminate pregnancy is a 'liberty' protected against state interference by the Due Process Clause of the Fourteenth Amendment.[190] The majority determined that *Roe v. Wade's* 'essential holding' should be reaffirmed because although it had attracted opposition, *Roe* had 'in no sense proven unworkable', there was significant reliance upon the rule; its central rule had not been left a doctrinal anachronism by subsequent decisions, and there had been no significant change in the factual underpinning of the decision. In contrast to *Payne*, the Court in *Casey* took a much broader approach to reliance in constitutional cases:

> The ability of women to participate equally in the economic and social life of the Nation has been facilitated by their ability to control their reproductive lives . . . The Constitution serves human values, and while the effect of reliance on *Roe* cannot be exactly measured, neither can the certain cost of overruling *Roe* for people who have ordered their thinking and living around that case be dismissed.[191]

It should be pointed out that in *Casey*, despite the apparent constraint imposed by what Chief Justice Rehnquist in dissent described as 'a newly minted variation on *stare decisis*',[192] the joint majority opinion also strayed from traditional adherence to precedent because it only affirmed the central holding of *Roe* rather than

---

[185] 473 US 402 (1997).   [186] 473 US 402 (1985).   [187] 473 US 373 (1985).
[188] 473 US 402 (1997).   [189] 410 US 113, 93 S Ct 705 (1973).
[190] Also see *Stenberg, Attorney General of Nebraska et al v. Carhart* 530 US 914 (2000).
[191] 112 S Ct 2791 (1992) at 2809.   [192] 112 S Ct 2791 (1992) at 2855 per Rehnquist CJ.

the decision in its entirety. The majority set out a new test for determining when a state can restrict the right to abortion without considering whether the old test had engendered reliance and whether a change in the test would produce uncertainty. This prompted Justice Scalia in dissent to comment: 'I confess never to have heard of this 'new, keep-what-you-want-and-throw-away-the-rest version ... of *stare decisis*'.[193]

The majority opinion explicitly acknowledged the role played by adherence to precedent in protecting the Court's legitimacy in adjudicating controversial civil liberties and civil rights issues in which Justices express 'principled disagreement' with previous interpretations of the constitution and display an inability to reach a consensus on 'what the law is'.[194] The majority stated that in such exceptional cases, prior rulings require:

... an equally rare precedential force to counter the inevitable efforts to overturn it and to thwart its implementation. Some of those efforts may be mere unprincipled emotional reactions; others may proceed from principles worthy of profound respect. But whatever the premises of opposition may be, only the most convincing justification under accepted standards of precedent could suffice to demonstrate that a later decision overruling the first was anything but a surrender to political pressure, and an unjustified repudiation of the principle on which the Court staked its authority in the first instance. So to overrule under fire in the absence of the most compelling reason to re-examine a watershed decision would subvert the Court's legitimacy beyond any serious question.[195]

Subsequently, in *Dickerson v. United States*[196] the majority of the Supreme Court justified its decision not to overrule *Miranda v. Arizona*[197] in similar terms. In *Miranda*, the Court had decided that certain warnings must be given before a suspect's statement made during custodial interrogation could be admitted in evidence. Chief Justice Rehnquist delivered the opinion of the Court in *Dickerson*, holding that the effect of *Miranda* was to announce a constitutional rule and a statute of Congress which made the admissibility of such statements turn solely on whether they were made voluntarily was an impermissible attempt to overrule *Miranda*. He also adopted an expansive definition of reliance upon constitutional precedents based on the disruption of public expectations and the corresponding damage to the Court's legitimacy and hence the rule of law:

Whether or not we would agree with Miranda's reasoning and its resulting rule, were we addressing the issue in the first instance, the principles of stare decisis weigh heavily against overruling it now ... We do not think there is such justification for overruling *Miranda*. *Miranda* has become embedded in routine police practice to the point where the warnings have become part of our national culture.[198]

[193] Padden (1994) at 1723; 112 S Ct 2791 (1992) at 2881.
[194] See Emery G Lee III 'Overruling Rhetoric: The Court's New Approach to Stare Decisis in Constitutional Cases' (2002) 33 *University of Toledo Law Review* 581.
[195] 112 S Ct 2791 (1992) at 2815.   [196] 530 US 428 (2000).
[197] 384 US 436 (1966).   [198] 530 US 428 (2000) at 441.

Justice Scalia, joined in dissent by Justice Thomas, once again took the 'wrongness approach' to *stare decisis*, taking the majority to task for failing to decide whether *Miranda* was wrongly decided:

It takes only a small step to bring today's legal opinion out of the realm of power-judging and into the mainstream of legal reasoning: the Court need only go beyond its carefully couched iterations that 'Miranda is a constitutional decision'... and come out and say quite clearly: 'We reaffirm today that custodial interrogation that is not preceded by Miranda warnings or their equivalent violates the Constitution of the United States.' It cannot say that, because a majority of the Court does not believe it. The Court therefore acts in plain violation of the Constitution when it denies effect to this Act of Congress.[199]

However, *Casey* and *Dickerson* reflect a central ingredient of judging, law and the rule of law itself that highlighted by Raz and Dworkin in their different ways. Judges do not come upon legal issues afresh with a vote count on their preferred view. That would make the Supreme Court a supra-legislative body appointed haphazardly by different governments with a huge incentive to stack the courts as a way of changing decisions they did not like. Instead, judges are a part of a tradition that interprets decisions that have already been made—including those that the judges do not agree with. While *stare decisis* does not mean that those earlier decisions cannot be changed, such change requires good reason. Such good reasons do not include a change of court personnel. Indeed, a change in court personnel is the very worst reason for changing a constitutional interpretation and conservative judges will reject attempts to do so merely because of such changes. This was a crucial feature of the *Second Territorial Senators Case*,[200] an Australian High Court case where two judges in a recent minority decision explicitly rejected the opportunity to overrule the decision from which they had dissented because of the opportunity created by the appointment of a like-minded judge. The *First Territorial Senators Case*[201] had ruled, by a narrow 5:4 majority, that the power of the Commonwealth Parliament Federal legislature to legislate for the representation of federal territories did include the power to create senators with voting rights. Two senators were elected from each of the two major territories (compared to the ten from each state), had sat and voted. In the intervening year, a Labor-appointed judge in the former minority had retired and been replaced by a new judge appointed by the incoming Liberal-Country party coalition. Two judges appointed by Liberal-Country governments who had been in the minority in the first case (Justices Stephen and Deane) defended the decision from which they had earlier dissented, increasing the majority from 4:3 to 5:2. I am not sure whether this featured as a consideration in the judges' minds but five out of the seven judges were coalition appointees, up from the previous four. The idea that the extension of a coalition appointed majority should allow for the overturning of decisions where the

---

[199] 530 US 428 (2000) at 444.
[200] *Queensland v. Commonwealth (Second Territorial Senators' Case)* (1977) 139 CLR 585.
[201] *Western Australia v. Commonwealth (First Territorial Senators' Case)* (1975) 134 CLR 201.

coalition appointed majority was smaller would make it look as if the government could stack the court and was in the process of doing so.

If the change in the court's decisions is seen as the result of politically driven appointments, the legitimacy of the court could be gravely affected. The problem for the current US Supreme Court is that there has been widespread pressure within Republican ranks to appoint judges who will reverse some of the major decisions of the 1960s and 1970s. These had yielded a court of seven Republican and two Democrat appointees. While Scalia J and others may seem impatient for the majority to assert itself, genuinely conservative judges will see such changing majorities as insufficient reason to reverse decisions reached by earlier courts— especially those which had a more even political balance of appointees.

We have seen that reliance arguments against overruling are at their strongest in common law and statutory precedents because of the direct practical effect on and potential unfairness to private parties who may have arranged their affairs in reliance on the previous rule. Statutory precedents are even more rigidly adhered to because of the twin arguments that first: statutory amendment should be left to the legislature not the courts; and second: parliament has effectively signalled its approval of the precedent by failing to amend the statute to effect an overruling.[202] Thus the majority opinion of Justice Brennan in *Johnson v. Transportation Agency*[203] took note of the fact that Congress had not amended Title VII of the *Civil Rights Act* of *1964* following the Court's earlier decision in *Steelworkers v. Weber*[204] which had determined that employer affirmative action plans did not impermissibly take into account the sex of the applicants in violation of Title VII. Justice Brennan took particular issue with:

Justice Scalia's dissent [which] faults the fact that we take note of the absence of congressional efforts to amend the statute to nullify *Weber*. It suggests that congressional inaction cannot be regarded as acquiescence under all circumstances, but then draws from that unexceptional point the conclusion that any reliance on congressional failure to act is necessarily a 'canard'. The fact that inaction may not always provide crystalline revelation, however, should not obscure the fact that it may be probative to varying degrees. *Weber*, for instance, was a widely publicized decision that addressed a prominent issue of public debate. Legislative inattention thus is not a plausible explanation for congressional inaction. Furthermore, Congress not only passed no contrary legislation in the wake of *Weber*, but not one legislator even proposed a bill to do so. The barriers of the legislative process therefore also seem a poor explanation for failure to act. By contrast, when Congress has been displeased with our interpretation of Title VII, it has not hesitated to amend the statute to tell us so. For instance, when Congress passed the *Pregnancy Discrimination Act of 1978* ... it unambiguously expressed its disapproval of both the holding and the reasoning of the Court ... Surely, it is appropriate to find some probative value in such radically different congressional reactions to this Court's interpretations of the same statute.[205]

[202] See Eskridge (1988).   [203] 480 US 616 (1987).   [204] 443 US 193 (1979).
[205] 480 US 616 (1987) at 629 fn 7.

In the United States, as in the United Kingdom and Australia, the argument based on reliance is also stronger in relation to retrospective criminal law. This is because the primary purpose of criminal law is to identify and attach penalties to certain proscribed forms of social behaviour which the lawmakers believe is socially damaging and deserving of the moral obloquy in order to deter citizens from acting in the ways proscribed. The threatened sanctions cannot be effective if not known in advance and it is unfair—indeed unconscionable—to impose moral obloquy on those who did not know that the behaviour was proscribed. The Supreme Court in *Bouie v. City of Columbia*[206] held that an unforeseeable retrospective judicial enlargement of a statute defining criminal conduct violated the defendant's right to due process, with the Court commenting that 'an unforeseeable judicial enlargement of a criminal statute, applied retroactively, operates precisely like an *ex post facto* law' and that 'if a state legislature is barred by the *Ex Post Facto* Clause from passing such a law, it must follow that a State Supreme Court is barred by the Due Process Clause from achieving precisely the same result by judicial construction'.[207]

Subsequent court decisions have substantially limited *Bouie* by conducting a foreseeability analysis and concluding that retrospective judicial change to criminal law was foreseeable in circumstances where a statute was ambiguous or conflicting precedents existed.[208] The Supreme Court has also declined to consider whether *Bouie* applies to retroactive judicial increases in punishment, even though logic suggests that when the judiciary acts in a legislative manner, it should also be bound by the *ex post facto* clause.[209] Kemphaus offers the following syllogism in support of such an extension:

(1) the judiciary acts legislatively when it modifies, changes or creates law

(2) the legislature is bound by the *Ex Post Facto* Clause, therefore

(3) the judiciary is bound by the *Ex Post Facto* Clause, when it modifies, changes or creates law.[210]

Kaatz argues that retrospective judicial increases in punishment should be treated the same way as retrospective legislative increases in punishment based on the three policy justifications behind the purpose of the *ex post facto* clause. First, the fundamental fairness justification in having government abide by rules of law established to govern deprivation of liberty, resulting in a defendant receiving a greater sentence retroactively, has equal force regardless of whether it is a legislative

---

[206] *Bouie v. City of Columbia* (1964) 378 US 347.

[207] Robert Kaatz, 'Is There an *Ex post facto* Prohibition on Judicial Decisions that Retroactively Enlarge Criminal Punishment' (2001) 47 *Wayne Law Review* 1367 at 1369, citing *Bouie v. City of Columbia* (1964) 378 US 347 at 353–54.   [208] See Kaatz, at 1371.

[209] Kaatz, at 1377, citing *Newman v. United States* (2000) 531 US 866.

[210] Nick J Kemphaus, 'Rogers v. Tennessee: Is the Judiciary Permitted to Violate the Ex Post Facto Clause of the United States Constitution' (2003) 30 *Northern Kentucky Law Review* 415 at 418 fn 36.

or judicial decision. Secondly, protection of the principles of notice and reliance in relation to legislation are applicable to judicial enlargement of punishment because individuals should be able to rely on the expected punishment attached to a crime when they are deciding whether to plead guilty or not. Thirdly, the *ex post facto* clause's role in restraining government power to enact arbitrary and vindictive legislation can be extended to protection against arbitrary judicial power, particularly in the United States where the judiciary in many states is elected and, like the legislature, is susceptible to electoral influence.[211]

5.6 Extending or distinguishing decisions

The application of existing rules to new situations was essentially the process by which the common law was developed and continues to be developed. These sorts of decisions are probably less surprising than those considered above because there will usually be no direct authority as to what rule should cover those situations. Any expectations that the rule will not be extended may, therefore, be irrational in the sense that it should have been possible to foresee that the court might decide to extend the existing rules by analogy to the new situation.

In *Attorney-General for the Northern Territory v. Kearney*,[212] the High Court extended the exception to the claim of legal professional privilege, which applies where the allegedly privileged communications arose in the furtherance of a crime or fraud, to communications which arise from an attempt to abuse a statutory power. In *Baumgartner v. Baumgartner*,[213] the High Court held that a constructive trust could be created by operation of law on grounds of unconscionability. The previous position had been that a constructive trust could only be created as a result of a proven common intention, while a resulting trust would only be created where there had been a financial contribution to the purchase price.[214]

Both of these cases would appear to involve reliance issues. In *Kearney*, the privilege case, both lawyer and client may have expected that their communications would remain confidential. Perhaps, the fact that the communications were in furtherance of an abuse of statutory power—and therefore at odds with the rationale of the privilege—is sufficient grounds for defeating that expectation. The fact that it would have been unconscionable, in the High Court's view, for the *de facto* husband in *Baumgartner* to deny any interest in the property to his spouse is also a sufficient answer to any argument he might advance that he had so arranged things as to ensure this very objective.

---

[211] Kaatz, at 1381–2.
[212] *Attorney-General for the Northern Territory v. Kearney* (1985) 158 CLR 500.
[213] *Baumgartner v. Baumgartner* (1987) 164 CLR 137.
[214] *Carr v. R* (1988) 165 CLR 314. See 'Criminal Law and Justice' (1988) 62 ALJ 1046.

The weight given to reliance in the above cases may be contrasted with *Caparo Industries v. Dickman*[215] in which the House of Lords refused to extend the duty of care owed by statutory auditors of a public company to shareholders or potential investors and 'predator' companies who may rely upon the accuracy of the financial statement/certified accounts in deciding whether to buy or sell shares in the company. Lord Bridge commented that this would be to subject the auditor to 'liability in an indeterminate amount for an indeterminate time to an indeterminate class' and to 'confer on the world at large a quite unwarranted entitlement to appropriate for their own purposes the benefit of the expert knowledge or professional expertise attributed to the maker of the statement.'[216] Lord Oliver stated that to hold otherwise would be to equate the relationship of 'proximity' with 'mere foreseeability' of reliance on the statement by another party.[217]

In *Cattanach v. Melchior*,[218] a High Court majority of 4:3 extended damages for economic loss in actions for negligence to include the cost of raising and maintaining a child born as a result of a failed sterilization procedure.[219] At the risk of simplification, the majority argued that to deny recovery of damages for this expenditure would be logically inconsistent with the existing uncontroversial head of recovery for the immediate hospital and medical costs of the birth; whereas the minority position was that the birth of a child could not be economically discounted or devalued at law because of an overriding public and legal policy upholding the inherent value of human life.

The majority's response to this was broadly that, in the absence of legislative guidance, it was very difficult for the judiciary to make assumptions as to public policy values in developing the common law, particularly in relation to arguments with theological origins (that is, the assertion that every child is a 'blessing'). The previous case law resulted in illogical and arbitrary distinctions, not applicable to any other type of medical negligence, between immediate and long-term costs when both were equally foreseeable consequences of the negligence. A general community acceptance of values respecting the value of human life, in the majority's view, did not translate into a demand that there be no award of damages by courts for the costs to the parents of on-going rearing and maintaining a child who would not otherwise have been born were it not for the negligence of the gynaecologist.[220]

Thus, it is seemingly ironic that, despite the majority's justifications for overturning previous decisions which had established recovery for initial costs of the birth but not for on-going maintenance, the Queensland legislature

---

[215] [1990] 1 All ER 568.   [216] Ibid, at 576.   [217] Ibid, at 593.

[218] (2003) 215 CLR 1. For discussion of this case see A Mason 'Legislative and Judicial Law-Making: Can We Locate an Identifiable Boundary?' (2003) 24 *Adelaide Law Review* 15 at 20; MH McHugh 'The Strengths of the Weakest Arm' (2004) 25 *Australian Bar Review* 181 at 188; and M Kirby, at 6 who notes that 'None of the judges in the case—not one—pretended that the path to his decision could be found solely by the application of logic and past legal authority'.

[219] Cf *McFarlane v. Tayside Health Board* [1999] 3 WLR 1301 in which the House of Lords overturned settled law to reach the opposite result.

[220] *Cattanach v. Melchior* (2003) 215 CLR 1 at 37, 53–4, 57–9 per McHugh and Gummow JJ.

responded to public criticism of the High Court's decision by passing amendments to the *Civil Liability Act 2003* (Qld) which prevent a court from awarding damages for the costs ordinarily associated with rearing or maintaining a child.[221] However, as McHugh J argues, an initial (and simplistic) reading of this case as illustrating 'the powerlessness of ultimate appellate courts within contemporary representative democracies' should rather be replaced with a more sophisticated analysis consistent with the understanding that judicial law-making can 'stimulate legislative action, thereby producing a democratic result'.[222]

A decision to distinguish precedent is essentially the converse of what has been described above as an extending decision; in the latter, it is held that there is a sufficient analogy between the situations covered by the existing rule and the new situation for the rule to be applied; whereas in the former, it is held that there is an insufficient analogy. The technique of distinguishing also enables the effect of precedent to be avoided without the court having to explicitly abrogate or over-rule the existing rule. Harris observes that 'the force of the doctrine of *stare decisis* has been such that courts have often preferred to strain to distinguish precedents when they should more appropriately have overruled them'.[223]

Thus, the House of Lords has rarely resorted to its Practice Statement in relation to overruling because of what Hodder terms its 'pre-existing skills in distinguishing inconvenient precedents'.[224] And the High Court has recognized the possibility of distinguishing a decision as a factor in the review of an earlier decision when considering whether or not to overrule.[225] Bueddu and Haigh observe that members of the High Court in constitutional cases have sometimes distinguished a decision on the bases that overruling it, although logically correct, would have had unacceptable repercussions, and have by this means somewhat annoyingly avoided the need to give effect to their interpretation of the Constitution.[226]

Therefore, a decision to distinguish a rule can be one of two things: it can either be a straightforward decision that the situation covered by the existing rule and the new situation are not analogous or it can be the covert avoidance of a rule which should, by analogy, apply to the new situation. An example of the former is *Fitzpatrick (AP) v. Sterling Housing Association Ltd*[227] in which the House of Lords distinguished between the situation of a surviving spouse to a stable homosexual partnership and the facts in *Carrega Properties SA v. Sharratt*[228] in which the House of Lords held that two people living and acting together as though they were aunt and nephew could not establish a familial relationship for the purpose of obtaining statutory succession rights to a tenancy. Lord Nicholls also noted that he would have been prepared to overrule *Carrega*, had the court in *Fitzpatrick* been asked to reconsider this precedent.[229]

---

[221] The amending legislation was the *Justice and Other Legislation Amendment Act 2003* (Qld).
[222] McHugh (2004) at 187–8.   [223] Harris (2002), at 412.   [224] Hodder, at 168.
[225] *Second Territorial Senators Case* (1977) 139 CLR 585 at 630 per Aickin J.
[226] Boeddu and Haigh, at 193.   [227] [2001] 1 AC 27.   [228] [1979] 1 WLR 928.
[229] *Fitzpatrick (AP) v. Sterling House Association Ltd* [2001] 1 AC 27 at 44.

The Australian Federal Court's decision in *Federal Commissioner of Taxation v. Gregrhon Investments Pty Ltd*,[230] arguably falls into the latter category.[231] In this case, the Court distinguished the High Court's decision in the famous case of *Slutzkin v. Federal Commissioner of Taxation*,[232] the facts of which had provided the model for 'bottom of the harbour' tax schemes. At the time, the outrage exhibited by some members of the tax profession certainly indicates that they regarded the decision as one of surreptitious overruling.[233]

In the United States, the process of limiting precedents and confining them to narrower ratios is commonplace. For example, some complain that the Rehnquist Court's approach to criminal procedure was less concerned with the overruling of precedent than with the undermining of precedent whilst 'giving the appearance of adhering to it': '[T]he Rehnquist Court has distinguished, created exceptions to, and reinterpreted such precedents. Rarely is this approach analytically elegant and, much of the time, makes criminal procedure quite complicated, if not a morass'.[234]

While many may disagree with the decisions and the effect it has on criminal procedure, the distinction and limitation of precedent is a time honoured way in which the law changes with limited retrospectivity, minimal changes to expectations and a signalling of the areas where reliance is risky.

5.7 Overruling lower courts

Where an ultimate appellate court overrules the decision of a court lower in the hierarchy, then expectations which are defeated are, at least arguably, less rational in that it can never be assumed that an ultimate appellate court will agree with the reasoning of a lower court. That is to say, the expectation should take into account the fact that the highest court in the land has not accepted the rule being relied on. Nevertheless, a decision that has stood for some time may have been acted upon in a way that militates against its reversal.

[230] *Commissioner of Taxation v. Gregrhon Investments Pty Ltd* (1987) 79 ALR 586.

[231] A further example from the United States Supreme Court is *City of Indianapolis v. Edmond* 531 US 32 (2000) in which the majority distinguished two precedents to hold that vehicle checkpoints to intercept unlawful drugs violated the Fourth Amendment. The dissenting Justices held that there was no valid basis upon which to distinguish the precedents. Interestingly, Justice Thomas in dissent stated that he would have overruled the previous decisions as being wrongly decided had he had the benefit of briefing and argument on the question of overruling, but in the circumstances he felt bound by the precedents.

[232] *Slutzkin v. Federal Commissioner of Taxation* (1977) 140 CLR 314.

[233] See 'Editorial' (1988) 17 Australian Tax Review 1; and AJ Myers QC, 'The Federal Court Decision in the Gregrhon Investments Pty Ltd Case' (1988) 17 *Australian Tax Review* 4. However, the ALJ Revenue Editor argued that if the decision in Gregrhon was a surprise, it was only because 'revenue practice tends to be so confining in its specialisation that its opinion formers may tend to lose touch with reality': 'Revenue' (1988) 62 ALJ 470 at 471.

[234] Stephen F Smith, 'The Rehnquist Court and Criminal Procedure' (2002) 73 *University of Colorado Law Review* 1337, p. 1358.

A good example of this is provided by the decision in *Babaniaris v. Lutony Fashions Pty Ltd*,[235] where by a majority (comprising Mason, Wilson and Dawson JJ, with Brennan and Deane JJ in dissent), the High Court overruled the decision of the Workers Compensation Board of Victoria in *Little v. Levin Cuttings Pty Ltd*.[236] That decision had held, in effect, that an outworker who was an independent contractor was covered by the *Workers Compensation Act 1958* (Vic), while an employee outworker was not covered. It was submitted, and accepted, that even if the decision was wrong it had been acted on since 1953, in that premiums had been assessed and paid on the basis that independent contractor outworkers were covered by the Act. There was considerable discussion of the doctrine of *stare decisis*,[237] all judges agreeing that where a statute was ambiguous an earlier decision should be left standing, even if the individual judge would have reached a different construction of the provision. The majority held that the provision was not ambiguous however, and that they, therefore, had no choice but to overrule the earlier decision. The minority, on the other hand, held that they were 'quite unable' to 'say positively that it was wrong and productive of inconvenience'.[238] They noted that:

If Little's case were now overruled, insurers would obtain a windfall liberation from the risk of undischarged liabilities to independent contractors against which the employers were insured. There is no practical injustice in leaving Little's case stand, especially as the operation of the Act will fall away as the *Accident Compensation Act 1985* (Vic) comes into effect.[239]

5.8 Judicial techniques to limit the retrospective effects of decisions

The maintenance of unjust or inefficient rules is not the only alternative to the retrospective application of better rules. The retrospectivity of judicial decisions may be modified by the exercise of judicial discretion in the award of remedies, by the principle of *res judicata* which often prevents the re-litigation of cases decided by reference to law which in a later case has been found to be incorrect, and, changes in the law may also be given prospective effect only. However, this leads us back to definitional problems with the concept of retrospectivity and questions of fairness, reliance and efficiency in deciding when a change of law should apply.

Court rules in most jurisdictions and the equitable laws governing the award of discretionary remedies provide some scope for courts to determine the date from

[235] *Babaniaris v. Lutony Fashions Pty Ltd* (1987) 163 CLR 1.
[236] *Little v. Levin Cuttings Pty Ltd* (1953) 3 WCBD (Vic) 71.
[237] (1987) 163 CLR 1 at 12–15 per Mason J; at 22 per Wilson and Dawson JJ; at 28–33 per Brennan and Deane JJ.
[238] (1987) 163 CLR 1 at 28, quoting *Bourne v. Keane* [1919] AC 815 at 874 per Lord Buckmaster.
[239] Ibid, at 31.

which orders should operate.[240] A court may decline to grant remedy on an application for judicial review even when it is satisfied that the act or decision is unauthorized or unlawful when, for example, the applicant is in some way at fault, or performance of the remedy by the respondent is impossible. In administrative review decisions, the Federal Court in considering whether the operative date of an order to set aside an administrative decision should be the date of the decision or a later date, the court may have regard to whether the applicant may have a claim of damages or restitution of money paid before the court's judgment.[241] Campbell gives the example of a court making an order that will have retrospective effect if the respondent has not taken corrective action by a specified date.[242] However, she also notes that the court's scope for modification of the retrospective effect of its decision is necessarily limited: for example, when the central issue for determination is whether the defendant had legal authority for a particular action/transaction, the court cannot postpone ruling on this issue until a later date.[243]

The principle of *res judicata*, which favours finality in the adjudication of a dispute, frequently bars re-litigation if the law applicable to the disputed action/transaction changes after judgment is final (all avenues of appeal are exhausted and statutes of limitations have expired). *Res judicata* was explained by the New South Wales Court of Criminal Appeal in *R v. Unger*:

> The trial having been concluded and the time for appeal having gone by, the general principle is that the matter is regarded as at an end. It is to be borne in mind that the effect of a conviction in a criminal court, no less than a verdict and judgment in a civil court, is to merge in that conviction or judgment, as the case may be, all of the material upon which it proceeded ... Although in pure theory the overruling or modification by judicial decision of previous conceptions of legal principle does no more than correct a departure from the timeless perfection of the law, the plain fact is that legal principle is constantly evolving and being moulded in the light of the changing and developing social context. Recognising this, there has always been an unwillingness to permit the re-opening of past decisions ... This finality of decision in each individual case leaves the court free to permit a judicial flexibility in the development of principle in later cases, free from inhibition lest such development may set at large disputes that have previously been resolved.[244]

Changes in the law may also be given prospective effect only; that is, may operate from the date of judgment or a later date rather than retrospectively. This brings us back to the difficulties inherent in the concept of retrospective law as discussed in Chapter 3: the indeterminate nature of retrospectivity as a concept

---

[240] See *High Court Rules* O 43 r 3.

[241] *Administrative Decisions (Judicial Review) Act 1977* (Cth) s 16(1)(a); *Wattmaster Alco Pty Ltd v. Button* (1986) 70 ALR 330. Discussed in Enid Campbell, 'The Retrospectivity of Judicial Decisions and the Legality of Governmental Acts' (2003) 29(1) *Monash University Law Review* 49 at 53. Campbell notes that despite s 16(1)(c), where an administrative decision is held to be invalid in that it was made under legislation which is *ultra vires*, the Federal Court would probably adopt the position that it had no alternative but to set aside the decision as from the time it was made (at 80).

[242] Campbell, at 53.   [243] Campbell, at 56.

[244] Campbell, at 57–8; *R v. Unger* [1977] 2 NSWLR 990 at 995–6.

and the flaws in the binary nature of the retrospective/prospective divide (prospective changes in legal rules can also affect prior transactions). Attempts have been made to distinguish between 'primary' retrospectivity, or laws altering the past legal effect of past conduct; and 'secondary' retrospectivity, laws affecting only the future legal effect of past conduct.[245]

However, Fisch and Kaplow have demonstrated the incoherence of this further distinction and observe that transition costs created by changes in rules are largely unaffected by whether a legal change can be slotted into the primary or secondary category.[246] Fisch gives the example of the retrospective imposition of a million dollars in liability on a manufacturer for past pollution having the same economic consequences as the prospective adoption of stricter pollution controls reducing the value of the factory by a million dollars. Her preferable approach, which we have adopted in this book, is one of distinguishing between 'nominally retroactive rules, which are explicitly directed at pre-enactment transactions, and nominally prospective rules, which expressly cover only post-enactment transactions but have some effect on prior transactions', or alternatively, 'classifying legal changes by degree and distinguishing between applications that have greater and lesser retroactive effects'.[247]

In the United States, the retrospective/prospective case law was somewhat confused for many years. For a time, the Supreme Court in the United States adopted a discretionary approach to departures from retrospective adjudication in criminal and civil cases in *Linkletter v. Walker* and *Chevron Oil Co v. Huson*.[248] These decisions have been analysed against 'the legal-philosophical landscape of the 1960s', with the rise of legal realism and the Court's perceptions of the judiciary as a legitimate and necessary law-making institution. The Court subsequently retreated from this position in such cases as *Griffith v. Kentucky*, *James B Beam Distilling Co v. Georgia* and *Harper v. Virginia Department of Taxation*.[249] The majority opinion in *Harper* seems to invalidate pure prospectivity (applying the new rule only to subsequent cases, not to the litigants in the law-changing case) on constitutional separation of power arguments, as well as selective prospectivity (applying a new rule in the case in which the new rule is announced but making the new rule otherwise prospective).[250] The Supreme Court also seems to have

---

[245] See Jill E Fisch, 'Retroactivity and Legal Change: An Equilibrium Approach' 110 (1997) *Harvard Law Review* 1058; K Roosevelt III, 'A Little Theory is a Dangerous Thing: The Myth of Adjudicative Retroactivity' (1999) 31 *Connecticut Law Review* 1075; and Stephen R Munzer, 'Retroactive Law' (1977) 6 *Journal of Legal Studies* 373 at 385–90.

[246] Fisch, at 1069; discussing Kaplow.   [247] Fisch, at 1069, 1072.

[248] *Linkletter v. Walker* (1965) 381 US 618; *Chevron Oil Co v. Huson* (1971) 404 US 97; *Griffith v. Kentucky* (1987) 479 US 314; also see *Teague v. Lane* (1989) 489 US 288.

[249] *Harper v. Virginia Department of Taxation* (1992) 509 US 86.

[250] This part of the majority judgment is arguably dicta (the case was not concerned with the question of pure prospectivity) and commentators note that a majority of the Court has never expressly recognized any constitutional limitation on prospective adjudication. However, the later Supreme Court decision of *Landgraf v. USI Film Products* (2004) 511 US 244 at 279 described *Harper* as creating 'a firm rule of retroactivity'. Fisch, at 1062.

reverted to a firm (bright-line) rule of retroactive application of the law in both criminal and civil cases on direct review, but not for collateral review of final decisions.[251]

Over the years the possibility of prospective overruling being adopted in the United Kingdom has been occasionally canvassed by some Law Lords[252] although until recently the majority consensus was that 'such a system...has no place in our legal system'.[253] Lord Browne-Wilkinson commented in *Kleinwort Benson Ltd v. Lincoln City Council* that although the unchanging theory of law had been rejected as a 'myth' and a 'fairy tale', 'its progeny—the retrospective effect of a change made by judicial decision—remains'.[254] As one commentator points out somewhat ironically:

Once it is accepted that the judges do change the law, then to reject prospective decision-making is not to limit, but rather to extend the judicial domain so as to include retrospective legislation, thus allowing the judiciary greater legislative power than the legislature itself.[255]

Two House of Lords decisions in which the rejection of prospective decision-making had arguably unjust or anomalous consequences were *Kleinwort Benson Ltd v. Lincoln City Council*[256] and *R v. Governor of Brockhill Prison, ex parte Evans*.[257] In *Kleinwort* the House of Lords abolished the common law distinction between mistakes of law and mistakes of fact, which had prevented recovery of payments made under a mistake of law. The rationale for overruling was that the distinction had been very difficult to discern, bringing the law into disrepute. In this case, payments were made to local authorities under contracts which, at the time, were understood by both parties to be valid and binding, so that the payments were believed to be lawfully due. Although all Law Lords recognized that the rule was no longer defensible, two believed that overruling it should be done only by legislation, so that it would not operate retrospectively. For example, Lord Browne-Wilkinson argued that the monies in this case should not be recoverable since at the time of payment the payer was not labouring under mistake: 'If, at the date of payment, the law was settled by clear judicial authority then a payment in accordance with such law was not made

---

[251] See Roosevelt; and Bradley Scott Shannon, 'The Retroactive and Prospective Application of Judicial Decisions' (2003) 26 *Harvard Journal of Law and Public Policy* 811 for a review of applicable case law; and David Lehn, 'Adjudicative Retroactivity as a Preclusion Problem: Dow Chemical Co v. Stephenson' (2004) 59 *New York University Annual Survey of American Law* 563.

[252] *Percy v. Hall* [1977] QB 924 at 952 per Schiemann LJ; *R v. Governor of Brockhill Prison, ex parte Evans (No 2)* [1998] 4 All ER 993 at 1002 per Woolf L (English Court of Appeal); *R v. Governor of Brockhill Prison, ex parte Evans (No 2)* [2001] AC 19 at 42 per Hobhouse L; at 26 per Slynn, L (House of Lords of Appeal).

[253] *Kleinwort Benson Ltd v. Lincoln City Council* [1999] 2 AC 349 at 379 per Lord Goff.

[254] [1999] 2 AC 349 at 358.

[255] 'Charnock—Overrulling as a speech act', article available at trinity.dit.unitn.it/ipra2005/uploads/Charnock_Overruling.doc (accessed 25 July 2005).   [256] [1999] 2 AC 349.

[257] [2001] 2 AC 19.

under a mistake of law even if the law has subsequently been changed by later judicial decision'.[258]

In *R v. Governor of Brockhill Prison, ex parte Evans* a convicted prisoner successfully sued for damages for wrongful detention after a judicial change in the law relating to sentencing, with Chief Justice Woolf of the Court of Appeal describing the result as 'highly artificial', while still holding that 'it is not open to this court to abandon the fairy tale'.[259] The plaintiff had been detained by the Governor for a period correctly calculated in accordance with the law as laid down in a series of Divisional Court decisions, which were subsequently disapproved by a later decision of the Divisional Court in which the plaintiff challenged the method of calculation and succeeded. The court set out a different method of calculation and stated on 15 November 1996 that her release date properly calculated was in fact 17 September 1996 (ie the plaintiff had been detained for 59 days too long).[260]

The Court of Appeal's judgment upholding the award of damages survived a House of Lords appeal, with the Law Lords suggesting by way of *obiter dicta* that the subject matter of the case (false imprisonment/deprivation of liberty) meant that it would never constitute 'such a very exceptional case' such that consideration of prospective overruling might be warranted. This was despite the fact that imposing liability on the defendant seemed unreasonable because he was merely acting in accordance with the view of the law taken by the courts at the time. Lord Slynn commented:

The judgment . . . follows the traditional route of declaring not only what was the meaning of the section at the date of judgment but what was always the correct meaning of the section. The court did not seek to limit the effect of its judgment to the future. I consider that there may be situations in which it would be desirable, and in no way unjust, that the effect of judicial rulings should be prospective or limited to certain claimants. The European Court of Justice, though cautiously and infrequently, has restricted the effect of its ruling to the particular claimant in the case before it and to those who had begun proceedings before the date of its judgment. Those who had not sought to challenge the legality of acts perhaps done years before could only rely on the ruling prospectively. Such a course avoided unscrambling transactions perhaps long since over and doing injustice to defendants.[261]

In the 2002 case of *Arthur JS Hall and Co v. Simons*[262] in which the House of Lords overruled previous case law establishing the common law immunity of advocates, Lord Hope stated that the decision should take effect only from the date when the House delivered its judgment because the Court of Appeal below had already held that the solicitors had not acted as their client's advocate and their conduct was not so intimately connected with the conduct of the case in court as to attract the traditional immunity. Lord Hope commented that: 'I consider it to be a

[258] [1999] 2 AC 349 at 362.   [259] (No 2) [1999] QB 1043 at 1058.
[260] *R v. Governor of Brockhill Prison, ex parte Evans* [1997] QB 443.
[261] [2001] 2 AC 19 at 26–27.   [262] [2002] 1 AC 615 at 726.

legitimate exercise of your Lordship's judicial function to declare prospectively whether or not the immunity—which is judge-made rule—is to be available in the future and, if so, in what circumstances'.263

Finally, in *National Westminster Bank v. Spectrum Plus Ltd*264 the Law Lords unanimously rejected the argument that prospective overruling was outside the constitutional limits of the judicial function. Lord Nicholls reviewed the arguments for and against prospective overruling and concluded that:

... there could be circumstances in this country where prospective overruling would be necessary to serve the underlying objective of the courts of this country; to administer justice fairly and in accordance with the law. There could be cases where a decision on an issue of law, whether common law or statute law, was unavoidable but the decision would have such gravely unfair and disruptive consequences for past transactions or happenings that this House would be compelled to depart from the normal principles relating to the retrospective and prospective effect of court decisions.

If, altogether exceptionally, the House as the country's supreme court were to follow this course I would not regard it as trespassing outside the functions properly to be discharged by the judiciary under this country's constitution. Rigidity in the operation of a legal system is a sign of weakness, not strength. It deprives a legal system of necessary elasticity. Far from achieving a constitutionally exemplary result, it can produce a legal system unable to function effectively in changing times. 'Never say never' is a wise judicial precept, in the interests of all citizens of the country.

Lord Hope stated that previous judicial statements by members of the House of Lords to the effect that prospective overruling had no place in the legal system could no longer be taken as definitive because the ability of courts to make prospective rulings was now recognised. He referred to limited powers in the Scotland Act 1998 and equivalent provisions in legislation dealing with the government of Ireland and Wales conferred upon the courts to limit the temporal effect of a particular class of decisions, and European Court of Justice statements that it can in exceptional cases limit the temporal effect of its judgments. Citing the recent *Pinochet* case in which the House of Lords held it had the power as ultimate court of appeal to rescind or vary one of its earlier orders to correct any injustice, Lord Hope concluded that '... it is for the House, as the ultimate court, to define the limits of its own jurisdiction' (subject to limitations imposed by Parliament compatible with treaty obligations under European Community law and with Convention rights).265

However, the House of Lords refused a request by counsel for *National Westminster Bank* to engage in prospective overruling in the case before it. The Court overruled *Siebe Gorman and Co Ltd v. Barclays Bank* which had been relied upon by lenders to establish that a charge over present and future book debts, where the debts were placed in an account but the charger was free to draw on the

263 [2002] 1 AC 615 at 710.   264 [2005] UKHL 41.

265 See *R v. Bow Street Metropolitan Stipendiary Magistrate (No 2), ex parte Pinochet Ugarte* [2000] 1 AC 119.

account for its business purposes provided the overdraft limit was not exceeded, was in law a fixed charge. The consequence of overruling *Siebe Gorman* was that such a charge was only a floating charge and thus, according to the relevant insolvency statute governing the rights of creditors when the assets of the company in bankruptcy were insufficient to meet all claims, was lower in priority than fixed charges (having the status of preferential debts). Lord Nicholls stated that *National Westminster Bank* was:

miles away from the exceptional category in which alone prospective overruling would be legitimate ... *Siebe Gorman* was a first instance decision. It cannot have been regarded as definitively settling the law in this field ... if the firm and unanimous decision now being given by the House were given prospective effect only, the result would be that in many existing liquidations preferential creditors would be deprived of the priority Parliament intended they should have.

On the basis of *National Westminster*, the House of Lords may consider prospective overruling in 'exceptional cases' although this is much more likely in respect to changes to common law rules in the interests of justice or certainty. However, the Law Lords were clear that prospective overruling would rarely if ever be appropriate in respect to the changed meaning or effect of a statute because this 'would be sanctioning the continuing misapplication of the statute so far as existing transactions or past events are concerned.'[266] As noted by several of the Law Lords, the decision in *National Westminster* brings the House of Lords more in line with European Court of Justice[267] and European Court of Human Rights[268] decisions limiting the temporal scope of judgments and also reflects the importance of section 3 of the *Human Rights Act 1988* in that UK courts must take into account decisions of the European Court of Human Rights in interpreting Convention rights.[269]

In *R (Bidar) v. Ealing London Borough Council* the European Court of Justice gave prospective effect to its judgment on whether UK rules governing financial assistance to students for maintenance costs were included within the scope of the EEC Treaty and outlined its jurisprudence of prospective overruling:

It is only exceptionally that the Court may, in application of the general principle of legal certainty inherent in the Community legal order, be moved to restrict the possibility for any person concerned to rely upon a provision which it has interpreted with a view to calling into question legal relationships established in good faith.... It is also settled in case-law that the financial consequences which might ensue for a Member State from a preliminary ruling do not in themselves justify limiting the temporal effect of the ruling....

---

266 [2005] UKHL 41 at para 38 per Lord Nicholls.

267 [2005] 2 WLR 1078, Case C-209/03 (Opinion of Advocate General Geelhoed 11 November 2004) available at European Court of Justice homepage <http://curia.eu.int> (accessed 28 June 2005).

268 See *Marckx v. Belgium* (1979) 2 EHRR 330, available at <http://www.echr.coe.int/echr> (accessed 28 June 2005).

269 [2005] UKHL 41 para 24–25 and 37 per Lord Nicholls; para 68 per Lord Hope.

The Court has taken that step only in quite specific circumstances, where there was a risk of serious economic repercussions owing in particular to the large number of legal relationships entered into in good faith on the basis of rules considered to be validly in force and where it appeared that both individuals and national authorities had been led into adopting practices which did not comply with Community law by reason of objective, significant uncertainty regarding the implications of Community provisions, to which the conduct of other Member States or the Commission may even have contributed.[270]

In Australia, Mason J (as he then was) noted in a case involving the overruling of a decision upon which there had been reliance, that 'some of the difficulties inherent in the problem under discussion might be avoided if the Court were to adopt the technique of prospective overruling... But the matter was not debated in argument and the technique is not without problems'.[271] In *Ha v. State of New South Wales*,[272] all members of the Australian High Court ruled that the Court had no power to overrule cases prospectively, on the basis that this would not be an exercise of judicial power and would contravene the separation of powers contained in Chapter III of the Federal Constitution:

Prospective overruling is thus inconsistent with judicial power on the simple ground that the new regime that would be ushered in when the overruling took effect would alter existing rights and obligations. If an earlier case is erroneous and it is necessary to overrule it, it would be a perversion of judicial power to maintain in force that which is acknowledged not to be the law. This would be especially so where, as here, non-compliance with a properly impugned statute exposes a person to criminal prosecution.[273]

Justice Kirby has subsequently suggested that *Ha's* ruling that courts in Australia may not declare prospective changes to law will act as a conservative influence when courts consider whether to change the common law. This is because courts will give greater consideration to the adverse effects of retrospective operation, in particular:

the extent to which any such change will affect a wide variety of public and private interests: exposing to liability those who previously may reasonably have assumed that they

---

[270] [2005] 2 WLR 1078, Case C-209/03, para 71 (Opinion of Advocate General Geelhoed 11 November 2004) available at European Court of Justice homepage <http://curia.eu.int> (accessed 28 June 2005). Also see *Banca Popolare di Cremona v. Agenzia Entrate Ufficio Cremona* (Opinion of Advocate General Jacobs 17 March 2005) Case C-475/03 available at European Court of Justice homepage <http://curia.eu.int> (accessed 28 June 2005) which concerned a preliminary ruling on whether a regional tax on production levied in Italy was caught by the Community's prohibition of national turnover taxes other than in accordance with the VAT system. The European Court of Justice noted at para 80 that 'an unlimited temporal effect might retroactively cast into confusion the system whereby Italian regions are financed'.

[271] *Babaniaris v. Lutony Fashions Pty Ltd* (1987) 163 CLR 1 at 15. For other High Court judicial statements as to the possibility of prospective overruling see *Trident General Insurance Co Ltd v. McNiece Bros Pty Ltd* (1988) 165 CLR 107 at 171 per Toohey J; *Oceanic Sun Line Special Shipping Co Inc v. Fay* (1988) 165 CLR 197 at 257 per Deane J; *Savass v. R* (1991) 55 A Crim R 24; *Bropho v. Western Australia* (1990) 171 CLR; and *McKinney v. The Queen* (1991) 171 CLR 468.

[272] *Ha v. State of New South Wales* (1997) 189 CLR 465 at 503–4 per Brennan CJ, McHugh, Gummow and Kirby JJ; at 515 per Dawson, Toohey and Gaudron JJ.

[273] Ibid, at 503–4 per Brennan CJ, McHugh, Gummow and Kirby JJ.

were not liable, or who may have arranged their affairs on the basis of established authority. In such cases, it is relevant to take into account the capacity of those affected to meet the enlarged liability and whether they have (or would be able in the future to procure) suitable insurance. The wider and more varied the class affected by any change, the greater the need for caution by a court invited to re-express the common law.[274]

Although *Ha* seems to settle the question of the validity of prospective *overruling* (applying the new rule only to subsequent cases) in Australia, the Court did not consider whether it had the power to *postpone* operation of its judgment, as requested by the State of New South Wales, which had argued that if its legislation was held to be unconstitutional, the High Court should postpone operation of the declaratory order for twelve months. The majority of 4:3 held the State's legislation to be unconstitutional in that it violated section 90 of the Constitution but did not find it necessary to overrule prior decisions on which the State had based the legislation because it considered that the legislation upheld in the previous cases was different in kind to the legislation being challenged before the Court. Campbell points to Canadian Supreme Court precedent allowing postponement in order to give the government the opportunity to bring legislation up to scratch with constitutional requirements, but only if:

A. striking down the legislation without enacting something in its place would pose a danger to the public;

B. striking down the legislation without enacting something in its place would threaten the rule of law; or

C. the legislation was deemed unconstitutional because of underinclusiveness rather than overbreadth, and therefore striking down the legislation would result in the deprivation of benefits from deserving persons without thereby benefiting the individual whose rights have been violated.[275]

5.9 What principles should apply in limiting the retrospective effect of judicial decisions?

Even assuming a separation of powers doctrine mandating temporal limits on judicial law-making, the indeterminate nature of retroactivity means that 'constitutional principles cannot definitively answer questions of legitimacy'.[276] Although the following arguments by Fisch are based upon the US constitutional text and doctrine, the same general principles apply to the United Kingdom and Australia. First, Fisch takes issue with Justice Scalia's circular argument in *Harper* that judicial power is, by nature, inherently retroactive, and that this is the principal

---

[274] *Brodie v. Singleton Shire Council* (2001) 206 CLR 512 at 595–6.   [275] Campbell, at 71.
[276] Fisch, at 1079.

distinction between judicial and legislative power (the same critique could be applied to the Australian High Court's reasoning in *Ha*):

> If, in contrast, the judicial power were defined to include prospective adjudication, the constitutionally derived lawmaking power of the courts could not be subjected to temporal limitations on the grounds that the judicial power is 'inherently' retrospective. This patent circularity is one of the most striking logical weaknesses of the separation of powers approach to retroactivity.[277]

Secondly, Fisch argues that this narrow conception of the judicial power is based upon a formalist approach to separation of powers doctrine, which fails to take account of the changing nature of the judicial power and, in particular, the expanded role of constitutional and statutory interpretation in which courts have taken on an increasing law-making function with policy analysis, traditionally the role of the legislature, forming an integral part of judicial decision-making.[278] Where the legislature has 'ceded the development of an entire field of law to the courts', there may even be a law-making 'partnership' between the legislature and the judiciary.[279]

Thirdly, although *stare decisis* and retrospectivity can both be viewed as doctrinal boundaries for judicial law-making, the former as a substantive limitation and the latter a temporal one, yet adherence to the doctrine of *stare decisis* is not considered to be a constitutional issue but a question for the discretion of the court. This is obviously inconsistent:

> A weak doctrine of *stare decisis* renders much of retroactivity analysis inconsequential by reducing the extent to which a judicial decision creates generally applicable legal rules that must be given prospective effect by later courts... If the Constitution does not address the extent to which the judicial power is affected by the choice of *stare decisis* principles, there is no reason to infer a specific temporal context to the Constitution's grant of judicial power.[280]

Finally, Fisch concludes that using the law of remedies to overcome supposed constitutional limitations on prospective application of new rules leads to unsatisfactory outcomes both for the litigant and doctrinally.[281] For the litigant, 'winning the application of a particular rule of law has little value unless the litigant is entitled to the relief justified by that rule'.[282] At the level of theoretical analysis, the Court relying on a remedial approach must still determine whether a rule is 'new' and then whether equitable considerations justify using the law of remedies to lessen its retrospective effect, with the same definitional problems that puncture

---

[277] Fisch, at 1080.

[278] Fisch, at 1081. Of course this is subject to the attack on so-called 'judicial activism'.

[279] Fisch, at 1081, referring to Richard A Posner (1985) *The Federal Courts: Challenge and Reform* (Harvard University Press, Cambridge, Mass.) 298–315.   [280] Fisch, at 1082.

[281] This theory of remedial discretion was developed by Richard H Fallon Jr and Daniel J Meltzer, 'New Law, Non-Retroactivity, and Constitutional Remedies' (1991) 104 *Harvard Law Review* 1731.

[282] Fisch, at 1083.

retrospectivity analysis and the same problems of what weight to give to policy considerations in limiting the effect of retrospective application of the 'new' rule.[283] Using the law of remedies to achieve a 'backdoor' prospective result is normatively suspect because it results in the separation of a 'remedy' from a 'right', perhaps to the point of denying any 'remedy' at all.[284]

Clearly, policy considerations other than constitutional limitations should ground the retrospective/prospective debate in judicial decision-making. In *Chevron Oil*, the United States Supreme Court developed the following balancing test controlling whether a new rule should be applied prospectively in the civil context:

First, the decision to be applied nonretroactively must establish a new principle of law, either by overruling clear past precedent on which litigants may have relied, or by deciding an issue of first impression whose resolution was not clearly foreshadowed. Second, it has been stressed that 'we must... [look] to the prior history of the rule in question, its purpose and effect, and whether retrospective operation will further or retard its operation'. Finally, we have weighed the inequity imposed by retroactive application.[285]

As Fisch observes, this test reflects the fact that prospective laws are typically thought to be more fair and retrospective laws more efficient. However, as we will see in Chapter 6, both these assumptions are open to challenge. It is commonly argued that prospectivity provides people with notice of legal change, enabling 'people to predict the consequences of their transactions and increases the influence of legal rules upon primary conduct',[286] and is more favourable to reliance interests. Applying the *Chevron Oil* test, a US court must specifically examine whether a litigant's reliance on a prior rule should be protected.[287]

The technique of prospective overruling seems most appropriate where a court is overruling an old precedent upon which people have or might have relied: the case of the better rule, rather than the uncertain rule. There is a *prima facie* case of unfairness in retrospectively overturning a rule upon which people have relied, even if the rule is a bad one; there is no unfairness in overturning such a rule prospectively. Dworkin's argument that an overruling decision is simply the best correct interpretation of the underlying law is 'cold comfort' for litigants who relied on precedent and also fails to take into account the role played by intervening decisions in altering the reasoning of judges in arriving at the best interpretation of the law:

[s]ince the body of preexisting law changes with intervening decisions, it seems clear that an intervening decision—even one not directly on point—can change the result in a pending case. In short, 'legal rights depend upon the temporal order in which cases are decided... [d]epending on which cases are decided between the transaction and its legal resolution, the "correct" result may vary'.[288]

283 Fisch, at 1084.   284 Shannon, at 844.
285 *Chevron Oil* (1971) 404 US 97 at 106–07, cited in Fisch, at 1055.   286 Fisch, at 1085.
287 Fisch, at 1085. See Chapter 6.
288 Roosevelt, at 1105–6 drawing upon Kenneth Kress's arguments in 'Legal Reasoning and Coherence Theories: Dworkin's Rights These, Retroactivity, and the Linear Order of Decisions' (1984) 72 *California Law Review* 369 at 373–4.

Yet Fisch rightfully observes that determining fairness in the context of civil litigation is problematic because of the 'zero-sum' nature of the game:

To the extent that some degree of fairness is achieved by prospective application of a change in law that would disadvantage one litigant, it is exactly matched by the unfairness of not applying the change in law to a litigant who successfully argued for legal change.[289]

Selective prospectivity, which allows courts to apply the new ruling in the case in which it is announced but to make the holding otherwise prospective, is particularly problematic from a fairness/equality perspective because it treats similarly situated litigants differently depending on who gets to the court first. It allows the court to apply the new rule to the first litigant to obtain a hearing and the old rule to others in the queue. The *Chevron Oil* test allowed courts to engage in this practice when considering the discretionary criterion of the extent to which particular litigants had relied on the original rule. The US Supreme Court on both constitutional and inequality grounds subsequently rejected the doctrine of selective prospectivity.[290]

Secondly, the actual degree of reliance varies from case to case based upon such factors as the nature of the rule, the reliability/predictability of the previous law, the extent to which expectations about the rule affected conduct and the extent to which these expectations were reasonable. In Chapter 6, we argue that more weight should normally be given to reliance upon substantive rules regulating conduct. Otherwise, there is the risk of rewarding reliance on procedural rules to avoid the effect of substantive ones. However, Fisch observes that the distinction between substantive and procedural rules is often unworkable because 'substantive rules are not inherently more important to a litigant than procedural rules; both can be outcome determinative'.[291] A good example is *Schriro v. Summerlin*[292] in which the United States Supreme Court by a 5:4 vote held that the *Ring v. Arizona*[293] ruling of 2002 that under the Sixth Amendment juries, not judges, should determine the existence of aggravating factors justifying the imposition of the death penalty, was merely the announcement of a new procedural rule. The majority opinion in *Schriro* engaged in the following word play:

This Court's holding that, because *Arizona* has made a certain fact essential to the death penalty, that fact must be found by a jury, is not same as this Court's making a certain fact essential to the death penalty. The former was a procedural holding; the latter would be substantive.[294]

Hence the *Arizona* ruling could not be applied retroactively to a criminal conviction that was already final but only to cases still pending on direct review. The immediate and seemingly completely arbitrary consequence of the thinly drawn procedural/substantive distinction in this case was that over 100 death row

[289] Fisch, p. 1087.   [290] *James B Beam Distilling Co v. Georgia* (1991) 501 US 529.
[291] Fisch, p. 1087.   [292] 542 US 348 (2004); 124 S Ct 2519; 341 F 3d 1082 (2004).
[293] 536 US 584 (2002).   [294] 124 S Ct 2519 at 2524.

inmates in at least five states were denied a new hearing before a jury.[295] *Schriro* prompted a spirited dissent from Justice Breyer joined by three other Justices:

Certainly the ordinary citizen will not understand the difference. That citizen will simply witness two individuals, both sentenced through the use of unconstitutional procedures, one individual going to his death, the other saved, all through an accident of timing. How can the Court square this spectacle with what it has called the 'vital importance to the defendant and to the community that any decision to impose the death sentence by, and appear to be, based on reason'?[296]

Thirdly, Fisch argues that changes in rules with nominally prospective effect can also have detrimental effects on reliance interests.[297] However, here the question should be whether the reliance is reasonable in the circumstances, particularly if the reliance was based on little more than an assumption that the law should not change.

Judicial decisions with strong retrospective effect are said to encourage greater efficiency based on utilitarian conceptions of efficient law making 'maximiz[ing] the net benefits of legal change', without regard for issues of distribution or who bears the inevitable losses or costs.[298] Such arguments are based on the assumption that the new rule is necessarily an improvement on the old one, thus justifying the application of that rule 'to as broad a class as possible'. If people can complete transactions prior to the operation of the new rule, the objectives of the new rule may be undermined.[299] However, in Chapter 6, we discuss, in some detail, the flaws in efficiency arguments favouring retrospectivity; and in particular the failure of law and economics theorists such as Kaplow to take sufficient account of market imperfections, transition costs and social costs arising from retrospective change. Indeed, prospectivity can reduce economic costs that constitute a barrier to change because the transition costs associated with 'changing the applicable rules midstream for past or pending transactions' are avoided.[300]

Given these concerns, how should a court make the decision between retrospective and prospective application of a change in law? We have already noted the theoretical and practical problems with a remedial analysis based on the law of remedies; indeed, some cases involving the retrospective application of a new rule might not concern the question of remedies at all.[301] Fisch's equilibrium model drawn from physics was described in Chapter 3. Broadly, where the existing law is settled (a stable equilibrium) change should be non-retrospective; where the law is unsettled (an unstable equilibrium) change should be retrospective. However, Roosevelt argues that Fisch's model gives insufficient attention to how it is that courts change the law (how courts would implement an equilibrium model in

---

[295] Death Penalty Information Center, 'Full Right to a Jury will not Extend to Older Cases', Press Release Thursday, 24 June 2004, available at <http://www.deathpenaltyinfo.org>.
[296] 124 S Ct 2519 at 2529 with reference to *Beck v. Alabama* 447 US 625, 637–638.
[297] Fisch, at 1087.   [298] Fisch, at 1088.   [299] Fisch, at 1089.
[300] Fisch, at 1089–90.   [301] Shannon, at 843.

practice). For example, would the avoidance of retrospectivity in disruptions to a stable equilibrium require pure prospectivity so that the new rule would not even apply to the parties in the case that changed the rule?[302] However, an alternative response could be to decide the case on narrow grounds or to signal that the law is in fact unsettled, indicating that a legal change may be on the way and it is risky to rely on the existing precedent.

Lehn has advocated courts taking a discretionary approach based on a cost-benefit test, including taking into account such factors as purpose, reliance and effect, with a rebuttable presumption in favour of prospectivity for disputes that arose prior to the change in law.[303] This discretionary test to be applied should, for the sake of equal treatment of litigants, be the same for a 'law-changing retroactivity question' (the disputed action/transaction in the law-changing court) and a 'subsequent retroactivity question' (all other disputed actions/transactions that preceded the law-changing decision, which decision intervened before these other disputes were litigated).[304]

The test should also be the same for pending (cases not yet final but the underlying action/transaction occurred prior to the rule change, for example, unfiled, in discovery, at trial, or on direct appeal at the time of the rule change) and final cases (all avenues of appeal exhausted and statute of limitations expired before the law-changing decision). Lehn observes that it is inconsistent for US courts to reject the law-changing/subsequent dichotomy underlying selective prospectivity yet maintain the pending/final case dichotomy, which mandates retrospectivity in pending cases and prospectivity in cases already final:

> The difference between a pending case and a final one also is often the result of 'accidental timing', which suggests that the pending/final dichotomy violates the principle of equal treatment as much as the law-changing/subsequent dichotomy does.[305]

Lehn argues that retrospectivity rules are rightfully conceptualized as a preclusion doctrine (akin to *res judicata* and *stare decisis*; but distinguishable); on this basis, the application of a discretionary cost-benefit test focussed on reliance might legitimately result in disparate treatment of similarly situated litigants, particularly to prevent the re-opening of final decisions:

> *Res judicata* and collateral estoppel protect reliance on a prior judgment, while *stare decisis* protects reliance on a precedent.[306]

Lehn rejects a mandatory regime favouring either retrospectivity or prospectivity as inefficient. He observes that mandating retrospectivity means that the court might be loath to change the law at all for fear of upsetting reliance interests. Conversely, mandating prospectivity so that a court can withhold a new rule

---

[302] Roosevelt, at 1109.
[303] David Lehn, 'Adjudicative Retroactivity as a Preclusion Problem: Dow Chemical Co v. Stephenson' (2004) 59 *New York University Annual Survey of American Law* 563 at 596–7.
[304] Lehn, at 596–7.   [305] Lehn, at 581.   [306] Lehn, at 588.

means that people may have no incentive to try to change the law since they will obtain no benefit from the change.[307] We would add that the policy arguments against making an overruling decision would be considerably weakened if the court had the choice of applying the new rule prospectively only: the court could thereby avoid depriving anyone of their right to a decision in their favour. This leads to one of the strongest arguments both for and against the practice of prospective rulings; it would undoubtedly remove one of the strongest inhibitions on judicial creativity and activism.

In contrast to Lehn, Shannon rejects a discretionary approach incorporating prospectivity, arguing for a firm rule of retrospectivity in all civil and criminal cases on direct review.[308] He states that:

It is an unavoidable implication of the adjudicative function that the cases considered by courts invariably involve conduct or events that occurred in the past... the usual rule is that a court is to apply the law in effect at the time it renders its decision.[309]

Shannon argues that a firm rule of retrospectivity is thus more in accord with the nature of the adjudicative function; it also maintains traditional understandings of the role of *stare decisis* and the distinction between the judicial holding/rule and dicta. Further, he argues that preserving a firm retrospective rule 'better furthers private ordering, fair and efficient adjudication, and public confidence in the judiciary'.[310]

Shannon's arguments are based on the equality, efficiency and reliance grounds in support of the retrospective application of judicial rules noted above: for example, that retrospectivity provides greater incentive for litigants to argue for legal change because the new rule will be applied in their case; it requires the court to (equally) apply the same rule of law to all similar cases not yet final; and avoids the potential for abuse and 'a disintegrating chaos of doctrine'[311] arising from judicial discretion in prospective approaches (including 'not only the ability to decide a case according to "incorrect" law, but also the ability to decide when such a decision is tolerable, or desirable').[312]

Shannon argues that an effective doctrine of *stare decisis* would mitigate against many of the inequities of retrospective judicial rule-change; factors such as reliance should be taken into account in the initial decision whether or not to change the legal rule and not deferred to considerations of application of the new rule to the parties before the court or, in subsequent cases, to parties contesting actions/transactions prior in time to the rule change. This would also remove the need for an unsatisfactory 'backdoor' prospective approach based upon the use of legal remedies.

If some particular change in the law would be so disruptive that it may not be justly implemented retroactively, that is not an argument in favour of prospectivity;

---

[307] Lehn, at 583–4, 599–60. [308] Shannon, at 836. [309] Shannon, at 839.
[310] Shannon, at 836–74. [311] Shannon, at 873. [312] Shannon, at 873.

rather, it is an indication that the law should not be changed, at least not in the current case. Therefore, considerations such as reliance interests must be balanced as part of the decision whether to change the law in the first instance. If a change is desirable but should not be applied retroactively, the solution lies not in a prospective announcement, but rather in the communication of possible change through the use of ordinary dicta.[313]

5.10 European echoes

Although this chapter is confined to a discussion of attitudes towards precedent and overruling in common law jurisdictions, similar issues arise on civil law systems generating similar solutions. Rorive's study of the Belgian *Cour de cassation* recognizes that the overruling of a previous ruling: 'it operates retrospectively and has an immediate impact in future on members of the community who were not parties to the litigation.'[314] Her summary of the *Cour de cassation*'s 'jurisprudence of overruling' in terms that could have been formulated by the House of Lords:

1. As a matter of principle, the *Cour de cassation* strictly follows its previous decisions.

2. The erroneous character of a decision of the *Cour de cassation* is neither a sufficient ground to depart from it nor a necessary prerequisite.

3. A departure in the case law of the *Cour de cassation* requires *prima-facie* a 'new fact' which can either be a lack of *paix judiciaire* understood in a broad sense (adverse reactions towards the previous decision from lower courts, academic writers or parliamentarians) or some material change in circumstances or in values.

4. Such a lack of *paix judiciaire* is however an insufficient ground to justify a departure in case law. There must be additional 'good reasons' for legitimizing the change, such as compelling considerations of consistency, justice and certainty or a misreading of the legislature's intention.

Even where there are good reasons, a change through case law may be rejected either because the legitimate expectations of individuals are at stake or the reform in question will be better dealt with in parliament.[315]

---

[313] Shannon, at 875. Shannon similarly states at 835–6: '. . . a proposed rule of law that is dramatically new and would seriously upset the reasonable reliance interests of one or more parties should not be regarded as a rule that should not be applied retroactively; rather, such a rule of law should simply be rejected as bad law, or a rule that cannot, as yet, be the law'.

[314] I Rorive, 'Diverging Legal Culture but Similar Jurisprudence of Overruling: The Case of the House of Lords and the Belgian Cour de cassation' (2004) 3 *European Review of Private Law* 321 at 344.   [315] Ibid, at 343–4.

5.11 Conclusion

This chapter has shown that judicial law-making remains controversial and some wish or will that it does not happen. It is not surprising to see that the form of judicial law-making that is most controversial is in criminal law[316] and the next most controversial is in taxation law[317] reflecting the most controversial areas of legislative retrospectivity.

This chapter also demonstrates the inherent retrospectivity of judicial decision-making and that senior judges have largely abandoned the pretence that it does not occur in favour of an open discussion of when they should engage and what principles should govern the exercise of this power. In setting out those principles, they recognize reliance interests, try to accommodate them but do not attempt to make them determinative.

The means by which courts respect reliance interests has varied. Some American judges sought to make their law-making retrospective and English and Australian judges toyed with the idea. However, the latter never got beyond a few *dicta*, and the former have essentially abandoned the idea. Instead, courts have attempted to provide guidance by setting out as clearly as they can a set of principles, reasons and precedents for when they will overrule, trying to provide fair warning of where law might be changed and where such change is unlikely.

There is a great deal of commonsense in the principles suggested and the eyes of a reader may glaze over when trying to decide which principles are to be preferred or whether, in true Aristotelian (or common law) mood, their application and combination should be a matter of 'judgement'. While each legal philosopher might have their own preference (ours are with those set out by Kirby J), our recommendation is not that judges should adopt 'one right principle' for over-ruling but the meta-recommendation that each court should openly and transparently develop its principles giving as much clarity and guidance as the matter can permit. It is better that each court has a clearly worked out and clearly expressed set of principles than that all courts should share a less clearly worked out set of principles. Having said that, it would be unsurprising if the principles adopted in different courts did not tend to converge over time—not only with each other but with legislatures that openly discuss when they will exercise their retrospective rule making power.

---

[316] See 'The Ladies' Directory Case', Shaw v. Director of Public Prosecution [1962] AC 220. The accused had published a directory containing names and addresses of prostitutes; one ground of prosecution was 'Conspiring to corrupt public morals by means of the Ladies Directory'. All judges with the exception of Lord Reid supported the conviction on this ground, with Lord Simonds at 268 asserting that the court possessed 'a residual power, where no statute intervened to supersede the common law, to superintend those offences which are prejudicial to the public welfare'. However, Lord Reid at 275 argued that 'where parliament fears to tread it is not for the courts to rush in'.

[317] Beginning with the Barwick High Court's decision in *Curran v. Federal Commissioner of Taxation* (1973) 131 CLR 409; see discussion in previous chapter under 'Retrospective Taxation Legislation'.

At the ultimate appellate level, where there are no superior courts whose decisions bind them, most courts have an ultimate preference for 'the better rule'—the legal rules and principles for which the reasons are strongest according to their approach to judicial reasoning.[318] While those approaches vary, none see themselves as coming to a view of the 'better rule' *de novo*. Most would have an anathema to the idea that they are 'making it up as they go along' and would endorse Raz's view that they are at the second stage of law-making, interpreting the law that emerges from other sources rather than starting afresh as a legislature has a right to do. The decisions of earlier judges provide reasons for their decisions because they are sources of law of which they have a duty to consider and apply where it seems appropriate. This is backed up by the genuine respect which virtually all judges give to the earlier decisions by other judges (including those of inferior courts). This could be derided as solidarity or a means of avoiding criticism but it is generally more than that, acknowledging the genuine effort that most other judges have made to reach an answer that fits, the possibility of reasonable disagreement, the possibility of error, the different contexts in which cases are decided, and the differential insights into the relevant rules that they bring.

This acknowledgement of other judges' decisions as sources of law and an independent respect for them does not abrogate their own responsibility to reach their own judgment and to come to a view that their approach to judicial decision-making has generated a 'better rule' that thereby has to be implemented. To some extent, the respect for the collective wisdom of other judges may lead them to overrule or progressively ignore decisions that are inconsistent or out of step with the broad direction that the law seems to be taking. In doing so, the law is made more coherent, consistent and worthy of respect (although none engage in what Dworkin rightly calls the 'Herculean' task of making the legal system as a whole the best it could possibly be).[319] However, judges are never forced to come to that conclusion and courts will often feel their way towards such a conclusion—using all their skills of distinguishing and failing to apply precedents, reformulating old rules in new verbal formulations, sending signals that show a rule is at risk of being overruled and that reliance on it is risky. This is not just to respect reliance but also to respect the work of other judges and an acknowledgement of the possibility of error when changes are introduced too hastily without proper thought. They need to have a high degree of confidence in their decision—needing new reasons in terms of new principles or the discovery of unintended consequences, be confident that the new decision will not, itself, be overruled. If the principles behind the original decision were not agreed or not clearly worked out, the court can feel more confident that the new rule really is a better one.

---

[318] We have chosen the word 'approach' as more neutral than 'practice' or 'theory' because of the differential extents to which judges consciously or deliberately follow conscious practices and the extent to which those practices are theoretically informed.

[319] See discussion in C Sampford, *The Disorder of Law* (Blackwell, Oxford, 1989). Chapter 4, of RM Dworkins, *Law's Empire* (Beknap, Cambridge, Mass., 1986).

Even when judges have come to the view that a new rule would be a better one, they will consciously consider whether or not they should adopt the better rule in the case and how far they will apply it in the instant case, sometimes using the many discretions they have as to orders. Those reasons will take into account the reliance that others would have placed on the continuation of the earlier rule—with the reasonableness and legitimacy of the reliance being either explicitly or implicitly taken into account. Reliance is implicitly supported by the respect for earlier decisions contained in the view as to whether a new rule is better and in whether, when and how the new rule is adopted.

6

Justifications for retrospective law

6.1 Introduction

Two things have become apparent in the course of our examination of retrospective law in the preceding chapters. Firstly, retrospectivity rule-making is widely practised, and often widely accepted, in the everyday business of law making. Secondly, an attitude of absolute opposition to retrospectivity is unwarranted. Because there is no normatively significant difference between retroactivity (express retrospectivity) and the retrospective effects of facially prospective legislation—and because such retrospective effects are a matter of degree—there is no bright line to be drawn between acceptable (prospective enough) and unacceptable (too retrospective) legislation. Although very many retrospective laws, including some of those discussed in Chapters 4 and 5, will be problematic for the reasons identified in Chapter 3, this will not always be the case. Sometimes retrospective law will be justified.

The question which remains to be answered is: *when* is retrospective law justified? The mere absence of decisive countervailing considerations is not sufficient; some positive argument must be given in favour of retrospectivity whenever it is to be used. In this chapter, we consider what reasons might be given in favour of retrospectivity—and whether these are good reasons. The most commonly seen justification for retrospectivity—that it is a 'necessary evil' under exceptional circumstances—concedes too much to absolutist opponents of retrospectivity. We argue that stronger justifications for retrospective law are available: indeed, that retrospectivity wisely used can serve to promote the values upon which a legal system rests. Retrospectivity, in other words, is an inherent and indispensable element of well ordered society under the Rule of Law.

6.2 Retrospective law as necessary evil

Perhaps the most common justification of retrospective law is some form of the argument that it is a necessary evil. This justification does not challenge the view that retrospectivity is always *pro tanto* undesirable. It holds that, in exceptional circumstances, the only alternative to the evil of retrospective law is an evil of even greater magnitude. In such circumstances, all of the available options represent a diminution in the values promoted by the law (justice, democracy, certainty, etc.), and retrospective law would result in the least such diminution: that is, it is the least worst option of those available.

Not only is this the most commonly used justification of retrospective law, it is often treated as though it is the *only possible* justification of retrospective law. Thus, Woozley, in arguing that some retrospective laws are justified, states that 'while it may be true that playing unfair is always bad, it does not follow that it is always wrong; and it will not be wrong in the case where, even if playing unfair is bad, playing fair is even worse.'[1] Fuller seems to imply a similar view when he describes the role of retrospectivity in the law as assisting us when we make mistakes:

Like every other human undertaking, the effort to meet the often complex demands of the internal morality of law may suffer various kinds of shipwreck. It is when things go wrong that the retroactive statute often becomes indispensable as a curative measure; though the proper movement of law is forward in time, we sometimes have to stop and turn about to pick up the pieces.[2]

In fact, most of the examples of controversial retrospective legislation considered in Chapter 4 were given this kind of justification. The *War Crimes Amendment Act 1989* (Cth) may be thought to be justified on the grounds that the alternative was allowing those guilty of heinous crimes (that is, gross violations of human rights) to go unpunished. Given the gravity of the offences, this might be regarded as too great an affront to common decency, and too great an injustice to the victims of these war criminals. Thus, a smaller injustice (subjecting war criminals to retrospective law) was to be preferred to a far greater injustice (denying recourse to their victims, and allowing the guilty to go unpunished for heinous crimes).

The 'necessary evil' justification is even easier to discern in the case of retrospective taxation legislation. One reason the Fraser Government gave for subjecting *Curran* schemes to backdated prohibition was the magnitude of the revenue losses caused by *Curran* schemes.[3] The same justification was offered for the bottom-of-the-harbour legislation. The Treasurer referred to the 'revenue implications' of the schemes, and the fact that they had lost the Commonwealth 'hundreds of millions of dollars' in revenue.[4]

Obviously, catastrophic loss of revenue could not be used as a justification for retrospective legislation against those tax avoidance schemes which did not represent a similar loss of revenue (for example, because they were not as widespread).

---

[1] AD Woozley, 'What is Wrong With Retrospective Law?' (1968) 18 *The Philosophical Quarterly* 70 at 53.	[2] Lon L Fuller, *The Morality of Law* (Yale University Press, New Haven, 1964) 53.
[3] Australia, *Hansard*, House of Representatives, 1978, vol. 108, p. 1245.
[4] JW Howard (Treasurer), Press Release, 25 July 1982. (Reprinted (1982) 11 *Australian Tax Review* 154–6.)

This particular 'necessary evil' justification, therefore, does not support the opinion of the Labor Shadow Treasurer at the time that *all* schemes covered by the legislation should be targeted retrospectively, on the basis of his doubts that 'the extent of tax avoidance involved in a particular scheme provides a sound basis for differential treatments as to operative dates for prohibitive legislation.'[5] However, other potential threats could possibly be used to justify the retrospective prohibition of these less 'costly' schemes: namely, the threat to the institution of taxation; distortion of the economy; and loss of respect for governments and the law by ordinary taxpayers.

There is no doubt that retrospective legislation could sometimes be justified on these grounds; it *is* always preferable to choose a lesser rather than a greater evil, especially where the greater evil represents a catastrophe. However, if this were taken to be the *only* possible justification for retrospective law, this means that retrospective legislation would only be justified in extreme circumstances; that is, when there is a real threat of catastrophe. And this is too limited a scope for justified retrospective legislation. A large amount of the legislation discussed in the previous chapter would be disallowed by such a standard, even though much of this legislation is uncontroversial.

Allowing only an 'extreme circumstances' justification for retrospective legislation would also encourage an *ad hoc* approach to retrospective law making. It must be decided by the legislature on a case-by-case basis whether the circumstances are exceptional enough to warrant retrospectivity, since it would not be possible or practical to develop a set of criteria which identify circumstances which are sufficiently exceptional to justify retrospective legislation. This could, in fact, increase the danger of legislative abuse of the power to legislate retrospectively. Such decisions would also be vulnerable to criticisms that the situation was not dire enough to warrant retrospectivity. This, indeed, is Walker's criticism of the Commonwealth's retrospective taxation legislation: he alleges that the 'emergency' which formed the basis for the *Curran* and 'bottom-of-the-harbour' legislation was 'no more menacing than a need to relieve governmental embarrassment'.[6] In short, this kind of justification for retrospectivity, while perhaps the weakest available justification, can be guaranteed to maintain the controversy surrounding retrospective legislation, rather than resolving it.

A more significant problem with the 'necessary evil' justification—whether or not it is seen as the only possible justification—is that it relies upon the view of retrospective legislation as a *pro tanto* bad. That is, it accepts that retrospectivity is always something to be regretted, even where the alternative is more regrettable. And this means that the possible beneficial uses of retrospective law will be ignored: such a view fails to see the integral part played by retrospective legislation

[5] Shadow Treasurer Ralph Willis, Australian Commonwealth, *Hansard*, House of Representatives, 1978, vol. 109, p. 1902.
[6] Geoffrey de Q Walker, *The Rule of Law: Foundation of Constitutional Democracy* (Melbourne University Press, 1988) 318.

in upholding the values on which the legal system is based. This justification is inadequate, in other words, because it fails to take into account the ways in which retrospective legislation can be a *tout court* good rather than a *pro tanto* bad.

As we saw in Chapter 2, it is impossible to have a legal system which completely and simultaneously fulfils all of the criteria of the Rule of Law. Raz's list included laws being: *prospective, open and clear, relatively stable; made under open, stable, clear and general rules; with accessible courts staffed by an independent judiciary exercising judicial review and observing rules of natural justice; and crime prevention agencies whose discretions do not pervert the law.*[7]

Often, one of these features can be promoted only by not simultaneously promoting the others: for example, more clarity may require less generality, or more certainty may require less clarity. Retrospectivity will not only be a requirement when we have made some kind of mistake that must be fixed up; rather, it will be an inherent feature of any legal system that seeks to uphold the Rule of Law. As such, retrospectivity can play a very important, even invaluable, role in furthering the Rule of Law within society.

The 'necessary evil' justification for retrospectivity is, therefore, somewhat misguided, especially if it is taken to be the *only* such justification. In order to use retrospective law wisely, and to its greatest potential, the potentially positive role of retrospectivity must be acknowledged. In the sections which follow, we consider four positive arguments for retrospectivity: the 'better rule,' 'better authority,' 'efficiency,' and 'fairness' arguments.

6.3 The 'better rule' justification

If we consider the possibility that retrospectivity can make a positive contribution to the Rule of Law (and other values associated with a legal system), a reason immediately arises for thinking that laws ought to be retrospectively applied in a far wider range of cases than traditionally has been allowed. This is that new legal rules are usually made because they are thought to represent an improvement (with reference to values like justice, efficiency, certainty, and so on) over the old rules. And if a new rule is a better rule—that is, one which better promotes the relevant values—then it would seem to be a good thing to apply it to as many cases as possible, including those in which its application would be retrospective.[8] This argument has a considerable pedigree. According to Savigny, 'a new law is always enacted in the persuasion that it is better than the former one. Its efficacy,

---

[7] Joseph Raz, 'The Rule of Law and its Virtue' (April 1977) 93 *Law Quarterly Review* 196, pp.198–201.

[8] Henry Hart and Albert Sacks saw retroactivity as a choice between an old and a new legal rule, a 'conflict of laws in time'. See HM Hart and AM Sacks, 'The Legal Process: Basic Problems in the Making and Application of Law' p. 616. Cited in Jill E Fisch, 'Retroactivity and Legal Change: An Equilibrium Approach' (1996–1997) 110 *Harvard Law Review* 1055 at 1056.

therefore, must be extended as far as possible, in order to communicate the expected improvement in the widest sphere.'[9]

This argument is, in fact, the reverse of the 'necessary evil' argument. Rather than viewing retrospectivity as inherently undesirable, to be used only in exceptional circumstances, the 'better rule' argument sees retrospectivity as inherently *positive*—as something which allows the wider application of a better rule instead of a worse one, and which therefore facilitates the improvement of the legal system which uses it. This view might even be taken to favour 'default' retrospectivity— that is, the adoption of a principle which states that new rules are to be applied retrospectively unless this is specifically disallowed, or unless there are compelling reasons against doing so.[10]

The 'better rule' argument, in fact, seems to be the reason why some kinds of retrospectivity (such as curative legislation, or retrospective legislation which confers a benefit) are non-controversial. If the old law contained an obvious and unintended defect, there is little to be said in favour of applying it instead of a new law in which the defect has been corrected.[11] And although curative legislation represents the strongest 'better rule' justification, the argument can also be made concerning new laws which are fairer and more efficient than the old ones. For example, taxation laws which close unintended loopholes exploited under the old law are better rules in more than one respect: they better reflect the intentions of the legislature; they better reflect the underlying justification for the law (and for the institution of taxation in general); and, they are better in terms of fairness and equity (since they stop some parties from gaining an unfair advantage over others).

This kind of justification for retrospectivity sometimes merges with another: 'efficiency'. It should also be noted that 'efficiency' is not used here in the sense which is often assumed. Rather, 'efficiency' here means 'lawmaking that maximizes the net benefits of legal change'.[12] The broadest possible application of a better rule is 'efficient'—it maximizes the benefits of the legal change—because it spreads those benefits as widely as possible. In general, however, the 'better rule' argument is unlikely to be decisive (except in the case of, for example, curative legislation or legislation conferring a benefit), since there will usually be strong reasons for protecting reliance on the old rule. In particular, there will be other 'efficiency'-based reasons in favour of protecting reliance: that is, the *overall* benefits of legal change will be maximized if a new rule is not applied retrospectively, even if it is a better rule.

The benefits that can be maximized by protecting reliance include all of those considerations discussed in Chapter 3. Firstly, and most importantly, protecting

---

[9] FC von Savigny, *Private International Law, and the Retrospective Operation of Statutes* (T. and T.C., Edinburgh, 1869) 344. See also Chapter 4.

[10] Lest this be seen as preposterous, it should be remembered that this is the approach to judicial retrospectivity discussed in Chapter 5.

[11] Jill E Fisch, 'Retroactivity and Legal Change: An Equilibrium Approach' (1996–1997) 110 *Harvard Law Review* 1055 at 1088. [12] Fisch, p. 1088.

reliance will help achieve the purposes of the law: guiding behaviour by indicating how state power will be used. Retrospective application of a new rule means that the law cannot achieve this purpose. Such application would also damage the ability of other laws to influence behaviour: if there can be no general reliance on the law that is applied being the law that was discoverable at the time a person's actions were chosen, then the incentives and disincentives built into other laws will be less effective. And secondly, there may be public costs associated with retrospective application: for example, as Fisch notes, 'retroactively changing a standard of civil liability may require the retrial of hundreds of cases.'[13] In such circumstances, the costs of retrospectively applying a new rule will outweigh the benefits of the broader distribution of legal improvements.

The 'better rule' argument will, therefore, only rarely be decisive where there has been reliance on an old rule and the reliance is reasonable. A related argument, however, may more often support retrospective application of a new rule. The 'better rule' argument involved the content of new rules. However, there is another way in which a new rule can represent an improvement over its predecessor: namely, in terms of the authority under which it is made. If a new rule has a stronger democratic mandate, then it might be classed as a better rule for that reason alone (although, of course, a rule which is more democratic will often also be better in terms of substantive content than one made by, say, a despotic regime).

It should be remembered that, in judicial retrospectivity, the 'better rule' argument dominates despite the retrospectivity of its application. As we saw in Chapter 5, attempts to limit its application through prospective overruling have effectively collapsed. While it is appropriate for judges to indicate 'stormy weather' where long established rules are in doubt and judges may sometimes feel their way to a new resolution through a series of cases, once they have come to their view of the better rule, they are expected to apply it.

6.4 The 'better authority' justification

Chapter 3 considered the possibility that retrospective laws were undemocratic because the enactment of such laws exceeded a legislature's temporal mandate. However, as we saw, this argument did not provide sufficient grounds for a blanket condemnation of retrospective law. Retrospective laws can be democratic laws under certain conditions. Indeed, they can sometimes be seen as having more democratic support than the laws they replace. And if we object to laws on the basis of their being undemocratic, then we should also prefer laws which are more democratic; democratic laws—all things being equal—are better laws. And this means that a new law which is democratic (in the sense of better reflecting the will

---

[13] Fisch, p. 1091.

of the people), is to be preferred to an old law which is not, or which is less democratic. This generates a distinctive version of the 'better rule' justification—'better' in terms of authority. This is, of course, central to judicial law making.

The 'better authority' argument might, therefore, condone the retrospective application of a new law, for example, where it can be shown that sufficient popular support for the new law existed in the relevant time frame prior to its enactment. As noted in Chapter 3 this may have been true of the Hawke Labor Government's attempts to retrospectively penalize bottom-of-the-harbour schemes where the previous legislature had not done enough to stop the practice. In such cases, the new law reflects not only the current will of the people, but also the will of the people at some time in the past—which, for whatever reason, was not reflected in the laws made at the time. By the same token, the old rule lacked an adequate democratic basis. The superior democratic basis of the new rule is a reason to prefer it.

The strongest version of the better authority justification occurs where a non-democratic regime (for example, a military dictatorship) is overthrown and a democratic government established in its place. When this occurs, a question arises as to the treatment of persons (government officials, soldiers, etc.) who performed actions—perhaps including torture and other human rights abuses—which may have been explicitly made legal under the old regime, but which are criminalized under the new, democratic, government. The 'better authority' argument might support the retrospective application of the new, democratic, laws, since the new laws have a democratic basis which the old laws lacked. (Of course, the new laws are better in many other respects as well: in particular, in relation to Rule-of-Law values as justice, fairness and certainty.) The prosecution of former soldiers in the former East German communist regime, as discussed in Chapter 4, was justified on such grounds.

This 'better authority' argument has a direct parallel in judicial rule-making. Consider the following hypothetical example of what happens all the time. The best authority for the interpretation of a pre-existing statute in 2003 may be a recent 2002 case in the Australian Federal Court (or English Court of Appeals) that has upheld a long line of cases at that level. The citizen acts on this understanding of the law. In 2004, the matter comes to the Australian High Court (or English House of Lords). If a court is called upon to determine the legal consequences of the citizen's actions in 2005, it will automatically and uncontroversially apply the later, higher authority despite the fact that the citizen relied, quite reasonably, rationally and legitimately, on the earlier decision. The difference between the legitimacy of the Court of Appeal and the House of Lords and the respect that they are due is miniscule compared to the difference in legitimacy and respect due to a repressive dictatorship as opposed to a subsequent democratically elected government.

Of course, the 'better authority' justification will often be unsuccessful for the same reason that the 'better rule' justification often fails: namely, that it is outweighed by the reasons in favour of protecting reliance. As with the 'better rule' argument, there will often be other 'efficiency'-based considerations—the public good, achieving the purposes of the law, economic efficiency—opposing the retrospective application of the new rule. (There will also, of course, be considerations of fairness; these will be discussed at the end of the next section.) However, as we noted in our discussion of these considerations in Chapter 3, such 'efficiency'-based reasons do not always count in favour of protecting reliance, which means that the better rule/authority argument might sometimes support retrospectivity. Additionally, as we now go on to show, these other 'efficiency'-based considerations will sometimes *themselves* support retrospectivity.

6.5 The 'efficiency' justification

Chapter 3 noted that efficiency was often used as an argument *against* retrospectivity: the uncertainty caused by retrospective application of new laws (ie a failure to protect reliance on old laws through mechanisms such as grandfathering) was said to create disincentives to investment.[14] It is perhaps surprising, then, that some commentators claim that there is a consensus that retrospective laws are generally more efficient.[15] In fact, there are a number of a ways—in addition to the wider application of a better rule—in which efficiency may be increased by the retrospective application of a new law.

Firstly, retrospective application of new laws often leads to greater administrative efficiency: that is, it makes it easier for officials to apply the law. As noted in Chapter 3, purely prospective legislation would result in multiple procedures having to be followed at any given time. Retrospective application of new laws means that only one procedure need be followed at any time, which reduces the complications officials must deal with. Retrospectivity also overcomes the problem of overcomplicated laws, which would often be required to guard against the exploitation of loopholes in a purely prospective system.[16]

Secondly, retrospective application of a new law is often necessary to achieve the purposes of that law. If people are aware that a particular legal protection will soon cease (or that conduct which is presently free of penalty will soon be penalized), and that reliance on the old law prior to the new law's enactment will be protected (eg through grandfathering), there is a temptation to rush into such activities before the law is changed, thus defeating—at least partially—the objectives of the legal change.[17] This is a strong argument for making new rules retrospective at least to the date of announcement: as Kaplow notes, failure

[14] Louis Kaplow, 'An Economic Analysis of Legal Transitions' (1985–86) 99 *Harvard Law Review* 509 at 527; Michael J Graetz, 'Retroactivity Revisited' (1984–85) 98 *Harvard Law Review* 1820 at 1824.   [15] Fisch, p. 1084.

[16] Stephen R Munzer, 'A Theory of Retroactive Legislation' (1982–83) 61 *Texas Law Review* 425 at 466.   [17] Fisch, p. 1089.

to do this 'might induce a flood of investment activity immediately prior to implementation—precisely the activity the reform was designed to discourage.'[18]

This means that efficiency can be used as an argument *for* the retrospective application of new rules. Indeed, it has been argued (in contrast to the contention above and in Chapter 3) that the protection of reliance interests—that is, a refusal to apply a new rule retrospectively—is almost always *in*efficient. Thus, Graetz and Kaplow, in a series of influential articles, claim that the most efficient policy concerning legal transitions is one which refuses any kind of mitigation (eg grandfathering, compensation, delayed effective dates) for retrospective effects of legal changes.

Firstly, both Graetz and Kaplow point out that while legal reforms can change the expected consequences of pre-existing investments, it is hardly true that these expected consequences would be certain to be realized in the absence of legal reform. There are many other sources of uncertainty, most of which fall under the category of 'market uncertainty'—changes in demand, technological development, natural disasters, and so forth. Graetz and Kaplow claim that uncertainty concerning the potential for legal reform is no different—at least in terms of normative implications—from 'market uncertainty'.[19] And since government mitigation of market risks is generally seen as economically inefficient, government mitigation of legal risk should be, likewise, regarded as economically inefficient.[20]

This, however, is merely an argument from analogy. Kaplow, therefore, goes on to explain why routine retrospectivity in legal transitions is more economically efficient than protection of reliance interests. Kaplow agrees that uncertainty concerning the future legal status of a current state of affairs might discourage investment. However, he claims that this is not problematic, because such investments *should* be discouraged:

> The efficient level of investment is that induced when investors bear all real costs and benefits of their decisions. Therefore, the encouragement resulting from the assurance that compensation or other protection will be provided in the event of change results in overinvestment.[21]

The reason why such investment is inefficient is that a promise of government compensation in the event of legal change 'shifts part of the long-run cost of private investment to the government and thus distorts an otherwise efficient decision making process'.[22] Investors do not have the proper incentive to take into account the risk of legal reform.[23] And this is a risk which, like market risks, ought to be taken into account: for all the emphasis on reliance and expectations on the part of opponents of retrospectivity, it is not—as noted in Chapter 3—reasonable to expect the law to remain constant. To protect such unreasonable expectations would be to encourage behaviour which is undesirable—and inefficient.

---

[18] Kaplow, p. 607.   [19] Kaplow, p. 520; Graetz, p. 1825.   [20] Kaplow, pp. 534–5.
[21] Kaplow, pp. 528–9. While I am sympathetic to Kaplow's arguments, I am not so easily convinced that compensation may not be a sensible alternative—see discussion in Chapter 6, s 1.4.
[22] Kaplow, p. 531.   [23] Kaplow, p. 531.

It will, therefore, be especially inefficient to protect reliance in areas of law which are known to be subject to change. Indeed, in such areas, it will often be desirable to encourage people to rely, not on the continuity of laws, but on the expectation of retrospective changes in the legal system. In other words, we should sometimes go beyond a mere failure to protect reliance, and create expectations that no such protection will be given. Kaplow illustrates this point by discussing the effect of expectations of future retrospectivity in relation to tort liability, saying that 'the expectation that future evolution in the law will be made applicable to harms arising, and factories built, prior to the announcement of new rules will have a desirable effect on behaviour;' namely, that owners will be more likely to avoid potentially harmful activities.[24] A similar point can be made concerning war crimes and human rights abuses in corrupt regimes: if those who are thinking of engaging in such activities believe that they will be punished under retrospective law under any return to democracy (or the Rule of Law), they may think twice. If they are deterred by the possibility of future retrospective laws, the potential retrospective law will have provided desirable guidance for the deterred torturer and protection for the spared torture victim.

In fact, the promotion of proper (socially desirable) incentives, according to Kaplow, sometimes favours more than just a refusal to mitigate for any retrospective effect of legal reform. Sometimes, express retroactivity (that is, specifically stating that a new rule is to take effect as of some date prior to its enactment) is required to achieve the desirable effects in question.[25] This may be the case with the retrospective taxation legislation discussed in the previous chapter: the knowledge that pre-enactment exploitation of loopholes can be retrospectively penalized discourages taxpayers from taking advantage of unintended effects— and discourages accountants and lawyers from making a living by seeking out loopholes and marketing schemes which exploit them.

There are, however, some criticisms of Kaplow and Graetz's view.[26] Firstly, Fisch points out that Kaplow's claims concerning economic efficiency depend 'on the contested empirical conclusion that the market is a better means of addressing the costs of legal change than are legal constraints on retroactive lawmaking'.[27] This conclusion seems doubtful, since market solutions may be unavailable, or impractical, in relation to many cases of retrospective legal change: 'for example, one might question whether market remedies such as insurance are viable options for addressing the impact of judicial decisions that retroactively eliminate sovereign immunity in tort for public officials.'[28]

In addition, a failure to prevent retrospective effects may create certain social costs. Thus, Ramseyer and Nakazato point out that inefficiency (and social

---

[24] Kaplow, p. 600.   [25] Kaplow, p. 551.

[26] There are also some significant differences between Graetz and Kaplow: Kaplow opposes *all* forms of transitional relief, whereas Graetz is opposed only to grandfathering.

[27] Fisch, p. 1090.   [28] Fisch, pp. 1090–1.

disbenefit) will occur in connection with a refusal to mitigate transition effects if, as seems likely, those affected by the proposed new rule will fight the changes:

Taxpayers do not sit idle as [the government] eliminates their tax benefits. . . . Many of those who can organize effectively will then do so. They will pay honoraria, organize grass-roots political organisations, and contribute to campaigns; to protect their projects from reform, they will coax, cajole and bribe.[29]

This means that a refusal to protect expectations will potentially result in the loss of the reform, and any benefit of the legal change being lost. Moreover, it will give legislators a perverse incentive to promise *not* to undertake legal reform. Promising to protect reliance interests will remove the motive to fight the reform, and will therefore be more efficient:

. . . under a [reliance-protected] regime, investors will not care whether Congress revokes their tax-favored status; under a [retrospective] strategy, they will care dearly. Accordingly, under the former they will lobby and bribe less than under the latter, and to the extent that happens, society gains.[30]

Goode similarly disputes the claim that grandfathering is always inefficient. He points out that where the government is deliberately trying to encourage certain kinds of investment, the use of grandfathering (and the creation of associated expectations of further grandfathering in the same and similar projects in the future) can be extremely useful in creating the right incentives: 'protection of such interests can be supported . . . as useful to avoid discouraging investment and particularly to preserve confidence in purposely legislated tax incentives.'[31]

These objections, of course, do not show that efficiency is *never* better served by retrospectivity; rather, they call for a closer look at the likely effects of a proposed reform. A more significant criticism is that Kaplow and Graetz's efficiency arguments (and, indeed, the 'better rule' argument) depend on an unrealistic view of legal change as invariably reflecting improvement in the law. As Fisch notes, 'efficiency arguments typically add an additional normative factor to the analysis: the assumption that legal change has occurred because of a determination that the new rule is an improvement.'[32] In fact, Kaplow explicitly asserts this assumption, stating that 'policy change is presumably undertaken in order to generate net gains in social welfare.'[33]

Many, however, dispute the view that legal changes are always improvements. As Fisch notes, 'fairness advocates generally doubt that legal change is either synonymous with improvement or consistent with any fixed objective. They are more apt to view legal change as the result of a power struggle, implementation of the values of a successful insurgent, or random experimentation in policy.'[34] And

---

[29] JJ Mark Ramseyer and Minoru Nakazato, 'Tax Transitions and the Protection Racket: A Reply to Professors Graetz and Kaplow' (1989) 75 *Virginia Law Review* 1155 at 1171.

[30] Ramseyer and Nakazato, p. 1174.

[31] Richard Goode, 'Disappointed Expectations and Tax Reform' (1987) 40 *National Tax Journal* 159 at 167–8.   [32] Fisch, p. 1088. See also Ramseyer and Nakazato, p. 1162.

[33] Kaplow, p. 552.   [34] Fisch, p. 1099.

according to Ramseyer and Nakazato, 'little reason exists to think Congress will necessarily improve the law.'[35] Indeed, some reason exists to think that it will not:

... if voters are rational and selfish ... they will not energetically work for a more efficient tax system for all. They will demand only lower taxes for themselves. And if a constituency for efficient tax reform does not exist, then few legislators will promote it.[36]

If legal changes are not improvements, then there are no benefits of legal change to be maximized. In this case, there is no efficiency argument in favour of retrospective application of new rules and we should be, at best, indifferent as to whether a new rule is applied retrospectively or not.[37] If legal reform does not represent the incremental improvement of the law, but rather represents the mere triumph of particular political interests, then concerns will arise about the fairness of retrospective application of that law. 'In a legal system in which change is random or politically generated, predicting legal changes is harder and burdening particular individuals with the costs of that change is more unfair.'[38]

We should be aware of setting up dichotomies between legal improvements and politically driven laws and putting all new laws in one or either camp. Not only are there examples of both kinds of change in any legal system, there may be new rules which are *both* politically generated *and* improvements, even predictable improvements. Indeed, it seems possible that Ramseyer and Nakazato could be charged with an almost naïve cynicism. Even if each individual voter is rational and selfish, this is not enough to show that the sum total of their aggregated votes cannot give rise to largely efficient legislative improvements. Moreover, even individual voters can be selfishly impelled to vote directly for fair legislation. If the only way a given individual can be free to engage in a particular lucrative activity is by allowing others to be similarly free, then such an individual may well be rationally and selfishly motivated to prohibit that activity for all. Thus, it may be that efficiency and fairness do not always conflict in decisions over whether to apply new rules retrospectively.

There is a more fundamental reply. Most countries are institutionally committed by their constitutions to having a legislature that updates laws on the assumptions that they will generally be improvements. That is why legislatures are created and given the power to legislate. The possibility of error and abuse of power are reasons for caution in giving them retrospective reach, but they are primarily reasons for improving those institutions to limit the likelihood of error and abuse.

The above debate leaves both efficiency and 'better rule' arguments standing and in potential conflict with fairness/unconscionability/rule of law arguments without a reason to believe that either should always take precedence when they conflict.[39] However, we should note that they will always conflict. As we have seen, efficiency may be better served by protection of reliance interests in some

---

[35] Ramseyer and Nakazato, p. 1162.   [36] Ramseyer and Nakazato, p. 1164.
[37] Ramseyer and Nakazato, p. 1166.   [38] Fisch, p. 1099.   [39] Fisch, p. 1096.

circumstances. Moreover, the next section will show that there are some circumstances in which fairness can be a reason *for* the retrospective application of a new rule.

6.6 The 'fairness' justification

We have seen that fairness/unconscionability/rule of law considerations are often assumed unequivocally to support the protection of reliance interests, and are, therefore, taken to count against retrospectivity. This assumption is challenged where the reliance is not reasonable, in which case there is no fairness argument in favour of protecting the interests of those relying on non-retrospectivity. But, it is possible to go further than this: sometimes fairness provides a positive argument in favour of retrospectivity. There are a number of situations in which the retrospective application of a new rule promotes fairness and equity.

Indeed, there may even be a fairness-based argument for a general refusal to protect reliance interests. This is that those granted protection against the adverse retrospective effects of legal reforms are more likely to be those who were wealthy and powerful enough to influence the legislature in establishing the original law.[40] Allowing the possibility of protection of reliance interests creates a situation in which the burden of legal change falls disproportionately on the less wealthy and powerful members of society, who are often least able to bear that burden; wealthy individuals, by contrast, are often much better equipped to deal with the adverse consequences of legal change.[41] It also creates the possibility that reliance interests will often be protected even where they are not reasonable.

In fact, the unfairness arising from the disproportionate political influence of the wealthy and powerful shows that fairness might be a reason for retrospectivity even when efficiency is a reason against it. In the preceding section, we discussed the possibility that protection of reliance might be more efficient because it removes the incentive for the wealthy and powerful to fight legal reform. However, this would seem to have the result that wealthy and influential groups will be accorded special protections merely because of their wealth and influence. However, while giving these protections may be more efficient, it could also be less fair.

The unfairness of protecting reliance (whether or not it is that of wealthy and powerful individuals) would be particularly pronounced in cases where the possibility of legal reform ought to have been reasonably expected: for example, where an intention to change the law has been announced, or the relevant area of law is subject to frequent change. In such cases, not only the fact of legal change, but also the nature of that change, will be predictable, and demands for protection of reliance seem no more than a cynical attempt to exploit the legal system. To

---

[40] Goode, p. 161; Fisch, p. 1089.   [41] Graetz, p. 1837.

protect such reliance would be unfair to those who properly ordered their affairs so as to avoid being burdened by the new rule, or those who elected not to take potentially profitable risks (for example, by exploiting tax loopholes) because of an expectation of legal change. It would essentially be to favour the interests of those who seek to undermine the purposes of the law, at the expense of those who respect the aims of the law.

A similar argument applies to those who committed heinous acts (such as human rights abuses) under an oppressive regime, then seek protection of their 'reliance interests' once the Rule of Law is restored. Such people act in ways which undermine the Rule of Law, then seek to enjoy the protection of the Rule of Law for those very acts. In these cases, although procedural fairness may favour the extending of protection to war criminals, substantive fairness (upholding the equity of the legal system, including securing justice for victims of war crimes) dictates that the new legal rules be applied retrospectively. Such retrospective application serves to promote democracy, fairness and the Rule of Law.

Fairness and reliance arguments may be made in favour of different groups in the one case. In civil law cases, we are used to there being two parties—frequently relying on the law as they understood it or had it expounded to them. The existence of two parties equally subject to disappointment of nurtured and apparently reasonable expectations may provide one of the reasons why judges are generally sanguine about the inevitably retrospective nature of their decision-making. However, it would be wrong to distinguish criminal, taxation and more generally public law on this ground—each party will rely on one interpretation of the law. One will be disappointed. Some may think that this is not relevant in matters of public law, taxation law, or criminal law. However, there are reliance interests at stake here too. The government relies on revenue laws in framing budgets and expenditures. Many citizens rely on the benefits that are funded from taxation revenue. When it comes to criminal laws, citizens rely on their consistent application for protection—especially against the most serious and/or heinous crimes of murder and torture.

If we express the reliance argument in its equitable form, all this is so much clearer. If the state has stated the way it will use its power with the intention and knowledge that individuals act on those statements, it would generally be unconscionable for the state to go back on its word where it would cause detriment to those individuals who have relied on the state acting as it said it would. Governments make statements about the enforcement of the criminal law to protect citizens and the provision of services and benefits from revenue. They expect citizens to act in reliance on such statements—not least in voting for them!

This does not mean that the government is placed in a dilemma as to whom it acts against unconscionably. The equitable doctrine includes some important limitations which would negate the unconscionability argument with respect to at least one group—where there was neither knowledge nor intention that citizens would rely on existing legal texts, where there was no actual reliance and where there was no actual detriment.

6.7 Some examples

In our earlier writings on retrospectivity,[42] three examples were given to illustrate different ways in which the considerations underlying reliance arguments—usually the strongest reason to reject retrospective laws—may in some cases provide the strongest reasons in favour of retrospective rule-making. Whereas we would generally want to encourage and protect reliance by prospective laws, the following examples show that there are some cases where we would want to actively discourage reliance through a deliberate policy of retrospective rule-making.

The Tasmanian murderer

The case of the Tasmanian murderer is based on a real case of a Tasmanian defendant accused of murder.[43] The defendant (Newell) was accused of murdering his wife at a time when guilty verdicts in murder trials had to be unanimous. In between the alleged offence and the trial, the rule was changed. In the actual case, the court decided that it was not intended that the rule act 'retrospectively'; however, the more interesting question is whether, if the provision had been intended to cover the defendant's case, such 'retrospectivity' would be justified. It is, of course, highly unlikely that Newell would have taken the procedures for securing verdicts into account in his decisions leading up to the alleged offence. If so, there is no reliance/fairness/equity argument generated by reasonable reliance on the requirement of a unanimous verdict. In such cases, there is no reason not to apply the 'better rule' test.

However, in the event that the husband had thought about the unanimous verdict requirement and taken it into consideration in planning his actions, he condemns himself. His prior consideration of the matter would be evidence not only of *mens rea* but also a high degree of premeditation. Such a claim would lead us to conclude that the husband had decided: 'this is not the perfect murder but it is good enough to fool one or two members of the average jury'.

A key feature of cases such as the 'Tasmanian Murderer'—where any appeal to reliance is foreclosed—is that the legal consequences of the action depend crucially on a lack of premeditation from the agent in question. The defendant is not estopped from claiming to rely on the law but the consequence of such a claim is to admit guilt.

Another example from criminal law is the crime of manslaughter. If an individual premeditated an action to the extent of studying the law of manslaughter before killing someone, then they should, in most cases, be facing the far graver crime of murder.

---

[42] Charles Sampford, 'Retrospectivity and the Rule of Law', *Law and Society Conference*, Brisbane, December 1990. (Later published in C Sampford and A Palmer, 'Retrospective Legislation in Australia' (1994) 22 *Federal Law Review* 217.)   [43] *Newell v. the Queen* (1936) 55 CLR 707.

Similar problems emerge for those who use reliance arguments against retrospective tort law. Consider a case where one party slips and injures themselves, and then proceeds to litigate against the local council. Immediately following the fall, new legislation retrospectively caps the potential payouts to litigants in such circumstances.[44] If the litigant were to say: 'I would not have slipped', or even 'I would have been more careful' or 'I would not have engaged in risky behaviour', they have blown their case under either the new or the old law. The only problematic response would be: 'I would have taken out personal injury insurance'. The litigant cannot plead that they were relying on the prospect of an open-ended payout when they decided to have the accident— because the very process relies on there being no such deliberate decision ever taking place.

In cases where a lack of premeditation plays a crucial role in legal assessment, there are still some reliance interests at play—particularly once a legal process has been set in place and a prosecution or litigation is underway. Even before this point, it is still possible to speculate that if the law had been very different, a person would not have taken similar risks or would have taken out insurance. However, such reliance interests are much thinner than the claim of, for instance, an investor who invested in a particular way on the basis of current law and Australian Tax Office guidelines, and who can clearly and unequivocally maintain that had the law been different, they would have acted differently. The individual charged with manslaughter or litigating on the basis of an accident cannot similarly and unequivocally claim that the relevant action would not have been performed if the law had been different.

More importantly, the more general reason why the 'Tasmanian Murderer' does not have an appeal to reliance interests is because, in this case, there is no change to the substantive law but rather to the *procedures* by which that law is executed. Reliance arguments become much less plausible when they are applied to legal procedures rather than substantive texts. For instance, the first criminals apprehended and charged primarily on the basis of DNA evidence—or indeed on the basis of fingerprint evidence, for that matter— could genuinely have claimed that had they known of the possibility that police and legal institutions could make use of such data, then they would have changed their behaviour, perhaps even deciding not to commit the crime. Yet, there is no plausible reliance argument to the effect that the criminal was justified in their expectation that police procedure would continue as it historically had done. To the contrary, a new police tool that apprehends criminals because it was not anticipated is to be praised for its efficacy rather than maligned for its failure to conform to the criminal's reliance on legal procedures.

---

[44] *Quod vide* Chapter 4.4 and *Justice and Other Legislation Amendment Act 2003* (Qld).

The Harbourside tax lawyer

The second example is the tax lawyers and accountants who fuelled Australia's tax avoidance boom of the 1970s and 1980s by constantly seeking what are colloquially called tax 'loopholes' through which they sought to drive as much of their client's income as possible before such loopholes were discovered and closed. The term is pejorative and would be resisted by the said lawyers and accountants who prefer to use the term 'tax planning'. However, the nature of their activity was to lower the tax that their clients would otherwise expect to pay by combing the increasingly complex tax legislation for 'unintended consequences' that lead to losses or deductions. Although intended consequences of complex legislation might be hard to determine in theory, they are fairly easy to determine in practice. As clients were prepared to pay fees on the basis of a proportion of tax avoided, both parties had a fairly clear idea of what the intended consequences of the law were—that they should pay the published rates of tax. Of course, virtually all tax regimes contain 'shelters' that deliberately favour some forms of investment over others. Whether or not one agrees with them, they are intended consequences. However, aggressive 'tax planners' seek ways in which these and other provisions produce reduced taxation for clients involved in other activities or much more significant reductions than are intended.

Practice dictates an easy distinction between intended and unintended consequences. One can easily pose the counter factual—would the Revenue consider tax outcome an intended consequence or would it move to have the act changed to remove this consequence? Whether or not the counter-factual is actually posed, the behaviour of the lawyers and accountants belies the expected answer. If they seek a prior ruling or other kind of clarification from the IRS, they think that it is intended or, at least, is in the range of intended consequences. The more they seek to complete the transactions that generate the lower level of tax the client wants and drive as much of their clients' money through those transactions, the more the lawyers demonstrate that testing the counter factual will reveal it as an unintended consequence.

This takes us directly to the positive reason for retrospective closure of tax loopholes—to discourage, indeed render pointless, the activity of trawling legislation for unintended consequences and then maximizing the extent of those unintended consequences. This sends a very clear message to the individuals and companies concerned. It also directs attention to the way in which professionals should deal with the law. If a lawyer or accountant finds a potentially unintended consequence in complex legislation, is it preferable to contact the relevant authority so that they can rectify this oversight? Or, if the consequence is intended or acceptable, should the professional confirm it by seeking a ruling so that clients can take advantage of it—legitimately, confidently and securely? Or should the professional push as much of their client's money through the loophole as possible before it is discovered? The former activity makes laws more certain, effective, consistent and, in all likelihood, more fair. The latter activity maximizes the extent of unintended consequences and makes the 'hunt for the unintended consequence' a highly lucrative business activity.

However, if it is made very clear that, in the absence of a prior ruling, retrospective legislation will be used to remove unintended consequences, tax professionals will be encouraged to check first. This will, interestingly enough, increase certainty and predictability for taxpayers because they will be losing the otherwise unfounded and illegitimate expectation that they could evade or avoid tax—an expectation that could in any case always be defeated by the courts or *ad hoc* retrospective legislation.

The South American torturer

Many coups lead to repressive regimes that engage in torture and other gross human rights abuses. This example of the applicability of retrospective law concerns a group of torturers in the Argentinean Naval School during the so-called 'dirty war' against leftists from 1976 to 1983. At the time that officials and the military authorized and engaged in torture, they had a rational expectation that no court would convict them. To the extent that this expectation was due to the intimidation of courts, or the lack of an available tribunal, this expectation was not based on any substantive law and was therefore not reasonable. To the extent that the expectation was due to the contents of relevant edicts of the repressive regime, reliance upon those edicts not being retrospectively amended is not worthy of protection. To the extent that they think about the possibility of future prosecution by a future democratic regime, they should be given good reason to fear prosecution and every reason to think twice about their participation in gross violations of human rights. Luckily, the threat of prosecution by a democratically-elected government in his own or another country is increasing. In January 2005, Adolpho Scolingo, an alleged torturer from the Argentinean Naval School, was put on trial in Spain.[45]

In the case of the South American torturer, arguments based upon 'efficiency', equity and fairness—which usually support the protection of reliance—suggest that retrospective legislation is highly desirable because we should seek to discourage rather than encourage reliance. This is not to deny that wherever possible, warnings should be given of what actions are liable to be prosecuted. In some circumstances, courts in exile might even try coup leaders and torturers *in absentia*.[46] Certainly, governments in exile should attempt to ensure that processes are as fair as possible. Coup leaders and torturers are entitled to a fair trial.

---

[45] *The Scotsman*, 20 January 2005.
[46] See C Sampford and M Palmer, 'International Responses', in Morton H Halperin and Mirna Galic (eds), *Protecting Democracy: International Responses* (Lexington Books, 2004).

However, members and supporters of the regime which ousted a democratic government with a functioning court system are estopped from complaining that the system under which they are tried is less than perfect.

6.8 Principles for justified retrospectivity

We have seen that there are many arguments which may be used to justify retrospectivity. Far from being a necessary evil justified only in extreme circumstances, retrospective law can often make a positive contribution to the values underlying a legal system. Indeed, the use of retrospective law can often be justified according to the very same considerations which are so often assumed to be reasons against it—as the three examples illustrate. Retrospectivity can, in some circumstances, serve the cause of democracy, of efficiency, and of fairness. Most importantly, guidance, the reason why retrospectivity is most obviously and generally criticized, may also be a reason for retrospectivity in some cases.

If that were all that could be said, we might be left without firm criteria for determining when retrospective law is justified. It might be thought that definitive criteria are not possible given that many of the concepts used in our analysis (including not only retrospectivity itself but also reasonable reliance, legal change, fairness) are matters of degree. The justifiability of retrospectivity might be another of those things that will be a matter of degree and ultimately an exercise in judgement. There are, however, a number of considerations which can be derived from the preceding discussion, and which can ground general principles by which to judge the justifiability of retrospective law.

In general, considerations of both fairness and efficiency should enter into judgements of the justifiability of retrospective law. These will sometimes—but by no means always—conflict. Sometimes fairness/equity arguments will not be relevant because no person will actually have relied on the pre-existing rule, no person could reasonably rely on the pre-existing rule and/or that any attempt to plead reliance will amount to an 'own-goal' confession to a more serious version of the alleged crime. Sometimes, however, both fairness and efficiency will point the same way: for example, where reliance on the old rule is unreasonable due to the probability and predictability of legal change, and protection of those reliance interests would be extremely costly. This will occur in areas where it is desirable to warn people *not* to rely too closely on the details of existing law: thus, the possibility of future retrospective changes produces an outcome—for example, deterrence from tax avoidance schemes, or from human rights abuses—which is both more fair and more efficient.

In general, the fairness of retrospectivity will increase or decrease in inverse proportion to the reasonableness of the reliance involved: the more reasonable the reliance, the less fair it is to fail to protect that reliance from retrospective effect. Conversely, where reliance is extremely *un*reasonable, fairness will come out in favour of retrospective application. There will probably be no clear point beyond which retrospectivity is fair, and below which it is unfair. One of the reasons for this is that there are often multiple parties involved. In Chapter 5, we noted Fisch's observation that much law is a zero-sum game where the interests of one party can only be met at the expense of others: 'if retroactive application of a new legal rule disfavours one litigant, it favors the other.'[47] Some litigants have more rational and/or legitimate expectations and hence more reasonable reliance interests. Some may have no reliance interest, hoping to secure a change in the direction of legal change (or ride a rising tide of legal change which has already gone a long way and which they hope will go further). However, there will be many cases where different reliance interests compete with each other and the direction of the fairness argument is uncertain. All three examples given in the last section involved strong reliance interests by persons other than the murderer, the torturer and the tax avoider (the victims of the first and the beneficiaries of programmes put at risk by the latter). Any 'balancing' of fairness and efficiency arguments may involve internal balances of fairness in which each side will have arguments of variable merit.

Efficiency will probably not bear the same proportional relationship to reasonableness of expectations, as does fairness. However, in general, it is probably true that where expectations are very unreasonable, it will be less efficient to protect them: not only will this be very expensive, it will also encourage people to rely unreasonably on the law (thus creating the circular argument for further protection of reliance). This will undercut the purpose of the law, prevent some of the benefits of legal change, and introduce more economic inefficiency. Conversely, the protection of very reasonable reliance is likely to be more efficient, since reasonable reliance is likely to occur in areas of law which are stable, or where the government is deliberately encouraging reliance in order to motivate investment in socially useful schemes.

The above discussion may seem to suggest that the justifiability of retrospective law must be decided on a case-by-case basis, by weighing up the competing considerations of fairness, efficiency, equity, and so on as an exercise of Aristotelian 'judgement'. It may be better (in terms of the overall predictability of the use of power and the operation of the legal system, social utility, and fairness) to adopt—and adhere to—a general set of principles to indicate when retrospective legislation is appropriate. This is consistent with the earlier discussion of the Rule of Law in Chapter 2: it is the system of laws, rather than each individual law, which is to be measured against Rule of Law standards; and a clear set of principles determining the use of retrospectivity will enhance the certainty and stability of the law.

---

[47] Fisch, p. 1085. Indeed, it is a negative-sum game as the costs of the litigation mean that the parties have a nett loss of welfare to the parties and a transfer to lawyers and the trial process. The state is generally a nett loser as well because of qualms about seeking full recovery of the costs of operating courts from the litigants.

We would propose the following as a (non-exhaustive) set of general principles to be adopted by legislatures in their retrospective law making endeavours. The first two principles indicate two important sources of guidance and the remainder are substantive principles derived in part from those sources and from the practical examples given above.

Draw on judicial analogies

In general, legislatures should consider the kinds of constraints that courts impose on themselves in overturning and developing the law. In a very real sense, all judicial decisions are retrospective as they affect actions that have already been completed. Unsurprisingly, no group of decision-makers have considered the issue of retrospective rule-making more deeply, consistently or thoughtfully than judges. The principles they have developed are not only generally appropriate for retrospective rule-making but they will address some of the reasons why legislatures are not as trusted with retrospective rule-making, as are judges. Guidelines based on judicial analogies should recognize:

(1) The main reason for judicial overturning is coherence. Retrospective rule-making is not just a matter of deciding that the new rule is better than the older one in isolation, something legislators properly do with any new prospective law. The main reasons for judicial overruling are that the decision overruled is not consistent with a general principle or because it is not achieving the effects intended or expected. This is very like retrospective legislation which limits or blocks unintended consequences which were defeating the stated purpose of previous laws.

(2) Legislators should recognize that the 'better rule' argument is the key issue for them as it is for judges. However, when it comes to laws with retrospective effect, the rule needs to be 'better' in terms of the criteria of coherence, consistency and better general guidance of citizens rather than the law merely being a 'good idea'. Thus overruling involves recognizing mistakes made in the past rather than enthusiasms for the future.

(3) Judges will overrule earlier decisions based on new reasons that lead to a changed view of the judges but not on the basis of an alteration of the composition of the bench.[48] While the whole point of democratic legislatures is that their majorities change at elections, this does not generally justify retrospective legislation. Like judges, legislators need new reasons that were not apparent at the time the original legislature made its decision.

(4) When judges develop new law, they usually do it gradually and incrementally, giving warning of the direction the law is headed so that they can start to adjust as the court feels its way (the closest that courts come to prospective

---

[48] See *Second Territorial Senators Case* (1977) 139 CLR 585 in Chapter 4.

rule-making). Where new law is likely to have retrospective effect (even in altering the future effects of past decisions such as the future returns on investments), legislatures should flag the possibility. The greater the effect, the greater the duty to warn as early and as comprehensively as possible.

(5) Like courts, legislators should recognize a hierarchy of sources. The outputs of democratically elected legislatures are to be given greater respect than the decrees of tyrants and other laws that were passed without democratic imprimatur. An incoming democratic regime (indeed any incoming regime) should provide a general savings clause that 'all laws continue until further notice' with immediate notice given of the particularly objectionable laws which are repealed, invalidated or suspended. However, the laws passed by non-democratic means are not accorded equal respect. They are tolerated and retained until further notice to prevent anarchy so that democratic legislatures do not have to re-consider all law instantaneously so as to ensure that citizens still have guidance about the legal rules that will be applied to them. However, their non-democratic origins should indicate that their continuity is less likely and citizens should be careful about placing too much reliance on them—especially those rules that it is unlikely that a democratic legislature would have passed. The above preference for prospective retrospectivity means that this is a risk that should be clearly flagged by an incoming democratic regime, but the failure to do so should not mean that citizens should not take into account the risk, or that democratic legislatures have to give equal respect to laws of non-democratic background.

(6) Equally, legislators, like courts, should recognize stability interests and they should particularly recognize that reasonable reliance on old laws (based on rational and legitimate expectations) does provide a good reason for limiting the application of new laws. Legislators are able to take account of reliance arguments more subtly than judges because they can choose the degree of prospectivity or retrospectivity through deciding the dates at which laws come into force, adopting transitional measures and various forms and degree of grandfathering or compensation. Of course, other considerations especially the rights and or interests of others can trump those reliance interests. But where reliance is reasonable, it should at least be taken into account.

(7) Legislators should also adopt a 'judicial' approach that avoids deliberately targeting, benefiting or discriminating against particular groups or individuals. The guiding principle must be the 'better rule' that serves coherence and consistency. Without adopting such a 'judicial mode', retrospective law could become a 'bill of attainder' or, more simply, payback and the passage of retrospective legislation could be seen as an abuse of legislative power. However, it should also be remembered that courts do not have the same ability to fine tune the degree and extent of

retrospectivity and have very imperfect mechanisms for prospective application of rules.[49] The judicial analogies are not offered to suggest that the legislature can engage in retrospective law making whenever a court would, merely that when they feel justified in doing so they should be guided by the limitations that judges put on themselves.

Draw on equitable analogies

Legislation is intended to guide citizens by giving a clear indication of how state power will be used and the legal consequences their actions will have. In deciding whether or not to alter such legislation retrospectively, legislators should consider the considerable body of equitable doctrine that indicates when it is unconscionable to go back on assurances of future action that others have relied upon (see Chapter 3.6). They should also be aware of the reasons that equity would provide for not acting on that promise—especially concerning whether or not it was intended that the citizen act in that way, the reasonableness of the expectation, and the actions of those seeking to claim reliance.

Equity emphasizes the keeping of promises—meaning that the arguments against retrospectivity may be weaker where the promise was not made by the legislature but by a predecessor. Although it could be said that the legislature and all predecessors are speaking for 'the state', democratic ideals of the 'sovereignty of the people' justify a strong distinction between the laws of democratically elected legislatures and those who were not chosen by the people of that state. Where the earlier lawmakers oppressed the people and sought to prevent them choosing their own governors, the equitable argument is also non-existent—a subsequent democratic legislature is quite entitled to say that the promise not to prosecute the torturer was not made by them.

However, the fact that the earlier law was made by a legislature dominated by a different party does not mean that this legislature is not bound. It is fundamental to democracy that the compositions of legislatures change on a regular basis but that laws continue despite that because the legislature is action on behalf of a sovereign people. However, it is also part of that system that such elections allow changes in the law so a promise not to change a law is not binding on subsequent parliaments.

'Clean hands' and the conduct of the party claiming reliance

Equity also directs our attention to the conduct of the person claiming reliance. In drawing the analogy to the maxim that those who come to equity must come with 'clean hands', we are not suggesting that the mere fact that relevant individuals were engaged in criminal or tortious behaviour that harmed others should mean

---

[49] As we saw in Chapter 4, attempts to make judicial law-making prospective have withered because of inherent difficulties and constitutional uncertainties.

new laws can be retrospectively imposed on them. What it does direct our attention to is any conduct by the person claiming reliance which made it difficult to pass prospective legislation. The Harbourside tax lawyer's conduct in searching for and then surreptitiously exploiting unintended consequences and the South American torturer's participation in a coup that suspended the operation of human rights laws are highly relevant. Similarly, anyone who bribes or otherwise pressures legislators to prevent the enactment of legislation regulating their behaviour prejudice any reliance claims they could otherwise mount against subsequent retrospective introduction of the kind of legislation that an unbribed or pressured legislature might pass.

Prefer 'prospective retrospectivity' to 'retrospective retrospectivity'

Although retrospective rule-making can be justified in some cases, the reasonable reliance argument provides a very strong reason for spelling out, in advance, the principles governing the making of retrospective law. This kind of 'fair warning' means that the normal reliance argument against retrospective rule-making does not apply. Those who have been warned that the rule might be changed between action and adjudication take a risk in so acting and they cannot complain if the risk materializes.

Indeed, if these principles can be set out clearly, then they can provide clear guidance in themselves—indicating the kinds of laws that may be reasonably relied on not to be changed retrospectively and those that actors should take note may well be changed—and, if possible, the ways that they may be changed. Obviously, the principles cannot provide certainty as to what new laws will be passed until the decision is made (at which time, the decision should be publicized as quickly as possible), but they can provide guidance where reliance on existing rules is risky and possibly foolish. Giving warnings about rules that may be changed discourages reliance on them and the adverse effects on individuals who have relied on a lack of retrospective change are minimized.

Where such warning is given, the retrospectivity can be seen as prospective. This can be contrasted to 'retrospective retrospectivity' where the legislators have previously eschewed retrospective rule-making. An example of such retrospective retrospectivity can be found in the tax legislation discussed in Chapter 4, which was initially treated as an exception rather than a precedent. This condemned the government to closing loopholes after the revenue had bolted, amending the Income Tax Act prospectively and increasing the complexity of the legislation thereby making it easier to find new loopholes. When 'bottom of the harbour' schemes subsequently emerged, the government felt compelled to introduce further retrospective tax legislation despite its earlier declarations that earlier retrospective tax legislation was a one-off exercise. We have already observed that the following three negative effects could have been avoided if fair warning had been given: loss of respect for the government; a massive increase in tax avoidance;

loss of revenue; economic distortions and the diversion of time and talent from productive activity.

Institutional and procedural changes should generally be implemented immediately and applied to all past behaviour

The case of the Tasmanian murderer points to a general principle of retrospective rule-making: changes to court procedures usually apply to all cases commencing after the new rules come into effect. Although there is generally a good deal of advance notice of rule changes, there is no 'grandfathering' of the rules to court actions initiated before the rules were either mooted or effected. As indicated in the case of the Tasmanian murderer, if the procedures are changed to make it more likely that guilty people are convicted, there can be no special case made for those who were alleged to have committed the offence before the procedural change. As we have indicated, the only relevance would be if a defendant could establish that they had relied on existing procedures in conducting their defence and were adversely affected by the change of procedures by not retaining evidence or making particular procedural moves.

The argument against retrospective rule-making is about the legal consequences that should flow from past behaviour. It is about the content of law rather than its process. The reliance interest is in having the consequences of one's behaviour judged according to text discoverable at the time; not in the means by which the courts determine those consequences. Even if the processes are heavily weighted to avoid some unintended outcomes over others (for example, 'it is better for 1,000 guilty men to go free than to convict one innocent man' or 'evidence extracted by torture should not be admitted in court'), this does not mean that the law is intended as a guide to guilty men concerning how to avoid having their guilt determined.

We have also noted that the greater difficulty in convicting Tasmanian murderers under the old rule could not be called a 'defect'— merely a procedural requirement (hurdle) which was relaxed by the new rule. In many cases, there are real procedural defects that prevent the application of publicly intended[50] legal consequences of the citizen's action. In some cases, the defects are not so much procedural but institutional. In criminal cases, there may be no police to arrest, no prosecutors willing to prosecute and/or no courts to convict, or no government willing to enforce convictions. In civil cases, there may be no means for citizens to enforce their rights. The case of the South American torturer can be seen as an extreme version of a lack of institutions to enforce intended legal consequences. Since Nuremberg, the lack of a permanent International Criminal Court has been an extremely serious institutional defect. The current Rome Statute establishing

---

[50] The term 'publicly intended' is used here in recognition of the fact that some regimes with inadequate legal systems pass laws that appear sound at face value, but in the knowledge that the laws will not be enforced.

the ICC has similar defects in that not all countries have signed up to institutions which will enforce the international law that they have either formally endorsed or are estopped from denying (because they have enforced those laws against others). Should procedures and institutions be created at a later time, there is no reliance argument that those who had earlier committed war crimes, crimes against humanity, or breaches of the Geneva or Hague conventions should not be tried because, at the time of the alleged offences, there was either no court available or the court had no jurisdiction.

Those who break laws because they do not think that they will be caught and tried because of limited or inadequate institutions are taking a risk—in a sense they make a wager with history. If the risk materializes and the court is created, they can expect no sympathy from the court and even less from the victims of their own lawlessness.

No reliance on unintended consequences

The case of the Harbourside tax lawyer points to another general principle; there should be no reliance interest placed on unintended consequences where the individual concerned had reason to believe that the consequences were unintended. The relevant reliance interest that needs to be respected and generally protected is, again, in those who seek the signalled protection or benefit of the law—based on the generally stated principles and the apparently intended consequences.

No reliance on criminally sourced immunity

All the justice and fairness and equity arguments for the rule of law are based on respect for human beings and it is on this same basis that human rights norms have been developed and adopted almost unanimously by sovereign states— norms that are much stronger than the countervailing reliance arguments. Although there is a general prohibition against retrospective criminal law in many human rights instruments, the *International Covenant on Civil and Political Rights* (1966) and the laws of some nations (for example, that of Germany), endorse 'retrospective' criminal statutes against acts that constitute a violation of international law.[51] And since the Nuremberg trials, notice has been given that individuals may be tried for war crimes that include crimes against humanity and various forms of human rights abuse. Accordingly, the reliance argument cannot be advanced without also accepting much stronger human rights claims and cannot be asserted against those rights claims.

---

[51] However, a statute would still be required, even a retrospective one. A restored democratic government could not simply stage its own Nuremberg-style trials by executive fiat without some kind of statutory authorization for the trial, conviction and punishment.

However, the ample reasons for prosecuting the South American torturer and the overdetermination of any such prosecution should not lead us to overlook another important principle—that reliance on criminally sourced immunity does not deserve protection—voiding any argument against retrospectivity and providing a good reason for it in discouraging the criminal act that is the source of the claimed immunity. To generalize from the case given: No coup leader can grant immunity from the laws of the constitutional democracy he overthrows. No incoming court of a restored democracy can be expected to honour such immunities. It can rightly consider the giving of the immunity and obedience to it as criminal acts. What is denied here is the sovereign right of whoever can terrorize their territory to make laws that are inconsistent with international law or the democratically expressed wishes of the majority. If 'officials' like the South American torturer cannot rely on the immunity, coup leaders are even less protected. They have no right to expect that they will be immune from prosecution by international tribunals or domestic tribunals trying them for breaches of what were the laws of the country. Their claims to make laws are based on the fact that he committed a series of what were, then, crimes (from trespass to buildings and, at the very least, threatening to kill or kidnap and illegally imprison officials who attempted to do his or her constitutional duty).[52] They cannot bootstrap a defence to prior laws on the basis that they have broken them. This is an admission of a further crime, not a defence!

Retrospective criminal law should be very rare and requires special justification

Although retrospective criminal legislation is sometimes passed and can be justified despite and even because of the reliance that individuals place on it, it should be a very rare phenomenon. Criminal law may take away some of our most important rights—to liberty and, in some jurisdictions, life itself. Even where a fine is imposed it has a different quality to the damages awarded in other forms of law.[53] Where tort, property, contract and employment law assign financial consequences to action—including a share of the fruits of productive activity and a share of the risks of daily life—a fine carries with it a moral condemnation. Criminal law does more than affect the consequences of human action. Many institutions affect the consequences of our actions—some more frequently and finally than the state and its law. However, the criminal law also attaches officially endorsed moral obloquy to the action. It purports to deliver retributive justice where other laws may provide a distributive and other forms of justice.

---

[52] See C Sampford and M Palmer, 'Who will rid us of these meddlesome generals?', in C Sampford et al (eds), *Asia Pacific Governance 2000* (Ashgate, London, 2002).

[53] With the exception of punitive damages in tort law that are imposed to show disapproval rather than as an indication of the probability of the damage being discovered or proven.

Income is not a crime and tax is not a punishment

None of the above applies to tax law. However much tax avoidance lawyers might want to draw analogies between tax and crime and to narrowly construe tax law against the revenue, there is a fundamental difference. States, societies and media in western democracies do not condemn earning income, spending or owning property. Such activities generate much more praise than criticism. The payment of tax is not a fine but is one of the legally determined consequences of economic activity. It is one of a series of laws and institutions that determine the way in which the fruits of economic activity are distributed (other laws including contract, property, employment, competition and corporations law and other institutions including joint stock companies, stock exchanges and families).[54] When a tax avoider is issued with an amended assessment that shows he earned one million pounds instead of ten, he is not being accused of criminality but of excess modesty in a society that so values income and wealth.

Other principles

The principles for judicial retrospectivity have been debated and litigated for decades. The above list is a first attempt at a suggested list of principles for legislative restrospectivity. It does not claim to be exhaustive of the principles a legislature might commit to if it issued a form of 'practice statement' similar to the House of Lords in 1966[55] but it is intended to initiate and advance the debate.

6.9 Conclusion

In this chapter, we have considered some of the possible justifications for retrospectivity. The common view of retrospective law as a necessary evil which is justified only in exceptional circumstances is, as we have shown, a misguided one. It puts unacceptable restrictions on retrospective law making and promises to create many of the problems commonly associated with retrospectivity. But most importantly, the view of retrospectivity as inherently negative is incorrect. Retrospectivity can play a valuable role in upholding and promoting the values which are central to the Rule of Law, including democracy, efficiency and fairness. We will develop this argument in more detail in the final chapter.

---

[54] C Sampford and D Wood, 'Rights, Justice and Taxation' in Sadurski, W (ed) *Ethical Dimensions of Legal Theory*, Poznan Studies in the Philosophy of the Sciences and the Humanities (Rodopi, Amsterdam, 1991) 181.
[55] *Practice Statement (HL: Judicial Precedent)* [1966] 1 WLR 1234.

7

Conclusions and consequences for
the Rule of Law

7.1 Introduction

This book has set out to challenge the common, easy and ready condemnation of retrospective law-making. The term conjures up an archetypical image of clear and simple injustice: of innocent citizens gaoled for an action that was perfectly legal at the time; and of tyrants who decide who they want to punish and make up the rules as they go along. When such examples occur, few can find reason to defend them and they have no place in any well-ordered society subject to the Rule of Law. This book has shown that the easy condemnation of retrospectivity rests on unrepresentative archetypes. In real world examples, we see that the retrospectivity is not always clear and that retrospective law-making is relatively common rather than exotic and rare. We have seen the many arguments against retrospectivity boil down to one very strong but not universally compelling argument about the Rule of Law and the reasons for protecting the reliance that citizens place on the laws that will be applied to their conduct.

This chapter will summarize conclusions that may be drawn from the earlier chapters, before moving on to the consequences that this has for our conception of the Rule of Law, an approach to retrospective rule making, the prevention of abuse and conclude with some comments on the application of these arguments in the international sphere.

7.2 Retrospectivity as an inevitable and justified part of law making in a well-ordered society under law

Retrospectivity is not so easily defined and is a matter of degree

One common refrain of this book has been that various concepts crucial to the retrospectivity debate are present in degrees rather than being an all-or-nothing matter. This includes not only retrospectivity itself, but also other concepts such as certainty, reasonableness of expectations, and conformity to the Rule of Law. These things are neither present nor absent; rather, they can be present to a greater or lesser extent in any given context. Just as importantly, it is not possible to achieve perfection in relation to many of them—and even if it were possible, it could well be undesirable. The reason for emphasizing these points is that all of these concepts play crucial roles in arguments about the justifiability of retrospective law making. The acceptability of a retrospective law will be a function of the interaction of all of these elements: the degree of retrospectivity, the extent to which legal change is predictable, the reasonableness of reliance, and the general conformity of the legal system or area of law with the Rule of Law.

The degree of retrospectivity involved is the extent to which a new rule alters the future legal consequences of past actions or events. We have already noted that this will not be tied to whether a rule is retro*active* or merely has retrospective effect: the extent to which consequences are altered can be the same (or greater) for a nominally prospective rule as for a retroactive one. The retrospective effect of a new rule will depend on the significance of the change; whether the past actions or events were undertaken as part of a long-term plan; the magnitude of the effects on individuals; and the extent to which individuals may have been able to avoid adverse consequences by reorganizing their affairs in anticipation of the new rule.

Finally, and most importantly, human action, especially the actions of individual rational actors following individual 'life plans' or collectively trying to set and articulate policy for common action, takes time to complete. The classic image is of a single completed action which is made illegal by the whim of a ruler—in which case each can be completed in an hour. However, in most of the areas where retrospective rule-making is contemplated, either the rule-making process or the pursuit of goals of importance to the individual takes time to play out. Frequently, this is true of both rule-making and the individual pursuit of goals. This means that the sequencing of action and legislation is not clear-cut and retrospectivity is inevitably a matter of degree.

The ubiquity of retrospective rule-making

Retrospectivity is a permanent feature of well-ordered societies under law for three important reasons. First, judicial retrospectivity is inevitable. Secondly, the inevitable imprecision of law means that clarification will be necessary and, for those who have had to act, the clarified law will be retrospective. Thirdly, retrospective rule-making is sometimes justified either in spite of its retrospectivity and, more rarely, because of it.

Judicial decisions involve an unavoidable element of retrospectivity. In all jurisdictions, a great deal of effort is taken to reduce the inevitable uncertainties and potential surprises that this will generate—especially in common law systems where principles are laid down for the overruling of earlier decisions. This leads to two historical observations. First, we have managed to get by with retrospectivity for time immemorial without the collapse of civilization. Indeed, civilization as we know it grew up with this element of retrospectivity. It has been with us from the communal campfires where we wistfully imagine disputes being discussed on the basis of reconstructed and re-imagined memories of stories from the real or mythical past to the modern version—Common Law precedent. Secondly, there has been a long-term trend to supplant such judicial law-making by legislation.

In Common Law countries, this seems to be a more recent phenomenon. When Montesquieu was praising the England of his imagination as having a tri-partite separation of powers with parliament making laws and the courts judging citizens on whether they had breached them, the judges, in the real England, were making most of the laws most of the time.

Since then, Parliament has taken on most of the law making and is the preferred law maker for several reasons:

- It possesses a significant degree of democratic legitimacy.
- It involves clearly defined and accepted procedures for changing or adding to legal rules (whereas the way that courts change laws is neither fully acknow-ledged nor fully accepted).
- It is able to initiate change (whereas courts are largely reactive and must wait for the parties to bring cases before them).[1]
- It has the capacity to research the potential effects of legal change and to con-sult with those who are likely to be affected (whereas courts must largely rely on the arguments of the parties).[2]

The vast bulk of the parliamentary legislation is formally prospective. With Parliament doing most of the law making, and doing most of it prospectively, this gives rise to a general model of prospective law-making and significantly reduces the level of effective retrospectivity.

However, it should not be surprising that, in some of the types of cases where judges would have made rules retrospectively, legislatures do as well. This limited degree of retrospectivity in legislation needs to be considered in the context of a relative decline in the extent of judicial retrospectivity and the general reduction in demand for judicial change by the provision of a legislative route.

At the same time there is an increase in new law making. This is not surprising. The creation of a largely rational, effective and legitimate means for changing the law means, in response to new information, new challenges. And, a changing social, political, economic and physical environment has meant that there has been much legislation. This does not lead to retrospectivity in the traditional sense but does affect the stability of law and the interests of many in the continuance of existing laws.

---

[1] Largely, because courts do signal potential changes and thereby invite litigation on points that they are prepared to change.

[2] Again largely, the High Court has, in particular, used its research staff to look at a wider range of literature and has encouraged barristers to present such material. However, even the most inquisitive and widely read High Court judge would suggest that this is a substitute for the kind of work that can be done by law reform commissions and commissioned research.

The second reason for the inevitability of retrospectivity is the imprecision of legal rules—something that has to be dealt with either by the courts or by the legislature. The courts will usually perform this task retrospectively through statutory interpretation. However, parliament will inevitably take a strong interest in the interpretation of laws and may seek to rectify what they see as judicial errors of interpretation. They will generally do so prospectively, and hopefully quickly, to minimize the effects of an erroneous interpretation. However, there remains a role for the legislature as the author of the rule and the possessors of their own legislative intentions to intervene and impose their own interpretation retrospectively. The ability to do this in cases of significant or continuing interpretations at odds with the parliament's intentions acts as a check on what could become a form of retrospective judicial nullification. Indeed, without this legislative check, the clearly intended effects of legal rules could be undermined by litigants actively seeking to generate judicially retrospective nullification of legislative intent and then (somewhat ironically) screaming 'retrospectivity' when the parliament seeks to return the law to what they clearly intended the law to be.

The justifiability of retrospectivity in at least some cases

As we saw in Chapter 5, there are some important arguments for retrospective rule-making. These include the efficiency of applying the same rule to all cases and the 'better rule' argument—that the latter rule is a better one in the eyes of those constitutionally charged with the responsibility of legislating. In some cases, the 'better legislature' (better authority) argument may also apply.

Put this way, one might wonder if there should be a presumption in favour of retrospectivity as there is in judicial decisions along the lines of: 'it is a pity that the better rule had not been thought of and enacted earlier but it is better to apply it to all cases now that this "better rule" has been discovered'.

There are good reasons against such a presumption but none are strong enough to support a ban on all retrospective laws. As we saw in Chapter 3, many arguments against retrospectivity are overstated or without merit. Those with merit largely boil down to one very important argument based on the rule of law—that it is generally desirable that people, when choosing how to act, should be able to rely on the fact that a court which subsequently decides the legal consequences of that act does so by using legal texts which existed and were discoverable at the time of the act. Even if the new rule is a better one, the response is: 'it would have been good if you had enacted the rule earlier but you did not'. In the meantime, people have relied on the rule and would suffer if the rule, through no fault of their own, were subsequently changed. This argument is a very powerful one but it is not definitive.

First, retrospectivity is a matter of degree—and determining this degree is by no means a simple matter. To condemn all retrospectivity would be to counter-intuitively condemn laws which have a small or benign retrospective effect, and which are universally regarded as uncontroversial and unproblematic. In general, a greater degree of retrospectivity will be more normatively significant, and will carry a greater burden of justificatory proof. But the justifiability of retrospective law does not *just* depend upon the degree of retrospectivity involved. Evaluation must also take into consideration the context, which includes not only the reasonableness of reliance and the predictability of legal change in any area of law, but also the extent to which the legal system as a whole conforms to the Rule of Law.

This brings us to the second and third points—the degree and reasonableness of the reliance. The degree of reliance and the reasonableness of the reliance may vary from law to law and from person to person. Many of those who are potentially affected will not be aware of the elements of the law that were changed and the extent of their reliance may be limited—with their actions determined by other reasons. Where reliance is rare but relatively easily proven, it might be more sensible to compensate those who actually did rely on the rule as it was rather than to delay the introduction of a rule which is seen as genuinely an improvement (and, if it is an improvement for the society as a whole in the sense of generating increased overall welfare, then compensation should be affordable).

In other cases, the reliance is very conscious and very deliberate. Where a tax minimization/avoidance lawyers have been successful in their 'search for the unintended consequence', they seek to maximize the unintended consequence by directing as much of their client's money through the loophole as is possible before it is discovered and closed down. In such cases, the reason why the new rule is a better rule is because it does not produce the unintended consequence. The reason why it needs to be passed is because those who have discovered the unintended consequence are seeking to benefit from it at the expense of the intended objects of expenditure from tax raised. The reason for the delay is that the tax minimization lawyers found it more profitable to keep this quiet until they could drive their clients' money through it. Rather than being innocent victims of the legislature's tardiness, they are exploiters of the legislature's ignorance.

A similar argument runs for those who seek to gain immunity from fundamental breaches of human rights by the wrongdoing of themselves and others. The laws that would bring them to account for their abuses are delayed: this is because of their own actions or actions by superiors, who are, at least, co-conspirators and more often, principals in the breaches. To the extent that they are the cause of the delay, they are estopped from complaining about suffering because of it.

The fourth point is that there are many people who rely on the law. Discussion of the Tasmanian murderer, the Chilean torturer and the harbourside tax avoider centres on the reliance placed by the killer, the torturer and the tax avoider that they would not be prosecuted or taxed. However, there are others who relied on the laws, as they had believed them to be—the killer's wife, the torturer's victims and the intentional beneficiaries of government expenditure. They had an interest in the enforcement of what they reasonably believed to be the law.

This draws attention to some important aspects of the reliance argument. It is based on the value of officials acting in a transparent, consistent and predictable manner and the ability of citizens to rely on such action in order to plan their lives. This is often expressed in the negative—in terms of constraints on official power. However, citizens also rely on effective official action to protect their rights and interests. In some cases, this may require giving them a degree of flexibility to achieve a clearly stated general goal. For example, criminals would be very happy to rely on consistency of police investigative procedures or tax audit procedures. But this would defeat the expectations of citizens who were relying on the ability of police to successfully investigate crime or collect otherwise avoided revenue. Accordingly, a broad, positive duty on officials to act to achieve certain purposes may fulfil more legitimate expectations than detailed constraints (although the latter are important to prevent abuse of human rights and to prevent miscarriages of justice).

A democracy thrives on predictability and transparency of government but depends crucially on the vagaries of the hidden ballot. The criminal justice system that assigns moral obloquy to some individuals as the breakers of laws must be very open and transparent about the laws it enforces and the rights that cannot be overridden during that enforcement. However, the methods of detecting law-breakers cannot be too transparent, open and predictable lest that predictability allows lawbreakers to avoid detection.

Accordingly, whether or not we think transparency and consistency are valuable features of some practices of government depends on the consequences of that transparency or consistency and, in particular, the place that these values play in the institutions and practices of a well-ordered society under law. We should not assume that reliance by citizens on a pre-declared official practice is intrinsically a good feature of a well-ordered society under law.

But sometimes it is not simply the case of deciding *whether or not* a particular reliance or transparency is valuable, but *which* particular reliance we most want to propound, or how to compromise efficaciously between different types of reliance. Many of the most accepted examples of retrospectivity are found where the intention behind the law (intent) is manifestly not expressed in the letter of the law (content). This intent/content bifurcation creates the impetus for all manner of retrospective legislation: curative legislation, validating legislation, beneficial legislation, criminal legislation and tax-avoidance legislation.

The issue arises of whether we should protect the expectations of those people who rely on the perceived purposes and principles behind the law or those who rely on the substantive wording of it. Is protecting reliance on intent more or less just or efficacious than protecting reliance on content?

Our earlier discussion of Rule of Law showed that a system of laws must be capable of providing guidance. So a key consideration is whether a system which protects expectations based on the intent of the law can provide guidance to citizens, and whether it does so more effectively than a system which protects expectations grounded in content. In the remainder of this chapter, we shall argue that, in many ways, protecting people's expectations based on the known intentions and principles behind the law provides more reliable guidance to ordinary citizens.

However, let us let this point lie for a moment. In fact, suppose it were untrue and that, in most cases, the specificity inherent in content provided better guidance than intent. Would there be other reasons for respecting reliance on the law's intent over its content?

There are two major problems with having a system focusing exclusively on protecting reliance on the content of the law. The first is that individuals may plan their actions based on the stated purpose and principle of the law, but suffer losses because the law was not drafted to achieve the stated effect. Barring such protection excludes the most basic curative and validating retrospective legislation. The second problem is that this system provides incentives for those who rely on the content of the law when it manifestly conflicts with the intention of the particular law or the fundamental principles behind the system of law—as exemplified in the cases discussed in the last chapter. A system of law that respects reliance on the intentions behind the law avoids both these problem areas. Such a system can defeat the reliance on anomalies, unintended consequences and criminally sourced immunity while protecting reliance on the stated intent of, and principles behind, the law.

On the other hand, there are some very practical reasons why our system of law should have this focus on intent over content:

1. Motivating respect for the law. One key reason citizens accept the laws that govern them is that they think the laws are morally justified by morally worthy principles and goals. Allowing such goals a primary recognition in the legal process (by respecting expectations and actions formed on the basis of knowledge of such goals and principles) strengthens the citizen's respect.

2. Motivating adherence to the law. There are many reasons why citizens obey laws.[3] But one important reason is a belief that the law reflects, furthers and instantiates morally worthy principles and purposes. This gives them a moral reason to obey the law even in those cases where it does not seem to them politically or pragmatically expedient to do so. In addition, the more that expectations, formed on the basis of known and morally worthy principles and purposes, are respected by the system of law, the less likely that the citizen is caught in the invidious position of being torn between moral imperatives and legal requirements.

3. Knowledge of the law. In an important way, the law 'tracks' morality. There is a significant correlation between legal and moral imperatives in any given

---

[3] See Sampford, *The Disorder of Law*, Chapter 8.

situation—even if this correlation is only in the negative sense that acts which appear morally obligatory are very rarely illegal. The closer that the law tracks morality the more citizens can be confident that acting in ways they consider morally obligatory will be legally acceptable. This last point allows for very powerful guidance about the law in myriad everyday situations where the individual has clear and unambiguous moral convictions but—as regularly occurs—has actually no substantive knowledge of the relevant particularities of the law governing their precise situation. While a perfect match between personal consciences and legal principles is impossible—given that we cannot find out about regulatory laws from our conscience, and that people's moral opinions differ on many issues—it is, nevertheless, true that the more correlation between basic moral principles and fundamental legal maxims (if such maxims are given primacy over the law's substantive content), then the more introspective reflection can serve as an approximate but highly reliable guide to legally acceptable action.

The suggested approach will highlight practical differences between the moral principles of individuals and the legal principles behind proposed legislation, generally stimulating debate before legislation is passed and increasing awareness by those who disagree that following their moral precepts may generate adverse legal consequences. It could be argued that this will increase acts of disobedience but this is unlikely. There are plenty of pressure groups who will ascribe bad principles to legislatures. The legislature will have the opportunity to put principles as they are intended rather than as they are demonized.

These above discussions provide strong arguments for respecting reliance on the principles and purposes underlying the law than its detailed content. In the next section, we will argue that this should be central to our conception of the rule of law.

An interest in the predictability of law

We have seen that both the proponents and opponents of retrospective law use human rights arguments. Some of those arguments have force but none are absolute. The right against retrospective criminal liability has some express reservations; the rights of others that laws are designed to protect may be limited by the rights of the accused.

Whether or not reliance interests rarely amount to a right, they are always strong *interests*. Individuals have a strong interest in the predictability of the consequences law imposes on their actions and on the protections the law affords them from the predations of others. This interest goes beyond limitations on retrospectivity. If citizens are to understand those likely effects, it is highly desirable that those consequences be clear so that they can be understood and internalized. They can also be better internalized if they are simple, general and based upon readily understood principles. All this is aided by stability in the laws—the initial concern of the Greeks discussed in Chapter 2. These interests in the stability of the law should be respected and taken very seriously when changes to law are considered. There can be no guarantee that the law will not change. For those making long-term investments, let alone Rawlsian 'life plans', the law is bound to change during the course of the investment/life and the ultimate consequences of our actions will be affected by the unpredictability of legal change just as they are affected by other changes in our environment. We cannot prevent that kind of 'retrospectivity' without banning all change. That would have been impossible in ancient Athens and ludicrous now.

However, the impracticality of avoiding all retrospectivity or all legal change should not blind us to the fact that changes to the law do affect the interests of those who have fashioned their investment and other plans on the law as they knew it. While such interests cannot always be protected or preserved, such interests should not be ignored. Laws should not be changed lightly; the consequences of change should be weighed carefully; and, fair warning should be given that stability is unlikely.

Stability of law is far from the highest value. However, it is a value and it should not be ignored because the opponents of change and the opponents of retrospectivity could not ramp their claims into indefeasible human rights.

Sometimes justice and efficiency will favour not only non-retrospectivity but also stability and an absence of legal change, prospective *or* retrospective. Sometimes, one or both of these considerations will count *in favour* of retrospectivity: a retrospective law will often produce a more just or more efficient outcome than a purely prospective law. And this is not just the case where retrospective law is the only way to avert a catastrophic outcome. Rather, retrospectivity will have an important and necessary role to play in upholding and promoting all of the values (or virtues) of a legal system, including those associated with the Rule of Law.

Recognizing stability and predictability as interests rather than rights raises the question of the extent and means by which these interests will be taken into account in law making. Sometimes the interest can be respected while still allowing retrospective variation. A ban on retrospectivity is not the only way it can be recognized, respected and partly protected. Grandfathering and compensation, partial or otherwise, are real possibilities. As we saw in Chapter 6, while Kaplow and Goode are against compensation for retrospective change, a good case can be made for it in some circumstances. Firstly, it could be argued that, if the overall change is beneficial to the general welfare, then the community can afford the cost of compensating those who lose out. Secondly, it could also be argued that the rulemakers should have an incentive to flag the change of rule as early as possible and to change the rule as soon afterwards as practicable. If the losses are borne by the individual citizens, then rulemakers have less of an incentive to bring on the change. As we saw in Chapter 6, one of the ways of characterizing the reason for retrospective rule-making is a recognition that the new rule was not thought of and implemented earlier. Thirdly, like many economic arguments, Kaplow and Goode's argument deals with overall 'welfare' rather than the distribution of benefits and costs. Finally, while a policy of uncompensated retrospective change may reduce the losses arising from the delayed introduction of the new law, forcing citizens to bear the risk of such change may mean that they are more reluctant to respond to the opportunities intentionally created by laws which, in fact, do not change. This returns to the central idea of the rule of law that laws are not only fairer but more effective if they give clear signals as to how citizens should modify their behaviour and that retrospective rule-making may undermine that.

None of the arguments for and against compensation are sufficient to ground a general rule. Sometimes, full or partial compensation will be a good idea. A flexible policy allows various means of respecting reliance—'no change', prospectivity, grandfathering and compensation—to be costed, compared and, in some cases, mixed. It also means that the claim for compensation can be carefully considered and potentially limited. The extent of the compensation should never be any more than the loss suffered because the individual would have acted differently if notice of the likely retrospectivity had been provided. Furthermore, where there are several changes to the law between the citizen's actions and the determination of its legal consequences, beneficial changes should be taken into account as well.

7.3 What does this mean for the Rule of Law?

This book has argued that retrospectivity is commonplace, frequently justifiable and has an important place in well-ordered societies under law. Given the oft-argued incompatibility between retrospectivity and the rule of law, one may wonder whether the acceptance of retrospectivity might lead to the abandonment of the rule of law just as some had argued that the acceptance of the rule of law must lead to the abandonment of retrospectivity.

Our response has been that, properly understood, the rule of law is compatible with retrospective rule-making. The purpose of the rule of law is (if anything) that State power should be exercised in a manner that is established in advance so that individuals may plan their lives with that degree of uncertainty removed. Laws instruct officials what to do about disputes and provide guidance to citizens in planning and executing life plans. While, in general, this is best achieved when rules are prospective, retrospective rule-making practices can provide some remarkably clear guidance. Prospective retrospectivity can deter people from attempting to undermine the purposes of the law. It can also reinforce the guidance of the fundamental principles of an area of law, by allowing correction of unintended consequences, and reducing the need for complicated laws which anticipate every contingency (and which are, therefore, less clear and less capable of offering guidance). Retrospectivity can, therefore, promote the Rule of Law and, indeed, is a necessary element in any well-ordered society under law.

While we have argued that the interaction of retrospectivity and the rule of law can lead to co-existence, compatibility and even mutual support, neither retrospectivity nor the rule of law emerge from the collision unchanged. The compatibility of the rule of law and retrospectivity suggests that the concept of 'the rule of law', and the law that rules, may need to be reconsidered. What was it about law and the rule of law which seemed so incompatible with retrospectivity? What does this compatibility tell us about law and the rule of law and the way that we may need to alter our understanding of them?

A reminder of the limitations of law

The term and most of the definitions of the rule of law include the word 'law'—hardly, in itself, a simple matter. The changing conception of law affects the concept of, and reliable meaning for, the rule of law. One of the largest of these changes relevant to the 'rule of law' is the relative indeterminacy of law. While the degree of determinacy conceived by our jurisprudential forbears may be exaggerated for the purpose of comparison, law has been assaulted on this point for most of the last century. Where it might once have been common to see law as providing a single right answer to legal questions—at least within its 'core'[4]—there is little such certainty now. Individual texts are subject to different interpretations and the same interpreter may find that different legal texts conflict. Interpreters will differ as to which texts are relevant and the weight that is given to them in the case in hand. Despite the attempt to provide clear rules about the relative authority of different legal texts, the methods to be used in interpreting and a hierarchy of appeals to sort out differences of interpretation, the complexity of rules in any functioning society means that legal certainty is impossible with a fixed set of texts. This is compounded by constantly changing legislation and appellate decisions.

Since the American realists removed the prop of legal certainty, attempts have been made to substitute other means of understanding and predicting judicial decisions. The realists themselves focussed on 'the law in action'—how officials would deal with citizens when matters came before them. While not developed into a new theory of the 'rule of law', this did focus an important element on the ideal—that the core value was predictability and the ability of citizens to rely on such predictions rather than the rules themselves. It is not just Holmes' 'bad man' who is interested in how officials will exercise their power but, as Holmes frankly admitted, people such as himself. This understanding relates directly back to the concern about the use of power that lies at the heart of the ideal of the rule of law.[5]

A second attempt concentrated on the values of judges. The 'jurimetric' movement sought to identify judicial values as a way to understand and predict judicial decisions. Political parties sought to appoint judges with like-minded values.

---

[4] As compared to the 'penumbra' of its meaning—a distinction once popularized by HLA Hart, *The Concept of Law* (Clarendon, Oxford, 1994) Chapter VII.

[5] For a discussion of Holmes' perspective of law see MDA Freeman, *Lloyd's Introduction to Jurisprudence* (Sweet & Maxwell, London, 1994) Ch 8, particularly pp. 655–670.

The third, and ongoing, attempt involved concentration on judicial decision making and the constraints involved in it. Dworkin highlighted and tried to explain the important internal constraints on judges that prevented them just 'making it up as they went along' and exercising a 'discretion', which he found deeply problematic—not least because such discretion would be so clearly retrospective.[6] In deciding 'hard cases', judges felt bound by a body of decisions already made and bound to make new decisions 'fit' within that body. Their own values inevitably play a part and Dworkin legitimates their role in choosing which 'interpretation' of existing statutes and decisions. However, they are not exercising raw discretion and merely deciding what the best result would be regardless of those earlier decisions. It involves a respect for law even while the law is insufficiently determinate to tell them exactly what to decide. They are making decisions within law so that their decision is a decision of law rather than of theirs alone. Raz encapsulates the most general form of this integrity or fidelity[7] to law. It involves a commitment to seeing law as a 'two-stage decision making process'. The first stage involves the attempt to make rules to guide future decisions of officials and the second stage involves an attempt to apply those rules. Even though the first stage cannot determine action at the second stage, what is required is a commitment to the idea that it is a two-stage decision making process and that the decision being made is at that second stage.

Critical legal scholars have taken the indeterminacy argument further—and used it as a direct attack on the idea of the rule of law.[8] In its simplest formulation, it argues that 'law is politics'.[9] A different view changes one letter of Clausewitz's one-liner to say that 'law is politics carried on by other means'.[10] The contenders may be the same and enjoy similar advantages, but difference in institutional means is important. The rich and powerful have a clear and obvious advantage in legal battles—as they have in political ones. However, that does not guarantee them success in either. Wars are not won by piling up the treasure on each side of the battlefield and awarding the result to the side with the largest pile. Treasure must be converted to material and trained soldiers and then used by generals who take into account the topography of the battlefield. Similarly, legal battles are not won just by throwing money at the case (at least not in those countries where bribery of judges is effectively checked). The skill of the lawyers and the way they use the existing legal terrain of laws and principles will often critically affect the outcome.

[6] Ronald Dworkin, 'The Model of Rules' (1967) 35 *University of Chicago Law Review* 14–46.

[7] J Raz, *The Authority of Law: Essays on Law and Morality* (Clarendon Press, Oxford, 1979) in RA Cass, *The Rule of Law in America* (John Hopkins University Press, 2001).

[8] See, generally, MDA Freeman, *Lloyd's Introduction to Jurisprudence* (Sweet & Maxwell, London, 1994) Ch 12.

[9] Unger's more sophisticated argument was that no firm dividing line could be drawn between legal and political disputes and that all attempts to do so had failed. See RM Unger, *Knowledge and Politics* (Free Press, New York, 1975).

[10] Karl von Clausewitz, *Vom Kriege (On War)* (1833).

The question that critical legal scholars rightly raise is: what institutional mechanisms are there to prevent law being another, largely undifferentiated, form of politics and what separates the law that rules from raw power? That is, indeed, the hope underlying the ideal of the rule of law.

Back to Fuller

While strident critics of retrospectivity seek to argue the complete incompatibility with the rule of law, it is important to remember the more complex and nuanced relationship between the two articulated by Fuller.[11] For Fuller, the rule of law was based on seven principles, none of which were absolute. Like many systems of rules and principles, there are several guidance principles and one is not lexically superior to the others—something that Fuller says by implication. The rule of law is a package of principles rather than a set of rules, any one of which breaches it. Indeed, one may accept that sometimes one principle is temporarily set aside for the larger principle—such is the argument about signalling retrospectivity in some cases to enhance the guidance that the law can provide the citizen.

First, one principle might override others in specific cases—clarity and generality might be preferred over retrospectivity. Secondly, substantive justice might be preferred over procedural desiderata such as prospectivity. Thirdly, the injunction against retrospectivity applies to law as a whole rather than to individual laws. If all laws were retrospective, there would be a failure of the rule of law and no law at all. However, there is no such failure just because some laws are retrospective and the rule of law may be enhanced by some justified retrospectivity. This should not make us cavalier. However, it reminds us that the virtues of the rule of law are more like Dworkinian principles about law-making rather than hard and fast legal rules. Law is not a set of fixed and unbreakable rules whose effects cannot be altered by retrospective and prospective change. They are rules that should, and generally do, provide guidance to citizens. Similarly, the rule of law is not a set of unbreakable rules but a set of principles which guide rule makers and other officials in the exercise of their powers.

A weaker/stronger conception of the Rule of Law

The relative indeterminacy of law means that it is not the kind of finely honed instrument that can deliver certainty. If law cannot rule in detailed certainty, its rule must take on a different character. One possibility that would appeal to opponents of retrospectivity is to say that even if the ultimate meaning and effect of texts is uncertain, at least we should know for certain what the texts are. At least, we will know what the textual battleground is in disputes about the legal

---

[11] See, generally, LL Fuller, *The Morality of Law* (Yale University Press, New Haven; London, 1964 (1969)). Also see Chapter 2.

consequences those texts have for individual citizens. However, this is a very poor substitute for certainty. It may be of only limited guidance to citizens. It is one or four lawyers removed from the guidance of citizens. Indeed, as we have seen, it may actually compromise or even contradict the guidance that law makers intend to provide and the legal consequences they intend to impose on particular outcomes. Sometimes, retrospective rule alteration of the text may be necessary if law is to have the effects that were intended and communicated to citizens as a guide for their behaviour. This suggests an alternative approach to the rule of law concentrating on the guidance provided to citizens. The central goal of law, and the rule of law that underpins it, is that law should provide clear indications about the behaviour that is encouraged and discouraged and thereby provide some fairly clear guidance to citizens in general. Consistent guidance and textual certainty are by no means incompatible and good law making seeks to set out general principles and make the detailed rules serve and further those principles. The suggestion, here, is to generalize the judicial approach to all rule makers—including the legislature. Good judicial interpretation gives strong preferences to interpretations of the legal text that conform to the general principles underlying the relevant statutes and precedents. However, where earlier precedents do not fit the articulated principles, judges will overturn them (or at least those they have the power to overrule). They have a preference for the general guidance of principles over the specific guidance of texts. Similarly, when it is discovered that the detail of a statute contradicts the principles underlying the legislation and communicated to citizens, legislatures might give preference to the principle. This would mean that both kinds of lawmakers[12] would have a consistent approach to law which subordinated precise guidance on the detail of legal rules to the general principles which govern the detail of those rules.

This is weaker than the traditional conception of the rule of law because it does not make claim to precise guidance on detail but it is stronger in that it can provide more effective general guidance to citizens. The guidance is for citizens through notice[13] of the general rules and principles that will be used to apply legal consequences to their actions rather than through certainty of which texts will be used to determine legal consequences. Indeed, if law could be specified in such detail, that detail could never be known by everyone—only highly specialized lawyers and those who understood what their lawyers said to them.[14] We are more concerned with the integrity of what the law represents to ordinary citizens than

---

[12] Given the wide range of official power in our community, it is important not to become too narrowly focussed on judges. Judicial power is only one form of power and not the most extensive or potentially the most damaging.

[13] It should be noted that guidance is more than mere notice. Laws are made with the intention that they will be acted upon by others.

[14] Ordinary citizens could never grasp all that detail because, as Karl Llewellyn observed, individuals can only respond to the purpose rather than the letter of the legal rule. See *The Bramble Bush*, p. 15.

with trying to ensure that the legal detail fits the general principles discussed in parliament and presented to the electorate.

This preferred construction of the rule of law shifts the emphasis from detailed rules to principles that can be understood by the population to which it is directed. It sees law as centrally a communication between the State and the citizens to whom it belongs rather than between the lawyers working for the State and lawyers working for citizens and corporations. This is not an attempt to 'cut out the [legal] middlemen'. Lawyers working in and for parliament, as judges and as practitioners, have a vital role to play in attempting to make the communication more effective and to give critical feedback from lobbying to litigation on the content and interpretation of rules. Lawyer-lawyer communication is important in assisting the communication between State and citizen but cannot be promoted at the expense of that which it is supposed to assist.

This guidance role should be taken seriously by the government and placed at the centre of its rule-making, for it goes straight to the heart of Fuller's rule of law. Most of the ways that King Rex fails to make law are failures of guidance. If there is too much secrecy, simplicity, incoherence and instability, then the citizen cannot be guided by it. Law can fail to provide guidance in any one of these ways. It makes little difference to the citizen whether the rule was secret or retrospective. Caligula's writing of rules in print too small and distant to be seen creates no less a problem than retrospective laws. For many people, the setting of laws in incomprehensible text that can only be accessed by paying unaffordable fees to lawyers is no more accessible or less opaque than Caligula's distant lettering.

The guidance of principles cannot be precise and comprehensive. Law cannot be a fully reliable guide like a complete and comprehensive street directory. It is more like a sixteenth-century map—with some parts very well drawn but not completely accurate despite the diligence and competence of the cartographer and other parts showing imagined and partially appreciated dangers. They show uncharted waters and indicate that you go there at your own risk. However, the analogy is not quite apt. A closer analogy might be attempts to chart sand bars in a river estuary with main channels that are deliberately dredged and other areas that are always of uncertain and shifting depth with the great danger coming from where the water is shallow rather than where the sand bar is showing. This analogy, too, misses something—the human dimension. To some extent, the sixteenth-century map is a better analogy because it shows the interaction between the cartographer's ideas, wishes, preferences and the known terrain.

Nevertheless, guidance is central to the whole enterprise. The rule makers (legislatures and appellate judges) seek to provide a dual guidance—to both the subjects of the law and the officials who implement it. Those who interpret and apply law recognize that they are at the second stage of Raz's two-stage decision-making process. They recognize that officials at the first stage have not just been attempting to make rules to add to the rulebook but have given undertakings on behalf of the State about the way that official power would be exercised. The officials at the second stage have a responsibility to attempt, as far as is possible, that they ensure those undertakings be fulfilled—especially where citizens have been guided by those undertakings and would be significantly disadvantaged if the State did not act as they had said it would.[15] The relative indeterminacy, opacity, incommunicability and voluminousness of law have a number of important effects for this process—though it does not render it either invalid or useless:

1. As indicated earlier, the guidance cannot be precise and certain; it cannot rely on fixed and certain rules but must involve principles.

2. Principles can be communicated to citizens more easily than a mass of detailed rules. However, such communication is neither direct nor automatic. It is dependent on second hand reports of the law from the media at a general level and the legal profession for citizens and corporations who want more detailed advice. If the guidance role is to be taken seriously, improved means of communication are necessary—such as authorized summaries of legislation and judicial decisions that allows citizens to understand the principles and their intended operation.

3. If parliament's central role is one of setting out the general principles, then there is much to be said for focussing on the principles when the Bill is being debated. Parliament should be the 'forum of principle' in which alternative principles are debated rather than a forum for the consideration of the detailed rules that attempt to implement those principles.

4. This does not mean that detail can or should be ignored. However, the detail of legislation can be filled out in one of three ways—in the principal act, in subordinate legislation, or by the judiciary. While the latter will always have a role, the scope of that role will depend on the extent to which the other two methods have been utilized. We would argue that the best approach is to concentrate on principle in the legislation and to provide most of the detail in subordinate legislation—with the proposed regulations being presented to Parliament so that all can see how the proposed detail is to be filled out. Scrutiny committees can consider both—giving feedback on the primary legislation to facilitate debate on the Bill and feedback on whether the detail of the subordinate legislation furthers the principles set out in the Bill.

5. This process requires a partnership between courts and legislators as the most common first and second order decision makers. But it is not Posner's development of an entire field of law.[16]

---

[15] These responsibilities of 'second stage' decision makers mean that the nature of the guidance given them is rather different to that given to citizens. A citizen's actions are guided by giving an indication of how officials will deal with them if they act in ways that are being actively encouraged/ discouraged. An official's actions are mandated. In a very real sense, the 'commands' issued in law are truly to those officials rather than to the citizens. However, the relative indeterminacy or law means that first stage decision makers can only effectively 'guide' rather than simply direct.

[16] R Posner, *The Federal Courts: crisis and reform*, 1986, pp. 298–315; discussed in Fisch, p. 1081.

6. The relative indeterminacy of law means that rule making and rule interpretation are never entirely separable and severable. Some of the details of common law are changed to fit in with the whole. However, it is still essentially at the second stage because judges are not expected to consider new rules in isolation but only to the extent that they are needed to conform more closely to the overarching principles in a particular area of law. When they do so, they are engaging in retrospective rule-making. That rule-making is only justified because the retrospective alteration of the detailed rules is only to make them conform to the principles that guide behaviour.

7. When legislators engage in retrospective rule-making, they should see the action as analogous to retrospective rule-making by judges. In this, legislatures need to learn more from judges than *vice versa* although the intellectual traffic should not be entirely one way. They are not introducing retrospective laws because legislators have changed their minds but because they want the laws to reflect the principles they had in mind and communicated when the law was passed (or at least most recently updated to reflect new thinking). Retrospective rule-making is a maintenance function, not an innovation function—keeping the details consistent and coherent to stated principles rather than striking out in new directions because of popular mandate, political whim or other drivers of political change.

8. Legislators and judges should each seek to give fair warning of the areas likely to change; the kind of change should be flagged. In any case, the policy on retrospectivity should be clearly articulated—as the House of Lords did in its practice statement on overruling.

There are two potentially strong criticisms of this approach which could be made on rule of law grounds. First, it might be seen as licensing the legislature to pass only very general rules and expecting the court to enforce these rules according to a very general spirit leading to uncertainty. This is not unlikely to arise as neither government nor legislature is likely to cede application entirely to the judiciary. These bodies are likely to specify the application of the principles in the kinds of situations that stimulated them to act and other situations where the drafters had clearly thought them through. General guidance will be sufficient for most. If not, the detail will assist those particularly affected (and possibly their lawyers) to identify the law's effects on them. However, they will know the general principle guides and so will be cautious about interpretations of the detail that do not fit with the general principle. In this way, the detailed legal content of regulations plays an important role in guidance.

The second objection is that a government that sought to persecute a particular group or ride roughshod over the rights of citizens might expect judges to interpret the text in the light of the government's overall goal and thereby deny those groups what little protection that their lawyers can glean and scrape from the law. We might claim protection on the basis that most governments do not want to state openly the goals of persecuting groups so that there is less danger in the stated principle than the devilish detail. But this will not always be the case. EP Thomson's famous line about the 'unqualified good' of the rule of law was a reflection upon a time when the stated purpose of the law was to deter crimes of the poor by the imposition of the heaviest sanctions—most notably through the widespread threat of the death penalty. Lawyers, finding loopholes in the language used or the procedures established, frequently defeated such intentions. The principles behind apartheid were clear—and some lawyers sought every means to use the detail of the law against its intention. There is now concern that the regimes created for alleged 'terrorists' and 'illegal immigrants' are profoundly unjust and motivated by principles that lawyers must fight rather than uphold. The criteria for good or bad principle or detail are inevitably contentious and difficult to apply. There is reason to believe that a 'bad' government, especially in a democracy, will be less outrageous in its publicly stated principle than in its legislated detail. Greater publicity leads to more scrutiny and more people that could be upset by taking too strong a line in any direction. The other is that a general policy will contain terms that have to be interpreted. If an act of parliament refers to 'terrorists' or 'illegal immigrants', independent judges will have to interpret the meaning of those terms. Such judges might find that targeted individuals are not 'terrorists' or 'illegal immigrants' according to any reasonable definition of the term.

One way of addressing the concern about the potential abuse of retrospective rule-making is to consider what integrity mechanisms are in place or could be put in place to reduce the likelihood of such abuse. Some of the integrity mechanisms that form part of 'integrity systems' in liberal democratic societies can assist in this and there are some specific integrity mechanisms that can, and in some jurisdictions do, address the issue of abuse of retrospective rule-making power.

7.4 Preventing abuse

Ideals and integrity systems

Concerns about abuse of power are not confined to the power to make retrospective rules. They are central to the rule of law and a set of values, norms, institutions and practices that have emerged in western societies over the last 400 years and have taken root in other countries where local democratic reformers found and emphasized the liberal and democratic strands of their own cultures.

This is not the time or place to set out that history and it has been retold many times in many different ways (and to 'prove' a multitude of points).[17] The original

---

[17] See, for example, C Sampford, 'State sovereignty and the common good and international intervention', in B Leiser and T Campbell (eds), *Human Rights in Theory and Practice* (Ashgate, London, 2001) and *Australian National Integrity Systems Assessment, Queensland Hand Book* (Transparency International, Australia, July 2001).

conception of a post-Westphalian state was highly authoritarian and justified as such by writers such as Hobbes. Philosophers and revolutionaries of the North Atlantic Enlightenment proposed a number of 'liberal democratic' values— including liberty, rights, democracy, equality, citizenship, community, welfare and the rule of law[18]—through which those highly authoritarian states could be 'civilized'.[19] Enlightenment *philosophes* insisted that states had to justify themselves to their citizens by furthering citizens' rights and by becoming accountable to the citizenry. Accountability was initially achieved through a right to revolution but was made more effective and regular through democratic legislatures and administrative law.

The rule of law was, in many ways, the first enlightenment value. It was realized in England earlier and more substantially than the ideals of liberty, democracy, citizenship and equality. But despite the fixation of some conservatives with the rule of law as a single and paramount value directed to avoiding the abuse of power, this approach fails to understand three critical connections that were established early on and which are central to the way we understand integrity systems. The rule of law is connected to other values, to the institutions which support it, and to the purposes for which law is supposed to rule.

First, the rule of law and other enlightenment values are, in most cases, mutually supportive. Most famously, Jefferson teamed up 'life, liberty and the pursuit of happiness'[20] and the French linked *liberté, egalité, fraternité*. We now recognize that the rule of law is supported by and generally supportive of other values such as citizenship, democracy and human rights. Indeed, as we saw in Chapter 2, some 'thick' theories seek to include some, or all of these, within the rule of law itself.

Secondly, values are not self-enforcing. Most enlightenment philosophers were fully aware that these values would not be realized without a set of institutional supports and the eighteenth century produced two of them: the US system of checks and balances and the Westminster system of parliamentary democracy.

From the beginning, the rule of law was crucially dependent on a number of norms, institutions and practices—in particular, a largely independent judiciary practising judicial review of executive action (commencing with the availability of prerogative writs to the British litigants from the seventeenth century) and a respect for their decisions by the executive. It was greatly strengthened by the

---

[18] The list of such values developed over the next 200 years. See C Sampford, 'The Four Dimensions of Rights', in B Galligan and C Sampford (eds). *Rethinking Human Rights* (Federation Press, 1997) 50–71.

[19] We are conscious of using such a loaded term in an area already overloaded with ideological rhetoric and cultural angst. However, the term is apt in that it emphasizes the importance of the control and marginalization of brute force, the importance of the citizen, the generation of civil society and its role in governance. It is interesting to note that what we would now call civil society was very strong in Western Europe in the seventeenth and eighteenth centuries and that this was influential in government even before universal suffrage made such nations democracies.

[20] *The Declaration of Independence of the Thirteen Colonies*, in Congress, 4 July 1776.

development of democratically elected legislatures, critical media, a professional civil service, government and non-government watchdog groups, non-government advocacy groups, administrative law reforms including the requirement to give reasons and 'freedom of information' (by which individual members of the public were given rights to access documents created by public institutions) and in many countries, federal division of legislative and executive powers. This dependence of the rule of law on supportive institutions and practices helps to explain the common tendency to define the rule of law in terms of such norms, institutions and practices (see Chapter 2). Such institutions are not part of the definition of the rule of law but are part of the legal machinery that constitutes a practical necessity in securing it.

These two lessons lie at the heart of the concept of integrity systems developed during the 1990s as the principal means of combating the abuse of power. The leading coalition against corruption, Transparency International (TI) defined corruption as the abuse of public (later 'entrusted') power for private (later including party political) gain. The best way to limit corruption was the adoption of a set of mutually supportive liberal democratic governance values and a range of mutually supportive institutions (independent judiciary exercising judicial review, independent prosecution decisions, elected legislature, scrutiny committees, freedom of information, whistleblower protection, free press, watchdog bodies such as ombudsmen and anti-corruption commissions), practices (including relevant constitutional conventions, legislative scrutiny and bureaucratic compliance) and ethical codes.

However, it is important that integrity systems and its components are not just about preventing corruption and other abuses of power. They are not just directed to avoiding bad governance but at promoting good governance. The reason is simple. If our only goal were to prevent the abuse of governmental power a simple, instantaneous, permanent and foolproof method is available—abolish government. While this solution is intermittently popular with anarchists of the right and left, few are attracted to it. The reason is that most of us want governments to perform a number of services—from the minimal internal and external protection of the 'nightwatchman State' to the expenditure of public funds for common purposes. This provides a conceptual link between 'integrity' and 'corruption'. We define integrity as the use of entrusted power for the purposes which are used to publicly justify the existence and exercise of that power. Corruption is an *abuse* of entrusted power in that it is used for other purposes. The integrity system aims to promote the former and limit the latter.

This is the modern version of a lesson learnt in the eighteenth century. Despite the abuse of power to which they had been subjected, few revolutionaries demanded an end to government. The emphasis was on finding the right system to ensure that the power was used for the purposes that justified it. For Jefferson, the purpose was far more ambitious, to further the 'inalienable' rights of 'life, liberty and the pursuit of happiness'. As governments were democratized, the purposes of government extended to the purposes which were supported by a majority of its voting citizens. These extensions were politically contested and remain a matter of legitimate public debate and decision by democratically elected legislatures. However, integrity systems are not designed to discriminate between the purposes that the State institutions should be publicly and legally directed to pursue. They are designed to ensure, as far as possible, that the power of public institutions are directed towards their publicly declared and legally endorsed purposes rather than abused for personal or other undeclared purposes.

Integrity systems are directed towards the inherent opportunities and threats posed by institutions. Institutions are created because their founders believed that they could more effectively contribute to the furthering of important values and would, on balance, benefit their members and the communities that authorized their creation and continued operation. They are sustained because their members (and those regulatory authorities which retain a say in the matter) continue to think that the institutions provide a net benefit to members and community alike (either with the original purposes that justify their establishment or new purposes that publicly justify their continuation).[21] This is not only true for governments but for any other group that is created to pool people and resources in the belief that they can achieve more collectively than individually and includes professions, churches and joint stock companies. However, the pooling of people and resources and the subsequent concentration of power provide a temptation to those who would seek to use that power for other purposes. Whether or not Lord Acton is correct to assert that power has a tendency to corrupt,[22] power certainly attracts the would-be corrupt, and integrity systems need to be designed to make abuses difficult and discoverable.

In placing power in the hands of individuals or groups, human communities are taking a risk—that the benefits to be gained from use for the justified purposes of the institution outweigh the risks of its abuse. Integrity systems are designed to increase the likelihood of the benefit of intended use and reduce the risk of the abuse.

One of the greatest powers handed to any group of individuals is the power to make laws for the governance of the community to achieve a number of large and important purposes expressed in many different and overlapping ways—to further their rights to life, liberty and the pursuit of happiness; to further the interests of the group as a whole; to protect the interests of the least well off; and to provide guidance to officials and citizens as to how the former should exercise their power

---

[21] For a discussion of institutions see C Sampford, *The Disorder of Law* (Blackwell, Oxford, 1989) Ch. 6. For a discussion of this aspect of them, see C Sampford, 'Law, Institutions and the Public Private Divide' (1992) 20 *Federal Law Review* 185.

[22] 'Power tends to corrupt, and absolute power corrupts absolutely. Great men are almost always bad men.' Lord Acton, letter, 3 April 1887, to Bishop Mandell Creighton (published in *The Life and Letters of Mandell Creighton*, 1904). See <http://www.theihs.org/libertyguide/people.php/75834. html. Accessed 4 April 2005>.

so that the latter can plan their lives in that light.[23] While this power is generally seen as justified by the benefits it can deliver to a community, the magnitude of the power generates a commensurate risk of abuse. Opponents of retrospective rule-making might seek to define retrospectivity as an abuse. However, this book has argued that retrospective law-making, whether legislative or judicial, is not necessarily an abuse but may be a legitimate exercise of law-making power to further the above purposes—including the last mentioned purpose of guidance. Indeed, it can correct or counter abuses of power—sometimes State power (the criminally sourced immunity) and sometimes other forms of power (including corporate power and the power of professionals). At other times, it is there to correct negligent and reckless mistakes. There is a general limitation that does not apply to prospective law-making (that is, making the existing law more coherent and consistent with the general principles that had publicly justified the pre-existing legal rules). Failure to conform retrospective rule-making to this key limitation is an abuse. However, it is only one of many possible abuses of retrospective legislation. Many of the retrospective rules that generate controversy appear to abuse legislative power in other ways that are equally as serious in prospective legislation. Accordingly, most retrospective legislation needs to be scrutinized in the same way and for the same reasons as other legislation. In any case, all changes in the law need to be justified on the basis that they are, overall, beneficial and that the net benefits outweigh the costs of change and the benefits of stability.

For these reasons, we would not generally argue for separate integrity mechanisms for retrospective rule-making but to have strong integrity mechanisms to reduce the risk of abuse of legislative power and to scrutinize legislation to see who benefits and who is disadvantaged by its introduction.

Of all the integrity mechanisms introduced in the last 200 years in western societies, few would doubt that the most important is the creation of a democratically elected legislature. For much of those 200 years, this was not only seen as the most important integrity mechanism but the only one needed. Indeed, it was not uncommon to argue that any other body should not check it. However, it is now recognized that parliamentary power can be abused and that the integrity system must include other accountability institutions and mechanisms.

Three kinds of integrity mechanism are commonly suggested to reduce the likelihood of abuse. First, to ensure that the legislature really is the popular choice, there are at least four requirements: provisions for free and fair elections (including limits on campaign donations and the use of government money for advertising government policy); an upper house controlled by neither government nor opposition; an electoral system that makes it more likely that the government chosen is preferred by a majority of electors; and an effective party system to frame and aggregate choices.

---

[23] Note, this is clearly stated here as a positive purpose of law making and not merely as a restriction on it.

Secondly, there are constitutional provisions that determine the extent of legislative power and an independent judiciary to determine whether law is within those bounds. (These may, or may not, include bills of rights although it can be argued that the most effective mechanisms are those that prevent legislation that breaches human rights being passed in the first place.)[24]

Thirdly, there are mechanisms that seek to reduce the likelihood that power will be used for the purposes of individual MPs or their backers: ethical codes and ethics committees to revise and interpret them; registers of interest; anti-corruption agencies; and a professional public service.

Fourthly, there are the mechanisms to promote informed debate on the actions of public institutions in the government and corporate sectors: freedom of information; a duty to answer questions asked in parliament; environmental and other impact statements generated by independent bodies; expert parliamentary draftspersons; scrutiny committees.

All this is supported by a rich and diverse set of non-government institutions that help stimulate debate within the community and a free media that brings to the public a wide range of views on legislation and other government action— noting that the power of the media can, itself, be seriously abused.[25]

These integrity mechanisms are designed to both prevent abuse of legislative power and to promote their use for the purposes which justify the existence and continuation of such power. These mechanisms are evolving and developing. They can certainly be improved—as they have been improved over the past 400 years. This is not the place to make suggestions for further improvements to integrity systems, in general, nor to integrity systems of individual countries, in particular. We will concentrate on some specific institutional reforms that might increase the guidance capacity of law and reduce the likelihood of abuse.

Reinforcing the guidance capacity of law

In proposing a modified version of the rule of law earlier in this chapter, we suggested that law should be seen, as first and foremost, a communication between State and citizens, and that guidance is central to the rule of law.

If law is to reflect this guidance role better, the guidance role should be taken into account at all stages of the legislative process. This could be seen as a plea for 'plain English'. Plain English is required, but this misses the key question: what

---

[24] C Sampford, 'The four dimensions of rights and their means of protection', in B Galligan and C Sampford (eds), *Rethinking Human Rights* (Federation Press, Sydney, 1997).
[25] C Sampford, 'Institutionalising Public Sector Ethics', in K Woldring (ed), *Business Ethics in Australia and New Zealand: Essays and Cases* (Thomas Nelson, Melbourne, 1995); C Sampford, N Preston with Carol Bois, *Public Sector Ethics: Finding and Implementing Values* (Routledge, London, and Federation Press, Sydney, 1998); N Preston, C Sampford with C Connors, *Encouraging Ethics and Challenging Corruption* (Federation Press, St Leonards, 2002); C Sampford, A Shacklock, C Connors and F Galtung (eds), *Measuring Corruption* (Ashgate, Aldershot, in press).

communications are to be put in plain English? If the communication is still directed at lawyers, this may be useful if the lawyers understand plain English better than the language used in law. There are undoubtedly times when the expression of some modern statutes is so convoluted and the purpose so obscure, that the attempt to use plain (or plainer) English may well help lawyers to understand it. However, those who read the current statutory output of legislatures and the reasons for decisions by courts of appeal will remain lawyers. Napoleon may have thought that the *Code Civile* could be bedtime reading for the *poilu* in his tent, but the soldiers and citizens of today give priority to other reading material. There is not a lot of point making legislation easier to read if the citizenry will not read it. If the 'plain English' terms are less clear than the legal terms that are more familiar to the lawyer, then the guidance provided by the law is reduced not enhanced.

Citizens understand the law from journalists and from word of mouth from their peers. Thus, the guidance offered by law to citizens is generally through third parties at the first instance and those parties are not necessarily the communicant's lawyers. Even when the politicians who introduced the legislation are talking about the laws, they may or may not have an interest in communicating the purpose and effect of the legislation (being more concerned with the purpose of re-election and the effects of the law's public reception on their chances of re-election). While legislatures and courts should not seek to 'cut out the middle man', they should certainly give attention to the way that laws are communicated.

Modern legislative practice has gone some way to address this issue, adding press releases and explanatory memoranda to the traditional second reading speech where the minister introducing legislation explains its purpose, rationale and justification. The authoritative version of the law is the Act of Parliament. The text of the explanatory memorandum and the minister's second reading speech are now used by most common law courts in interpreting the authoritative text of the Act—especially for divining the purpose of the legislation. However, if there is a conflict between the two, the more widely read and disseminated text is ignored.

We are strongly in favour of reversing this approach. We would argue that parliament should take the prime responsibility for providing explicit guidance to citizens about the intended effect of the law and how they can act to take advantage of the benefits conferred by the law and avoid actions where the law seeks to impose sanctions. It should write a 'binding summary' of the legislation on which it expects citizens to rely and which can act as an authoritative guide. While such texts would explain where there is detail and when the citizen may need detailed legal advice, the burden should be on the drafters to make the principles clear. By so doing, citizens will have a better chance of understanding the law and making and acting out life plans on the basis of that understanding. If the citizen can rely on the principles communicated in the public statement overriding detailed rules to the contrary, the law will be much more effective. This is not only reasonable but also equitable (see Chapters 3 and 6). The 'binding summary' becomes a statement of how State power is going to be used and, as a matter of equity, the State should act as it has indicated where the citizen reasonably relies on it.

While the purpose of such a text is that it can be read reliably and separately from the main text of the Act, the best place, constitutionally, for such a text is in the first chapter of the main Act. It is then easy to include an interpretative section which indicates that all the detailed provisions of the Act should be read in the light of the summary and that any inconsistencies be read in favour of a citizen relying on the summary and acting in good faith on its apparent requirements.

Such a regime would impose a significant and useful discipline on the State in formulating legislation and the principled statements of rationale for that legislation. Those politicians who are formulating policy and those lawyers who are drafting legislation to give it effect are forced to articulate and think through the purposes of legislation and the internal consistencies in the principles behind it.

The creation of 'binding statements' would support and be supported by other elements of current 'best practice' and some developments of that practice. These might include the principles (underlying what the Queensland Electoral and Administrative Reform Commission called 'high quality legislation') that were enshrined in the *Legislative Standards Act 1992* (Qld) as subsequently amended.[26] Achieving those ends requires that:

- The purposes of legislation are defined.
- The means are identified.
- The proportionality of the means to that end are considered.
- Drawbacks are identified.
- Alternatives to legislation are considered.
- The supporting measures are considered.[27]

A well-staffed, effective bi-partisan scrutiny of legislation committee is particularly valuable. While the United States Congress has long established substantive committees that examine legislation on substantive topics such as defence, foreign affairs or the environment, an apparently Australian innovation from the early 1980s was the establishment of Scrutiny of Legislation Committees. The initial impetus was to scrutinize proposed legislation to determine whether it breached human rights. This was partly because Australia lacks a bill of rights which could invalidate legislation that breached international human rights norms. However, it can also be argued that it is better to create a parliamentary remedy before passage of the Bill than afterwards when rights have actually been breached. In Queensland, the Scrutiny of Legislation Committee was given oversight of all legislation and a brief to not only prevent legislative breaches of human rights norms but to seek to improve the standard of Queensland legislation through the

---

[26] See C Sampford, 'Fundamental Legislative Principles: Their Meaning and Rationale' (1994) 24 *Queensland Law Society Journal* 531.

[27] In order to achieve policy goals, it is usually necessary to do more than pass a law.

encouragement of 'high quality legislation' (meeting the criteria above and being consistent with a non-exhaustive list of fourteen 'fundamental legislative principles' defined as: 'principles relating to legislation that underlie a parliamentary democracy based on the rule of law').[28] These principles cover matters such as the onus of proof, rights of entry, natural justice, and retrospectivity. One principle which the Committee is required to look at is whether the legislation 'is unambiguous and drafted in a sufficiently clear and precise way'. Such committees are most effective if no party has a majority and would benefit from being structured to deny that possibility.[29]

Whatever body is responsible for scrutinizing legislation, it is highly desirable for the retrospectivity criteria to be developed and raised to the status of ethical principles about the use of legislative power—drawing on the judicial practice of overruling in which the key issue is the coherence of the relevant law and the rational and legitimate expectations created by the earlier law and governmental actions. The Committee would develop and apply those principles and report to Parliament on whether or not it considered the proposed retrospective legislation fell within those principles.

It may also be worth extending, slightly, the powers of such committees. Currently, ministers are obliged to respond in a timely fashion to the concerns of the committees, and to provide answers to specific questions. However, in certain cases, legislation may be passed through Parliament before the scrutineering bodies have had a chance to assess the legislation, or before the relevant ministers have responded to enquiries. In such cases, ministers can choose not to respond to such enquiries, given that the scrutineering body is now, in any case, *functus officio*. Notwithstanding this point, there may, nevertheless, be merit in requiring ministers to go on record regarding their reasons for the more worrisome aspects of their legislation. This would force relevant ministers to be upfront about whether or not they accept the Bill to be retrospective, and, if so, what reasons they are willing to give for this. At the very least, ministers would come to learn that there is a dialogic process that must be undertaken if one wishes to enact retrospective legislation—regardless of whether the party holds the numbers in Parliament.

However, the work of parliamentary scrutiny committees in considering retrospective legislation should not be pursued in isolation. As indicated earlier, legal rule-making is a partnership between legislators, judges and the legal profession. While parliament plays the central role (especially in using the reports of scrutiny committees), the judiciary and the profession should consider their respective roles and the way they interact with each other.

---

[28] *Legislative Standards Act 1992* (Qld) s 4(1). Section 4(2) states that 'these principles include requiring that legislation has sufficient regard to: (a) rights and liberties of individuals; and (b) the institution of Parliament'. Sections 4(3) and 4(4) provide a non-exhaustive list of such 'fundamental legislative principles'.

[29] Our suggestion would be for such a committee to have equal numbers of government and opposition members with an independent non-parliamentary chair agreed by both parties.

The judiciary and the legislature

Judges have considered the principles governing when they will overrule earlier decisions and when they will not. This is done in the time honoured sequence of precedents in which judges give reasons for their own decisions based on the earlier decisions of courts. While this common law approach to the development of the principles for overruling common law precedents is entirely appropriate and does not need to be replaced, this does not prevent some more collective consideration of judicial retrospectivity by the judiciary and associated judicial commissions and training institutes across a number of issues:

1. How do the practices of judicial overruling vary across different jurisdictions?

2. How do such judicial approaches to overruling compare to the approaches that different scrutiny committees adopt to retrospective legislation?

3. How do the practices of 'flagging' possible changes in the law vary across jurisdictions? (Note that such practices can provide some important guidance to citizens in warning against reliance on the rules and precedents questioned. These practices indicate where citizens should 'play it safe' and avoid reliance on contested interpretations of the law.)

4. Can the judicial and legislative roles be mutually supportive in the development of legislation? For example, the judiciary might be encouraged to state where legislation does not appear to provide clear guidance through a lack of clarity or because it generates consequences the judges find difficult to believe were intended. On the other hand, where judicial interpretations of statutes are being constantly overridden (whether by prospective or retrospective legislation), judges should take note that something may be wrong with the communication process so that they are failing to understand the intended meaning and consequences of the legislation that they are interpreting.

The executive—guidance through rulings

The executive also has a role to play in improving the capacity of laws to provide guidance. This is obviously the case when a ministry is considering legislation and drafting it for introduction to Parliament. However, where a public agency is a potential litigant, it should flag, as much as possible, the view it takes of existing law. Inland revenue services have long provided rulings on their view of tax law—including 'binding private rulings' that indicate the view that the agency will take of a particular transaction. There is no better guidance that the citizen can gain as to the legal consequences of their intended actions. Indeed, it can achieve the elusive goal of 'certainty'. It is superior to the legal advice of a citizen's own lawyers who can only predict what will happen in court. The public agency's ruling informs the citizen of whether they are going to have to face court and the view taken by what is generally the only potential litigant. The citizen can achieve a degree of certainty that no lawyer can provide. There are, inevitably, complaints about the provision of rulings—the time taken to issue them and the fact that the interpretation of the law tends to favour the State. The time taken reflects, in part, the fact that the rulings are provided free of charge. But there is no reason, in principle, against charging for rulings. Given the fact that public agency rulings provide a certainty that highly paid legal advisors cannot (including those advisors who are paid to seek the ruling), citizens should value them and be prepared to pay. Claims of state favouritism can always be tested in court.

As rulings improve the capacity of law to guide citizens, their extension beyond revenue to other government agencies would improve the capacity of other areas of law to guide citizens.

The legal profession—the citizen's traditional guides

Lawyers are the 'front line' of guidance to the citizen about the intended consequences of law for their action. In most cases, they are in partnership with the courts and legislatures—playing the vital role of disseminating intended consequences of laws so that citizens can more reliably make plans (whether Rawlsian 'life plans' or more prosaic business plans) and act on them. However, in some cases, lawyers are engaged in a different kind of game—seeking to defeat the purposes of the law and the consequences intended for the citizen's action. In repressive States, this may be necessary—and it can never be the choice of the State to determine when such necessity arises. However, the better developed the integrity system is to prevent the abuse of legislative power, the less frequently such guerrilla action against the purposes of the law will be required.

7.5 The international dimension

This book is about retrospective law-making within the independent jurisdictions of sovereign states. However, it is salutary to remember that discussion of retrospectivity was stimulated after World War II by the Nuremberg trials which imposed retrospective individual liability for 'crimes against humanity'. Most of the discussion for the next 60 years, including this book, has been about retrospectivity in domestic legislation. This book is devoted to that context in which most issues of retrospective law-making will continue to arise (as that is where the vast bulk of law making itself will occur for the foreseeable future).

The three cases justifying retrospective rule-making are issues for domestic jurisdiction. Even the case of the Chilean torturer in breach of fundamental human rights was considered in the context of potential domestic retrospective legislation on the return to democratic rule. Despite the fact that he breached internationally recognized human rights, the first and primary resort should be in the domestic law of states applying domestic law—whether the law ratified the international treaties or the other, long-standing, domestic laws covering aggravated assault, false imprisonment and murder.

Although there are now other avenues (foreign courts exercising universal juris-diction, *ad hoc* tribunals and the International Criminal Court), as a matter of theory and practice, domestic courts remain the principal means for prosecuting breaches of humanitarian rights laws. General Pinochet, the very real boss of very real South American torturers was arrested and faced extradition to a Spanish court. He was not extradited, but the case gave added impetus to Chilean author-ities to bring Pinochet to trial in Chile and to strip him of the retrospective immun-ity that his own regime had given him. The International Criminal Tribunal for the Former Yugoslavia (ICTY) has achieved a number of successful prosecutions although its legitimacy has suffered because it is funded by countries which became belligerents in the former Yugoslavia. While the International Criminal Court (ICC) is much more promising, it, too, is intended as a backstop where the relevant State cannot, or will not, prosecute its resident war criminals. This is the appropriate role of international institutions and international action—to pro-vide a backstop for failed domestic prosecution and, in doing so, to provide encouragement to domestic prosecution and discouragement to domestic inertia. The first goal must be to encourage nation states to take seriously the commit-ments they make when signing international human rights instruments and to impose penalties and create risks for those who toy with the idea of breaking them.

When international tribunals or foreign courts exercising universal jurisdiction hear cases for breaches of international law, there is no need for retrospectivity. The Nuremberg trials may well stand as one of the greatest examples of the retro-spective creation of criminal laws. At the very least, they imposed, on the Nazi elite, laws that had not been previously articulated. However, those trials and the many subsequent international human rights treaties and conventions have estab-lished a rich body of international law.[30] Since then, the major need has been to find institutions and mechanisms to enforce existing rules rather than create new ones, retrospectively or otherwise. *Ad hoc* successors are always established after the alleged crimes they are established to adjudicate but these bodies can rely on international law that predate their creation. The Rome Statute created the ICC lists and defines a number of crimes—but does not purport to create them. It con-fers jurisdiction over 'the most serious crimes of concern to the international com-munity as a whole'—genocide, war crimes, torture and aggression (Article 5). There is ample authority for the existence of these crimes prior to 1998.

While the jurisdictions of the ICJ and ICC are limited to the countries that have signed up to them, both courts can adjudicate matters that occur before a country signs up to them.[31]

---

[30] Including the Hague and Geneva Conventions, international treaties such as the Torture Convention and the Genocide Convention and the United Nations Charter itself.

[31] Countries which have not accepted the 'compulsory jurisdiction' of the ICJ can consent to the court's hearing a dispute between them arising out of actions that have already occurred or, as is often the case, ongoing actions. The ICC has no jurisdiction over the crimes listed in Article 5 that occurred before the court's establishment on 1 July 2002. While later signatories are generally only

None of this involves retrospectivity. As argued in Chapter 5, the creation of an institution to enforce a pre-existing law does not make it retrospective. Even if it were, there can be no legitimate expectation that breaches of law will not be prosecuted.

The international community is not a 'well ordered society under law'. However, it does possess the key legal and institutional elements for such a society and the international rule of law is a meaningful ideal.[32] It has institutional elements to create laws (through treaty making, international custom, ICJ decisions) and to apply them (the ICJ, the ICC and the WTO). There is no need to develop a radically new concept of the rule of law for the international community— merely to apply the rule of law in its most rudimentary form.

Future prosecutions of those who start and fight wars contrary to international law would be neither retrospective nor in breach of the international rule of law. The Kellogg-Briand pact of 1928 by which 'The High Contracting Parties solemnly declare in the names of their respective peoples that they condemn recourse to war for the solution of international controversies, and renounce it, as an instrument of national policy in their relations with one another' was enshrined in the United Nations Charter.

Interestingly, the three countries which contributed troops to the 2003 invasion of Iraq[33] were all parties to the Kellogg-Briand pact[34] and the War Crimes Trials held in Nuremberg and Tokyo. Accordingly, they are long estopped from denying the existence of the crime of aggression.[35] Even though the ICC does not have jurisdiction over the crime of aggression until it is further defined (Article 5.2), this does not mean that the crime does not exist or that it could not be tried by an *ad hoc* tribunal or by courts in countries that have given themselves universal jurisdiction over war crimes such as the crime of aggression.

Of course, the American politicians who authorized the Iraq invasion, and the Chiefs of Staff who planned it, might consider that their chances of being tried before an independent tribunal for the crime of aggression are very limited. The United States does not subscribe to the jurisdiction of the ICJ or ICC and has pressured other countries not to sign or, if they do, to exempt the United States

---

bound from the dates of its acceptance of ICC jurisdiction, a mechanism is expressly created by which states may accept ICC jurisdiction for crimes committee after 1 July 2002 while they were not a State party.

[32] C Sampford, 'Reconceiving the Rule of Law for a Globalizing World', in S Zifcak (ed), *Reconceiving the Rule of Law* (Routledge, London, 2004); C Sampford, 'Sovereignty and Intervention', Invited Plenary Paper, World Congress of Legal and Social Philosophy, New York, June 1999 published in B Leiser and T Campbell (eds), *Human Rights in Theory and Practice* (Ashgate, London, 2001).

[33] The United States, the United Kingdom and Australia: the so-called 'coalition of the willing'.

[34] Britain signed on its own behalf and on behalf of the (then) Dominion of Australia.

[35] Note that they could not repudiate the Kellogg-Briand pact even if they wanted to, as the ban on the use of force other than in self-defence or UN sanction is a peremptory norm of international law and a fundamental element of the Charter.

from its reach. The US administration has also made loud noises about 'rescuing' American soldiers and citizens from international tribunals seeking to try them for war crimes. However, the Pinochet case reminds us that we may live long enough for the international climate to swing towards prosecution of past misdeeds and that the domestic climate may switch even more firmly. Even if the expectation of non-prosecution for lack of a tribunal is rational, it cannot be legitimated and is no more worthy of consideration than someone saying that 'he did not expect to be caught'. As in domestic law, those who are accused of war crimes deserve a fair trial—no less. The international rule of law demands that they receive no more. The greater the likelihood of such trials, the less likely politicians are to engage in wars of aggression and the less likelihood that their soldiers will fight such wars. The British Attorney General, Lord Goldsmith, contemplated the possibility of such a trial in his confidential advice to the Prime Minister on 7 March 2003—though he failed to mention this to Parliament, the Cabinet or Chiefs of Staff despite the fact that at least some of the latter two bodies might be potential defendants in any such trial.[36]

7.6 Concluding remarks

The bulk of this book sought to examine the nature and practice of retrospective rule-making and the arguments for and against the practice. The strongest, and most interesting, arguments were the systemic ones that saw it as inimical to the law and its rule. Most writers see it as a mercifully rare but necessary evil. Some see it as not law at all.

It is always very interesting when a phenomenon that is supposedly inimical to a system is actually commonplace within it. Whether this is because of misinformation, misunderstanding, hypocrisy or long redundant taboo, studying the phenomenon may provide considerable insights into the system. This chapter has explored what some of those insights might be and used retrospectivity as a lever to understand law and its rule.

First, it makes us realize that much discussion of the rule of law does not really take into account modern understandings of law and its relative indeterminacy. This makes retrospectivity inevitable in both legislation and judge-made law. However, its inevitability means that institutions that have to deal with the rule of law on a day-to-day basis have developed means of dealing with it. Judges who have confronted it for the longest time and in the most systematic manner have much to offer legislatures in dealing with the indeterminacy of their own law and the need to occasionally retrospectively adjust it.

Secondly, the discussion emphasizes the centrality of citizen guidance in the rationale for law and its effective operation. Putting this at centre stage helps us to

---

[36] See C Sampford, 'More and More Lawyers but Still no Judges' (2005) 8 *Legal Ethics* 16 at 19ff.

understand why retrospectivity is frequently unjust but why it is sometimes entirely appropriate. It also emphasizes that law is intended to be a communication between lawmaker and citizen and it is the role of lawyers to serve not dominate.

Thirdly, in denying that retrospectivity is necessarily an abuse of law-making power, it acknowledges that it can be abused and that the dangers of abuse need to be addressed. However, this shifts the focus from a ban on retrospective law-making to integrity systems that prevent the abuse of power generally and the abuse of legislative power in particular.

Fourth, it reinforces the institutional dimension of law and its rule—domestically and internationally.

Finally, it reminds us of the development of international law and especially its application to individuals—from something that had to be largely invented in 1945 to something that needs institutional support 60 years later.

Bibliography

anon 'Charnock—Overruling as a speech act' available at trinity.dit.it/ipra2005/uploads/ Charnock_Overruling.doc.

—— 'Criminal Law and Justice' (1988) 62 ALJ 1046.

—— 'Current Topics' (1987) 61 ALJ 759.

—— 'Editorial' (1978) 8 *Taxpayer* 99 (Australian Taxpayers Association).

—— 'Editorial' (1988) 17 *Australian Tax Review* 1.

—— 'Editorial', *Australian Financial Review*, 3 June 1983.

—— 'Government's Action Sets Dangerous Precedent for Taxpayers' (1990) 25 *Taxation in Australia* 546.

—— 'Howard Rules Out Retrospective Terrorism Laws', 23 February 2004, available at <http://www.smh.com.au/articles/2004/02/22/1077384621312.html>.

—— 'Recent amendments to the *Income Tax Assessment Act 1936*; the issue of retrospectivity' (1978) 52 *Australian Law Journal* 299.

—— *Australian National Integrity Systems Assessment, Queensland Hand Book*, Transparency International and Key Centre for Ethics, Law, Justice and Governance, Griffith University, Australia, July 2001, available at <http://www.griffith.edu.au/centres/kceljag/>.

—— *The Scotsman*, 20 January 2005.

AAP, 'Difficult and messy appeal will send Amrozi to firing squad: expert', *Sydney Morning Herald*, 8 August 2003.

Ackland, Richard, 'Why throw Hicks to the wolves', Sydney Morning Herald, 21 January 2005.

Acton, Lord, 'Letter to Bishop Mandell Creighton, 3 April 1887', published in *The Life and Letters of Mandell Creighton*, 1904, available at <http://www.theihs.org/ libertyguide/people.php/75834.html>.

Alcorn, Gay, 'Northern Territory: Australia's Final Frontier' (February 1995) *Independent Monthly* 48–9.

Alcorn, Gay, 'NT Minister Rejects Law Criticism by Amnesty', *Melbourne Age*, 12 February 1993.

Amankwah, HA, 'Judicial Legislation: A New Phase? John Pfeiffer Pty Ltd v. Rogerson [2000] HCA 36 (June 21, 2000)' 7 JCULR 254.

Austin, J, *The Province of Jurisprudence Determined* [1832], David Campbell and Phillip Thomas (Eds), (Aldershot, UK, 1998).

Australia, 'Senate Resolution of 8 November 1988 reproduced in Australia', *Work of the Committee During the 38th Parliament*, SSCSB, 1997 Chapter 2, pp. 10–11, available at <http://www.aph.gov.au/senate/committee/scrutiny/work38/report/c02.htm>.

Australia, *109th Report*, Australian Senate, October 2000.

Australia, *Alert Digest 15*, SSCSB, 4 December 2002.

Australia, *Alert Digest 9*, SSCSB, 2004.

Australia, *Annual Report 1986–87*, SSCBS, Parliamentary Paper No 443 of 1987.

Australia, Attorney-General Philip Ruddock, News Release (127/2004), Parliament House, Canberra, 23 July 2004.

Australia, *Bills Digest No 120 2003–4*, Anti-terrorism Bill 2004.

Australia, *Economics Legislation Committee*, Senate, 13 November 1997, E 75.

Australia, *Eleventh to Eighteenth Reports of 1987*, SSCSB, Parliamentary Paper No 442 of 1987.

Australia, *First to Twenty-First Reports of 1989*, SSCSB, Parliamentary Paper No 466 of 1989, Australian Parliament.

Australia, *Hansard*, House of Representatives, 13 April 2000.

Australia, *Hansard*, House of Representatives, 1977, vol. 106.

Australia, *Hansard*, House of Representatives, 1978, vol. 108.

Australia, *Hansard*, House of Representatives, 1985, vol. 140.

Australia, *Hansard*, House of Representatives, 1987, vol. 155.

Australia, *Hansard*, Senate, 1982, vol. 96.

Australia, *Hansard*, Senate, 1985, vol. 107.

Australia, *Hansard*, Senate, 20 September 2001.

Australia, *Hansard*, Senate, 24 September 2001.

Australia, *Hansard*, Senate, 25 September 2001.

Australia, *Official Committee Hansard Senate Legal and Constitutional References Committee Reference: Migration Legislation Amendment (Further Border Protection Measures) Bill 2002*, submission of Mr James, Lecturer in Law, p. 26.

Australia, *Senate Debates*, vol. 82, 1979, pp. 629–30.

Australia, *Senate Official Hansard No 13*, Thursday 20 September 2001, Australian Parliament.

Australia, *Senate Official Hansard No 13*, Wednesday 26 September 2001, Australian Parliament.

Australia, *Seventh Report of 1990*, SSCSB, 7 November 1990, Australian Parliament.

Australia, *Work of the Committee During the 38th Parliament*, SSCSB, 1997 Chapter 2, available at <http://www.aph.gov.au/senate/committee/scrutiny/work38/report/c02.htm>.

Australia, *Work of the Scrutiny of Bills Committee During the 38th Parliament*, Standing Committee on Regulations and Ordinances, Senate, 1997, chapter 2.

Australian Taxation Office, *Administrative Treatment of Retrospective Legislation*, 1994, available at <http://www.ato.gov.au/taxprofessionals/content.asp?doc=/content/45130.htm>.

Babington, Anthony, *The Rule of Law in Britain: From the Roman Occupation to the Present Day* (3rd edn, Barry Rose, England, 1995).

Bailey, G, *From Revolution to Reconstruction: A Biography of William Blackstone (1723–1780)*, available at <http://odur.let.rug.nl/~usa/B/balckstone/blackstone.htm>.

Balkin, JM (ed), *What Brown v. Board of Education should have said: the nation's top legal experts rewrite America's landmark civil rights decision* (New York University, 2001).

Bannon, Mike, 'Draft ATO rulings offer immunity from penalties', *Canberra Times*, 16 July 2000.

Beaumont, Brian, 'Managing Litigation in the Federal Court', in Brian R. Opeskin and Fiona Wheeler (eds), *The Australian Federal Judicial System* (Melbourne University Press, 2000).

Bell, J, *Policy Arguments in Judicial Decisions* (Oxford University Press, Oxford, 1983).

Blackstone, Sir William, *Commentaries on the Laws of England*, 1765 (repr. University of Chicago Press, Chicago, 1979, vol. 1).

Bleich, J David, 'Judaism and Natural Law', in Martin P Golding (ed), *Jewish Law and Legal Theory* (New York University Press, 1993).

Boeddu, Gian and Haigh, Richard, 'Terms of Convenience: Examining Constitutional Overrulings by the High Court' (2003) *Federal Law Review* 167.

Boeddu, Gian, and Haigh, Richard, 'Our Perfect Constitution' (1981) *56 New York University Law Review* 353.

Boyle, Peter, 'Vic Labor allowed to hang on—for now' (12 June 1991) 15 *Green Left Weekly* 5. Reprinted at <http://www.greenleft.org.au/back/1991/15/15p5.htm>16 March 2005.

Broadbent, David, 'Wrong Way: No Going Back', *The Age*, 24 October 2004.

Buchanan, James M and Tullock, Gordon, *The Calculus of Consent: Logical Foundations of Constitutional Democracy* (University of Michigan Press, 1962).

Caldarone, Richard P, 'Precedent in Operation: A Comparison of the Judicial House of Lords and the United States Supreme Court' (2004) 759 *Public Law*.

Calvin, John, *Institutes of the Christian Religion*, Geneva, 1539, Book 2, Chapter 8, Section 1, trans. (Henry Beveridge, Eerdmans, Michigan, 1989).

Campbell, Enid, 'The Retrospectivity of Judicial Decisions and the Legality of Governmental Acts' (2003) 29(1) *Monash University Law Review* 49.

Carrigan, Frank, 'A Blast from the Past: The Resurgence of Legal Formalism' [2003] *Melbourne*.

Cass, Ronald A, 'Judging, Norms and Incentives of Retrospective Decision-Making' (1995) 75 *Boston University Law Review* 941.

Clark, Gerald J, 'Military Tribunals and the Separation of Powers' (2002) 63 *University of Pittsburgh Law Review* 837.

Clarke, Ross, 'Retrospectivity and the Constitutional Validity of the Bali Bombing and East Timor Trials' (2003) 5(2) *Australian Journal of Asian Law* 2–32.

Crawford, James, 'Australian Law After Two Centuries' (1988) 11 *Sydney Law Review* 447.

Dawkins, John (Finance Minister), 'Retrospective Legislation Against Tax Avoidance' (28 April 1983), Press Release: reprinted in (1983) 17 *Taxation in Australia* 1006–7.

Death Penalty Information Center, 'Full Right to a Jury will not Extend to Older Cases', *Press Release*, 24 June 2004. Available at <http://www.deathpenaltyinfo.org>.

Devlin, Lord, *The Judge* (Oxford University Press, Oxford, 1979).

Dicey, AV, *Introduction to the Study of the Law of the Constitution* (10th edn, Macmillan, London 1924).

Dickins, Jim, 'Fears of tax office corruption', *Courier Mail*, 7 November 2000.

Downer, The Hon Alexander (Minister for Foreign Affairs), Transcript of Interview 6 September 2004, ABC Radio 5AN, available at <http://www.abc.net.au>.

Driedger, Elmer A, 'Statutes: Retroactive Retrospective Reflections' (1978) 56 *Canadian Bar Review* 268.

Dworkin, RM, *Law's Empire* (Duckworth, London, 1986).

Dworkin, Ronald, 'The Model of Rules' (1967) 35 *University of Chicago Law Review* 14–46.

Dworkin, Ronald, *Taking Rights Seriously* (Duckworth, London, 1987).

Edin, Douglas E 'Rule Britannia', 2002, available at <http://www.utpjournals.com/product/utij/523/523_edlin.html>.

Ely, John Hart, *Democracy and Distrust: A Theory of Judicial Review* (Harvard University Press, Massachusetts, 1980).

Eskridge, William N Jr, 'Overruling Statutory Precedents' (1988) 76 *Gerogetown Law Journal* 1363.

Eule, Julian N, 'Temporal Limits on the Legislative Mandate: Entrenchment and Retroactivity' (1987) 379 *American Bar Foundation Research Journal*.

Evans, C Stephen, 'Apologetics in a New Key: Reviving Protestant Anxieties over Natural Theology', in Mark McLeod and William Lane Craig (eds), *The Logic of Rational Theism: Exploratory Essays* (E Mellen Press, Lewiston, NY, 1990).

Evans, Simon, 'Immigation Law—Ruddock v. Vadarlis (The Tampa Litigation)' (2003) 1(1) *International Journal of Constitutional Law* 123.

Fabro, Allesandra, 'Tax Office flaws revealed', *Australian Financial Review*, 17 November 2000.

Fallon, Richard H Jr. and Meltzer, Daniel J, 'New LAW, Non-Retroactivity, and Constitutional Remedies' (1991) 104 *Harvard Law Review* 1731.

Fisch, Jill E, 'Retroactivity and Legal Change: An Equilibrium Approach' (1997) 110 *Harvard Law Review* 1055.

France, Anatole, *The Red Lily* [1894] (The Library Press Limited, London, 1925).

Frank, Jerome, *Law and the Modern Mind* (Brentano's, New York, 1931).

Freiberg, Arie, 'Ripples from the Bottom of the Harbour: Some Social Ramifications of Taxation Fraud' (1988) 12 *Criminal Law Journal* 136.

Fuller, LL, *The Morality of Law* (Yale University Press, New Haven; London, 1964 (1969)).

Gifford, DJ, *Statutory Interpretation* (Law Book Co, Sydney, 1990).

Glueck, Sheldon, *The Nuremberg Trial and Aggressive War* (Knopf, New York, 1946).

Graetz, Michael J, 'Retroactivity Revisited' (1984–1985) 98 *Harvard Law Review* 1820.

Hancock, Nathan, 'Current Issues Brief 2001–2: Refugee Law—Recent Legislative Developments', Law and Bills Digest Group, Department of the Parliamentary Library, 18 September 2001.

Harrington, James, *The Prerogative of Popular Government* (1657) and *The Commonwealth of Oceana* (1656).

Harris, JW, 'Final Appellate Courts Overruling Their Own "Wrong" Precedents: The Ongoing Search for Principle' (2002) 118 LQR 408.

Harris, JW, 'Towards Principles of Overruling—When Should a Final Court of Appeal Second Guess' (1990) 10 *Oxford Journal of Legal Studies* 135.

Hart, HLA, *The Concept of Law*, 2nd edn (Oxford University Press, 1997).

Hart, HM and Sacks, AM, 'The Legal Process: Basic Problems in the Making and Application of Law', University Case Book Series (revised and edited by W Eskridge and W Frickey) (West Publishing, 1993).

Hayek, FA, *The Constitution of Liberty*, (Routledge, London, 1960).

Hayek, FA, *Law, Legislation and Liberty Vol 1: Rules and Order* (Routledge and Kegan Paul, London, 1973).

Hayek, FA, *The Road to Serfdom*, (University of Chicago Press, Chicago, 1944 [1975]).

Hebert, Julie E, 'State Ex Rel Oliveri v. State: The Scarlet Letter of Protection—A Constitutional Analysis of Louisiana's Megan's Law Statutes' (2002) 48 *Loyola Law Review* 327.

Heydon, JD, 'Judicial Activism and the Death of the Rule of Law' (2003) 23 *Australian Bar Review* 1.

Hobbes, Thomas, *The Behemoth* (in *The English Works of Thomas Hobbes*, 2nd edn, vol. 6, John Bohn (London and Scientia Verlag Aalen, Germany, 1966 [1840])).

Hodder, Jack, 'Departure from "Wrong" Precedents by Final Appellate Courts: Disagreeing with Professor Harris' [2003] *New Zealand Law Review* 161.

Holmes (Jnr), Oliver Wendell, *The Common Law* (Little, Brown and Company, Boston, 1881).

Honore, AM, 'Real Laws', in PMS Hacker and J Raz (eds), *Law, Morality, and Society: Essays in Honour of H.L.A. Hart* (Clarendon Press, Oxford, 1977).

Howard, Colin, *The Constitution, Power and Politics* (Fontana/Collins, Melbourne, 1980).

Howard, J (Treasurer), 'Second Reading Speech', *Hansard*, Australian Commonwealth, House of Representatives, 1978, vol. 108, p. 1245.

Howard, JW (Treasurer), Press Release, 25 July 1982. Reprinted (1982) 11 *Australian Tax Review* 154–6.

International Commission of Jurists, *The Rule of Law and Human Rights: Principles and Definitions* (International Commission of Jurists, Geneva, 1966).

International Commission of Jurists, *The Rule of Law in a Free Society* (International Commission of Jurists, Geneva, 1959).

Jacobs, Andrew M, 'God Save This Postmodern Court: The Death of Necessity and the Transformation of the Supreme Court's Overruling Rhetoric' (1995) 63 *University of Cincinnati Law Review* 1119.

James, Angus, 'Submission to the Senate Legal and Constitutional References Committee: Migration Legislation Amendment (Further Border Protection Measures) Bill 2002', Australia Commonwealth, 2002.

Kaatz, Robert, 'Is There an *Ex post facto* Prohibition on Judicial Decisions that Retroactively Enlarge Criminal Punishment' (2001) 47 *Wayne Law Review* 1367.

Kanstroom, Daniel, 'Criminalizing the Undocumented: Ironic Boundaries of the Post-September 11th Pale of Law' (2004) 29(4) *North Carolina Journal of International Law and Commercial Regulation* 639.

Kaplow, Louis, 'An Economic Analysis of Legal Transitions' 99 (1986) 99 *Harvard Law Review* 509.

Kelman, Mark G, *A Guide to Critical Legal Studies* (Harvard University Press, Massachusetts, 1987).

Kelsen, Hans, *The Pure Theory of Law* (University of California Press, 1967).

Kemphaus, Nick J, 'Rogers v. Tennessee: Is the Judiciary Permitted to Violate the Ex Post Facto Clause of the United States Constitution' (2003) 30 *Northern Kentucky Law Review* 415.

Keyzer, Patrick, 'When Is an Issue of "Vital Constitutional Importance"? Principles Which Guide the Reconsideration of Constitutional Decisions in the High Court of Australia' (1999) 2 *Constitutional Law and Policy Review* 13.

Kirby, M, 'Judicial Activism? A Riposte to the Counter-Reformation' (2004) 24 *Australian Bar Review* 1.

Kitson, Danielle, 'It's an Ex Post Facto Fact: Supreme Court Misapplies the Ex Post Facto Clause to Criminal Procedure' (2001) 91 *Journal of Criminal Law and Criminology* 429.

Lacey, W, 'Judicial Discretion and Human Rights: Expanding the Role of International Law in the Domestic Sphere' (2004) 5 *Melbourne Journal of International Law* 108.

Law Council of Australia, 'Legislation by Media Release' Media Release of 18 July 1988.

Law Council of Australia, 'Submission on Legislation by Media Release', attachment to Media Release of 18 July 1988; Law Council of Australia, 'Views of Taxation Commissioner Condemned', Media Release of 5 October 1988.

Law Council of Australia, 'Views of Taxation Commissioner Condemned', Media Release of 5 October 1988.

Lee, Emery G III, 'Overruling Rhetoric: The Court's New Approach to Stare Decisis in Constitutional Cases' (2003) 33 *University of Toledo Law Review* 581.

Lehn, David, 'Adjudicative Retroactivity as a Preclusion Problem: Dow Chemical Co v. Stephenson' (2004) 59 *New York University Annual Survey of American Law* 563.

Leithart, Peter J, 'Natural Law: A Reformed Critique' (29 February 1996) 3(2) *Premise* 4.

Llewellyn, Karl, *The Bramble Bush* (Oceana Publications, New York, 1960).

Logan City Council, 'Anger at Valuation Role Fee', Wednesday, 23 June 2004, at <http://www.logan.qld.gov.au/LCC/logan/news/NewsArchive.htm>.

Logan, Wayne A, 'The Ex Post Facto Clause and the Jurisprudence of Punishment (US Supreme Court rules against ex post facto clause) (1998) 35 *American Criminal Law Review* 1261.

Lombardi, R and Martin, S, 'Acts Without Power?' (1991) 65 *Law Institute Journal* 75.

Lynch, Andrew, 'Dissent: The Rewards and Risks of Judicial Disagreement in the High Court of Australia' [2003] *Melbourne University Law Review* 724.

Lynch, W (Treasurer), 'Budget Speech', *Hansard*, Australian Commonwealth, House of Representatives, 1977, vol. 106, p. 54.

Lyons, David, *Ethics and the rule of law* (Cambridge University Press, 1984).

Maher, G, 'Statutory Interpretation and Overruling in the House of Lords' (1981) *Statute Law Review* 85.

Malkan, Jeffrey, 'Retrospective Justification' (1990) 6 *Touro Law Review* 213.

Martyn, Angus, 'The Amrozi Bali Bombing Case: Is Indonesia's Anti-Terrorism Law Unconstitutional?', *Research Note No 14*, Australian Parliamentary Library, Canberra, 7 October 2003, at URL <http://www.aph.gov.au/library/pubs/rn/2003-04/04rn14.pdf>.

Mason, A, 'Legislative and Judicial Law-Making: Can We Locate an Identifiable Boundary?' (2003) 24 *Adelaide Law Review* 15.

Mason, Sir Anthony, 'The State of the Australian Judicature' (1989) *Law Institute Journal* 977.

McHugh, M, 'The Law-Making Function of the Judicial Process—Part II' (1988) 62 ALJ 116.

McHugh, MH, 'The Strengths of the Weakest Arm' (2004) 25 *Australian Bar Review* 181.

Morris, Sophie, Shanahan, Dennis and McGarry, Andrew, 'Latham backs off new law for Hicks', *Weekend Australian*, 21–22 February 2004.

Mount, Ferdinand, *The British Constitution Now: Recovery or Decline?* (Heinemann, London, 1992).

Munzer, Stephen R, 'Retroactive Law' (1977) 6 *Journal of Legal Studies* 373.

Munzer, Stephen R, 'A Theory of Retroactive Legislation' (1982–83) 61 *Texas Law Review* 425.

Munzer, Stephen R, 'A Theory of Retroactive Legislation' (1982) 61(3) *Texas Law Review* 463.

Myers, AJ (QC), 'The Federal Court Decision in the Gregrhon Investments Pty Ltd Case' (1988) 17 *Australian Tax Review* 4.

Neier, Arey, 'The Military Tribunals on Trial' (1992) 49(2) *The New York Review of Books*, available at <http://www.nybooks.com/articles/15122>.

O'Loughlin, Toni, 'Private tax rulings may be published', *Sydney Morning Herald*, 26 July 2000.

O'Loughlin, Toni, 'Secret rulings: PM defends department', *Sydney Morning Herald*, 29 July 2000.

Padden, Amy L, 'Overruling Decisions in the Supreme Court: The Role of a Decision's Vote, Age, and Subject *Matter in the Application of Stare Decisis after Payne v Tennessee*' (1994) 82 *Georgetown Law Journal* 1689.

Paterson, AA, 'Lord Reid's Unnoticed Legacy—A Jurisprudence of Overruling' (1981) 1 *Oxford Journal of Legal Studies* 375.

Pearce, DC, *Statutory Interpretation in Australia* (2nd edn, Butterworth, Sydney, 1981).

Pearce, Dennis C and Geddes, RS, *Statutory Interpretation in Australia* (3rd edn, Butterworths, Sydney, 1988).

Plato, *The Laws* 644, trans. Trevor J Saunders (Penguin, Harmondsworth, 1970).

Posner, Richard A, *The Federal Courts: Challenge and Reform* (Harvard University Press, Cambridge, 1985).

Preston, N, Sampford, C, with Connors, C, *Encouraging Ethics and Challenging Corruption* (Federation Press, St Leonards, 2002).

Queensland, 'Comments by Mr Lucas', *Hansard*, 20 July 2004, p. 258.

Queensland, 'Question to Minister for Local Government and Planning', *Hansard*, 11 May 2004, p. 793.

Queensland, 'Scrutiny of Legislation Committee (Qld): Alert Digest 11', 26 November 2002, p. 22.

Queensland, 'Second Reading Speech', *Hansard*, 26 November 2004.

Queensland, 'Third Reading Debates', *Hansard*, Thursday 25 November 2004, p. 3837.

Queensland, 'Transport and Other Legislation Amendment Bill Second Reading', *Hansard*, 13 May 2004, p. 1005.

Queensland, 'WorkCover Queensland Amendment Bill Second Reading', *Hansard*, (Lester, V) 27 November 2002.

Queensland, *Hansard*, 23 November 2004, pp. 3618–19.

Queensland, *Hansard*, 25 November 2004, p. 3837.

Queensland, *Hansard*, 27 November 2002, p. 4869.

Queensland, *Hansard*, 5 October 2004, p. 2669.

Queensland, Scrutiny of Legislation Committee, *Alert Digest 11*, 26 November 2002, p. 35.

Rajanayagam, V, 'The Tampa Decision: Refugee Rights versus the Executive's Power to Detain and Expel Unlawful Non-citizens' (2002) 22 *University of Queensland Law Journal* 1.

Ramseyer, JJ Mark and Nakazato, Minoru, 'Tax Transitions and the Protection Racket: A Reply to Professors Graetz and Kaplow' (1989) 75 *Virginia Law Review* 1155.

Rankin, Geoff and Hedge, John, 'Bankruptcy Amendments Target High-Income Earners', available from Allens Arthur Robinson website at <http://www.aar.com.au/pubs/insol/foinsjun04.htm>.

Ratner, Michael, 'Moving Away from the Rule of Law: Military Tribunals, Executive Detentions and Torture' (2003) 24(4) *Cardozo Law Review* 1513.

Rawls, John, *A Theory of Justice* (Harvard University Press, Massachusetts, 1971).

Raz, J, *The Authority of Law: Essays on Law and Morality* (Clarendon Press, Oxford, 1979).

Raz, J, *The Concept of a Legal System: an introduction to the theory of legal system* (2nd edn, Clarendon Press, Oxford, 1980).

Refugee Convention, Centre for Comparative Constitutional Studies and the Institute for Comparative and International Law, 'International Law and the Tampa Affair: A Legal Twilight Zone', Centre for Comparative Constitutional Studies and the Institute for Comparative and International Law, The University of Melbourne, 11 October 2001, p. 5.

Rehnquist, James C, The Power that Shall be Vested in a Precedent: Stare Decisis, the Constitution and the Supreme Court' (1986) 66 *Boston University Law Review* 345.

Reicher, Harry, 'Legislation by Press Release' (1978) 7 *Australian Tax Review* 32.

Richard Goode, 'Disappointed Expectations and Tax Reform' (1987) 40 *National Tax Journal* 159.

Richardson, AT, 'War Crimes Act 1991' (1992) *Monash Law Review* 73.

Robertson, Geoffrey, *The Justice Game* (Vintage, London, 1999).

Roosevelt III, K, 'A Little Theory is a Dangerous Thing: The Myth of Adjudicative Retroactivity' (1999) 31 *Connecticut Law Review* 1075.

Roosevelt, K and Shannon, Bradley Scott, 'The Retroactive and Prospective Application of Judicial Decisions' (2003) 26 *Harvard Journal of Law and Public Policy* 811.

Roosevelt, K, 'Legal Reasoning and Coherence Theories: Dworkin's Rights These, Retroactivity, and the Linear Order of Decisions' (1984) 72 *California Law Review* 369.

Rorive, I, 'Diverging Legal Culture but Similar Jurisprudence of Overruling: The Case of the House of Lords and the Belgian Cour de cassation' (2004) 3 *European Review of Private Law* 321.

Rubenstein, Kim, 'Citizenship, Sovereignty and Migration: Australia's Exclusive Approach to Membership of the Community', paper presented to seminar 'Boundless Plains to Share? Australia's Response to the MV Tampa Asylum Seekers', Institute for Comparative and International Law, University of Melbourne, 11 October 2001.

Sabin, Lori N, 'Doe v. Poritz, A Constitutional Yield to an Angry Society' (1996) 32 *Californian Western Law Review* 331.

Sagoff, Mark, *The Economy of the Earth: Philosophy, Law and the Environment* (Cambridge University Press, 1988).

Sampford, C and Palmer, A, 'Judicial Retrospectivity' (1995) 4 *Griffith Law Review* 170.

Sampford, C and Palmer, A, 'Retrospective Legislation in Australia' (1994) 22 *Federal Law Review* 217.

Sampford, C and Palmer, M, 'Strengthening Domestic Responses', in Morton H Halperin and Mirna Galic (eds), *Protecting Democracy: International Responses* (Lexington Books, 2004).

Sampford, C and Palmer, M, 'Who will rid us of these meddlesome generals?', in C Sampford et al (eds), *Asia Pacific Governance 2000* (Ashgate, London, 2002).

Sampford, C, 'Institutionalising Public Sector Ethics', in K Woldring (ed), *Business Ethics in Australia and New Zealand: Essays and Cases* (Thomas Nelson, Melbourne, 1995).

Sampford, C, 'Fundamental Legislative Principles: Their Meaning and Rationale' (1994) 24 *Queensland Law Society Journal* 531.

Sampford, C, 'Law, Institutions and the Public Private Divide' (1992) 20 *Federal Law Review* 185.

Sampford, C, 'Media Ethics Regimes and Ethical Risk Management in Australia' (2004) 19(2) *Journal of Mass Media Ethics* 86–108.

Sampford, C, 'Reconceiving the Rule of Law for a Globalizing World', in S Zifcak (ed), *Reconceiving the Rule of Law* (Routledge, London, 2004).

Sampford, C, 'Review of Walker's The Rule of Law' (1989) 16 *Melbourne University Law Review* 174.

Sampford, C, 'Sovereignty and Intervention', Invited Plenary Paper, World Congress of Legal and Social Philosophy, New York, June 1999.

Sampford, C, 'State sovereignty and the common good and international intervention', in B Leiser and T Campbell (eds), *Human Rights in Theory and Practice* (Ashgate, London, 2001).

Sampford, C, 'The four dimensions of rights and their means of protection', in B Galligan and C Sampford (eds), *Rethinking Human Rights* (Federation Press, Sydney, 1997).

Sampford, C, Preston, N with Carol Bois, *Public Sector Ethics: Finding and Implementing Values* (Routledge, London, and Federation Press, Sydney, 1998).

Sampford, C, Shacklock, A, Connors, C and Galtung, F, *Measuring Corruption* (Ashgate, Aldershot, in press).

Sampford, C, *The Disorder of Law* (Blackwell, Oxford, 1989).

Sampford, C and Palmer, M, 'International Responses', in Morton H Halperin and Mirna Galic, (eds), *Protecting Democracy: International Responses* (Lexington Books, 2004).

Schlag, Pierre, 'Normativity and the Politics of Form' (1991) 139 *University of Pennsylvania Law Review* 801.

Scott, Samuel P (trans.), *The Civil Law: Including the Twelve Tables, the Institutes of Gaius, the Rules of Ulpian, The Opinions of Paulus, the Enactments of Justinian, and The Constitutions of Leo* (Central Trust Co., Cincinatti, 1932).

Shadow Treasurer Ralph Willis, Australian Commonwealth, *Hansard*, House of Representatives, 1978, vol. 109, p. 1902.

Sheridan, Greg, 'Constitutional Terror', *The Australian*, 28 August 2004.

Silverii, Jason, 'Bankruptcy Bill to be Revised [Bankruptcy Legislation Amendment (Anti-Avoidance and Other Measures) Bill 2004]' (2004) 78(9) *Law Institute Journal* 24.

Simpson, AWB, *Invitation to Law* (Blackwell, Oxford, 1988).

Sinnar, Shirin, 'Patriotic or Unconstitutional? The Mandatory Detention of Aliens Under the USA Patriot Act' (2003) 55(4) *Stanford Law School* 1419.

Slawson, W David, 'Constitutional and Legislative Considerations in Retroactive Lawmaking' (1960) 48 *Cal. Law Review* 216.

Smith, Stephen F, 'The Rehnquist Court and Criminal Procedure' (2002) 73 *University of Colorado Law Review* 1337.

Somerville, JP, *Politics and Ideology in England, 1603–1640* (Longman, New York, 1986).

Spriggs, James F II and Hansford, Thomas G, 'Explaining the overruling of US Supreme Court Precedent', University of California Center for the Study of Law and Society Jurisprudence and Social Policy Program, at <http://repositories.edlib.org.csls.Iss/9>. Accessed 17 October 2005.

Spry, ICF (QC), 'Retrospective Legislation for Company Tax' (1982) 11 *Australian Tax Review* 152.

Starmer, Keir, 'Two Years of the Human Rights Act' (2003) 1 *European Human Rights Law Review* 14.

Stewart, Cameron, 'Nowhere man: While alleged terrorist David Hicks sits in a cage in Cuba, his case sits in the too-hard basket of international diplomacy', *Weekend Australian Magazine*, 6–7 April 2002, pp. 15–17.

Stone, Julius, *Legal System and Lawyer's Reasonings* (Stanford University Press, California, 1968).

Tate, Michael, 'The Operation of the Australian Senate Standing Committee for the Scrutiny of Bills, 1981–1985', Australian Parliament, Parliamentary Paper No 137 of 1985.

Taylor, Greg, 'Retrospective Criminal Punishment under the German and Australian Constitutions' (2000) 23(2) *University of New South Wales Law Journal* 196.

Thomson, EP, *Whigs and Hunters: The Origin of the Black Act* (Penguin, London, 1990).

Toohey, John (Justice),'A Government of Laws, and Not of Men'? (1993) 4 *Public Law Review* 158. Posner, Richard A, *Problems of Jurisprudence* (Harvard University Press, Massachusetts, 1990).

Troy, Daniel, *Retroactive Legislation* (American Enterprise Institute, Washington DC, 1998).

US, 'Companion Guide to the Department of Justice's Report from the Field: The USA Patriot Act at Work', Bill of Rights Defense Committee, available at <http://www.bordc.org/companion>. Peter Walsh, 'Sir Garfield Barwick, Dishonourable Judge', *Labor Herald*, October 1977, p. 8.

Vince, JH (trans.), *Against Meidias, Androtion, Aristocrates, Timocrates, Aristogeiton*, Loeb Classical Library No 299, (Harvard University Press, Mass., 1951, vol. 3).

von Clausewitz, Karl, *Vom Kriege (On War)* (Dummlersverg, Berlin, 1833).

von Savigny, FC, *Private International Law, and the Retrospective Operation of Statutes*, (T. and T.C., Edinburgh, 1869).

Waldron, Jeremy, *Law and Disagreement* (Clarendon Press, Oxford, 1999).

Walker, Geoffrey de Q, 'Ending Constitutional Drift: A Democratic Agenda for Change,' in Suri Ratnapala, Geoffrey de Q Walker and Wolfgang Kasper (eds), *Restoring the True Republic* (Centre for Independent Studies, St Leonards, 1993).

Walker, Geoffrey de Q, *The Rule of Law: Foundation of Constitutional Democracy* (University Press, Melbourne, 1988).

Walsh, Peter, *Confessions of a Failed Former Finance Minister* (Random House, Sydney, 1995).

Walsh, Peter, *Hansard*, Australian Commonwealth, Senate, 1978, vol. 77, p. 2417.

Walters, Mark D, 'Common Law, Reason, and Sovereign Will', 2003, available at <http://www.utpjournals.com/product/utlj/531/531_walters.html>.

Walzer, Michael, *Thick and Thin: Moral Argument at Home and Abroad* (Notre Dame University Press, Indiana, 1994).

Willis, Ralph, *Hansard*, Australian Commonwealth, House of Representatives, 1978, vol. 109.

Woozley, AD, 'What Is Wrong With Retrospective Law?' (1968) 18(70) *The Philosophical Quarterly* 41.

Yakley, Louise, 'Mark Latham Suggests Retrospective Anti-terror Laws', Friday 20 February 2004, available at <http://www.abc.net.au/pm/content/2004/s1049998.htm>.

York, Barry, *Australia and Refugees, 1901–2002: An Annotated Chronology Based on Official Sources* (Social Policy Group, 16 June 2003).

Index